BROTHER TO THE SUN KING

BROTHER TO

The Johns Hopkins University Press   *Baltimore / London*

THE SUN KING

Philippe, Duke of Orléans

Nancy Nichols Barker

© 1989 The Johns Hopkins University Press
All rights reserved
Printed in the United States of America

The Johns Hopkins University Press
701 West 40th Street
Baltimore, Maryland 21211
The Johns Hopkins Press Ltd., London

The paper used in this publication meets the minimum requirements of
American National Standard for Information Sciences—Permanence of
Paper for Printed Library Materials, ANSI z39.48-1984.

Library of Congress Cataloging-in-Publication Data

Barker, Nancy Nichols.
Brother to the Sun King, Philippe, Duke of Orléans.

Bibliography: p.
Includes index.
1. Orléans, Philippe, duc d', 1640–1701—Family.
2. Louis XIV, King of France, 1638–1715—Family.
3. France—Princes and princesses—Biography.   4. France—
History—Louis XIV, 1643–1715.   I. Title.
DC130.073B37   1989   944'.033'0924[B]   88-46061
ISBN 0-8018-3791-x (alk. paper)

To my late husband,
Stephen Barker,
again and always

Contents

GENEALOGICAL CHARTS

Illustrations

William of Orange in the Dutch War. How could so insignificant a prince have led a French army to victory? Perhaps, I began to think, Philippe deserved a closer look.

At that point the appeal of Monsieur's personality and the uniqueness of his position in the court of the Sun King asserted themselves. Younger brother of the most powerful king France has ever known, the prince was perceived as a threat to the throne and was deliberately thrust into the background. An intelligent, gifted man, he could not be permitted to excel and was with few exceptions denied honorable service to the Crown. Only two years younger than Louis, he was the perpetual loser in a lifelong sibling rivalry. His life was the classic history of an underdog, a term that might have made its way to the title page of this book had such colloquialisms been appropriate in a scholarly publication.

Monsieur has no previous biographer in English. The only biographer of him in the French language has written with much grace but, having designed his book for the general public, he confined his research primarily to memoirs of the period.[1] The present study of the prince is the first to make extensive use of archives and other manuscript sources. The family papers, deposited in the Archives Nationales by the count of Paris, present head of the house of Orléans and available to scholars with his permission, are indispensable for reconstruction of financial management. The archives, manuscript collections, and other resources of the Ministry of War, the Ministry of Foreign Affairs, the Bibliothèque Nationale, the Bibliothèque Historique de la Ville de Paris, and in London, of the Public Record Office, among other repositories, have helped me to follow the prince as he went to war, built his palaces, married his wives, and fathered a family. With the exception of the Public Record Office, where are deposited the letters Philippe wrote to his brother-in-law, King Charles II of England, no collection of the prince's letters is known to exist. Although he wrote them by the hundreds, not many have survived, and those that have are widely scattered. In my quest I feel fortunate to have unearthed not a few that had previously escaped the notice of scholars of the period.

The present biography has a psychological dimension, but as any psychohistorian would readily agree, it is not a psychobiography. Trained as a historian, I have been unwilling to place theory of personality at the axis of my investigation of Philippe's behavior and character. I have not subordinated factual evidence gathered from contemporary sources of information to a theoretical model or to cognitive assumptions. I have not attempted to make the historical data fit a theoretical procrustean bed. On the other hand, when psychological theory was compatible with verifiable evidence, I have used it as a tool to increase my understanding.

I soon came to realize that in studying an individual so singularly placed in society and so deeply demoralized as was Monsieur, the commonsense psychology employed by the conventional biographer would not suffice. The use of psychological theory has, if nothing else, prompted questions that I would otherwise not have thought to ask. It has suggested possibilities that otherwise would have gone unperceived. As a historian, I tend to be a cultural relativist, committed to acknowledging profound differences between centuries, cultures, regions, social classes, and even families. Yet I can agree that to a degree human biological development is more or less timeless. What Freud has called man's "long childlike helplessness and dependence," for example, is merely one of the inevitable sociological realities common to mankind in all periods of its history. Without attempting to resolve the controversy between the psychoanalytic reductionist and the historical relativist, I have on occasion resorted to the theory of personality in order to sharpen and broaden my biographer's sense of reality. Throughout the writing of this book I have been exceedingly grateful to my colleague formerly at the University of Texas at Austin, Dr. James Bieri, professor of psychology and practicing clinical psychologist, who has read it in its entirety and given me the benefit of his specialized knowledge.

Other colleagues and friends, both in this country and in Europe, have generously placed their knowledge and time at my disposal. Ruth Kleinman, professor of history at Brooklyn College, CUNY, and author of the scholarly and perceptive *Ann of Austria: Queen of France*, read the manuscript in an early stage and helped me enormously to place the prince in proper historical perspective. Several of the themes throughout the work evolved in part from her inspiration. Georges Dethan, associate director of the Archives of the French Foreign Ministry and author of scholarly books on Gaston d'Orléans and Mazarin, guided me through the archives to a number of letters of Monsieur that I might otherwise have missed. Orest Ranum, professor of history at the Johns Hopkins University and a great seventeenth-century specialist, offered wise counsel along the way on solving a variety of archival problems. Virginia Crosby, professor of French literature at Pomona College, who now resides mainly in Paris, helped me especially in the acquisition of prints and in the search for data on the lost château of Saint-Cloud. Special thanks are also due Mme Yves Bercé, conservateur of the Bibliothèque du Ministére de la Culture, to Georges Molvinger, secrétaire général adjoint des Amis du Parc de Saint-Cloud, and to Mme André Schmitz, wife of the former conservateur du Domaine National de Saint-Cloud for help in research on the prince's palaces and châteaus, and to A. D. K. Hawkyard in London for furthering my research in the Public Record Office. Throughout the several years of preparation of this manuscript, the deans of the Graduate School and the College of Liberal Arts at the University of Texas at Austin, William S. Livingstone and Robert D. King, have been generous in affording me financial support and leaves of absence for uninterrupted writing.

For encouragement when it was much needed, as well as for medical expertise, I am grateful to my brother, Dr. M. M. Nichols, professor of medicine at the University of Texas at Galveston. My sister-in-law, Margaret Nichols, whose gift for understanding people can scarcely be equaled, and who is no mean stylist, read the entire manuscript to my immense benefit. Always in my thoughts was the memory of my late husband, Stephen Barker, without whose love and support I should not have written this or any other book.

BROTHER TO THE SUN KING

•

ONE

Brother of Le Dieudonné

THE NEW DUKE OF ANJOU

On Christmas night 1639 Louis XIII, king of France, allegedly startled his court with the order to prepare his bed in the chamber of the queen. The result of this rare conjugal visit was the birth on September 21, 1640, of Philippe, duke of Anjou, later duke of Orléans, founder of the house of Orléans of modern times.

The baby prince was the son of the king and the queen, Anne of Austria (so styled owing to her Habsburg lineage) and the younger and only brother of the dauphin, Louis, whose "miraculous" arrival only two years earlier had earned him the epithet le Dieudonné, the gift of God. The succession to the throne, so long in peril, was now doubly assured.

The joyful news traveled quickly to Paris, which erupted into celebrations nearly equal to those that had greeted the birth of the dauphin. The bells of the Palais Royal, which sounded only for *enfants de France* (legitimate children of kings) played a gay carillon; the guns of the Arsenal and the Bastille boomed; the city fathers gave official thanks; citizens danced in the streets and lit fires before their portals. A solemn Te Deum was celebrated by the bishop of Meaux at the cathedral of Notre Dame de Paris. The official *Gazette de France* wrote fulsomely of the two princes as twin "pillars" on which the future glory of France would rest. Even Louis XIII roused from his customary moroseness and joined in the general rejoicing, jubilant to see himself the father of two sons, "he who had feared to have had none at all."[1]

The happy event was a strange contrast to the tormented family history that lay behind it. His Most Christian King Louis XIII and the infanta Doña Ana Maria Mauricia, daughter of Philip III of Spain, were in their teens when they married in 1615. From the first the relationship was strained and unhappy. The neurasthenic Louis proved a reluctant bridegroom and fulfilled his marital duties with an infrequency that not only dismayed his wife but alarmed the court and ministers, all of whom were keenly aware of the necessity of an heir. Although not overtly homosexual, he was apparently repelled by female contact and on occasion showed unnatural attraction to males at court. Absorbed in his cares as ruler, frequently absent on campaign or on hunting trips, he neglected his wife and at the same time suspected her of all manner of immoral and treasonable conduct. According to contemporary stories, a singular combination of events had been necessary to produce a dauphin for France: the exhortations of the king's confessor, the good offices of a young nun who urged on Louis the need for reconciliation with his wife, and a rainstorm that caught him far from home and obliged him to accept the queen's hospitality for the night. Inevitably, there had been amazement and gossip surrounding the circumstances of this birth, which took place eighteen years after the marriage of the parents.

The birth of a son and heir to the throne consolidated Anne's position as queen of France but did not noticeably improve her relations with her difficult husband. Despite occasional visits to the marital bed, Louis made her life unhappy by dismissing her friends at court and giving his affections to the young marquis de Cinq-Mars, to whom he became strangely attached. Even during Anne's second pregnancy Louis did not hesitate to cross her, and only a few days before she gave birth he reduced her to tears by threatening to remove the dauphin from her care.

It is true that Anne's record was not unblemished, even though excuses for it are easy to find. As a foreigner, she found her position at court difficult from the start. Rejected by her husband, who disliked Spaniards, she ran the risk of being repudiated for failing in her duty to provide an heir to the throne. In her predicament, her behavior was at times foolish and indiscreet. Regarding her husband's chief minister Cardinal Richelieu as her personal enemy, she became involved to one degree or another in plots against him.[2] Suspicions mounted against her: her letters to her brother, Philip IV, were accounted treason; her dalliances with the duke of Buck-

ingham and others were judged infidelity. A beautiful and exquisitely feminine woman, even her appearance was against her. Moreover, she loved to dance, to gamble, to attend the theater, and even
to read ribald literature. She rose late, ate too much rich food, drank
too much chocolate, and gave every impression of idleness and frivolity. Worst of all, however, were her alleged conspiracies with
Gaston, duke of Orléans, scapegrace younger brother of Louis and,
in the continued absence of a dauphin, the immediate heir to the
throne. Louis deeply suspected the pair of engaging the help of
Spain in a plot to place Gaston on the throne and to make Anne his
queen once the deed was done. Kings of France had always to be
on their guard against rebellious brothers, who more than once had
imperiled the royal authority and the unity of the realm. His anger
at Anne was the greater because it was strongly tinctured with jealousy of the prince who, lighthearted, debonair, successful with the
ladies, was everything the king was not. What woman would not
have preferred this charmer to the dour Louis? Moreover, it was
only too true that Gaston hoped one day to be king and was an
inveterate if less than resolute conspirator. With the income from
his proprietary possessions, from his large appanage, and from his
governorship of the states of Languedoc, Gaston was in a position
to mount a formidable challenge to the authority of his brother.[3]

Yet Anne had a strong, dutiful aspect to her character that deep-
ened with the passage of time. A pious woman with deep moral
convictions, she weathered the bleak years before her children were
born, outgrew much of her frivolous behavior, and matured into a
responsible queen and mother. Neither her religious scruples nor,
for that matter, the close surveillance under which she lived would
have permitted marital irregularities. No one close to the court ever
seriously questioned the paternity of Louis and Philippe. Although
her longtime friend and confidant at court, Mme de Motteville, criticized Anne for having defied her husband and opposed Richelieu,
she well understood the struggle the queen had gone through: "She
was born to make the late king her husband the happiest man in the
world, and if he had so wished he no doubt would have been, but
that fate that seems always to separate the hearts of sovereigns,
came between the king and the queen. The love that she could have
given to that prince, she gave to her children."[4]

The baby prince was born at the old château of Saint-Germain
outside Paris in the presence of the king and the great ladies of the
court, Mme la Princesse (de Condé), Mme la Connétable (de Mont-
morency), and the duchess of Vendôme, while crowds of courtiers
pressed at the doors. An hour later the infant was baptized privately

by the bishop of Meaux and received the name of Philippe. Although Louis at first seemed inclined to favor the title of count of Artois, in honor of the recent French victory at Arras in that county, he followed royal tradition in creating his second-born duke of Anjou, the title borne by the brothers of Louis IX (Saint Louis), Charles V, and Charles IX. The new duke was then removed to the apartments prepared for him, where were admitted the ladies and gentlemen of the court.

Like his brother, he was a vigorous and beautiful infant, although, in contrast to the blond dauphin, he had dark eyes and black hair. The princes' physical health and beauty, it has been suggested, were perhaps the result of their unusual heritage: the crossing of genes of the Burgundian Valois, Habsburgs, Medicis, and Bourbon families at fortuitous moments in the past.[5] Ferdinand and Isabella of Spain, Charles the Bold of Burgundy, Lorenzo the Magnificent, Emperor Charles V and his son Philip II, and the celebrated Bourbon king Henry IV were among their famous ancestors. And if their father were sickly and short-lived, their mother exuded a vitality and earthy beauty rarely seen in queens of France.

As soon as Philippe was born, arrangements were made for his household. Like most royal children of the seventeenth century, he occupied a nursery apart from his parents and his brother, although, being only two years younger than Louis, he shared the same governess. In addition, he had his own assistant governess, wet nurse, chambermaids, physician, and steward. The only difference between his household and that of the dauphin seems to have been that whereas Philippe had one wet nurse, Louis had two.[6]

Like Louis, and in accordance with accepted practice, Philippe would remain in this household in the care of women for some seven years, after which he would be placed under the governance of men. The position of the governess was thus a very important one. She was a respected personage at court and lived in intimacy with the royal family. Her duties were to watch over the health of her charges, to form their tastes and habits, and so far as it was possible with children of that age, to inculcate in them principles of honesty and moral rectitude.[7]

In thus setting up the households of her children and giving them over to wet nurses, Anne was of course following the accepted practice of her day for royal and other highborn families and was not at liberty to indulge her own inclinations. Even the choice of the all-important governess was not hers, the position falling to Françoise de Souvré, marquise de Lansac, who had the support of Richelieu and the king. Even so, Anne was far from relinquishing her influence in the nursery, which became the center of existence. Much evidence exists that despite the governesses, the wet nurses, the servants that might seem to have been a human wall dividing mother from sons—to say nothing of the separate apartments they occupied—she maintained a close and loving relationship with her children. Unlike the king's mother Marie de Medici, who rarely saw her children, Anne constantly watched over Louis and Philippe. A few months after the birth of the dauphin, an attendant wrote: "The queen hardly leaves him. She takes great pleasure in playing with him and taking him out in her carriage whenever the weather is fine; it is the whole of her amusement."[8] After Philippe appeared, she continued to live a quiet life in the old castle at Saint-Germain with only the exceptional visit to Paris.

A few historians cling to the myth that Louis and Philippe were neglected as children and were raised principally by servants of low birth who allowed them to play recklessly and eat unheathfully.[9] In support of these allegations, except for the superficial testimony of the abbé de Choisy, who played with Philippe as a child, and that of Saint-Simon, who was not yet born when the royal brothers were children, there are only the stories told by Louis XIV to Mme de Maintenon, the companion of his old age. But if the king could recall shabby linen and indigestible treats purloined from the kitchens, not too much faith should be placed in the reminiscences of a septuagenarian. To the contrary, the little princes were continuously surrounded by an attentive staff and watched over by a loving mother, all of whom were quite aware that not only the future of the realm but their own positions at court depended upon the lives and health of their precious charges. If there were danger, especially for Louis, it lay in constant adulation rather than in neglect.

Within a year or so of Philippe's birth, Anne began to think seriously about the education of the princes and consulted a number of learned and pious authorities. One of them, whose identity is not known but whose views almost certainly reflected those of the queen, wrote for her a treatise entitled "Maxims of Childhood Education and Direction."[10] It was addressed specifically to the training of the dauphin, but because many of the maxims were of a general nature, they would presumably have applied to Philippe as well. The emphasis was above all on religion and moral development but also included prescriptions for physical health and daily activities. Suggestions were made on the means of explaining to a small child abstractions such as charity, justice, evil, and virtue. He must love God and his parents, for example, because they love him. Evil and sin are those things that displease them and that he must thus avoid.

Devotion he would learn by simple prayers, but above all by the reverent example of his mother and father. Instruction in reading French and even Latin might begin at age five, but such lessons should be brief, informal, and enjoyable. Coercion and threats should be avoided, and praise rather then censure should be used to encourage his efforts. Corporal punishment should be used only as a last resort, since the author believed that a child's fear of the displeasure of those he loved was more powerful than his fear of a beating as an incentive to improve and to learn.

The whole document is noteworthy for its insistence on teaching by example and has a remarkably modern ring. Very likely it is evidence not only of the sound maternal judgment of the queen but also of the evolution of attitudes toward the treatment of small children that took place during the course of the seventeenth century.[11] The author's appeal to the child's senses and affection is in marked contrast to the harsh discipline, including brutal beatings, that had been imposed on Louis XIII as a child on the orders of his father Henry IV, who believed that he himself had profited enormously from frequent caning as a boy. And in fact, so far as can be known, neither Louis nor Philippe was systematically beaten, although evidence exists that neither entirely escaped corporal punishment.

LE PETIT MONSIEUR

Philippe was still a toddler when it became clear that his father had not much longer to live. By the spring of 1643 the king was in the last stages of what was probably intestinal tuberculosis, and the deathwatch began. The child could have had no understanding of the portentous events taking place, although possibly he sensed something was amiss from the solemnity of the adults around him and the tenseness of his mother as she alternated visits to the king's chamber and counsels with the ministers.[12] Contemporary accounts make little or no mention of Philippe at this time, although they abound with dramatic stories of the young Louis in his last meetings with the dying king. According to one of them, almost certainly apocryphal, when his father asked him his name, the child replied, "Louis XIV." To which the dying man responded, "No, my son, not yet." If the anecdote were false, at least it was an accurate reflection of the focus of attention on the heir to the throne as the court waited in suspense for the transition to take place. Except for a farewell visit to his father's bedside to receive his blessing,

Philippe must have remained out of sight in his apartments with his household.

The end came on May 14, 1643. Philippe was not yet three years old—thirty-two months precisely—and Louis was not yet five. The old order, of which the prince could scarcely have had conscious memory, had passed away to be replaced by the one he would know to the end of his life. The reign of the Sun King had begun. His mother was now regent; Philippe was now the younger brother of the king and the immediate heir to the throne. Those in court would henceforth refer to him as Monsieur (in fact, he was usually known as le Petit Monsieur to distinguish him from Gaston). That very night his signature as duke of Anjou, along with those of Anne, Gaston, and other relatives and high dignitaries, was affixed to the death certificate of his father as a guarantee of his recognition of the accession of his brother.[13]

The new life began immediately as Anne, surrounded by the dignitaries of the court, knelt in homage to her older son, who was now her sovereign. "The king is dead, long live the king." The next day she left Saint-Germain with her sons and rode with ceremony in an open carriage to Paris.[14] As he was to do so many times in the future, Philippe looked on while his brother and mother received the applause of the crowds and the blessings of the clergymen who greeted the cavalcade entering the capital. A few days later the child-king made his first official appearance at the *lit de justice* in the Grand Chamber of Parlement (a high court of law), where he was carried to his high throne by a peer of the realm.

Once in Paris Anne faced immediate and formidable problems. Although regent in name, by the terms of her late husband's will she was severely limited in the exercise of sovereign power. Distrusting his wife to the end, Louis XIII had named Gaston lieutenant general of the realm and had created a council of regency composed of powerful royal relatives and ministers whose decisions were binding on the queen.

Where would the new focus of power lie? In theory, of course, it was situated in the king, revered as a kind of visible deity. But although he was treated with elaborate respect, as a small child who could not yet even write his name, Louis could count for little in reality. The traditional opponents of the Crown—the *parlements*, especially the Parlement of Paris (possessing the power to register royal decrees, its members, owning their offices, tried to assert the right of judicial review), the provincial governors, and others of the greater nobility—could be expected to lay claim to privilege and to a role in the government. Henry IV (1589–1610) had begun in earnest to curtail the authority of these powerful groups and had laid the foundations for the later transformation of France into an absolute monarchy. Louis XIII (1610–43), his successor (after the regency of his mother, Marie de Medici), chiefly through the wily and ruthless Richelieu, had truncated the rights of the Protestants and had subdued defiant nobles in the provinces. Largely owing to the work of the cardinal, Louis XIV would later be able to make his greater nobility into sycophants in his court. Richelieu had also extended the practice of sending royal intendants across the land to enforce the king's will in matters of police, taxation, and justice, thus going far toward creating a centralized government. But the long battle of the Crown to extend the law of the king was still not won.[15] With the death of Louis XIII the restrained centrifugal forces would be released again.

As regent for a minor king, Anne would also face the demands of a crowd of relatives and other fortune seekers hoping to detach for themselves some part of the royal patrimony—offices, lands, benefices, whatever—that they claimed was their due. In Anne's case the situation was especially difficult. Not only was she inexperienced in public affairs, but she had the reputation of being too weak and lazy to inform herself or to impose her will. Nor could she turn to Richelieu, who had died five months before Louis XIII. Even if he had opposed her in the past, the cardinal would certainly have rallied to the cause of preserving the royal authority of the child-king. Now all of the minister's past enemies and victims as well of those of the late king flocked to court to clamor for revenge. Their hopes were the greater because in the regent herself they recognized a former accomplice.

The court proper was still relatively small, the Crown not yet having established itself as the sole source of favor and benefits. Its permanent members comprised first the households of the king, the queen, Monsieur, le Petit Monsieur (Philippe), the princes of the blood, and other members of the royal family. Next came those great nobles whose interest and connections required their residence near the king, and finally all the favorites and creatures of these personages. Only much later, when the mature Louis XIV had extended his authority, did the court swell to comprise most of the great families of France.

Of all these persons with whom Anne would be obliged to treat there was, first and foremost, Gaston, with his long record of conspiracy, inconstancy, and incapacity. In the last days of his reign Louis had named him lieutenant governor in the council of the future regency with the intention of using one enemy, his brother, as a check on another, his wife. The prince was not sufficiently black of heart to be suspected of planning the murder of his nephews in order to usurp the throne; but at best he would be demanding, and at worst he would be a possible locus of future rebellion.

Among other potential sources of discord was Henry II of Condé, head of the other cadet house of Bourbon. A fearsome prince in his prime, former fomenter of civil war and butcher of Protestants during the minority of Louis XIII, he was now basking in the glory of his son, the duke of Enghien, who had won a great victory over the Spanish at Rocroi only a few days after the accession of Louis XIV. On the death of his father in 1646, Enghien would take his place as first prince of the blood, with the title "Monsieur le Prince." Owing to his successes in war, he has gone down in history as the Grand Condé.

Also in the "family" were the legitimized descendants of Henry IV, the Vendômes, father (César de Vendôme) and son (the duke of Beaufort), both ravaged by the jealousy members of a bastard line felt for the legitimate relatives of the king. Additionally, there was a long list of returnees to the court, many of whom had been friends of the queen in her rebellious youth and were hoping to profit from that fact—Mme de Chevreuse, Mme de Hautefort, M. de la Porte, and others. These, known as the "important ones," coveting the lands, offices, and pensions once held by the favorites of the late king and his minister, could be expected to push their own interests even at the expense of the monarchy.

They were soon to be disenchanted. Anne moved quickly to break the testament of Louis XIII and take to herself the right to govern the kingdom "with full power and freedom" during her son's minority. Exploiting the enmity that had existed between the *parlementaires* and the late king and his chief minister, the regent had no difficulty in persuading the Parlement of Paris to override the last wishes of its old enemy. The members were only too ready to demonstrate that their authority was sufficient to set up the machinery of the new government. Consequently, by the time the boy-king held his first lit de justice on May 18, all was arranged. Anne alone was declared responsible for the person and education of the king and for the administration of the realm. She could set up her own council and appoint her ministers. Gaston retained the title of lieutenant general but was subject to the authority of the regent.

The queen proceeded relentlessly to blast the hopes of the "important ones" and to punish would-be fomenters of rebellion. In her new position as regent, Anne changed her political identity. She

now took the cause of the Bourbon monarchy as her own and became the enemy of those with whom she had collaborated in the
past to thwart the will of her husband and Richelieu. Her goals were
to preserve and extend the power of the Crown for the benefit of
her son. Now she would carry on the struggle to assert the royal
prerogative. She must govern so as to ensure the grandeur of Louis
XIV's future reign. As a pious Christian mother, Anne wanted
Louis to grow up to be a good man; but even more, this Habsburg
granddaughter of Philip II of Spain wanted him to become a great
king. Passing one day before the portrait of the late cardinal, with
whom she had often clashed, she is said to have remarked aloud:
"If you were alive today, never would you have been as powerful!"
Even if the anecdote is not true, it could have been, for Anne herself
was well aware of her change of heart and policy.

Where had Anne acquired the political wisdom to maneuver so
adroitly and to consolidate her authority as regent so quickly? The
answer was chiefly to be found in the remarkable man who had
served as Louis XIII's chief minister in the last few months of his
reign: Cardinal Jules Mazarin. A protégé of Richelieu, Mazarin had
been a diplomat for the Vatican before entering the service of the
French court. His intelligence, ambition, and devoted work, to say
nothing of his charm, had earned him the esteem of the king, who
had done him the signal honor of making him godfather of le Dieudonné. Mazarin had been known to Anne at least slightly since
1634, when the late cardinal had presented him to her with the
insolent remark: "He will please you, Madame, he is much like
Buckingham," an allusion to a scandal of the 1620s caused by the
English duke's indiscreet advances to the young queen. Buckingham aside, Mazarin did have the qualities to appeal. About the same
age as the queen, handsome and cultured, he had sojourned in Spain
and could converse in her native language. Elegant, worldly, but
with refined tastes and habits, he understood how to flatter both the
queen and the woman. But more than anything else, knowledgable
and experienced in public affairs, devoted to the cause of the monarchy, he was there when Anne needed him. It was he who had
guided her in the crucial maneuvers to break the testament of the
late king and to consolidate her authority as regent.

In foreign affairs as well Mazarin was invaluable. It would be he
who would persuade the queen to place the interests of France
above her pro-Spanish proclivities. When Anne became regent the
kingdom was openly involved in the so-called Swedish-French period of the devastating Thirty Years War in the Germanies and was
following a tortuous diplomatic course. Richelieu, although sup-

porting the Spanish alliance that had arranged the marriage of Louis XIII with the then-infanta Anne and Catholic religious unity within France, had been strongly anti-Habsburg. He had been determined to contain Spanish power, even when that meant aiding Protestant Sweden in Germany and making war on Spain. Now Mazarin was to make it plain to Anne that Richelieu's policies must be carried on. Under his guidance Anne became, if not a bellicist, at least a proponent of continuing the war against Spain to a victorious conclusion.

As Anne continued to take Mazarin's counsel in long tête-à-têtes nearly every evening—the doors carefully left open for the sake of appearances—the returning aspirants to court began to feel alarmed, well knowing that he would stiffen her resistance to their ambitions and claims. Mme de Chevreuse and the duchess of Longueville, sister of Enghien, with others, thought to end his influence by telling the queen the scandal his visits were creating. In vain. Although Anne "blushed to the whites of her eyes," she turned more and more to his guidance. By the time the troubles and uncertainty of the transition were passed and the policies of the Regency laid down, Mazarin's ascendancy over the queen and her government was an established fact at court.

Philippe, of course, could have known nothing of these plays for power attendant on the beginning of the new reign. But very early he must have come to sense that although as Monsieur he was a very important person indeed—he outranked even the princes of the blood—he ran a very distant second to his brother the king.

At the time of his birth the *Gazette de France* had indeed written of the princes as two "pillars" supporting the monarchy; but the pillars were by no means of equal stature. Philippe's position of inferiority was rooted in the law of primogeniture, which conferred upon the firstborn the exclusive right of inheritance. Even had he been born into less exalted circumstances, he would have suffered in comparison with an older male sibling. The privilege of the child favored by primogeniture or by his parents' choice was firmly fixed in the economic and social framework of early European society. It enabled the family to prevent the division of its estate and the derogation of its assets and honor. Younger sons were sacrificed to serve the interests of the one, usually the oldest male, designated to carry on the interests of the house and pass the inheritance intact to the next generation.[16] Not until the very late seventeenth and early eighteenth centuries did moralists and educational theorists begin to preach the concept of equal rights of children.

If the cadet in households of relatively modest means could expect discrimination, how much worse the fate of younger sons of royalty. At stake was the unity of the realm and the sovereign authority of the Crown. Obviously the throne could accommodate only one occupant at a time.

The marked preference that Anne had shown for her firstborn from the very beginning was thus based, at least in part, on what she must have perceived as her duty. But according to those who observed her, it also flowed from inclination. Although the queen loved Philippe very much, noted Mme de Motteville, Louis was her idol, toward whom she displayed "an infinite tenderness."[17] It was his birth, after all, that had made her mother of the heir to the throne and ended her humiliating position at court. Now that Louis was king, she rose when he entered her presence and to others referred to him formally as "the king, Monsieur my son." In speaking of Philippe, however, she said simply "my son."

The relative positions of the two children are vividly preserved for us in an anonymous contemporary engraving (see plate 1) designed to commemorate the accession of Louis XIV and the Battle of Rocroi. With the battle scene depicted in the background, the seated Anne holds a laurel crown in one hand and with the other hand supports the arm of the child-king, who holds aloft a scepter. Although the figure of the regent occupies the near center of the picture, Louis, clad in an ermine-trimmed robe and seated beneath an imposing drapery, is the center of attention. On a cushion to his right rests the crown of France. Off to one side on the left of the queen and ignored by her stands Philippe. Wearing a dress decorated with a single ribbon, he reaches out to touch his mother's skirt as if to remind her that he too is a member of the family.

That Philippe is dressed in skirts in this and other tableaus of those years should not be misinterpreted. In the seventeenth century small boys customarily wore dresses until they were "breeched," that is, clothed in the breeches or trousers worn by men, an event that usually took place about the time they were taken from the custody of women. Louis, too, wore skirts when very young. Historians have often mistakenly concluded that Anne was deliberately cross-dressing her younger son as part of a plan to render him effeminate and thus submissive to his brother. The error is the easier to make because Anne did tend often to treat Philippe more like a daughter than a son, calling him "my little girl," and when the time came for his education to begin, acquiescing to a much less rigorous program than that designed for Louis. Thus the representation of the prince in skirts, although perfectly in accordance with the practice of the day, can be seen as symbolic of his mother's attitude toward him and of his later role in life.

Her preference for Louis was never more apparent than in the way she responded to the occasional illnesses of the two children. When in the autumn of 1647, for example, Philippe fell ill with measles complicated by a dangerous dysentery, Anne left him in Paris with his household and, though alarmed, nonetheless went off to Fontainebleau with Louis for a change of air. Following the advice of Mazarin, she hid her concern for political reasons and returned to Paris to the bedside of the prince only when he took a turn for the worse. But soon persuaded that he was improving, she left after three days on hearing that Louis was lonely for her. When the court returned to the capital in mid-October, she found Philippe so thin and pale as to be almost unrecognizable. Even so, again probably for political reasons, she went ahead with plans for a ball. A similar incident took place the following year when Philippe contracted smallpox and was left alone for a short time with his household in Paris. At that time the revolt known as the Fronde had just begun, and Mazarin, desiring to remove the king from the danger of popular violence, used the risk of infection (even though Louis had already had smallpox) as an excuse to spirit him and his mother out of the capital, leaving Philippe behind.

When Louis took sick, on the other hand, it was a very different story. In 1647, while Philippe was still convalescing from his long illness, Louis had come down with smallpox. There was no pretense this time that all was well; nor were excuses found to leave him alone until he recovered. Anne hastened to his bedside, where she remained night and day until he was out of danger. All at court could see how differently she reacted when Louis, not Philippe, was the patient. Imperiling her own health by her vigil, she later confessed that had she lost the king she would not have had the strength to go on living. After he recovered, she ordered public rejoicing and religious celebration. In January 1648 and again the following April, Louis, acclaimed by the crowds, went in state to the cathedrals in Paris and Chartres to render public thanks for the return of his health.[18] Philippe, present on both occasions and nearly eight, was old enough to have noticed that no such ceremonies were ever held for his benefit.

Anne made no attempt, as a modern mother might do, to lessen or play down the distinction in rank between the two brothers. Quite the contrary. From earliest childhood, even in play, Philippe was required to defer to and to obey his brother the king and made to understand that only in that manner could he earn his mother's love and approval. Submission was the price of social acceptance. Louis, on the other hand, was made constantly aware of what was his due as king and of the distance between him and his subjects, including his brother. The decision to instill in the cadet the need for obedience and submission was a conscious one on the part of the regent and Mazarin, since they were well aware of how often in French history younger brothers had mounted rebellions against the Crown and plunged the country into civil war. Always there was the living and lamentable example of Gaston before their eyes. The minister was devoting his life to completing the work of Richelieu—destroying the enemies of the monarchy. Louis XIV could never become a great king if he had a second Gaston at his side.

The lessons of regent and minister seem to have had early and complete success. According to the Venetian ambassador, by the time Louis was five years old he was clearly conscious of his majesty. "In his relations with the duke of Anjou, his brother aged three, he [Louis] wishes to be respected and obeyed," he wrote. "He understands and recognizes that he is king and he wishes to be treated as such. And if sometimes his mother scolds him, he answers that there will come a day when he will be master."[19] Apparently the older brother, at least at this stage of his life, was encouraged from his vantage point as king not so much to disdain or belittle the younger boy (as he was later to do), as to use his authority to protect and watch over him. There is considerable evidence that as children they could play harmoniously together. But it was less the relationship of brother to brother than of father to son. In one of the letters Louis wrote to Philippe during their childhood, he asked earnestly about his health and, after assuring him of his own, closed: "Believe me always your affectionate and good little papa. LOUIS."[20]

The efforts of Anne and Mazarin to efface Philippe may have been at least in part inspired by a genuine concern lest he outshine his older brother. By all accounts the prince developed into a handsome, active little boy with fine, regular features, bright black eyes, and an abundance of dark, curly hair. He was much shorter than Louis and promised never to be very tall, but he was exceedingly well proportioned. "The prettiest child in the world," was the verdict of his cousin, la Grande Mademoiselle, daughter of Gaston.[21] And whereas the king was quiet and reserved ("dignified" and "noble" in the vocabulary of the memoirists), Philippe was affectionate and vivacious. "As soon as he learned how to talk, this prince displayed a lively intelligence," wrote Mme de Motteville.[22]

Moreover, according to the same source, he was not without a will and ideas of his own, which he could express very clearly when he wished. Once, she related, when Philippe was convalescing in 1647 and found his room crowded with visitors who tired him, he begged his mother to get rid of them. When she refused, explaining that they were ladies of quality whom she could not offend, the child riposted: "But Madame, what difference does that make? Are you not the mistress? What good is your crown if it cannot get you your way? You chase me out often enough when it suits you, I who am your son. Why shouldn't they have their turn?"[23] If the story is true, and there is little reason to doubt it, it reveals on the part of the seven-year-old not only a well-developed facility of expression but also a precocious if naive understanding of the pecking order about him.

On public occasions, too, Philippe was much more likely to speak out while the king remained silent. Louis's confessor, Father Paulin, described an incident in 1650 when the two brothers and their mother were traveling in Burgundy in an effort to pacify the provinces by showing the people their king. On being received by the dignitaries at Dijon, Louis listened to their speeches in silence and made no reply ("he preferred to observe and reflect," wrote the good father). Philippe, on the other hand, "less inhibited by grandeur," and apparently not intimidated by the crowd, "let all admire his graceful manner of speech."[24] Coming from the pen of a man who owed his post and position in life to his devotion to the king, this evidence is impressive. This occasion and no doubt others like it may well have truly alarmed Anne and Mazarin and been at least one reason they tended more and more in future years to leave Philippe behind with the court during their official travels across France with Louis. No one could be permitted to upstage the king.

As le Petit Monsieur was ready to leave his female attendants, what can be said of the start he had made, or been given, in life? Obviously, as the account above reveals, the record of those early years so precious to theorists of personality is far from complete. Although we know Philippe was suckled by a wet nurse, for example, we do not know for how long, or under what conditions. Yet certain facts are clear. Philippe was born in highly unusual circumstances: his father was a king and his brother would soon be one. He was a healthy infant and an active child. Small for his age but well proportioned, handsome, intelligent, even precocious, he seems to have had every grace of mind and body. The child lost his

TWO

·

The "Education" of a Prince

THE TEACHERS, THEIR DUTIES, AND THEIR THEORIES

In the spring of 1648, when Philippe was nearly eight years old, within the space of a few weeks he was taken from the care of women and baptized publicly in an elaborate ceremony attended by the king and queen, other members of the royal family, and high dignitaries of the court.[1] It was an important transition in the life of the prince, marking the beginning of his participation in the public life of the court and of a supposedly serious preparation for his position as brother of the king and heir to the throne. Henceforth he would take his dinner with Louis each evening and appear by his side at many of the court functions, lay and religious.

The public baptism (as opposed to the private one he had received at birth) took place on the afternoon of May 11 in the chapel of the Palais Royal, the residence of the queen and her children in the heart of Paris. Presiding was the bishop of Meaux, and serving as godparents were his uncle Gaston, duke of Orléans, and Henriette of France, queen of England, wife of the deposed Charles I. The ceremony was a fairly long and complicated one for which the prince had been carefully coached and which, at least according to the official account, he carried off faultlessly.[2] It involved, among other things, taking his place on an elevated seat before the assembled court and chief prelates of the church, voicing a request for the rite of baptism, accepting anointment with holy oil, and answering in Latin the questions put to him. The prince, "beautiful as an angel," displayed throughout such "marvelous attention and devotion" and made his answers so distinctly and correctly that all were impressed; and several of the ladies, unable to contain their admiration for the solemn child, cried out repeatedly, "Oh, how beautiful he is!"

Such accounts, of course, cannot be taken too literally. Comments and phrases like "beautiful as an angel," for example, were standard for baptismal rites. Much the same thing in many of the same words had been said of Louis at the time of his public baptism in 1643.[3] And it is not difficult to agree that both children, handsome and exquisitely dressed, must have cut appealing figures as they stood alone before the great altar and faced the impressively gowned and mitered prelates. In the case of Philippe, a graceful performance may have come quite naturally. All his life he was to enjoy ceremony and to insist upon its correct observance in every detail. Later in life this pleasure may have derived from his realization that it represented one of the few areas of public affairs, if not at times the sole one, in which he was allowed to participate. But if in this early day he could find satisfaction in it, so much the better. A lifetime of ritual and ceremony lay ahead of him.

The next step after baptism was confirmation, which Louis and Philippe received together in December 1649.[4] This ritual was preparatory to first communion, which newly confirmed children normally received the following Easter. Anne, however, wishing to emphasize the unique relation of a king by divine right with the King of Heaven, arranged for Louis to receive his first communion alone on Christmas Day and, rather than in the private chapel inside the Palais Royal, in his parish church of Saint-Eustache. Philippe's role in the ceremony was limited to holding one of the four corners of the cloth laid across the communion table.[5] His own first communion followed not the following spring but, delayed owing to the civil uprising in Paris, on Easter Sunday of 1651.[6]

These events, however, constituted but a small part of the religious life of Anne and her children. Devout in the Spanish way, by which the French meant that she attached great importance to external forms and religious ritual, the queen was tireless in visits to churches, convents, and monasteries. She especially favored Val-de-Grâce, where she had constructed an impressive baroque chapel, the cathedral of the Virgin at Chartres, to which she made frequent pilgrimages, and their parish church of Saint-Eustache. The reli-

gious calendar was meticulously observed, with all the saints receiving their due. The schedule was especially crowded in the week
before Christmas and in the spring during Lent, when, in addition
to daily mass, the court participated in special prayers, vigils, processions, visits to shrines, or other forms of Catholic worship. During Holy Week in 1647, for example, the *Gazette* reported that on
Palm Sunday "the king and Monsieur, his brother, went to hear
mass at the house of the Capuchins on rue Saint Honoré, where His
Majesty received the palm from the hands of the Capuchin general."
Three days later Anne, Louis, and Philippe heard high mass at the
cathedral of Notre Dame, after which the king and queen washed
the feet of twenty-two beggars and served them at table. A separate
table of thirteen services was set up for "Monsieur, only brother of
the king, who wished to take part in the ceremony." And the following day Louis, candle in hand, was present at the procession of
the Holy Sacrament, "Monsieur, his brother at his side."[7]

Consider, too, that in addition to these public services, stunning
to modern readers in their frequency and duration, Philippe heard
mass daily in his own household and received the ministrations and
exhortations of his chaplain and private confessor. It all added up to
a childhood fairly steeped in religion. Not surprisingly, it seems to
have made a lasting impression on him, as it did on Louis. Although
neither was ever even slightly interested in questions of theology,
and each was perfectly capable of separating his personal morality
from religious practice, as adults both were unfailingly dutiful in
observing the outward forms of Catholic worship. As for Philippe,
he carried over to adulthood not only a liking for exercises of religious piety—even funeral services—but a belief in the efficacy of
amulets, medals, and chaplets. Also, his love of jewelry and dress,
which manifested itself while he was still a child and grew with the
years, was undoubtedly stimulated by the brilliance of the vest-
ments of the clergy and the gold and silver, jewel-encrusted ecclesiastical vessels.

The lay, as opposed to the religious, education of princes was a
totally masculine sphere. Princesses, Anne included, received only
that instruction deemed necessary to produce dutiful wives and
mothers, and their lessons usually did not extend much beyond
religion and the social graces. It was only natural, then, that the
regent should turn to Mazarin when the time came for Louis and
Philippe to leave the custody of women and begin their formal education. In March of 1646 when Louis was seven years old, she appointed Mazarin to the newly created office of superintendent of the

education of her sons, with the power to designate the governors, assistant governors, preceptors, and other members of the princes' educational staff who would serve under his authority.[8]

This appointment was a critical one for current and future reasons. At stake was not only the appointment of the personnel of the households of Louis and Philippe, matters involving finances and patronage, but the larger question of the quality of the children's education and the shaping they would receive. By controlling the nomination of these educators, Mazarin had in his power the development of the character and intelligence of the king and the immediate heir to the throne and, by extension, the power to influence the future of the monarchy itself. So vital a position was bound to be controversial, and it was especially so when it was held by a man who accumulated as many enemies as did Mazarin. And while certainly many of the charges made against him were spurious and motivated by a desire for spite or revenge, others, especially those relating to the shaping of Philippe, merit consideration. There is in fact good reason to question whether he always made responsible use of the trust placed in him.

At the top of the list under Mazarin was the governor, who was at least in theory the real director of his charge's education and of the formation of his character. His duties were to supervise the conduct of the prince, to preserve him from corruption, to raise him in virtue, and to teach him to direct his life and to be a judge of men. He was supposedly to guide by example, as he was to live in close association with his student, sleeping in his chamber and accompanying him in his carriage when he rode out. Always the governor was a personage of high rank and birth, and more often than not he was an army officer, perhaps even a marshal of France. The military profession not only enjoyed the general esteem of the court but was considered especially suitable for one called upon to direct the education of a prince, whose most important subject of study was military science. To assist him and to replace him if he were called away, the governor of both Louis and Philippe had two assistant governors, who were also usually men of high military rank.

The actual teaching of a prince was undertaken by the preceptor, whose duty was to develop his student's intelligence by the study of the arts and sciences. This person was usually a man of erudition with a reputation as a savant and would most likely have a connection with the church. He would be assisted by a battery of instructors in specific subjects and skills. However, his goal was not to make the prince into a scholar but to give him the kind of education

that would enable him to rule wisely and well. Latin and Greek
would be of far less use than knowledge of the army, of horsemanship, of drawing, of fencing, even of dancing. These rather than
scholarship would command the respect of the nobility in times of
war and peace. Even so, Latin, history, literature, mathematics, and
foreign languages were not to be entirely neglected; the king must
be a civilized and cultured prince, not merely a crude and ignorant
soldier. Still, the emphasis was definitely on the practical rather than
the intellectual, on applied knowledge as opposed to the humanities
or liberal arts. Such general principles reflected the ideas of Mazarin
and also no doubt a growing perception in the seventeenth century
of the noble as a man of gentility versed in the arts of civilization as
well as of war.[9]

In choosing the principal educators of Louis in 1646, Mazarin had
adhered closely to these general guidelines. The marquis de Villeroi, who became the king's governor, was a highly regarded army
officer. Louis's preceptor was Hardouin de Péréfixe, a scholarly cler-
gyman.[10] Under their ministrations, the king developed rapidly and,
notwithstanding the many criticisms then and since of the education
to which he was exposed, acquired the accomplishments essential
to his royal craft.

When Mazarin set about creating Philippe's household of mentors, he seemed to repeat this pattern, and superficially, at least, his
selections were impeccable. Chosen as governor was César de
Choiseul, count of Plessis-Praslin, whose qualifications were impressive. A marshal of France, renowned for bravery and a specialist
in artillery and siege warfare, he had long been an esteemed figure
at court, having been one of the children of honor when Louis XIII
was the dauphin. The assistant governors, Millet de Jeure and
D'Aluimar, were also high-ranking officers in the army.[11] The preceptor was François de La Mothe Le Vayer, who, though a married
man and not an ordained priest, was a member of the French
Academy and admired for his scholarship. He was to write essays
on geography, rhetoric, and morals in 1651 and an undated *History
of France* that was addressed specifically to Philippe.

Despite the impressive credentials of these men, their appointments were questionable in a number of ways. In the first place,
Mazarin was in no hurry to make them. Plessis-Praslin did not take
office until 1649, when Philippe was nearly nine years of age, and
even then, owing to the outbreak of civil war that required his active service in the army, he was not generally available to fulfill his
duties until 1653. The other members of the household were not in

place until 1651 or later. In the meantime, Philippe was placed under the tutelage of Louis's governor, Villeroi, but in fact he seems
to have been allowed to fritter away his days in foolish games with
the ladies of honor and their daughters in the service of the queen.
Mme de Motteville, although she regarded the prince with tender
affection, remarked with regret his penchant for wasting time and
concluded: "It would [have been] desirable if an effort had been
made to remove him from the idle play that was allowed him in his
youth."[12] Although Philippe may have shared some lessons with
the king, he did not truly enter upon his formal education until
1653, after the end of the Fronde.

In the second place, both governor and preceptor were men who
had earlier tried and failed to win appointment in the service of the
king. The reasons for the rejection of Plessis-Praslin as Louis's governor are not entirely clear, although they may be guessed at from
difficulties that arose when he was nominated to serve Philippe. In
the case of La Mothe Le Vayer, an element of "pyrronism," of the
"vice" of Protagoras, a Greek Sophist, was allegedly present in his
scholarly work and was held against him. The mentor of His Most
Christian Majesty could not be permitted to introduce into his mind
even the shadow of doubt or questioning of the truth of Catholic
orthodoxy. The result could be a fatal loss of self-confidence and
destruction of the king's qualities of leadership. It may be, however,
that this objection was not taken too seriously by Mazarin, since
La Mothe Le Vayer was permitted at times to instruct the king and
has been credited with influencing his intellectual development as
much as his own governor, Péréfixe.[13] Yet the fact remains that for
Philippe's two most important teachers, Mazarin chose men he had
rejected for the service of the king.

Plessis-Praslin's appointment was vulnerable from other points
of view as well. Disappointed not to be accepted as Louis's mentor,
he was less than enthusiastic about taking second best. In the end
he accepted the office, which of course was a venal one, because it
was very important to him financially. There is good reason to think
that he was much more interested in making his fortune than in
instructing his charge. Plessis-Praslin has been criticized for having
been the creature of Mazarin, which to a degree he must have been,
and for having too slavishly followed his direction;[14] but in fact
there was hard feeling between the two, which had its root in
money. Mazarin too, when he had accepted the office of superintendent of the education of Louis and Philippe, had been thinking in
terms of financial gain, since it carried with it the right to receive a

commission from the recipients of posts in their households, educational and other. A problem of jurisdiction arose when Plessis-Praslin asserted that as governor he had within his purview the post of the prince's superintendent of finances, claimed also by Mazarin, with the right to collect the provisions attached to it. The sordid side of the affair came to light when Jean Baptiste Colbert, to whom Mazarin had entrusted the care of his personal finances, advised the cardinal to double the offices of Philippe's household in order to turn a better profit and to remove Plessis-Praslin from jurisdiction over half of them. "Thus I have caused to be created a second provision of intendant," wrote Colbert. "And if you want to believe me, you will do the same thing for the post of secretary of commands; I shall sell them profitably; just rely on me." In the same letter he was at pains to put the cardinal on guard against the governor who, he averred, "can never be one of your friends." He continued: "[Plessis-Praslin] thinks he has a right to half of the money that you will derive from those offices; and when I speak of money, it is his God and his veritable soul, and the same can be said for his wife."[15]

Despite this dispute, the manner of whose resolution is not known, Plessis-Praslin held on to his office. When he began to fulfill its duties in 1653, he became the subordinate of Mazarin, to whom he reported daily on the conduct and progress of his charge.[16] It was thus the cardinal and not the governor who had overall control of the direction and purpose of the prince's education, what ideas and principles he should emphasize and what subjects he should avoid. Plessis-Praslin followed Mazarin's instructions carefully, which, he wrote, "he [the governor referred to himself in the third person in his memoirs] found very reasonable." Always, he added, "He devoted himself entirely to the training of the prince who had been entrusted to his care . . . . he encouraged him as much as possible in the direction of piety and study; he engendered in him the sentiments of respect and of tenderness that he owed to the king and made him understand that his true greatness consisted in being in the good graces of His Majesty, and that he should never permit even a hint of misplaced ambition to give rise to doubt of his loyalty." Expanding on this theme, he continued: "Brothers of kings cannot have too much greatness of soul, nobility of sentiment, or elevation of view, but all of these must be subordinated to what they are duty bound to owe their sovereigns, *for even while being their brothers, they do not cease to be their subjects.*"[17]

The governor was very likely perfectly truthful when he wrote that he found Mazarin's instructions sensible. He had, after all, just been through the Fronde of the princes, in which once again Gaston had rebelled against royal authority. As a marshal of France, Plessis-Praslin had participated in the military defeat of the Frondeurs and had served as negotiator with the prince to obtain his submission. No need to instruct him in the dangers of a disloyal younger brother.

Despite Plessis-Praslin's conviction of the need to teach Philippe his duty of submission to Louis, he chafed at the limitations placed upon his governance after 1653 when he took up his duties. By this time his charge was entering his teens and in the opinion of the old soldier should begin to learn the arts of war and other "quantities of things" proper to his rank. He knew that Mazarin was constantly initiating the king into his life's work. Louis was now permitted to sit in the royal council and was often taken to the army, not only to improve its morale, but to enable him to learn about its organization and operations. Meanwhile Philippe was left behind with the queen and her ladies. Plessis-Praslin complained, but to no avail. Governors of princes, he observed, are not always masters of their conduct, and when obliged to submit to the will of "superior forces," he kept silent and remained with Monsieur at court. Even so, he protested that Philippe was much too old by this time to live apart from men and that the prince himself was much displeased at the idleness of his life.[18]

By "superior forces" the governor had of course referred to Anne and Mazarin, but of the two he really meant Mazarin, who made the decisions on the education of Louis and Philippe and indeed on virtually everything else. Now the confidant as well as first minister of the queen, he governed her life and the business of the state as well. Whenever separated, the two wrote to each other constantly and in terms that leave no doubt that there was more to their relationship than that of minister and regent. In 1653, in a sort of code they had worked out to refer to themselves, Louis, and a few others, Anne wrote: "15 [Anne] cannot have other designs than those that please 16 [Mazarin] and, to show him that there is nothing in the world equal to the attachment [*amitié*] that 22 [also Anne] has for 16, 15 does not wish to displease him even in her thoughts."[19] Historians are still not in agreement on the exact nature of their relationship, Louis's foremost biographer arguing that they were man and wife (the cardinal was not an ordained priest and could have married within the church), while Anne's most recent biographer has concluded that Mazarin's position as godfather of Louis ruled out the possibility of marriage (according to the church, marriage of the mother to the godfather of her child was incest).[20]

An Arrested Development

However it may have been, what is certain is that the education Philippe received is the education that the all-powerful Mazarin intended for him. What were those intentions, and what plans did he entertain for the future of Monsieur, heir to the throne? Submission to his brother was obviously lesson number one. But was that the entire story? At court the accusation was frequently heard that the cardinal, out of fear lest the cadet outperform the king, instructed La Mothe Le Vayer to retard the prince's academic progress. Elizabeth Charlotte of the Palatinate, Philippe's second wife, was almost certainly repeating that view—and perhaps that of Philippe as well—when she related Mazarin's alleged reprimand to the preceptor on an occasion when his pupil had performed well: "What can you be thinking of, Monsieur La Mothe, in making a clever man of the brother of the king! If he becomes more learned than the king he will no longer be able to obey him blindly."[21] The upshot reportedly was the cardinal's order to the teacher to cease his lessons and send the prince off to play.

Little came of the bright promise that the prince had shown as a small boy. When Mademoiselle returned to court in 1657 after an absence of several years, she was astonished at how little the prince had changed. While the king was entering his manhood, brimming with confidence and actively engaged in the affairs of the army, Philippe was still living the life of a feckless child. Rather than going to the army or sitting in on councils, he was splashing in the river with the ladies of the queen and amusing them with puerile pranks.[22]

The problem of Philippe's education must have been difficult for Mazarin from both a personal and a political point of view. In his close daily association with Anne and Louis, he had come to regard himself as a surrogate father to the king, to whom he had become totally devoted. Anyone who has read his letters cannot doubt the genuineness of his love for Louis or fail to realize that for the cardinal, even more than for Anne, Louis came first. Yet as chief minister of state, he must have been aware of his responsibility to ensure the future governance of the kingdom. Until the time Louis married and had a son, Philippe was next in line to the throne.

Given the high mortality rate in the seventeenth century, especially of children, the possibility that Philippe would become king was no remote one. Simple prudence required his preparation for that eventuality. And even if he did not assume the crown of France, there were other thrones the brother of the king of France might be called upon to ascend. When Philippe was six years old, the only son of the widowed king of Spain died. Anne thought of pressing her own claim to the throne on behalf of her younger son, a project that fell through when the Spanish king remarried and his queen gave birth to the future Charles II.[23] Some ten years later Mazarin, hoping to evict the Habsburgs from their possession of the imperial crown, suggested Monsieur as a potentially suitable emperor.[24] And Philippe himself in the decade of the 1660s aspired at least briefly to be king of Naples. Of course, if Monsieur were to rule a country other than France, his ignorance and resulting incompetence would pose less of a danger and might even be advantageous to the French king. But in failing to groom Philippe to succeed Louis, Mazarin must have known he was taking great risks.

Of course, it could be argued that even if the prince had received exactly the same training as Louis he might still have grown into the same puerile, self-indulgent adolescent he in fact became. Perhaps he might have defeated the efforts of the most diligent and exacting mentors. The causes of the prince's arrested development can never be known with certainty. This much admitted, it is still undeniable that Philippe received an education and training in many ways more befitting a princess than the heir to the throne. Mazarin so feared he might pose a threat to Louis that he did not submit him to a serious program of study or offer him an apprenticeship in the métier of a king. He was left to his games, and his boyish indolence was fostered rather than combated. And as he fell further and further behind his brother, games and indolence would themselves become a refuge from the humiliation and failure he was to experience in competition with Louis.[25]

What enduring marks did these pedagogical theories and practices leave on the young Philippe? If Saint-Simon, the celebrated memoirist of the later years of the reign of Louis XIV, is to be believed, they were disastrous: "With more affability [du monde] than intelligence and no learning whatever, although with an extensive and precise recollection of family trees, births, and marriages, he was capable of nothing. No one so soft of mind and body."[26] But Saint-Simon knew the prince only from a distance and in the last years of his life. This merciless pen portrait, drawn when Philippe was prematurely aged in body and broken in spirit, tells us nothing about the man in his prime.

Despite certain unfounded horror stories to the contrary, the prince did not remain a functional illiterate well into his teens. A letter in his hand, or rather scrawl, to his uncle Gaston congratulating him on the birth of a son in September 1650 is incontrovertible proof that he could read and write at least serviceably, if not correctly, by his tenth birthday (plate 6).[27] Even so, subsequent correspondence evidenced less improvement than one might expect if the student had been more diligent or the teachers more demanding. He was never to master the grammatical structure of the French language; his spelling was faulty and his handwriting remained so poor that he frequently could not read it himself. "Here Madame," Liselotte (the family name of Elizabeth Charlotte) later remembered his saying: "you are accustomed to my handwriting. Read me this; I do not know what I have written." Both thought it a joke and would enjoy a good laugh over his dilemma.[28] Here no doubt he differed little from most of the nobility of his day. As a rule, the higher the rank, the more illegible and ungrammatical the hand. (Louis, however, was at least one exception; even if his orthography were poor, he learned to handle French correctly and even with elegance.) Certainly Philippe derived no pleasure from the written word and had no gift for literary expression. He wrote no memoirs and although, as brother of the king, he was obliged to write letters by the hundreds (not many of which have survived), he usually kept them as brief as possible. Except for the rare occasion when he gave vent to emotion, perhaps pent-up rage and frustration, his letters make use of a limited vocabulary and colorless formula. Most are chiefly remarkable for triteness of expression and banality of thought.

In speaking, however, as in early childhood the prince continued to command an easy flow of words and often an apt turn of expression. When he was close to fourteen one of his chaplains published a little book, *Les dits notables de Monsieur Philippe de France*, in which some of his most noteworthy expressions were set down. Extremely laudatory, indeed to the point of ridiculousness, much of it can be written off as sheer flattery. The alleged purity of the prince's speech, his modesty, piety, and virtue came in for special praise. When someone expressed surprise at Philippe's short stature, the prince supposedly replied in a clever play on words "that princes were always somewhat *grand* [tall or great], but as for himself he wanted only to grow *grand* in wisdom.[29] Nonetheless, the choice of this particular form of adulation was undoubtedly a reflection of Philippe's articulateness and wit. No one ever composed a similar encomium on the more reserved Louis at this or any other time of his life. The prince was always to have a reputation as a great talker (often without having said very much). Later he was said to have been a veritable chatterbox and incapable of keeping a secret.[30] "Oh!" Louis would remark scornfully, "if anyone could talk as much as my brother."

Philippe seems to have made no formal study of languages other than French, although he became reasonably fluent in Spanish. He probably learned most of it from Anne, who reportedly spoke Spanish to her children in the intimacy of family life. Shortly before Louis's marriage to his Spanish cousin Maria Theresa, the prince joined his brother in working on the vocabulary that would be useful in the exchanges of protocol. On that occasion he was able to converse successfully with the bride and her father,[31] but subsequently he seems to have made no use of the language except to show off his knowledge on occasion before the dutifully admiring ladies of the French court.

Philippe was anything but a student or scholar. In any case, Mazarin did not desire to give him, or the king, for that matter, an education in the humanities. The few books that he was known to have read—or at least that were written for his express benefit—were tracts by La Mothe Le Vayer on, in addition to the history of France, geography, rhetoric, and ethics. But dry and colorless, they must have repelled him rather than attracted him to the printed page. He seems never to have been introduced to classical literature. A translation of Florus from the Latin was published under his name, but it was almost certainly mostly or entirely the work of a tutor. As an adult he was never known to have read or referred to any of the great Latin essayists, poets, or statesmen. Nor was he known to take any interest in the literature of his day. Although for many years he was a friend of Mme de Sablé, hostess of a celebrated literary salon, he was not a part of her literary circle, which included La Rochefoucauld, nor, to judge from his letters, did he discuss literary subjects with her. The world of belles lettres was closed to him. Louis, too, of course, was never bookish either as a boy or as an adult. But whereas the king was instructed personally and daily by Mazarin in the craft of statesmanship and was soon obliged to spend long hours reading, writing, and analyzing government papers, Philippe was shut out of these adult pursuits. Thus he could not acquire the vast practical knowledge of politics, diplomacy, and organization of government that distinguished his brother. Nor was he ever trained to approach a question analytically and to pursue it systematically. Contemporaries noted his inability to concentrate long on any given subject. Such habits of thought and expression were no doubt the inevitable results of what Philippe's chaplain, Daniel de Cosnac, bishop of Valence, summed up as "an education disproportionate to his rank."[32] Not that the prince was devoid of wit or knowledge. However, such accomplishments as he came to possess were of the kind that could be acquired more through observation and instinct than by systematic study.

Foremost among them were his talents and achievements as a collector of paintings, gems, and objets d'art and as a builder of gardens and châteaus. For these occupations he had to thank above all his innate love of beauty and his artistic gifts, which evinced themselves early in a childish fascination with jewelry and adornment. He also was soon greatly beholden to the cardinal who, himself a connoisseur of the arts and owner of an incomparable palace in Rome, probably took a spontaneous pleasure in gratifying a kindred spirit and fostering and shaping his aesthetic tastes. In addition, Mazarin must soon have realized that the prince's artistry could serve his purpose very well. Not only could his interests and energies be thus diverted into areas that posed no political threat to his brother, but his gratitude and obedience to Louis's will could be ensured through timely gifts to feed his passion for building and collecting. A discernible pattern emerged during Philippe's adolescence. Whenever the prince appeared to kick against the pricks, a gift (some might say a bribe), great or small, ranging from the magnificent property of Saint-Cloud on the Seine down to a small sum of money or a painting or two would effect a reconciliation and bring him to heel. Another, and no doubt unintended, result of this policy was the fostering of a spirit of acquisitiveness in Philippe. It was probably no accident that in his adult life he was to demonstrate a passion not only for collecting works of art but for amassing wealth and material possessions of all kinds. By then it may have become a means of securing gratification or compensation for other satisfactions that had escaped or been denied him.[33]

As for physical activity, Philippe was taught, or at least exposed to, all the skills usual in boys of high rank: horsemanship, hunting, shooting, fencing, and dancing.[34] The enclosed garden of the Palais Royal was a splendid playground, and in it Mazarin had constructed a miniature fortress in which Louis and Philippe played at war with a selected group of children of honor. He was barely six years of age when a letter of the cardinal informs us that he was being taken to the hunt. And according to the *Gazette de France*, in summer he often joined Louis in swimming in the Seine.[35] He must have been a good dancer, since he frequently appeared in the ballets that were one of the highlights of the court in the 1650s and 1660s.[36] Even in later years, according to his second wife, "he danced well" and enjoyed attending balls and masquerades.[37] On these occasions, again according to the *Gazette de France*, his performance was graceful and accomplished, though never, of course, equal to that of the king, who was always the star. He also must have become a skilled equestrian. He took prominent roles in the extravagant pageants and tests of equestrian skills that Louis staged in the early years of his adult reign and later, when with the army in Flanders, thought nothing of spending entire nights in the saddle.

Nonetheless, during his adult life Monsieur displayed a marked aversion for physical activity of any kind. In contrast to his brother and to the tradition of his Bourbon ancestors, he had no taste for the hunt. "Were it not for war," wrote Liselotte, "[Monsieur] never in his life would have mounted a horse."[38] Perhaps he was sedentary by nature. But it could not have been much pleasure for Philippe as a child to compete with Louis in sports and exercises. The older boy possessed all the natural advantages of age—superior strength, coordination, and skill—and was a natural athlete to boot. He was also the king, who had to excel at everything and to whom all the children had to defer. He probably would have prevailed even had the game not always been rigged. To Philippe fell the role of perpetual loser. Small wonder he preferred the company of women and girls for games and play. With them competition was absent. In any case, outranked by the prince, they deferred to him just as he was obliged to yield to the king. One need not be a psychologist to understand that an increasingly marked preference for female companionship, reinforced by the slackness of the educational program designed for Philippe, was in part the result of the demoralization he felt in competition with Louis. His seeming laziness could easily have been a means of avoiding being put to the test.[39] Perhaps also as an adult he decided, consciously or unconsciously, that this was one humiliation he could forgo.

THE SOCIAL GRACES

Except during the years of the Fronde, the court in which Louis and Philippe grew up was lively and full of gaiety. Although in her middle age Anne took seriously her duty to God and her responsibilities as regent, she had by no means lost her taste for a good time. From the Spanish court, where Lope de Vega had performed, she had brought a well-developed interest in the theater. In France she became a devoted patron of Corneille and Molière. Mazarin broadened her taste by importing Italian opera and ballet. Theatricals were only a small part of the social life of the court. Receptions, balls, banquets, masquerades, and pageants succeeded each other at a dazzling pace. Especially during the winter months, the social calendar was crowded. In addition, on evenings when no special entertainment was planned there was always the gaming table, which never aroused any religious scruples in Anne. Both she and the cardinal were avid gamblers and, in line with attitudes typical of their century, probably saw nothing wrong in permitting small children to play games of chance, even for money.[40] Certainly Louis and Philippe could have come by their gambling habits early in life. It was later a staple feature in Louis's court and became almost a passion for Philippe during his mature years.

Anne presided over these festivities with the ease and practice of a natural hostess. She understood the importance of the social graces in the life of a court and believed her sons' training in them could not begin too soon. Both children began appearing at receptions and dinners for visiting dignitaries as soon as they left the custody of women. By the time they were ten or eleven they were already hosting small afternoon gatherings or early evening suppers for selected children of the court.

In these affairs Philippe was a willing and gifted pupil. Naturally gregarious and sociable, he enjoyed mixing with people and going into society. Even more than attending parties, he loved giving them and in time became a celebrated host. He was still in his teens when his cousin, la Grande Mademoiselle, after attending a reception in his quarters while traveling with the court, noted his "special talent for doing the honors of his house."[41]

Philippe had opportunities aplenty to perfect his social skills. After the Fronde he moved away from Anne and Louis and set up a separate household in the Tuileries, vacated by Mademoiselle, then in disgrace for her role in the rebellion. There, while the pace of court social life increased in the return of domestic peace, Philippe began to preside over more elaborate entertainments and participated with Louis in the round of gaiety. Consider, for example, the month of January 1655, when the prince was fifteen years old. The year began with a ball given by Louis at the Louvre, his residence after the Fronde, in honor of his mother in the traditional feast of kings. The next day there was a supper at the adjacent palace of Mazarin during which Louis and Philippe entertained the company with "a very gallant improvised masquerade." On January 7 Philippe invited all the ladies of the court (with escorts, of course, including the king) to a ball and comedy followed by a late collation. The eleventh saw a hunt at the forest of Vincennes, the fourteenth an Italian comedy at the Louvre. On the seventeenth Philippe again hosted a great ball and buffet at the Tuileries. The festivities of the month drew to a close when Louis and Philippe at the head of a band of young nobles, all in disguise, trooped to the lodging of Henriette, princess of England, to sing a serenade, after which they descended on the mansion of Chancellor Séguier. Recognizing his august visitors and reacting quickly, the chancellor spread a feast. So delighted were the invaders that they asked to return, which they did two evenings later to be offered a ball, comedy, music, and banquet.[42]

THE FRONDE AND ITS EFFECTS

The civil war known as the Fronde—in French literally a slingshot used by boys—was far more serious and complex than its name would imply. Lasting nearly five years, it involved a fundamental challenge of the authority of the Crown: among others, its right to control taxation, its right to direct foreign policy, its right to dictate to the Parlement of Paris, and its ability to sweep aside the grievances and ambitions of a nobility that desired to share the royal prerogative. The leaders of the Fronde lacked a well-formulated ideology of revolt and offered no clear alternative to absolutism. But many of their grievances and demands were to reappear 140 years later in only slightly altered form in the origins of the great French Revolution. In the seventeenth century as in the eighteenth, these conflicts were fought out in a larger context of class struggle, widespread economic deprivation, popular violence, and a royal treasury desperate for revenue. The rebellion is usually divided into two phases, the parlementary Fronde of 1648–49 and the Fronde of the princes of 1651–52.[43]

From the very beginning the Fronde involved a clash of persons in high places and a network of intrigue and conspiracy that often masked the significance of the important questions at stake.[44] To Anne the revolt reduced itself to disobedience to her beloved son, her firstborn and her sovereign. It was also, of course, an attack on her own person and authority as well as on those of Mazarin, whose direction of affairs of state she upheld. Both came in for vilification of the grossest kind. In her desire for forceful suppression of the disorders and punishment of its perpetrators, she reacted with the outrage of a mother as well as a regent. Bad enough that the parlementaires, for whom she had nothing but contempt, should rebel. Far worse and infinitely more dangerous was the disloyalty of members of the high nobility and of the king's own family. Cadet branches of the royal family, both legitimate and illegitimate, formed the nucleus of cabals reaching down to their creatures and other ambitious place hunters. Possessed of provincial governorships and enormous financial resources, the princes were capable of fomenting and leading armed rebellion across the land. When joined by the Grand Condé, Louis II of Bourbon, first prince of the blood, and by that prince of conspirators, Gaston, duke of Orléans, they posed a formidable threat to Louis's throne. Thus, to the already complex political situation were added the strains of a family feud, all exacerbated by the wounded maternal instincts and pride of the regent.

Philippe had not yet passed his eighth birthday and was ill with smallpox when disorder broke out in Paris in the summer of 1648. He could, of course, have had no comprehension of the issues involved. Perhaps in his childish mind the early events of the Fronde were no more than a jumble of frightening impressions and experiences: his feverish sufferings, an inexplicable separation from his mother, mysterious arrivals and departures in the middle of the night, and terrifying hours shut in the trunk of a carriage as it jolted and rocked through the streets of the capital.

The violence erupted when Anne and Mazarin, who had been negotiating in vain with the demands of Parlement and other sovereign courts in Paris, ordered the arrest of three of their most prominent members. The poor—the *menu peuple*—incited by the courts and always on the edge of starvation, poured into the street and erected barricades around the Palais Royal and across the city. Paris was out of control. In the Parlement proposals were heard to seize the king, to shut the queen up in a convent, to create a regency for Gaston, and to dismiss Mazarin and replace him with Monsieur's closest adviser, abbé de la Rivière.[45]

Fearing for the safety of Louis, Mazarin used Philippe's illness as a pretext for removing the king from Paris while the Palais Royal was cleaned to rid it of the danger of infection. On September 13 Anne took Louis first across the river to Rueil, the estate of Richelieu's niece, and then to Saint-Germain. Philippe, still feverish, remained in Paris with his household as a sort of hostage of the Parisians, who were "delighted to have this precious pawn in their hands."[46] Only after nine days, on September 22, was Anne able to devise a rescue. One of her gentlemen, making what was ostensibly a courtesy call on the prince, managed to spirit him out of the palace, hide him in the trunk of his carriage, and successfully arrange his transportation to Rueil.

This flight was but the first of many subsequent departures of the court, which was to live an almost nomadic existence for the next four years. After yielding to virtually all of Parlement's demands and returning to Paris late in October, Anne and her children were obliged to flee again the following January. Roused in the small hours of the night, Louis and Philippe were bundled into a carriage with their mother, Gaston, and his daughter and taken outside the city to Saint-Germain. So great had been the need for secrecy that no preparations of any kind had been made. Sleeping on cots or on straw, the royal party camped out as best it could in the unheated, deserted palace.[47] Although the government signed a treaty with the Frondeurs in March, the Treaty of Rueil, which again yielded to all their demands except for the dismissal of Mazarin, the court did not return to the capital until the following August.

During these confrontations with the parlementaires Anne and Mazarin had been not a little uneasy over the attitude evinced by Gaston. Partly owing to his popularity in Paris and partly because of his position as lieutenant governor of the kingdom, they had chosen him to negotiate with Parlement while representing the position of the government. But from the very first Monsieur had proved entirely too sympathetic with the demands of the Chamber of Saint Louis, an irregularly constituted body of delegates from the courts. Presented with the October "charter" that Gaston had negotiated and that yielded on all points, Anne was outraged, signing it only when Mazarin explained that it was a temporary expedient that could be set aside later, once peace with Spain had been achieved. Nor was the Treaty of Rueil any improvement. As Monsieur's biographer has so perceptively observed: "The victory of Parlement was to some extent [Gaston's] own."[48] What did the prince think he was doing? Anne and Mazarin must have asked themselves. What was he really aiming at?

Their fears were not set to rest during the ensuing year when cabals of the princes began to provoke uprisings in the provinces and when Condé, who had sided with the government during the parlementary Fronde, decided his efforts had not been sufficiently appreciated and began to make unreasonable demands. Caught between a capital still far from pacified and the threats of armed rebellion led by the formidable soldier-prince, whose governorship and other resources lent him enormous potential power, Anne and Mazarin had perforce once more to turn to Gaston. While the regent and her sons toured the provinces, showing them their king in an effort to regain their loyalty, Monsieur remained in Paris, charged with maintaining order, and given authority to administer the kingdom temporarily with the title of "lieutenant general of the king in all his provinces and armies." Never had the prince enjoyed such power or such popularity as, debonair and regal, he dispensed justice, presided over civic ceremonies, and basked in the confidence of Parlement and of the people. When in August the news was announced that his wife had given birth to a son, the expressions of public joy were almost the equal of those that greeted the birth of an heir to the throne.[49]

With the arrival of this long-desired son and heir (all his other children were daughters) and with his newly achieved influence in the capital, was Monsieur aspiring to share the authority of the king more permanently? So Anne and Mazarin must have feared. And the tenor of their remarks on his person and character can readily be grasped from a letter he received at this time from his small nephew, who well proved the truth of the adage "Little pitchers have big ears."

"Sir my good-for-nothing rascal [*Monsieur mon pendart*]," began Philippe. "I am delighted to have a brother-in-law [he meant to write cousin]. I should like very much to see him and that all this business at Bordeaux [where he was with Anne and Louis] was over. I am, Sir my good-for-nothing rascal, your very affectionate servant and good-for-nothing rascal. [Signed] Philippe."[50] (See plate 6.)

What were the effects of the Parlementary Fronde on Louis and on Philippe? The effects on the king, historians have agreed, were both vivid and permanent and were the root of his later distrust and fear of the capital. In the words of a recent biographer, "In his *Mémoires*, in his letters, and in his conversations for the rest of his life, traces of the fears and terrors caused by the barricades and rebellion always remained."[51] He had learned from experience how quickly a great city can become ungovernable and how vulnerable can be the position of the royal family. When he later built the permanent residence and showcase of his reign, he chose Versailles over Paris and came to the capital as infrequently as possible.

However accurate this hypothesis may be as an explanation for Louis's later aversion for Paris, it works not at all when applied to Philippe. Although his memories of the rebellion must have been just as frightening as those of his brother or perhaps even worse, they did not turn him against the capital. To the contrary. As an adult, until he completed the building of the château of Saint-Cloud, he habitually made the Palais Royal his principal residence outside the court. And to the end of his life he came often to Paris, where he could enjoy the theater and bask in the attention of his own court and circle of friends. He was always popular with the Parisians, to whom he dispensed largess with a princely hand. It was during the lifetime of Philippe that Paris and the Palais Royal became identified with the house of Orléans.

Why did he react so differently from his brother? Perhaps, in his childish mind, he began to associate Paris with his uncle, whom he greatly loved and with whom, as his letter to Gaston proves, he had begun to identify himself. They were both "good-for-nothing rascals." Not only was Monsieur his godfather, but he too was the younger brother of a king. Monsieur and his nephew had always been close. They even looked alike, their delicate dark beauty perhaps a throwback to their Medici ancestors. "Don't be astonished," Gaston had remarked when others marveled at the comeliness of his nephew. "I was as pretty as that."[52]

Perhaps Philippe was beginning to feel a bond of sympathy for a prince who had dared to challenge the same authority to which he was subjected. After the Fronde, when Gaston was exiled in disgrace, the prince continued to write to his uncle in terms of love and affection. "I beg you to treat me without ceremony," ran one such letter, "for the sincerity of the friendship that you have promised me and that I have pledged to you permits us to take this liberty." Never would the disgrace in any way, he concluded, diminish the "perfect esteem" and "very strong love" that to the end of his days he would bear for him.[53]

Gaston was popular in Paris, and the Parisians had revolted against the king. Already, at least unconsciously, the boy may have begun to associate the capital with a desire for independence, if not rebellion, that he was helpless to express in the regimen of his life in his brother's court. His descendants most certainly came to view the city in that light. Philippe's talented son, regent for the child Louis XV, made the Palais Royal the site of his brilliant court. Under his son and grandson, until the French Revolution, the palace became the visible focus of the spirit of anti-Versailles. Nor can one forget that in the 1780s the then duke of Orléans, the great-great-grandson of Monsieur, later better known as Philippe Egalité, exploited his popularity with the Parisians and used the Palais Royal in the heart of the capital as his political base from which to conspire and revolt against his cousin Louis XVI.

If in 1650 when Gaston was still professing loyalty to the Crown he was a "good-for-nothing rascal" at court, what must they have called him a year later when he decided to throw in his hand with Condé and join the Fronde of the princes? The quarrel of both men was principally with Mazarin, whose power over Anne and the minor king, and hence over the state, was all but absolute. Yet Condé was a dangerous adversary. With his courage, with his talents as a soldier, and with his governorship of Languedoc, alliances with other noble families, and extensive control of patronage, he was capable of inciting rebellion across much of the south of France.[54] Moreover, he was not averse to seeking an alliance with his former enemy the Parlement (sealed in the so-called Treaty of the Two Frondes) and even with Spain, with whom France was at war. At first the cardinal had the upper hand, and in January 1650 he ordered the arrest of the prince, his brother Conti, and his brother-in-law Longueville. A year later he bowed to Condé's superior combination, released the three from prison, and himself went into exile.

As for Monsieur, his intentions were never entirely clear. Certainly he was jealous of the power wielded by Mazarin, but whether he intended to supplant him or merely to dilute the authority of the Crown perhaps not even he was entirely sure. While Mazarin was absent, advisers were not lacking who urged him to seize the person of the king, confine the queen in a convent, and place himself at the head of the state. But Gaston declared himself satisfied with his title of lieutenant general and avowed his intention never to oppose the will of the regent.[55] At the same time he called repeatedly for the convocation of the Estates General, an action that in itself carried a challenge to the royal prerogative and to which no sovereign could be expected to consent except under extreme duress. Monsieur seems in fact to have been reluctant to make open war on the Crown; he also greatly disliked Condé, whose ambitions he distrusted. Yet when Mazarin returned to the side of Louis and Anne early in 1652, his hand was forced. Calling on his revenues from the states of Languedoc and from his proprietary holdings, he began assembling an army to take up arms against the king.

During the course of this conflict it was Mademoiselle, more than her father, who moved to the center of the stage. By now twenty-five years of age and still unmarried, she saw herself as a tragic heroine caught in the trap of unkind fate. No one, she was to declare, had ever suffered as much as she. She has told us her story herself in memoirs (she fancied herself a writer) whose appealing naiveté and honesty are offset by an insensitivity and pride of birth offensive and even comical to the twentieth-century reader. Her principal interest in life was what she called her "establishment," by which she meant marriage, and by that, in turn, a throne. The question was no easy one. For the granddaughter of Henry IV and the richest woman in France (sole heiress of Gaston's first wife), not just any crown would do. In an age when dynastic marriages were a prime instrument of diplomacy, the disposition of her hand involved considerations of state as much as the satisfaction of Mademoiselle's personal *gloire*. Over the years one marriage project after the other had been launched only to fall to the ground.

This ill success did not unduly disappoint the princess, however, for ever since childhood she had above all hoped to become queen of France. When Louis was born, even though he was nearly twelve years her junior, she had shocked Richelieu by calling the baby her "little husband." Mazarin and Anne had been no more encouraging, since both saw the interests of France best served by the king's marriage with a Spanish infanta. Now came her father's adhesion to the Fronde, an event that, to the undiscerning mind of the princess, seemed designed to serve her purpose: a victory of the Frondeurs over the Crown would, she somehow believed, induce Anne to consent to her marriage with the king.[56]

Such was the background of Mademoiselle's exploits as Amazon and Frondeuse. In her eager pursuit of glory and her royal husband, she far outpaced the indecisive and hesitant Gaston. In the Loire valley, finding the gates of the town of Orléans closed to the army, she crossed the river by herself, contrived to enter by a rear gate, and persuaded the town officials to accept the authority of the princes. A few months later, when Condé's army was pressed by the forces of the king against the walls of Paris, Mademoiselle, who was inside the city, went herself to the towers of the Bastille and ordered the guns of the fortress turned on the king's army while Condé and his men marched to safety through the gates of Saint-Antoine.

Successful in war, the princess was a failure in love. The reaction of the court to these acts of armed rebellion was just the opposite of what she had anticipated. Mazarin, who had again returned from exile and with Louis was watching the action of Mademoiselle from a nearby hill outside Paris, sized up the situation to perfection: "With that cannon," he remarked, "Mademoiselle has shot her husband."

The three-thousand-odd soldiers recruited by Monsieur performed no great military feats; yet when added to the armies of Condé, those of his princely allies, and the Spanish regulars brought in from Flanders, they sufficed to battle the army of the king for nearly a year. Their time ran out only when their alliance with the Spanish enemy became clear and the moderates in the Parlement of Paris went over to the Crown. Perhaps they were destined for defeat from the first. During most of the seventeenth century, despite the discontents and grievances of the courts and nobility, there was probably no viable substitute for the absolute state.[57] On October 21, 1652, Louis was able to make a formal reentry into the capital. The Fronde of the princes was at an end.

The restoration of domestic peace meant the return of the entire court to Paris and to the rhythm of its usual life. It also spelled the departure of Gaston and his daughter in disgrace on the orders of the king, Monsieur to his estates in the Loire valley, Mademoiselle to a distant château on her property at Saint-Fargeau. Both must have been sorely missed by Philippe, for they were his favorite relatives. Meanwhile Condé refused to sheathe his sword and withdrew to Flanders with the Spanish army.

If the end of the Fronde spelled no immediate or dramatic change in the lives of the royal family, its effects were substantial and long lasting. Even more than from the first Fronde, Louis drew lessons from this rebellion that made an indelible mark on his character and on his later direction of the state. As for Philippe, for the remainder of his life he was to pay, and to pay heavily, for the rebellion of his relatives.

To Louis and to Mazarin the spectacle of the princes and great lords of the land at the head of their private armies must have seemed a throwback to the civil wars of the sixteenth century. It underscored the critical need to build a royal army on whose loyalty and strength the sovereign could count to punish disobedience to the Crown. Many years later in memoirs designed for the instruction of his son, the king recalled the near anarchy of those years: "The terrible rebellion across the land . . .; a war with a foreign enemy in which the domestic troubles cost it dearly; a prince of my blood and a very great name at that at the head of my enemies. . . . Everywhere civil war reigned supreme."[58]

The Fronde had also served to remind him of the need for constant vigilance against the pretensions and ambitions of members of his own family. "It could reasonably be asked," he wrote, "if a prince does not have as much need to protect himself from the pretensions of his own allies, of his own subjects, *and even of his own family*, as from the attacks of his enemies."[59] Hence the highest praise he could give to his mother was her willingness, when he reached the age of decision making, to give over freely and entirely the reins of sovereign power into his hands, "for thus she let me know that I had nothing to fear from her ambition."[60]

Brothers, he recognized from the example of Gaston, could present a special problem, and he warned his son (at the time he wrote Louis still hoped for additional male heirs) to be on his guard and "to raise yourself above them and make the whole world recognize that you merit this rank [as dauphin and future king] given you by birth alone."[61] The inference was clear: exclude them from positions of authority in the government and never permit them to possess lands or other resources that they could use as a base to mount a challenge to the authority of the Crown. "Sons of France [i.e., male children of kings]," he concluded succinctly, "must never have any other shelter than the Court nor any other refuge than in the heart of their brother."[62] And even these precautions might not suffice. Better yet if he who ruled were elevated over brothers and other members of the family not only by his station and his power, but also by his character and habits of work. "The greatness and firmness of his [the sovereign's] soul is irradiated by the contrast of the laxity to be found in theirs [the relatives]; and his love of work and of true glory is all the more illuminated by the soft idleness and frivolity to be found in them."

The implications of these royal dicta for the future of Philippe are too clear to require commentary. Symbolically, at least, the difference between the ranks of the king and his brother had already been demonstrated publicly in the ceremony of the king's majority on September 7, 1651. On that occasion, after Louis had proclaimed his intention of taking on himself the governance of the kingdom and Anne had renounced her authority as regent, according to the official account, "Monsieur, only brother of His Majesty, approached to the feet of His Majesty to bend his knee, kiss his hand, and profess his fidelity.[63]

As in public, so in private. In the wake of the Fronde, the elevation of the king and the abasement of his brother were to be ever more pronounced. Truly Gaston, Mademoiselle, Condé, and the others had done Philippe an ill turn. The humiliations, failures, and consequent demoralization of the prince were just beginning as he entered the troubled years of adolescence. It was ever more difficult to be the younger brother of the Sun King.

THREE
·
Le Roi Manqué

When the court returned to Paris in the autumn of 1652, the royal family no longer lived as a unit. As was customary with younger brothers of kings, le Petit Monsieur was established in his own household. Henceforth Philippe resided in the Tuileries, vacated by Mademoiselle on the orders of the king, while Anne and Louis, on the insistence of Mazarin, moved into the old Louvre, which could be more easily defended against popular violence than the Palais Royal.

The result, no doubt unintended, of this separation of Philippe's household from that of his mother and brother was an even greater isolation and exclusion of the prince from the inner circle composed of Anne, Louis, and Mazarin. Although the Louvre and the Tuileries were not far from each other, they functioned as independent units, with the king and prince following different regimens. From the descriptions one of Louis's gentlemen servants gave of the king's daily life during his teens (no comparable account exists for Philippe), we learn that now he neither dined, exercised, nor studied with his brother. And while the king saw his mother daily, visiting her apartment and often dining with her, he seems not to have been in the company of Philippe except on social occasions.

Who was there now for Philippe besides his mother and brother in the way of family and daily companionship? Gaston was at Blois,

Mademoiselle at Saint-Fargeau. With Condé still in rebellion, of Philippe's immediate relatives only the prince of Conti, who had declared his penitence, was at court. There were also the queen of England and her daughter, Henriette, and the queen of Sweden, when she was in France, and of course Mazarin and his family of nieces. But he had never had close ties with any of them.

At this period of Philippe's life probably the cardinal was the most important person in defining his position within the inner family. Even if Mazarin were not married to Anne, he was on such terms of love and affection with her and with Louis as to be in fact head of this close-knit family of three. For the cardinal, Philippe had always been at best a distant second to Louis. We have seen how during the Fronde, for example, he was willing to leave the prince behind in Paris while he spirited Louis and Anne to safety outside the walls. Moreover, in the dozens of letters he wrote at that time, he not only betrayed no anxiety for the welfare of the prince, who was then seriously ill with smallpox, but made no mention of him at all. In one he wrote that "their Majesties came to take the air in this place," and in another that the entire court was present at Rueil.[1] If this was not strictly accurate, Philippe being at the time in Paris, still it was a remarkable disclosure of who truly counted in the mind of the cardinal.

In the years after the Fronde Mazarin's indifference to the prince evolved into a poorly concealed hostility. The indispensable source of information on these emotions and on his feelings for Anne and Louis as well is again the cardinal's correspondence. A steady stream of letters containing a constant outpouring of love and affection (in the words of Louis's recent biographer, that of a "teen-age girl" and her "boyfriend"[2]) flowed between Mazarin and Anne while he traveled with the king and the army. It was understood that any letter to or from either of them, or from or to Louis, was meant for all three. The main topic of interest, aside from the mutual assurances of devotion, was unfailingly the Confident, their code name for Louis: his health, his prowess on horseback, his presence of mind in inspection of the troops, and his messages of esteem and affection for one or the other. Philippe, on the other hand, when he appears at all in these missives, is referred to simply as "my son" by Anne or as "Monsieur," by Mazarin, the term of respect unmistakably tinged with irony. "The Confident sends many embraces to 22 [Anne], and I promise you that he is entirely yours. He wishes much to be remembered to Monsieur, whose very humble servant I am,"[3] wrote the cardinal in 1653. Two years later, after assuring Anne of Louis's good health and his indefatigable performance with the army, he added: "I beg you to permit me to assure Monsieur of my very humble respects."[4] Or still again: "I beg you to say to the Confident that I think only of him and of the person [Anne] whom he loves the most, and I beg both of them to take a few moments to remember the absent [Mazarin]." And coldly he added in conclusion: "I entreat you to be so kind as to present my very humble respects to Monsieur."[5]

Anne's letters, far fewer of which have survived, as a rule speak of Philippe in his relationship with Louis and Mazarin. They may perhaps explain, also in a tone of irony, that the prince is much too busy playing with the ladies of the court to be bothered to write. Even so, she continued to keep him much in her company. To the continuing displeasure of Plessis-Praslin and over his protests, the prince habitually passed the spring and summer months with Anne and the court while Louis and Mazarin traveled to the front. (An exception was the year 1657 when Anne, despite the discouragement of Mazarin, permitted Philippe to make a brief appearance at the siege of Montmédy.[6]) He also accompanied his mother to religious services and convents so often as to cause the *Gazette de France* to remark that he was doing his best "to walk in the footsteps of such a perfect and distinguished model of piety."[7] Yet despite this frequent association of mother and son, Anne's letters, beyond her outpourings of devotion to Mazarin, were chiefly concerned with the health and safety of Louis. They as well as those of the cardinal are proof that neither of the two adults most important in Philippe's life took much interest in his problems or in his development. Unlike Louis, he could not be sure of their affection and support in the stressful years of adolescence. Unlike Louis, the prince came first in the heart of no one in his immediate family. Philippe was in fact caught in a game he could not win. If he strove to excel, he earned not the approval of his mother and her minister but their displeasure, stemming from fear lest he outshine the king. If he played along with their program, submitting with docility and learning little, he invited their disrespect if not their contempt for his childish ways and idle games.

THE CORONATION

This fissure within the innermost circle of the royal family was nowhere apparent in the consecration of Louis in the cathedral of Reims that took place June 7, 1654. The greatest ceremony in the reign of any French king, it not only was a celebration of his per-

sonal glory and absolute power but, through his anointment with
the holy oil said to have been sent by heaven for the consecration
of Clovis, a confirmation of the sacerdotal quality of the monarchy
and the king's unique religious prestige and authority. It also was
a dramatic exaltation of the person of the monarch, who stood
above every subject, high and low in his realm, and received token
of their submission. For Philippe, who played the role of the dean,
most senior of the lay lords, it was the occasion of the most dramatic demonstration of his obedience to his sovereign brother.

Elaborate preparations had been made to stage as magnificent a
spectacle as possible.[8] Within the cathedral the richest tapestries of
the Crown draped the galleries, choir, nave, and transepts. The
steps at the foot of the great altar were covered with Turkish rugs,
and the altar itself was adorned with precious stones and satin embroidered in gold. Before the altar on a dais was placed an imposing
armchair for the king. To his right were banked seats for the ecclesiastical peers and a raised tribune for Anne, the queen of England,
and other royal dignitaries. To the king's left and somewhat to his
rear was a lower dais with a smaller chair destined for Monsieur,
who represented the duke of Burgundy, one of the original peers
of the realm.[9] To his left were banks of seats for the other lay
peers. Dominating all, in the middle of the entrance of the chancel
was raised the high throne on which the king would sit after his
consecration.

From start to finish, of course, it was Louis who was the focus
of all eyes and the star of the entire performance. Philippe, although
set apart and slightly above the other lay lords, was cast in a supporting role. While the lords, lay and ecclesiastical, together with
Anne and other queens and dignitaries, took their places in the cathedral at dawn on the day of the consecration, Philippe remained
with the king to accompany him to the ceremony in the procession
headed by the bishops of Beauvais and Châlons and the grand
chamberlain. Once they were in their places, the prince advanced to
kneel before his brother and to place on his heels the spurs of gold
that had been brought from Saint-Denis. There followed a long
and complicated ritual climaxed by the consecration, coronation,
and enthronement. Just before the king received the crown of
Charlemagne, the peers, Philippe at their head, were called upon
to declare their presence at "this act." Placed on his high throne,
the king was "adored" by all present. While doves fluttered and
swooped in the rafters and trumpets sounded fanfares, Monsieur
again led the peers in kneeling before the throne, kissing the feet
of the monarch, and chanting *vivat rex*. After the reading of high

mass, the king emerged from the cathedral to the acclaim of the people. The following day, again "accompanied by Monsieur," he went to the church of Saint-Rémy where, like the thaumaturgical princes of the Middle Ages, he "cured" three thousand (the figure given in the *Gazette de France*) victims of scrofula with "the touch of the king."

What the fifteen- and thirteen-year-old adolescents may have been thinking or feeling as they went through the exhausting ritual, the historian has no way of knowing. They could not have failed to be impressed by the magnificent pageantry and religious solemnity of the occasion. Philippe, with his eye for beauty and love of adornment, probably took pleasure in the jewels, the rich fabrics, the gold and silver of the ecclesiastical vessels, and the monstrance with the Host. He must himself have cut a handsome figure in an ermine-trimmed mantle of violet satin and a diamond-encrusted ducal crown. Perhaps he managed to be proud rather than resentful of his subordinate role in the ceremony. It was, after all, no new thing for him to bend his knee to his sovereign. From his earliest memory he had been drilled in his duty of obedience to his brother. In any case, investigative reporting not yet having been invented, the numerous contemporary accounts give us not the slightest insight into the human side of the unfolding drama and lead us to suppose that from the time the king arrived in Reims until his departure nearly a week later, he and the rest of the cast, like statues come to life, performed faultlessly, with cool precision.

ADOLESCENT REBELLION

If in public Philippe could master the role of loyal subject, in private he was not always in such command of himself. The prince was entering that critical period of transition from childhood to adulthood when the individual must throw off his dependence and find for himself some sense of direction and purpose. Although the concept of adolescence as developed by twentieth-century personality theorists, with its attendant "identity crisis," no doubt did not yet exist, the prince was exhibiting behavioral problems identified with this period of the developmental cycle that have been described across the ages.[10] By the time he was seventeen his social attitudes were still so childish as not only to amaze Mademoiselle, meeting her cousin for the first time in five years, but to dismay even the cardinal and Anne, who saw that his occupations were in no way normal for a boy of his age.[11] Today they would probably be called regression, a defense mechanism, or escapism. Whatever the label or whatever the century or culture, they can easily be understood as a logical reaction to the subordinate and humiliating status in the family and the court that he was helpless to change.

The flight from reality, however, was on occasion interrupted by episodes of rebellion. The evidence is sparse but is probably sufficient to permit us to perceive the resentment and rage seething beneath the veneer of childlike insouciance. Although infrequent, these episodes were acute and usually assumed a physical form. Their outcome, of course, was never in doubt. Disgrace, punishment, and submission were the prince's inevitable lot.

As a young boy Philippe already had a reputation for a quick temper that more than once got him into trouble. One day while dancing a ballet he tripped over his partner's skirt and saw one of the ladies of the queen break into laughter. Furious, he slapped her. Not long after, he struck one of the daughters of a lady of honor who had quarreled with his nurse. By the time he was twelve, the adults about him seem to have hoped that he was properly cured of these childish bouts of temper. Father Paulin, writing Mazarin, soon to return to court from exile during the Fronde, could report as follows: *"The King is always in good spirits, well behaved, and very pious, loving well his Mother, the Queen our Sovereign, and the little Monsieur his brother is a now a delightful charmer. No longer does he have temper tantrums. Your Excellency will not know him.*[12]

This letter may have reflected a particularly egregious outburst by the prince, this time directed against Louis, that had taken place earlier in the year. The episode, as reported by the king's valet La Porte, who witnessed it, would strike us today as a normal and hilarious scuffle between two young boys. But involving as it did a physical attack on His Majesty, it was a matter of no small importance and reverberated through the court. The brothers, who were traveling with their mother, had slept in a small room in beds side by side. On waking the king, apparently without thinking, spit on the bed of Monsieur, who immediately retaliated in kind. Angered, Louis spit in his brother's face. Not to be outdone, Philippe leaped on Louis's bed and urinated, an act that was also repaid in kind. "Having nothing more with which to spit or piss," related the valet, "they set about tearing up the sheets and soon began to fight." Only the entrance of Louis's governor put an end to the fray.[13] "Monsieur became angry more quickly than the king," noted La Porte in conclusion, "but the king was more difficult to appease than Monsieur."

Perhaps Paulin was right in believing that the fallout from that affair, which by implication was emphatic but was nowhere spelled out, had been sufficient to quell the prince's temper. Not until Philippe was sixteen does the historian learn of another occasion on which he brought down on himself the opprobrium of the adult world, and that was caused not by loss of temper but by adolescent foolishness. His reaction to their wrath is one of the few evidences we possess of his sense of pride and his own worth natural to his age. According to a source usually well informed on the gossip of the court, some of the daughters of the ladies of honor had complained to the queen that when the prince encountered them, he would make as if to lift their petticoats while offering suggestive remarks. Anne, failing to see any humor in the situation, confronted the culprit and commanded that he be whipped. Easier said than done. Neither the governor nor his assistant would carry out the order. "Advised of this," wrote the informant, Philippe "said to the queen that they had done well not to accept the commission, that he was past the age to be beaten and that anyone who tried it could be assured that he would run his sword through his body."[14]

A far more serious row took place the following spring, again probably triggered by adolescent bravado. It was Lent, and Philippe, no doubt with the intention of shocking his mother and brother, helped himself to a bowl of meat broth at table and declared his intention of eating it. Properly horrified, Louis retorted "Bet you won't" and tried to take the plate from his brother's hands. In the puerile scuffle that followed, the king threw drops of the broth on Philippe's hair and clothing. Suddenly beside himself with a fury he could not control, the prince threw soup and plate in His Majesty's face. Louis, his vanity piqued by the outcries of the ladies-in-waiting, became angry in turn and declared that save for the presence of his mother he would kick his brother bodily from the room. Disgraced, the prince withdrew to shut himself in his room for the remainder of the day.

As the news traveled, the court buzzed like a beehive. The heir to the throne had struck the sovereign. According to some, the prince was beaten for his act of lèse majesté; others speak only of an incomplete and painful reconciliation effected the next day by Anne and Mazarin. Daniel de Cosnac, Philippe's future chaplain, was so impressed by the prince's show of spirit that he decided on the spot to serve him. Seeking out the cardinal to arrange to purchase the post of chaplain, he declared: "I had thought that the prince was nothing but a pretty boy, but now I see he has it in him to be a man. With all my heart I shall enter his service."[15] Mazarin's reaction can be easily imagined.

Philippe was much embittered by the humiliating experience and unburdened himself to Mademoiselle, of all those at court the one who could best understand what was going on within him. "Much later," she wrote, "he told me of the terrible grief and resentment he had felt at the manner in which the king had treated him." The first time Philippe saw his cousin after the fight, he warned: "Don't say anything to me, they will think we are talking of what happened." Like the prince, she too was an outsider who, as daughter of Gaston and herself a Frondeuse, lived beneath a persistent cloud of disapproval. Even before the Fronde, when Mademoiselle was reprimanded by the queen for an excessive independence of conduct, the little boy had instinctively taken her side. "Cousin," he told her at the age of eight, "I am always for you, and I shall stand up for you against the whole world."[16] When she returned to court in 1657 she had made her peace with Anne and Mazarin, but with her always were the memories of her father's disgrace and her own rebellion.

Now the cousins began to seek out each other's company to the point that Mademoiselle, from whose mind marriage was never very far, began to consider the prince, child though he seemed, as a possible husband. "A young prince, handsome, well built, brother of the king," she wrote, "seemed to me a good match." Nothing came of the thought, of course. The queen and cardinal had other plans; but they were well aware of the sympathy the two cousins bore one another. It must have been easy to recognize the attraction of one underdog for another.

Can a deeper meaning be read into these episodes of rebellion? In psychoanalysis a fundamental dictum is the constant presence of antitheses: that every passion or emotion signals an underlying conflict in which an opposite passion is unconsciously at play. As Freud stated it, "Antitheses are always closely connected with each other, and often paired off in such a manner that the *one thought is conscious too strongly; its counterpart, however, is repressed and unconscious.*"[17] The individual is a bundle of conflicting emotions. At the same time he loves and hates, desires to destroy and needs to embrace. Molded by his culture, he is also stifled by it. One need not accept Freudian psychology in its entirety to perceive its applicability here. Outwardly loving and obeying his brother, unconsciously Philippe hated him and wished to destroy him. His feelings were ambivalent. A psychoanalyst would see the presence of an oedipal conflict. In the triangle of Philippe, Anne, and Louis, the king would have represented the surrogate father with whom the prince competed in a hopeless love for his mother. While hating Louis and wishing to remove him as his rival, he would at the same time have felt for him a "measure of tenderness" that would have caused him to submit to his authority so as to gain his love and approval.[18] Louis, on the other hand, as surrogate father would have seen Philippe as a hated and loved rival, and as older brother he would have sought to retain or to reaffirm the privileged position that he had once enjoyed first as only child of his mother and second as the stronger sibling who could dominate in every respect.

The unique positions of the two brothers as king and direct heir to the throne would have exacerbated these passions. According to seventeenth-century thinking on monarchy, a king did not die. As Bishop Bossuet was to phrase it, "Man dies, it is true, but the king, we say, never dies: God's image is immortal."[19] Or put another way, "The king is dead; long live the king!" As direct heir to the throne for eighteen years, Philippe menaced Louis with supplanting him as sovereign. He was a daily reminder to the king of his human mortality, and that in an age when death was no stranger. And while the king felt threatened, Monsieur, at least unconsciously, would have been envisaging himself as lord of the realm.

Such, of course, is the stuff of which great drama has been made. In Shakespeare and in English history the aging father is jealous of the young and ambitious son and heir. In the history of France more usually it was the struggle of brother against brother that had caused blood to flow. Early in the summer of 1658, only a few weeks after the king and the prince had nearly come to blows, they were themselves caught up in the drama of life or death that would decide which of the two would wear the crown.

THE WOULD-BE KING

Late in May 1658 Mazarin and Louis went again to the army, this time, after the fall of Dunkirk, to an encampment near Mardyck on the coast. It was an unhealtful spot, hot and humid, fetid with the stench of rotting corpses. Anne had protested their going to so dangerous a place, and once there the cardinal too had to admit its discomforts. Nonetheless, he wrote, Louis remained in good health and refused to heed his advice to leave.

Philippe had remained with his mother and her court at Calais. According to the cardinal he had been invited, even urged, to accompany his brother (Plessis-Praslin reported just the opposite).[20] But Mazarin must have sensed, in the bitter aftermath of the quarrel earlier in the spring, what the prince's answer would be. Mockingly, the cardinal wrote to Anne: "God [must have] inspired him not to come here, as it would be almost impossible for him not to fall sick; and as for boredom, he would have enough to last him a long time."[21] Seemingly without a care in the world, Philippe had retreated again to his play world to romp with the ladies on the beach and to feast on the sweetmeats and other delicacies sent by the English as a compliment to the queen.[22]

A few weeks later Mazarin was mocking no longer. On the last day of June Louis took to his bed complaining of a headache. A high fever followed, and within a few days the king was at death's door. Probably it was typhoid fever. While the doctors purged him, bled him, gave him enemas, and fed him herbal teas, the clergy exposed the sacred Host, recited special public prayers in churches all over France, and led religious processions. Transported to Calais early in July where he could be near his mother, Louis took communion and prepared for extreme unction. A special detachment of soldiers was ordered to come from Paris to bear and escort the body of the king to the capital in the expected event of his death. Not until July 11 did the fever break. Two days later Louis was convalescent at last.

During the nearly two weeks of crisis, Anne and Mazarin were in despair. The mother exhausted herself in constant vigil at the bedside of her son, deaf to all pleas that she conserve her strength.[23] Later she told Mme de Motteville that had the king died she would have left the world and retired to Val-de-Grace.[24] Mazarin, whose growing grief and ensuing joy can be followed in his letters, struggled to master his anguish and forced himself to make provisions for a future he could not bear to contemplate. "It is not only the king my master ... who is dangerously sick," he wrote on July 5, "but the best friend that I have in the world. May God not punish this kingdom in taking from us the one who brings us joy."[25] Three days later Mazarin had all but given up hope and tried to accept an event "that I dread more than my own death."[26] "I lack the strength to think that the king may die, but since he is mortal and extremely ill, wisdom and prudence dictate that we prepare for what may happen."[27]

At first Mazarin was inclined to think that the conduct of affairs would go on much as before, "for despite the desire of the queen to retire [in the event of Louis's death], I am assured that Her Majesty will do what I shall have the honor to counsel her, and I am certain that Monsieur will abide completely by her wishes."[28] A few days later his confidence was badly shaken. Not only had a peasant uprising occurred on the outskirts of the city of Orléans,[29] but—infinitely more serious—a number of the former princely Frondeurs, followers of Condé, were allegedly preparing to renew their revolt against the authority of the cardinal should the king die. Colbert, in Paris, was sending alarming reports that the great families of Retz, Brissac, La Trémouille, and others were known to be in collusion and were almost open in their demonstrations of joy at the king's illness.[30] On the instructions of Mazarin he fortified the royal garrisons at Vincennes and the Bastille, warned all the ministers, public officials, and those provincial intendants and others known to be special friends of the cardinal, and secured as best he could the safety of his palace with its treasures. But worst of all was the news of a cabal that had formed around Philippe, whose members were exploiting his antipathy for Mazarin and jockeying for positions of favor and power in what they believed would soon be the new reign. Allegedly with ties to the disloyal princes, they planned to move with king Philippe from Calais to Boulogne, push the queen aside, and arrest the cardinal, divesting him of his great wealth.[31] The ringleaders of the conspiracy were a group of women, notably Mme de Choisy, wife of Gaston's chancellor, the princess palatine, Anne of Gonzaga, sister of the queen of Poland, and a young adventuress with a reputation for avarice, Mme de Fiennes, lady-in-waiting of the queen of England.[32] Mazarin also believed that Philippe's governor, Plessis-Praslin, was involved as well as the comte de Guiche, son of the marshal de Gramont, known to be a close friend (much too close, from the point of view of Anne and the cardinal) of the prince.[33]

Just how effective these conspirators might have been in realizing their plans can never be known. But there is no doubt that the cardinal took them seriously. "The person who spoke to you about the movements afoot during the illness of the king," wrote Mazarin, "is entirely correct, and I am persuaded that those who are named were up to no good, no matter what they may now say."[34] In addition to the security measures taken on his orders by Colbert, he seems to have paid Mme de Fiennes to play a double game and at the same time managed to intercept letters of the most damaging kind written to Philippe from Mme de Choisy.[35] By late July, Louis having recovered, the minister began to make a clean sweep of the offenders, evicting them from court and exiling many to their provincial estates.

What of the prince himself during the critical days of his brother's illness? What emotions was he experiencing, and what plans if any was he making for the future that seemed to be opening for him? Mme de Motteville, who had her information from Anne, wrote that Philippe "showed all possible love [for his brother] and appeared extremely fearful of losing the king." When the queen told him that he could not go near Louis for fear of contagion, "he began to weep and with such terrible despair that for a long while he was unable to speak." The queen, she continued, was so very much moved by his goodness of heart "that from that day forward she loved him more tenderly than she had ever done in the past"[36]—a confession that, incidentally, reveals most tellingly the reservations in Anne's love for her younger son.

Motteville's testimony need not be set aside or discredited in order to accept Philippe's complicity to one degree or another in the cabal. Although there is no evidence indicating that he initiated the plot, even if he had done no more than read the letters and listen to the proposals of ambitious intriguers, he was culpable. He should immediately have informed the queen and Mazarin of his correspondents' malevolent intentions. Instead it was left for the cardinal, using bribery among other means, to unmask the culprits. Loving and hating at the same time, Philippe could have grieved over his brother's possible death while hoping and planning in private to supplant him. What might be regarded as perhaps an excess of emotion in his reaction to Louis's illness might have been rooted in his guilt over his secret desire.

No letters from the prince during these critical days have survived, but those of Mazarin to the queen reveal that at first the cardinal believed only that others had attempted to use the prince for their own selfish purposes. "I am the very humble servant of Monsieur," he wrote on August 7, "who I am persuaded has always been well disposed toward me, notwithstanding all the idiot things to the contrary they write from Paris."[37] A few days later, however, he had evidence in his hands that convinced him of the prince's guilt and ill will. Referring to unidentified letters that had come to light, he wrote: "And the Confident and you will see that the son [Philippe] of 22 [Anne] wants badly to hurt the sea [Mazarin]." The prince believed, he added, alluding to the sentences of exile he was passing out to the conspirators, that Mazarin was "the sole cause of the misfortunes experienced by those he loves. But . . . I shall do my duty no matter what may happen."[38]

A crisis of this gravity could not blow over without leaving its mark both on the course of events and on the individuals concerned. Its most immediate consequence was to reveal to Mazarin and to Anne the urgency of Louis's marriage. In the past mother and minister had seemingly shut out of their minds, as too terrible to entertain, the possibility of the king's death. Now that possibility had come very close to being reality. Their distraught reactions during the crisis of Louis's illness must have stemmed in part from their knowledge that they had failed to groom the heir to the throne for the role of king. The solution was obvious: Louis must marry, and quickly too. Forthwith, the minister began to seek ways to bring the king of Spain to the peace table and his daughter, the infanta Maria Theresa, to the throne of France.

For Philippe the effects were of a much more personal nature. He had been apprehended in the midst of a plot of a most heinous kind. How could he face those he loved? On what terms could he live with the cardinal, again all powerful, whose ruin he had at least contemplated? What, if any, self-respect or pride of person could he salvage from the hideous debacle?

He could, first of all, try to run away, to turn away from life and its demands. Early in August, to judge by a letter from Anne, he was attempting to do just that. "My son [Philippe] has asked me to thank you for your care of him and to assure you of his affection," she wrote the cardinal, "and except that he is too busy enjoying himself with all the ladies we have here to take a minute to write, I think he would have done so [i.e., written to Mazarin]." She closed: "I have so many things to tell you that cannot be set down on paper."[39]

Mazarin, however, refused to let the matter rest there. A few weeks later, after the prince had been prevailed upon to put pen to paper (his letter has not survived), he showed himself generous in offering his friendship and respect while at the same time making clear to the prince where his path of duty lay. With great good sense, even though obviously failing to comprehend the reasons for the demoralization of Philippe's personality, the minister understood the necessity of coming to terms with the one who was still direct heir to the throne. To Anne he wrote: "Monsieur has written me a very kind letter. In my reply I spoke with perfect sincerity and without exaggeration. He has only himself to blame if he is not the happiest prince in the world."[40]

He had, in fact, written: "No one more than I wishes with more sincerity and eagerness to serve you well and to merit your good graces; time and events will convince you of this truth." Others may flatter you more, he continued, but no one can serve your interests better than by telling you what you should do: "that is to say, to love the king and queen with all your heart . . . [and they] have and will always have all the affection for you that you may desire."[41]

Mazarin may have sensed that more than lectures would be necessary to overcome the humiliation and resentment of the prince, and perhaps he truly felt sorry for him. He was also undoubtedly aware that court gossip ascribed Philippe's hostility to the cardinal's alleged parsimony that denied the brother of the king, a fils de France, a style of life befitting his rank.[42] In any case, while he was delivering these stern admonitions, he very likely had already put on foot the negotiations for the purchase of a gift that he knew above all would give the prince pleasure: a villa and gardens bordering the Seine west of Paris at Saint-Cloud. Early the following October, when the royal family and Mazarin were again in Paris, they went as a group to visit the property. The villa itself had been built in the previous century by Jérôme de Gondi and was then the property of Barthélemy d'Hervart, controller of finances and a long-time associate of the cardinal. Especially notable were the sweeping views of the river and the gardens with hydraulic fountains. Philippe, who knew of Mazarin's intentions, was transported with joy. The sale was arranged on the spot for the price of 240,000 livres. Within the week the duke of Anjou was proudly doing the honors of his new establishment.[43]

Apparently Mazarin's method of financial carrot and verbal stick met with success. Again from his correspondence, we know that he was able to elicit from the prince some kind of promise or assurance of his goodwill.[44] In the ensuing months the cardinal continued to build on this beginning and to keep open the channel of communication he had established. During the late summer and early autumn of 1659, when he traveled to Saint-Jean-de-Luz on the Spanish border to negotiate the king's marriage, he corresponded with Philippe more or less regularly, something he had never done before. Some of the letters do not say very much, and their style still verges on the mocking. "I feel myself covered with glory at the kind wishes that you have been pleased to send me," he wrote, "and to assure you once again that none of your servants to whom you dispense your favors can be more devoted or can wish to serve you more truly and passionately than I."[45] Others again preached to the prince his duty of loving his brother and mother. Even so, they were unvaryingly friendly and, even more important to a prince who had no income whatever except that doled out to him by the Crown, they continued to offer the promise of financial assistance. "I am terribly grieved that you have lost [at the gaming table]," he wrote. "You can depend on me to do all in my power to help you repair your misfortune."[46] One of the last in this series of letters, written shortly before his return to court, hinted at more substantial expenditures in behalf of the prince. "On my return, which will be soon," he declared, "you and I shall settle our accounts together, if that is your pleasure, and I am certain as of now that you will be satisfied ... [for] you will not recognize Saint-Cloud when you see it."[47]

That Mazarin had succeeded in getting through is proved by a letter from Philippe, the only one we have for this period, written from Bordeaux in September 1659. The prince was with Anne, Louis, and the court while Mazarin was still engaged at Saint-Jean-de-Luz in the marriage negotiations. It is a pathetic document, a reflection of his loneliness and sense of rejection. Although Philippe made no mention of the cardinal's generosity, he was clearly on better and more intimate terms with his former antagonist than with his mother and brother.

"I fear my letter will be very boring for you, having nothing pleasant to write from here," began the prince. "I assure you that everyone misses you very much, and I in particular am in despair, for you know that when you are here how I torment you for news, and no one tells me anything ... [and] it seems an infinity of time since I have seen you. I say this not just to compliment you, for I should not say it if it were not the truth. ... They tell me nothing, which makes me furious [but] I do not complain because the king and queen are very good to me." As an afterthought he closed: "I beg you not to write the king or the queen that I have said I am told nothing, for perhaps they would be angry with me."[48]

Understandably, Anne and Louis found it much less easy than the cardinal to forgive Philippe's seeming treachery and to admit him to their confidence. Mademoiselle reported that in the months following his convalescence the king constantly taunted his brother. In a typical episode, she wrote, Louis had jeered:

If you had been king, you would have had a terrible time of it. Madame de Choisy and Madame de Fiennes would not have gotten along, and you would not have known which one to keep with you. Probably it would have been Madame de Choisy; she it was who gave you Madame d'Olonne for a mistress. She would have been the sultan's queen, and while I was dying, that is what Madame Choisy was calling her.

Monsieur became very upset on hearing this [recounted Mademoiselle] and said to the king in a tone that seemed sincere enough, that he had never wished for his death, and that he had too much affection for him ever to make up his mind to lose him.

"And I believe you, too," replied the king, but immediately went on: "When you are in Paris will you be in love with Madame d'Olonne? According to what they write from Paris, the comte de Guiche promised it."

Monsieur blushed, and the queen chimed in angrily: "What a stupid thing to promise your friendship like that. If I were in your place I should be ashamed. . . . A fine figure you will cut."[49]

Mademoiselle herself had been greatly saddened by the whole affair. "All of Monsieur's true friends," she wrote, "were very angry at what had happened . . . for it was said that it [the cabal of the ladies] was the way to turn him against women."[50] Nor had she been happy at the prospect of Philippe as king, close to him as she was. "He was too much of a child to rule . . . . It is not that Monsieur was not intelligent, but he was still immature. . . . The state would have been badly governed."[51]

The more she thought over the whole affair the more disappointed with her cousin she became. She noticed that the following autumn the prince no longer showed the same eagerness to be with her. "But to tell the truth," she wrote, "I did not much care. The more I knew him the more I found him to be a man who thinks more of his clothes and his appearance than of making something of himself and of distinguishing himself. So that although I loved him very much as a cousin, I could never have loved him as a husband."[52]

Mademoiselle's change of heart may, of course, have been a bad case of sour grapes, her thoughts of marriage to the prince having come to nothing. It may also have had another cause. The prince she regarded so coolly in the autumn and winter of 1658–59 was not the same person who had greeted her on her return to court a year and a half earlier. In the aftermath of the king's illness and the machinations of the cabal, Philippe now seemed almost to glory in his disgrace. And among other things, the homosexual tendencies that had been latent and covert had now become open and avowed. Monsieur no longer made any secret of his attraction for men. To use the jargon of a later day, he had "come out of the closet."

Le Goût Abominable

Any historian broaching the subject of homosexuality is immediately in deep and murky waters. Not only are authorities in profound disagreement on its etiology, but the literature is too vast and the proliferation of theories so rapid as virtually to defy description or summarization.[53] And even if the correct theory were not in doubt, how does the historian apply it to the past? In attempting to do so he verges, however unwillingly, on the discipline of "psycho-history," as it is usually called, itself a field of notorious controversy. "How does one psychoanalyze the dead?" it is instantly asked. The historian is not dealing with living human beings who come to his office to relate the details of their private lives. He must rely instead on evidence from the past, which as a rule—certainly for the seventeenth century—is not only sparse but often of dubious reliability. Memoirs must be regarded with suspicion. Their authors, whether intentionally or unintentionally, were often careless of the truth and conspicuously unfair. They may have written long after the event, forgotten much, remembered only what they wished to, and from the perspective of hindsight imposed on the past an interpretation totally absent at the time. Letters, when one is fortunate enough to have them, are often capable of conveying more than one meaning.

But as partisans of the psychohistorical method remind us, historians have always written about psychology, often without being aware of it. "The professional historian has always been a psychologist—an amateur psychologist," the prominent American historian Peter Gay recently wrote in his strong argument for the use of the psychological dimension in history. "Whether he knows it or not, he operates with a theory of human nature; he attributes motives, studies passions, analyzes irrationality and constructs his work on the tacit conviction that human beings display certain stable and discernible traits. . . . He discovers causes, and his discovery normally includes acts of the mind."[54] The biographer who is to enter at all into the "personality" of a subject must inevitably account in some manner for the development of character. Even a pragmatist such as John Wolf, Louis's recent and perhaps ablest biographer, careful as he is to eschew theory, devotes chapter on chapter to the king's childhood and youth and on occasion is not averse to using "personality theorists" to help him understand the "ego-identity that both allowed and forced him [Louis] to play out the role of king."[55]

It is impossible for the biographer of Monsieur to avoid the subject of homosexuality. Not only did his sexual preference develop into a cardinal aspect of his character, his lovers at times governing his life, but owing to the loathing and contempt with which homosexuality was regarded by his contemporaries, in great measure it defined his reputation for posterity. In the ultimate "degradation" of his character, the brother of the king became the symbol or the epitome, in the words of Saint-Simon, of le *goût abominable*.

It must be said at the outset of any such discussion that even during his lifetime the subject of Monsieur's homosexuality was charged with suspicion and controversy. Many believed, and others have been repeating it ever since, that Mazarin, with Anne as a willing accomplice, deliberately emasculated the prince in order to unfit him for public office.[56] According to this view, a rebellion of the cadet against the sovereign was deemed so dangerous to the safety of the realm that both the cardinal and queen agreed that extreme measures were necessary. The abbé de Choisy, a notorious transsexual who had played with Philippe when they were children, wrote in his memoirs: "And all this [the emasculation of the prince] was done, so it was said, on the orders of the cardinal, who wished to render him effeminate so that he would not be a threat to the king as Gaston had been to Louis XIII."[57] Later the legend grew up that Anne of Austria let one of her sons disappear behind the iron mask, sacrificing his liberty for reasons of state. At the time the two were believed, with less theatricality but no less calculation, to have turned the younger son in the direction of effeminacy and then, the appropriate moment having arrived, to have arranged his seduction. A nephew of Mazarin, the duke of Nevers, was the individual most often named as "the first to [have] corrupted Monsieur."[58]

Mademoiselle, who had heard this gossip on all sides, came close to repeating the accusation to the cardinal's face. When in the spring of 1658, shortly before Louis's illness, Mazarin complained to her of the prince's effeminate habits—his love of dressing up as a girl and his distaste for the activities normal in a young man of his age—the princess demurred, although as discreetly as possible. She thought, she said, that "one" was only too satisfied with this behavior, and that "one" did not want him to lead another style of life. To which the cardinal retorted: "On the contrary, the queen and I passionately wish that he will ask to go to the army."[59]

Why, it may well be asked, were Philippe's contemporaries so ready to believe that Anne and Mazarin would resort to this particular method of destroying the cadet? Was it merely because the prince was already showing signs of effeminacy? If so, how should one account for the rumor that the cardinal had earlier attempted to perpetrate the same crime on Louis, supposedly to ensure his dominance of affairs of state, even though the king did not exhibit any overt tendency toward inversion? The accusation was preposterous, of course, and may be dismissed out of hand. Its source was the valet La Porte, an old servant of Anne who detested Mazarin and would say anything to blacken his reputation.[60]

The most logical answer seems to be the general abhorrence of homosexuality and homosexuals in the seventeenth century. According to the dictates of religion, sodomy was considered contrary

to nature and the most heinous of sins, likely to consign its perpetrators to the fires of hell. Until the end of the Old Regime it was
even punishable by death, although, since the vice was thought to
be confined principally to the clergy and the nobility, the ultimate
penalty was rarely invoked.[61] Even so, "corruption" of an individual
was accepted as an especially effective means of destroying him in
the public eye. In that climate of opinion, just as there was rever-
ence for the sacred and the "pure," there was loathing for the pro-
fane or the "impure," of which bastardy and sodomy were dichoto-
mous parts. If bastardy were a distortion of procreation, then
sodomy, according to the thought of the time, was a perversion of
sexuality and was thus impure.[62] The terms contemporaries used to
allude to homosexual practice well reflected the pejorative view-
point: the "Greek vice," the "Italian vice," or Saint-Simon's *goût
abominable*, among others. One can even read into the medical treat-
ments of the time, which relied heavily on purging, the opposition
of anal elimination to anal entry. The former, with its healing benefits, was desirable; the latter, as in sodomy, was repulsive. Moreover, those who engaged in homosexual activity were more often
than not said to be involved in other especially loathsome deeds.
Bastardy, sodomy, and murder by poison were frequently linked.
Thus, the chevalier of Lorraine, later the homosexual lover of Monsieur, was the one who allegedly negotiated the marriage of Monsieur's son to Louis's bastard daughter, Mlle de Blois, a union regarded as especially repugnant since the bride was herself the
product of a double adultery (Louis and his mistress having both
been married to others at the time of her conception). Or—a connection with murder—the chevalier and his shadow the marquis
d'Effiat, another of Philippe's lovers, were thought to have arranged
the alleged fatal poisoning of Monsieur's first wife, Henriette of
England. And again, the chevalier was assigned to conduct the oldest daughter of Monsieur, married to the king of Spain, to her
throne in Madrid where she subsequently died, again allegedly of
poison. The list of examples could easily be extended.[63]

When Mazarin told Mademoiselle that he and Anne deplored
Philippe's effeminate ways and wished he would take up soldiering,
he may well have been telling the truth. He and the queen may have
had no idea how demoralizing had been the effects on the prince of
their years of "parenting." True, they had not trained him to under-
study Louis in the role of king; but no tangible evidence has ever
been found substantiating the accusation that they deliberately attempted his emasculation. In any case, the historian and biographer
need not accept the thesis of the cardinal's and the queen's action to

account for Philippe's homosexuality. With the help of the psychological dimension, the data available on his childhood can shed much light on the development of this aspect of his personality.

While it is true that one school of thought maintains that "exclusive homosexuals"—people unable to achieve erotic satisfaction with members of the opposite sex—are the products of a physiological anomaly present at birth (perhaps in their genes or in their endocrine glands, for example),[64] most experts view homosexuality as an acquired condition usually arising from "early and profound disturbances in the mother-child relationship."[65] They accept the Freudian premise of the "original predisposition to bisexuality" of all human beings, whose sexual orientation does not take place until after puberty.[66] Consequently the experiences of the child, especially in his relationships with his parents, will have a determining effect upon his later sexual behavior.

A review of the pertinent record of Philippe might go as follows. Having lost his father before he was three years old, he was from earliest childhood much in the company of women, and as an older boy he continued to prefer their company and pastimes to those of boys. Anne encouraged this pattern, acquiesced in a lax program of training, and in fact raised him more as a daughter than as a son. "My little girl," she would call him. When he was old enough she made him her constant companion in her religious observances and still later kept him at court with her while Louis went with Mazarin to the army. Philippe early and easily fell in with this existence. According to Motteville, Philippe "liked to be with women and girls, to dress them up and to arrange their hair; he knew more about the style of feminine dress than most women, and his greatest joy was to adorn them."[67] When the prince did play with boys, it was often with the son of Mme de Choisy, François-Timoléon de Choisy, the future abbé de Choisy, a notorious transsexual, whom she was raising as a girl. Recounted the abbé:

> They dressed me as a girl every time the little Monsieur came to play, and he came at least two or three times a week. I had my ears pierced, diamonds, beauty spots, and all the other little affectations to which one becomes accustomed so easily and that later are so difficult to do without. Monsieur, who liked all that, was always very friendly with me. As soon as he arrived, followed by the nieces of Cardinal Mazarin and the ladies of the queen, they began to dress him and arrange his coiffure.... His jacket was removed so that he could put on the coats and skirts of women.[68]

Such details on Philippe's childhood would agree with the layman's usual view that male homosexuals tend to have possessive mothers who smother their sons, keep them tied to their apron strings, and crush their early attempts to assert their independence. In contrast, the fathers either are absent or are remote figures who take little interest in their sons. More strongly identified with their mothers than with their fathers, they tend to play more with girls and are likely to eschew the competitive, active games boys prefer. Such was certainly the experience of Philippe who, many theorists would say, was following the virtually "classical" pattern of childhood of the male homosexual.[69]

Yet Philippe was by no means an "exclusive homosexual." Episodes in his youth and adolescence clearly show that at times he was attracted to the opposite sex. When he was about twelve years old, learning that one of the young ladies of the court (in fact the one he had once slapped) had inexplicably retired to a convent, the prince was reported to have rushed off in great agitation, secured her release from the authorities, and returned with his beauty to court. During his adolescent years he was supposed to have been in love with her and to have made her expensive presents.[70]

At the age of sixteen he had been caught lifting the petticoats of the ladies-in-waiting. During the same year, while Mazarin was objecting to the prince's attentions to one of his nieces, Mme de Mercoeur, others reported that he was courting the affections of a certain duchess of Roquelaure.[71] And at the time of Louis's nearly fatal illness in 1658, as we have seen, he apparently already possessed a mistress. Other examples could be cited.

On the other hand, the tendency toward homosexuality was undeniably present before the summer of 1658. It was not just the effeminate behavior of the prince that troubled Anne and Mazarin. They so disliked the friendship that had developed between Guiche and Philippe that the cardinal warned Guiche's father in private to keep his son away from court, and Anne forbade the prince to see the young man without others present.[72] According to Mademoiselle, the prince managed to get around this order through the good offices of Mme de Choisy, who arranged to have "Monsieur see Guiche secretly, . . . as one would have done with a mistress."[73] And, of course, Anne and Mazarin must have been aware that there were homosexual "nymphs" at court who would have been only too eager to accommodate the wishes of the king's brother. One of Louis's and Philippe's childhood playmates, Louis-Henri de Brienne, has recounted in his memoirs: "Monsieur liked me even more than the king [and] called me his friend; without, however, anything wrong taking place between us, although I was much on the alert and well aware of what went on among the young schoolboys and the pages."[74] On one occasion, related Brienne, the prince made unmistakable advances to which the other, allegedly embarrassed, did not respond, being unwilling, he wrote, to "avail himself of what the world would call his good fortune."[75] We also have two letters in Philippe's hand written to a friend, the young duke of Candale, during his early teen years that hint of a sexual relationship, although what kind is not completely clear. In one he scolds the duke for having repeated to others what the prince had said "regarding the flesh [*cuisse*]," since "that would have gotten me in trouble with the king [if he learned of it] and is not what a friend should do."[76] In another he complains of an unidentified illness from which both he and his correspondent suffer. "I hope, nevertheless," he wrote, "that [the illness] will not prevent you from enjoying yourself in Paris . . . [and as for me] since I have been sick I have become very devout."[77]

After the king's nearly fatal illness in the summer of 1658 this homosexual aspect of his personality, which Philippe had striven to keep private, came out into the open. Guiche not only began to see the prince in public but ruled over him with an arrogance that scandalized the court and enraged the queen. Philippe seemed to glory in his humiliation, even when, as at a costume ball in December of the following year, it exceeded the bounds of decency. According to Mademoiselle, she and the prince, disguised as gypsy women, had gone to the party together and found Guiche already present. Pretending not to recognize Monsieur, the young man pulled the prince out on the dance floor, pushed him about roughly, and kicked him several times in the rear. The princess was shocked at this disrespect to the brother of the king. But Monsieur, she remembered, "liked" everything that Guiche did.

Word of the incident got back to Anne, who confronted the two cousins the following day. When Mademoiselle, not wishing to do Philippe a bad turn, pretended she had seen nothing, the queen retorted: "You are too discreet, Mademoiselle, the thing is public knowledge." Shamed and angry, she scolded her son for letting people laugh at him, all of which made no impression on Monsieur, wrote the princess, except that he was sorry his mother did not like Guiche.[78]

Philippe had taken a long step, at least in the public eye, toward conforming to the image of Monsieur, the king's brother, that is known to posterity, the effeminate and pathetic figure of the later and imperishable pen portrait of Saint-Simon: "A little man propped up on heels like stilts; gotten up like a woman with rings, bracelets, and jewels; a long wig, black and powdered, spread out before; ribbons wherever he could put them; and exuding perfumes of all kinds."[79] The handsome, precocious, active child was on his way to becoming a sort of court buffoon. When he was twenty years of age the court musicians were openly singing the ditty of Isaac Benserade, poet and salonist:

J'étais un fort joli garçon
Et j'avais toute la façon
Qu'on voit aux royales personnes
Qui touchent de près les couronnes,
Quand, à force de m'attacher
Au beau sexe qui m'est cher,
En m'habillant comme il s'habille
Je suis enfin devenu fille.[80]

Was it mere chance that the prince made known his homosexuality in the months that followed Louis's nearly fatal illness and the abortive cabal? Proponents of the nature (as opposed to nurture) theory of inversion might say so. As biologists, they would regard as relatively unimportant any emotional disturbance he might be undergoing or the interaction between the brothers and the mother. The physiological anomaly that must have been present in him since his birth and that was probably inherited would be seen, the age of puberty being passed, to be manifesting itself. Not for nothing, these experts might add, was Philippe d'Anjou the son of his father, the nephew of César de Vendôme, and the grandson of a Medici, all of whom, if not avowedly homosexual, were sexually attracted to males. And indeed, the hypothesis cannot be easily ruled out. Most experts of nearly every school agree that homosexuality has no single cause.[81]

Proponents of the nurture theory (psychologists of one school or another) would see the case in an entirely different light. For them the manifestation of the prince's homosexuality would have been triggered by the guilt and consequent desire for self-punishment engendered by the traumatic events of the spring and summer of that year. According to modern psychological theory, the prince would appear as a once extraordinarily gifted and ambitious child who by his teen years had become thoroughly demoralized by the hopelessness of his rivalry with his brother. Unable to dispossess Louis in the affections of his mother, constantly subordinated to him both in the family and symbolically in public functions as first male subject of the Crown, he felt himself doomed to mediocrity and inadequacy. While seeming to run away from life and its demands, he had turned inward upon himself those drives that he was helpless to express otherwise.[82] The incident of the plate of soup revealed both the prince's usually suppressed hatred of the king and his desire to destroy him. Soon thereafter Louis nearly died, and Philippe's guilty fantasy of supplanting him almost became reality. His collusion in the cabal would have exacerbated the need for self-punishment (Freud would say the ego was masochistic while the superego was sadistic) and at the same time the need to be loved by the one he had wanted to destroy. Hence the homosexuality, in which he would find satisfaction in feminine passivity and self-humiliation.[83] Glorification in the count of Guiche's tyranny over him was the result.

Most personality theorists stress the narcissistic quality of homosexual love. Philippe's effeminate interest in his coiffure and dress, his use of perfumes and cosmetics would be seen as exhibitionist traits of self-love and as self-defeating efforts to compensate for his sense of guilt and inferiority. If the individual as a child has suffered "traumatic onslaughts ... on his self-esteem," as an adult he "will tend to vacillate between an irrational overestimation of [him]self and feelings of inferiority, and will react with narcissistic mortification to the thwarting of [his] ambitions."[84] At the same time the resemblance between the lover of the prince, Guiche, and the king is unmistakable. One who knew Guiche well in court described him as "the handsomest young man at the court, well built, gracious, gallant, bold, brave, [and] of elevated rank and station. . . . He was haughty of attitude, but all recognized that no one had more merit than he."[85] Guiche was close to Louis in age. With his male beauty, high social position, and confident, disdainful air, he could almost have been the king's twin. Most of Monsieur's subsequent lovers were of similar appearance and temperament. One and all, they governed his life. And one and all, they were always to appear the most dominant and commanding during those periods in which Monsieur's humiliations at the hands of his brother were most acute.

As the 1650s drew to a close, the identities of the two brothers appeared clearly defined. Louis was the aggressive and confident ruler, seemingly sure of his sexual identity and ready to enter on his glory years as the Sun King. Philippe was the passive subject, tormented by feelings of guilt and inadequacy, desiring approval but knowing it would always elude him. In a court that abhorred homosexuality, he was known as "one whose heart could never be won by woman."[86]

In the past most theorists have held that personality is definitively formed and permanently fixed by the end of adolescence (some said by five years of age). In recent years, however, there has been a growing belief that behavior and personality continue to change over the entire course of life. The rationale is that although the early experiences of childhood do indeed shape personality, subsequent events and influences can modify behavior, which in turn affects the personality in a continuing "interactive cycle."[87] In line with these theorists, then, Philippe's inner drives and dispositions would indeed have been fixed; but the new and varied demands, responsibilities, and opportunities of his adulthood would exert fresh societal pressures. They in turn would mold and shape the direction of his daily life and the future development of his personality.

FOUR

·

Minette

RITES OF PASSAGE

The years 1659 to 1661 were momentous ones in the history of France and in the lives of the king and of Monsieur. In 1659 Mazarin had traveled to the Spanish border to begin negotiations for peace and after months of bargaining had signed the Treaty of Pyrenees with Spain in November of that year. For the first time in decades the kingdom of France was not at war. The long dynastic struggle with the Spanish Habsburgs as well as the internal divisions of the Fronde were now things of the past. France was on the eve of her glory years.

During these years both the private and public lives of the king were transformed. The treaty with Spain had brought not only peace but an infanta to France: Maria Theresa, daughter of King Philip IV of Spain, whom Louis married in the church of Saint-Jean-de-Luz on June 9, 1660. Anne (henceforward the queen mother), Philippe, Mademoiselle, Mazarin, and much of the court were in attendance. The match was a purely diplomatic and dynastic one; the young couple had not laid eyes upon one another until after the bride had already been married by proxy on the Spanish side of the border several days before the French ceremony. If the young queen were lacking in the beauty, wit, and vitality needed to win and hold the affections of the king it mattered little, at least on the official level. Her duty was to produce an heir to the throne, an obligation she fulfilled by giving birth to the grand dauphin the following November 1661.

Husband and father, Louis was by now also head of his government in fact as well as in name. For if he had gained a wife and son during these months, he had lost the only "father" he had ever really known. Mazarin, who had returned to Paris exhausted and ailing after his long negotiations in the southwest, died on March 9, 1661, after a month of illness. The event caused Louis not only personal sorrow (anyone who has read the details of the cardinal's last weeks and Louis's letters after his death cannot doubt the sincerity of his grief) but a transformation in his life as king. Determined in the future to serve as his own first minister, he began immediately to gather into his own hands the reins of the government formerly controlled by his mentor. It is unnecessary to add that Louis neither consulted his brother nor made a place for him in his government. Just as before, the prince was totally excluded from affairs of state.

Although the passing of Mazarin had less impact on the emotions and life of Philippe than on those of Louis, the events of these years were also of great consequence for the prince, even if they in no way altered the fundamental impotence of his position in the court and government. During them there took place the metamorphosis of the adolescent duke of Anjou into the young adult, duke of Orléans, husband, head of his household, possessor of an appanage, and soon-to-be father. The birth of Louis's son deprived Monsieur of his title of heir presumptive and removed him one step from the throne. But before this event took place the death of Gaston, duke of Orléans, in February 1660 had opened up the probability of succession to his uncle's title and of at least a small degree of financial independence. The late duke not only had enjoyed an independent fortune from his first marriage to Marie de Bourbon, duchess of Montpensier, but also had been the holder of a sizable appanage from the Crown and of the governorship of the province of Languedoc. Mademoiselle, the only child of this marriage, would inherit the proprietary holdings of the house, but as a female she could inherit neither the title of duke of Orléans nor the appanage that by law was reserved for male heirs. Nor, of course, could she be appointed governor of a province. Because Gaston's only son had predeceased him, the appanage would revert to the Crown. Philippe was the late duke's closest male relative, and he was also, like Gaston, the younger brother of the king, with the right to possess an appanage. Thus Monsieur could expect to receive his uncle's title and appanage and perhaps the governorship as well.

The death of the family black sheep not only raised questions of inheritance and rank but also opened up old wounds from past battles between the brothers. How much grief Philippe experienced on the passing of this uncle with whom he had once identified cannot be known with any certainty, but it must have been considerable. Although he had seen Gaston rarely if at all for nearly eight years, the duke having lived in seclusion and semidisgrace in his château at Blois, despite his aversion for letter writing he had continued to correspond with him on terms of affection. Only a few weeks before his death the prince had assured his uncle of his "constant devotion," of his "perfect esteem," and of the "passion" with which he remained his "most affectionate nephew."[1] Louis, on the other hand, remembered only his uncle's rebellion and his brother's love for him. For him Gaston was the enemy and Philippe his accomplice. Not only did he profess not to believe in his brother's grief, but through the disguise of mockery he saw it as a threat. It was Mademoiselle, sincerely mourning her father's death, who unwittingly bore the brunt of the sibling animosity. On presenting his formal condolences to his cousin, the king remarked: "Tomorrow you will see my brother trailing a long mantle. I think he is delighted at the death of your father just so that he can have the pleasure of sporting it." Seemingly as an afterthought, he alluded to the idea that probably was never far from his mind: "Lucky for me that he was older than I; otherwise my brother would have wished for my death instead of his so that he could put it on."[2] It was true, Mademoiselle admitted, that the next day Monsieur appeared with a train of "furious length";[3] but the princess was hurt and angry at the king's seeming lack of respect for her sorrow.[4] What she had failed to perceive was the hostility between the two brothers that had prompted it.

In the end it was Mazarin, still in control of affairs in 1660 when Gaston died, who decided with Louis on the disposition of the late duke's legacy. The two made no difficulty over the transfer of the title to Philippe, who immediately began to style himself duke of Orléans. They knew, too, that Philippe had a sound claim to his uncle's appanage, which according to the jurisprudence of the day was an indemnity to cadet branches of royal houses for the sovereignty of which they were deprived.[5] On the other hand, problems arose involving the timing of the award, which customarily took place at the time of the appanagist's marriage, and its size, which would determine its revenues. This last consideration was especially delicate, since the last thing either Louis or Mazarin desired was to afford Philippe a basis of financial independence that would free him from the shackles of the royal will. Moreover, the income Philippe might receive from an appanage would be entirely different from the grants and pensions he was currently receiving from the Crown. By law an appanage, once in the possession of the appanagist, could revert to the Crown only in the absence of a male heir on his death. It was therefore very nearly irrevocable, unlike the royal grants, and its usufruct would provide the duke of Orléans over his lifetime with an income sheltered from the whim of the sovereign.[6]

In reality, however, the concern over the revenues of the appanage were of more symbolic than practical importance. Although Gaston's appanage had yielded an annual income of some 200,000 livres, which made it one of the most remunerative in France during the entire Old Regime,[7] it had constituted only a small fraction of the duke's enormous revenues, which were well over two million livres each year.[8] Even for Philippe, who of course possessed none of the other proprietary possessions of his uncle, the sum would be far less than he was then receiving from the royal treasury. Nonetheless, Louis could not resist some cheeseparing. Although Mazarin wrote that the king wanted "to treat Monsieur well" and Anne too was reported to be urging generosity,[9] Louis resolved to retain Chambord and Blois, the two choicest châteaus of the appanage, and to substitute something else supposedly of equal value. When finally constituted, the appanage yielded annual revenues of slightly less than 150,000 livres.[10] As for the timing, it was decided not to make the award until the occasion of the prince's marriage, which would be arranged as soon as possible in accordance with the interests of the state.[11]

The governorship of Languedoc, which Philippe much desired and expected to receive, was a more substantial issue with political as well as financial ramifications. It was true that governors of provinces could no longer challenge and imperil the royal authority as in the distant past. After the civil wars of the sixteenth century, forts and châteaus of rebellious nobles had been razed, and the king's intendants had tended to become more powerful than the provincial governors. In the seventeenth century major governors were more court oriented, as Gaston had been, and rarely if ever visited their provinces. Even so, they continued to exercise considerable authority and, owing to the financial rewards in their control, they could exploit their provinces as a base for gathering to them men willing to serve under their banner. The use both Gaston and Condé had made of their provinces during the Fronde was recent proof of their potency in aiding rebellion. As a financial asset, too, a major governorship such as Languedoc was far more substantial than an appanage. During the sixteen years that Gaston had occupied the post he had received on the average of 500,000 livres annually from the province, chiefly in the form of "pensions"—in reality bribes—paid by the estates of Languedoc and other local institutions to induce the governor to represent local interests.[12] This was no small item in the budget of even a great prince such as Gaston and had been an important factor in building his long record of rebellion and conspiracy.

Given these considerations, Philippe should not have been surprised when he learned that the post was awarded not to him but to Conti, brother of Condé. True, this prince had been a Frondeur, but he had later begged the pardon of the king, married a niece of Mazarin, and become *dévot*, living only for his religious devotions. From Louis's point of view Conti was powerless, therefore harmless. In making the decision the king reportedly acted on the advice of Mazarin,[13] but he probably did not need it. In his dealings with his brother throughout their lives and long after the death of the cardinal, Louis held fast to the principle that an enfant de France should have no haven except the court and no base of support except in the heart of the king. He never faltered in his resolve to deny Philippe a governorship or any other position in the realm that would have afforded him any true independence. Hence the utter futility of the angry protests of the prince, whom Mazarin sought to mollify by his usual practice of gifts of objets d'art to satisfy his collector's soul. But the real prize had escaped him, and everyone knew it. Philippe was now the duke of Orléans; he could wear a long train, and he would soon marry and enter on the possession of an appanage. But he was financially dependent on the Crown and carried no weight in the court or the government. "Monsieur does nothing [and] knows nothing," was the reported verdict of Mazarin.[14] In the words of another observer: "Monsieur, young and handsome, ... who thought only of his pleasures, counted for nothing."[15]

TOUT À FAIT AMOUREUX?

Although Monsieur was a cipher in the conduct of public affairs, as brother of the king only once removed from the throne he was from a biological point of view of great importance to the dynasty and hence to the interests of the state. The marriage he would make and the children he would sire would doubly ensure the legitimate succession of the monarchy and serve its high policy in Europe. Philippe of course understood as well as anyone else that his own preferences in the matter would receive scant attention if any. Personages of such rank were obliged to consider themselves at the disposition of the realm. If Mazarin had not viewed Philippe's marriage with the same urgency as that of the king, he still wanted it to take place in the very near future. Even while working out the details of Louis's wedding to the infanta in the spring of 1660, he was thinking ahead to the establishment of the cadet.

The choice of a bride presented few problems. She was already living at court, was Roman Catholic, was pleasing or at least acceptable to all parties concerned, and—the most important consideration—admirably served the needs of Louis's and Mazarin's foreign policy. This was Philippe's cousin Henriette of England, seventh and youngest child of the late and unfortunate Charles I of England and Henrietta Maria of France, and youngest sister of Charles II. Born at Exeter on June 16, 1644, in the midst of the English Civil War, she had been brought to safety in France when she was barely two years old. True, Mazarin in general had little liking for the house of Stuart, and after the beheading of the English king in 1649 he had negotiated an alliance with Cromwell, an arrangement that had helped bring Spain to the peace table on terms advantageous to France. Nor had Louis ever looked at the English princess as other than a poor relation, and a very unattractive one at that, too young in years and too thin of body to excite his interest.[16] During his teen years his mother had no little difficulty in obliging him to be polite to the little girl on occasion and to dance with her at balls. But the death of the English Protector and the restoration of Charles II to his throne in May 1660 cut short the Anglo-French collaboration and immediately caused the king and the cardinal to view the princess in a much more favorable light. They needed some inducement to prevent England from gravitating out of the French orbit and toward the Spanish. A dynastic alliance could be most useful. "The marriage of my brother [with Henriette]," Louis later explained in his memoirs, "served to keep [Charles] on my side."[17]

The English relatives of the princess were only too pleased to agree to the match. Charles, insecure upon his newly reestablished throne and facing severe financial problems, easily envisioned a number of advantages in having the king of France as his brother-in-law. He also knew that his mother, Henrietta Maria of France, queen of England, daughter of Henry IV, strongly favored the match, and he may also have believed that little Minette, his affectionate name for Henriette, to whom he was always tenderly attached, may have desired it as well.[18] The mother, who had been living in exile with her daughter in the French court on the charity of her relatives for nearly fifteen years, had eagerly received Anne's formal request for her daughter's hand for Philippe and had promised to write immediately to her son for his permission.[19] She had long ago given up any hope she might have had that Henriette might become queen of France. During the long years of her exile as the mother of a crownless and penniless king, she had failed to attract even minor royalty such as the dukes of Savoy and Tuscany as suitors for her daughter. Her son's restoration to the throne had, of course, entirely changed the picture, immeasurably enhancing the marriage prospects of the young princess. Even so, she settled willingly for Monsieur, only brother of the Sun King, still the immediate heir to throne at the time of negotiation of the match, and one of the most eligible princes in Christendom.

The wishes and feelings of the principals themselves can be described with less certainty. In the case of Henriette, the existing evidence is both sparse and ambiguous. In reporting the French proposal to Charles, Henriette's mother was content to describe the princess "as by no means upset [*faschée*] over the prospect."[20] Charles, on receiving the news, was said to have known that he would "make his sister's happiness in giving her to Monsieur."[21] These statements, inconclusive though they are, may have been a fair reflection of the princess's state of mind, which in any event would have carried little weight with those making the decision.

Unlike many royal persons about to marry, Henriette was acquainted with her intended husband, whom she had known since early childhood, although apparently without having formed any special tie of friendship with him. They had appeared at the same balls, danced in the same ballets, and known the same people. She could not possibly have been unaware of the court gossip concerning Philippe's sexual preferences. It must have afforded her serious and unpalatable food for reflection—provided, that is, that in her youth (barely sixteen in the summer of 1660) and inexperience, the result of a closely guarded upbringing, she understood very clearly what all the talk was about.

In any event, the marriage undeniably held out such dazzling attractions to the princess that it is small wonder if she entered into it willingly. Monsieur was young (twenty years of age in September 1660) and very handsome. He was also giving every appearance of the ardent suitor, "altogether in love [*tout à fait amoureux*]," in the words of Henriette's mother,[22] doing everything possible to win his bride and to advance the day of the wedding. He must have seemed to the young girl like a prince out of a fairy tale when, mounted on a magnificent white horse and resplendent in a coat of embroidered silver, he had trotted beside Maria Theresa's carriage in August 1660 on the occasion of the young queen's official entry into the capital. His pause beneath the windows from which Henriette and her mother were watching the procession, and his salute to the ladies above, was not lost upon the observers of the court.

Marriage to Monsieur would be an entry to an enchanted land. Rather than endure the discomforts of cold rooms in a dilapidated, shabby palace and fret over the cost of proper clothes in which to appear at court, she would reside in lodgings second in magnificence only to those of the king and preside over a huge household of officers and servants. Unlike poor Maria Theresa, she would not be obliged to move to a strange country and adapt herself to different customs and dress. Nor would she need to struggle with a foreign language. Although styled Henriette of England and the sister of the king of England, the princess was thoroughly French. Brought to safety in France when she was barely two years old, she had never known her English father and had been raised by her French mother in the French court, the only home she had ever known. What knowledge of the English language she possessed was so slight that when she traveled to England in the winter of 1660–61 to receive the blessings of Charles and a dowry from the Parliament, while professing an "English heart," she was obliged to express her thanks and gratitude in her native French.[23]

Moreover, once married, gone would be the morose governance of an embittered mother, who was religious to the point of bigotry and relentless in her discipline. It had been Anne, moved by the plight of the young princess in her poverty and isolation, who had provided the only joys of her youth by including her as much as her mother would permit in the social events of the royal family. In the future as Madame, as henceforth she would be styled, instead of a poor relation on the fringe of the court Henriette would be in its center, even its uncrowned queen. Certainly little competition could be expected from the dumpy, dull-witted queen or from the aging queen mother. A foretaste of what she might expect in her new dignity was provided by the cardinal, who honored the betrothal of the pair by a lavish banquet replete with dozens of violins, musicians imported from Rome, and a Spanish theatrical piece.[24]

As for Philippe, could he truly have been "altogether in love," as

Henriette's mother had averred? Evidence abounds that the prince earnestly desired to marry and had chosen his English cousin as a bride. Even before the princess's brother was restored to the English throne, Philippe had been urging Mazarin to arrange the match. Louis had marveled at his brother's ardor. "Come, cheer up!" he had jeered. "You will marry the princess of England. No one else wants her. M. de Savoy has turned her down. So has M. de Florence, so I am sure you will have her in the end."[25] Once formally betrothed, Philippe urged forward the date of the wedding. When Henriette and her mother left for England in the autumn of 1660, the prince appeared the picture of dejection. While she was gone he moped about, lost weight, and wrote letter after letter to his future mother-in-law pleading for their immediate return.[26] Partly in response to his importunities and against her better judgment, the mother set out with the princess from England in the dead of winter on what proved an uncomfortable and perilous cross-channel voyage, during which Henriette fell dangerously ill with fever. On learning of her safe return and convalescence, the prince went forth eagerly to greet her.[27] Louis, meanwhile, continued to taunt his brother on his haste "to wed the bones of the Holy Innocent" (a reference to the future bride's extreme thinness).[28]

Certainly it was possible, both physiologically and psychologically, that Philippe's profession of love was sincere. In the past he had at times shown susceptibility to the attractions of the opposite sex. In the future the six (some say eight) pregnancies of Henriette during the nine years of their marriage were to be ample proof of his ability to perform his *métier d'époux*—his husbandly duty. Much later, when relations between the spouses were at their worst, Philippe was to confide in Mademoiselle that he had loved Henriette only for a fortnight,[29] a confession that, if true, at least was evidence of a real tenderness for his wife, however transitory.

On the other hand, considering the character of the prince and his position vis-à-vis his brother and at court, the suspicion arises that motives having little to do with the inclinations of his heart may have lain behind his desire to wed. Until the time of his uncle's death, Philippe had evinced no special tenderness or affection for his English cousin. To the contrary, he had seemingly regarded her with contempt. Late in 1658, not many months before he was to profess his desire to marry Henriette, he had rushed to the defense of Mademoiselle, who was being reprimanded by Mazarin for having upstaged and humiliated the English princess. "And so if [Mademoiselle] did do it, would she not have been right?" Philippe had riposted. "We have come to a fine state of affairs when people like that [Henriette and her mother], who owe their bread to us, go in before us. Why don't they go live somewhere else?"[30]

Certainly it is highly suspicious that Philippe's desire to wed did not show itself until after the death of Gaston and the reversion of the uncle's appanage to the throne. According to law and tradition an appanage was awarded to an enfant de France at the time of his marriage to enable the appanagist to provide for his house and whatever male children might result from the union.[31] The prince was probably as aware of these facts as anyone else, and even if he had not been, he would have learned from Louis that the appanage was not his by right owing to the death of the duke of Orléans. "[Philippe] thinks he will inherit [Gaston's] appanage; he thinks of nothing else; well, he doesn't have it yet," the king had jeered to Mademoiselle.

In addition to the appanage, marriage could be expected to bring other benefits, both tangible and intangible. Not only the confirmation of his adult status, it would mean the establishment of his house and of his family, wherein he could exercise an authority denied him elsewhere. With a wife beside him whose social gifts, as it would turn out, equaled or surpassed his own, he would preside over his own court and entertain on a scale far more lavish than before. On the material side, he could count on greatly enhanced revenues from the Crown: for himself, the household of Madame, and any male heirs born of the union. For Philippe as well as for Henriette, marriage promised to be the beginning of better days.

BRIDE AND GROOM

Despite Monsieur's eagerness to claim his bride, the wedding did not take place until March 31, 1661. Delayed by the princess's voyage to England and her subsequent illness and by the deaths of one of her brothers and one of her sisters, it was put off again by the prolonged sufferings of Mazarin and his death on March 9, after which, on the orders the king, the court went into full mourning. Three weeks later, although the princess was still in deep mourning,[32] a simple marriage ceremony took place. On March 30 the bride and groom made their confessions and witnessed the signing of their marriage contract by Louis, Maria Theresa, and Henrietta Maria, queen of England. The following day at noon the couple were married in the chapel of the queen of England in the Palais

Royal in the presence of their immediate family, Mademoiselle, Condé, and a select group of court dignitaries. A small wedding supper given by the bride's mother was the sum total of the festivities. Henriette then went to live with her husband in his quarters in the Tuileries.[33]

From its very beginning, observers of this marriage have expatiated on the matchless qualities of Madame, extolling her sweetness of character, her delicacy, spirituality, vivacity, and exquisite charm. "Never has France seen so adorable a princess as Henriette d'Angleterre. . . . Never was a princess so affecting or so endowed with the power to please."[34] Physically, it had to be admitted, there were certain defects: a face a trifle too long, a body thin to the point of emaciation. A few could detect through the artifice of her toilette a hunchback that even the groom did not perceive until after the marriage.[35] But her grace of spirit more than compensated for the lack of conventional beauty. From Mme de La Fayette (who wrote the story of her life at the princess's dictation) to Molière, whom she befriended, from Bishop Bossuet, whose eulogy immortalized her name ("Madame is dying; Madame is dead!"), through Voltaire, Michelet, Sainte-Beuve, Anatole France, and a host of others, Henriette has gone down as the ornament of the court, a paragon of taste and charm, martyred and wasted in wedlock with the unfortunate, if not despicable, Monsieur. Philippe was the heavy, the husband who was unable to appreciate either the physical or the intellectual allure of his wife, yet who went into paroxysms of jealous rage when she turned her irresistible glance elsewhere.

Yet in a number of ways Henriette and Philippe could be said to have been well suited to each other. They had many of the same likes and dislikes and shared many of the same pleasures. Both had an aversion for the outdoors and eschewed the hunting parties that were so important to the king's enjoyment. Although by all reports Madame was an accomplished equestrian and could display her skill and grace in pageants and parades, she was too frail of health to endure or enjoy rigorous physical exercise. As for Monsieur, although physically robust in his youth, as an adult he rarely mounted a horse except during war or on ceremonial occasions. Both sought their amusements in society. The ballroom, the salon, and the theater were the world they enjoyed and in which they excelled. Intelligent, well endowed with the social graces, each had a well-developed artistic sense and a strong interest in the arts. It could be expected, given the almost limitless financial resources placed at their disposal, that they would make their mark on the society and culture of their day.

Indeed, for a few short weeks the marriage gave every appearance of being a brilliant success. The cream of the court flocked to the Tuileries; Madame and Monsieur were the stars of the social season. Banquets, promenades, and soupers succeeded each other. Monsieur, beside himself with pride and joy, entertained his guests with theatrical pieces, musicals, gambling, and dancing. "In short, everyone partook of every imaginable pleasure and threw off all restraint."[36] Ingenuously, the host basked in the accomplishments of his bride and took special care that Guiche, whose close friend he remained, should admire her perfection.

This happy passage came to an end when Louis, in need of diversion from the company of the queen, now in an early stage of pregnancy and even duller than usual, invited the couple to join him at Fontainebleau. As April drew to a close Philippe and Henriette obeyed the royal summons. With them went their household and, it was said, all the "joy and pleasures" of the season. Once there the charms of the princess, of which the prince was so proud, exerted themselves in a fashion that not only revealed a less lovely side of her character but destroyed forever any chance of happiness the marriage had ever had.

For even in the best circumstances, Henriette could not have been an easy person to live with. Delicate and high-strung, she ate little and slept less. Today her behavior appears characteristic of anorexia nervosa, an eating disorder consistent with her heredity and upbringing: high intelligence, a domineering and restrictive mother, and an absent or passive father.[37] She was also an incipient tubercular.[38] Unable to work off an excess of nervous energy, another symptom of the anorectic, she passed her days and nights in endless search of diversion. Moonlit evenings would find her promenading in the park or bathing in the river, unable to find repose after the daylong round of pleasure. So frenetic a pace might have been harmless enough, except for the toll on her health, had it not been for the provocative behavior and amorous play that always attended it. Her coquetry was seemingly ingrained and insatiable. Despite her tender years—she had not yet passed her seventeenth birthday on her wedding day—and closely guarded upbringing, Madame was no child and was well aware of the power of feminine charm and the use that could be made of it. During her voyage to England she had managed so to infatuate both the duke of Buckingham and Admiral Montague, who commanded the vessel on which she was a passenger, as to bring them to the point of blows. On her return to France, Buckingham still in tow, she had first experienced the jealousy of Philippe, who was at length placated by the reassurances of his mother and the enforced departure of the English duke.

"Madame was weary of the vexations and constraints that she had experienced in her life with her mother, the queen," wrote Mme de La Fayette.[39] The adolescent girl was in the act of freeing herself from the mother's despotic tutelage. How better to retaliate than to collect men's broken hearts and, like trophies, display them for her mother and all to see?[40] And what greater trophy could there be than the heart of the king? What sweet revenge for humiliations she had suffered at his hands and in his court! And what more favorable ambience could she have found than the libertine atmosphere of the court of Apollo? Certainly it would be a mistake to infer that Louis and his companions devoted all their waking hours to the pursuit of pleasure. Little that Louis did was without calculation, and many of his most extravagant fetes and pageants served some ulterior purpose. Nonetheless, the rising sun of Louis XIV revealed a court of gilded, superb youth—licentious, cruel in its passions, and amoral in its behavior. According to a witticism of the day, "It is extremely useful to die in God's grace, but it is extremely boring to live in it." And Louis in that summer of 1661 at Fontainebleau, bored with the society of his queen, was in a mood to be receptive to the charms of the young sorceress.

The king and Madame were constantly seen in each other's company. While Maria Theresa languished in her chamber with her Tia, the couple explored the grottoes, bathed in the river, and on moonlit evenings promenaded to the sound of violins around the canal.[41] How innocent were these pleasures? It is impossible to know with certainty. In any case appearances were such as to give rise to an enormous amount of gossip and a budding scandal.

The effect his wife's behavior had on Philippe is not difficult to imagine. In vain did he expostulate with Henriette, "whose receptiveness to [the king's] gallantry was greater than he would have wished."[42] To be publicly cuckolded and made a figure of ridicule during the first weeks of his marriage were bad enough. Worse still, the lover of his wife was his own brother,who once again in their long rivalry, and in the most humiliating form possible, had scored and beaten him.

The budding scandal came to a close only when Anne joined forces with Philippe and Henriette's mother and attempted to bring the couple to their senses. The force of the resulting maternal reprimands caused the guilty young people, who were still not entirely freed from parental governance, to resort to ruse rather than rebellion to continue their dalliance. In place of Henriette as the object of his affections, Louis would pretend to substitute one of her ladies,

Mlle Louise de La Vallière, chosen, it would seem, for her innocence and naiveté. Probably it was a surprise to all three when the decoy became the real thing, the secret mistress of the king.

The proud Stuart had been supplanted by the little provincial from Blois! Now Madame was humiliated while Monsieur tried again to hold up his head. But Henriette was not yet finished for the summer. A fresh conquest was needed to assuage her wounded vanity.[43] Her victim, she decided, would be none other than Guiche, who, she was aware, had paid her discreet attentions in the past but who had stepped aside in deference to the king's gallantry. Occasions for encouraging his suit were not difficult to find. During rehearsals for the *Ballet des saisons*, in which they both danced, Guiche was brought to express the feelings of his heart, which of course were already all too clear to the avidly observant court. Immediately it was whispered that Philippe was cuckolded again, this time not by a male gallant, but by his own wife, whose beauty was preferred over his own by his cherished friend.

The position in which the prince now found himself was ridiculous and humiliating beyond description. To be the unsuccessful rival in love of his own wife! His abasement in the eyes of the court was complete. Useless to upbraid his faithless friend for his treason. Guiche, treating the prince in his usual high-handed fashion, "had it out with him in no uncertain terms and broke with him as if he had been his equal."[44] Horrified at the implications of his son's behavior, Marshal Gramont ordered his son to go to Paris and not return to Fontainebleau.

Was revenge within Philippe's grasp? Always, of course, there was the bedroom, where he could exercise his marital rights. We have reason to believe that things had gone very badly in that department from the start. The very first night of the marriage Philippe, eager to consummate the marriage, had been furious at the unwelcome appearance of "Monsieur le Cardinal" (a seventeenth-century euphemism for the menses), who had "slammed the door" in his face.[45] When the "cardinal" disappeared and Philippe was able to perform in due course, he had for reasons unspecified been unable to "entertain" his bride to her satisfaction. But no matter, as a husband he could still command his rights, and he may well have used them as his means of retaliation. Sometime during that month of July, even while Henriette was engaged in her flirtation with Guiche, Philippe rendered her pregnant with their first child. Considering the circumstances, the suspicion is strong that its conception was an act of vengeance rather than of love. If so, the same may have been true of the subsequent pregnancies in this loveless marriage. Each took its toll on the beauty and grace of the princess, whose health was fragile to begin with, and each effectively curtailed the exercise of her charms for extended periods of time.

Within a period of four months the marriage of Henriette and Philippe, which probably never had much of a chance, was in shambles. It is clear now that although superficially the young people had much in common they had been tragically mismated. Henriette, in full rebellion against a despotic mother, found gratification in seductive behavior. When Anne and Philippe also became her censors the strong hate she felt for her mother was transferred to them. In seducing Guiche she could strike at the prince and through him at his mother. For a personality already as demoralized as Philippe, whose self-confidence had already been effectively destroyed, the effects of her provocative behavior were fatal. Nor can Louis's role in the ruin of the marriage be ignored. Despite Henriette's undeniable charms, the king could not have been seduced against his will. Moreover, he had carried on his romance in the full view of the court without the slightest attempt to conceal it from his brother, whose humiliation he no doubt unconsciously savored. In subsequent years he did not hesitate to sow discord between the two, and in the last drama of Philippe's and Henriette's life together once more it was Louis who came between them.

The result of these marital tensions would be the intensification of the prince's hatred of Louis, the rival he could never best and who always defeated him, and of his desire for self-punishment for the guilt he could never admit. The homosexual inclinations that from the start of the marriage had been an exacerbating influence would be reinforced. Henriette's flirtations and especially the king's response tilted the balance of Philippe's bisexuality toward a homosexual pattern. The result was a marriage that became a grotesquerie.

The Facade: The Household and Diversions of Monsieur and Madame

But for better or for worse, the marriage was a fact with which Philippe and Henriette had to live. The establishment of their household was their first concern. Louis placed at their disposal the Palais Royal, home to the king and Philippe as children and subsequently to Henriette and her mother, and gave them permission to execute badly needed repairs and to renovate and decorate it to fit their needs and tastes. Sometime early in 1662[46] the couple left the

Tuileries and took up residence in the great palace that henceforth was to be the focal point of their life together and of the house of Orléans in the future. Monsieur and Madame did not cease to live periodically at court, and on occasion they hosted elaborate fetes at Saint-Cloud and other ducal residences. But in the royal presence they had perforce to follow the lead of the king; at Saint-Cloud as then constituted they had as yet insufficient space to accommodate their growing households. The vast Palais Royal, on the other hand, with its theater and its location in the heart of Paris, afforded the possibility of creating a circle of their own in an urban setting. Independent of the king's court, it would have a pace and tone peculiarly its own. For the remainder of his life Philippe, who retained his fondness for the capital, frequently took up residence in the palace and prolonged his visits for weeks during the winter social season, "a fact that did not fail to earn him the affection of the Parisians."[47]

The Palais Royal was far from a fashionable center when the young duke and duchess moved in. Constructed by Cardinal Richelieu[48] during the reign of Louis XIII and bequeathed to the Crown in his testament of 1636, it was a massive quadrilateral formed by a central building and wings giving on the rue Saint-Honoré in front and on an immense walled-in garden in back. If in size and grandeur it had been worthy of a prince of the church and minister of the king, it had been a failure as an urban project. Richelieu had induced his creatures to build impressive *hôtels* in the neighborhood, but he had been unable to breathe life into the quarter. The small, uniformly built houses that enclosed the garden, hiding it from public view, clashed meanly with the magnificent dwellings surrounding them and sold poorly. The adjacent streets were quiet and uninteresting.[49] Even though the quarter had been the political and courtly center of France during the life of the cardinal and again under the regency, when Anne had taken up residence with her children, it had never acquired cachet. Compared with the palace of the Luxembourg and the hôtels of the parlementaires on the Left Bank, it lacked elegance, while it never attained the smartness and cultural vitality of the *marais* across the river on the Right Bank. After the departure of the court in 1652 and during the residence of the poverty-stricken queen of England and her daughter, it took on a half-abandoned appearance and fell into sad disrepair.

The introduction of the households of Monsieur and Madame must have brought movement to the nearly empty streets. Although relatively modest in size at first (the word relatively must be emphasized, since even in the early years they numbered in the hundreds), the staffs of both husband and wife expanded enormously as the decade progressed. Their salaries, which have been estimated to have reached 800,000 livres annually,[50] were in large part paid from the royal treasury.[51]

In 1663 "L'éstat général de la maison de Monsieur" listed nearly five hundred officers and servants: twenty ecclesiastical officers; over one hundred maîtres d'hôtel, chefs, waiters, pages, and other servants; over one hundred gentlemen and servants of the bedchamber; over two dozen doctors, surgeons, and barbers; nearly fifty masters of the horse, huntsmen, stableboys, and grooms; a military guard of close to 150, and a council of over twenty members whose most important personages were the chancellor and the superintendent of finances.[52] By contrast, the staff of Madame for the same years appeared modest: four ecclesiastical officers; six ladies-in-waiting; some dozen servants of the bedchamber; two maîtres d'hôtel, and one doctor. A military guard of ten together with other assorted servants brought the total to forty-three.[53]

Nine years later, in 1669, the household of Monsieur numbered over one thousand retainers, while that of Madame was well over two hundred. For Monsieur all areas of service grew appreciably, although increases in the stables and the council were proportionally the most pronounced. Appearing on the list for the first time were architects, lawyers, an interpreter, a historiographer, and a *grand maître des eaux et forêts*, offices that reflected the prince's greater financial resources and responsibilities. The household of Madame of 1669 showed no such introduction of specialists but rather experienced its greatest increases in the kitchen, dining, and bedroom service, an indication, it appears, of a general elaboration of lifestyle.[54]

The installation of Monsieur and Madame in the Palais Royal was no simple affair. The building needed not only thorough cleaning and redecorating but structural repair as well. Parts of the roof had caved in, and water had damaged floors and walls. Moreover, the rooms had to be reassigned and their interiors redesigned to fit the needs and tastes of the new occupants. The work went on over a number of years; in fact, it may be said never to have been completed. During the lifetimes of Monsieur and of his descendants in the eighteenth and nineteenth centuries it was in a nearly constant state of renovation and repair.

The palace being still in the possession of the Crown, the king supposedly picked up the bill. However, the expenditures recorded for its maintenance in the *Comptes des bâtiments du roi* for the 1660s (a total of 63,836 livres with an annual average of slightly over

9,000 livres)[55] may not have been sufficient to finance the extensive
renovations undertaken, and Louis may have obliged his brother to
contribute from his own purse.[56] Receiving priority were the apartments of Monsieur, Madame, and their first child, the anterooms,
and the public salons. The most prominent artists and craftsmen of
the day were employed. The *chambre de Madame*, situated on the
east facade of the main building, received parquet floors worked
with copper and pewter by Jean Macé and friezes by the sculptor
Mersy. The apartment of Monsieur, on the west of the same facade,
was decorated by the painter Errard, a member of the Academy,
and was notable for a deep and heavily ornamented alcove containing the bed. Noël Coypel was engaged to design and paint the ceiling of Mademoiselle, the firstborn. The *galeries des objets d'art* of Richelieu's day were made over into the new *grands appartements*,
while the cardinal's *galerie des hommes illustrés* was restored to its
former magnificence. In these salons were hung not only a wealth
of Gobelin tapestries but also the core of what was to become one
of the most celebrated collection of paintings in Europe: among
them canvases by Van Dyck, Titian, Tintoretto, Mignard, and
Veronese.[57]

When the young couple took up residence in 1662 the transformed palace entered one of the most brilliant decades of its existence. In fall and winter during the theater season and the festivities
surrounding the new year, Monsieur and Madame held court unin-
terruptedly for weeks at a time. Their salons were crowded with all
of Paris and many from the king's court as well.

These evenings at the Palais Royal were especially gratifying to
Philippe, who basked in the attention of his guests. The material
advantages attendant on his marriage helped provide much-needed
self-esteem. Here for the first time he was obliged to defer to no
man, and he took a naive pride in the size of the crowds thronging
his rooms.[58] As his role in his brother's court became increasingly
painful, he found his urban palace a refuge. He also began to consolidate the special bond he had long felt with Paris and the Parisians, who responded affectionately to this prince who would live
among them.[59] What a contrast to the king, who disliked the city,
always associating it with the humiliations of the Fronde, and almost never came there. According to the second Madame, who said
she had it from the king himself, the popularity of Philippe in Paris
irritated and even alarmed Louis, who for that reason always defended Henriette's flirtatious behavior so that Philippe might have
something to think about other than affairs of state.[60] There is no
doubt that the long love affair between Paris and the house of Or-

léans, an attachment that was to play so important a part in the political and social history of the eighteenth century, began during the lifetime of Monsieur.

With the great palace in the heart of Paris ready for occupancy in the early spring of 1662 and the Maison Gondi at Saint-Cloud on the outskirts of the city refurbished and landscaped, Monsieur and Madame began to entertain on a scale that compared in grandeur and frequency even with that of the king and queen. In these early years of his personal rule, before he had built his great château at Versailles and settled there, the king could make good use of the hospitality of Monsieur, since he helped supply the pageantry and entertainment desirable for the court of Apollo. With Louis and Maria Theresa, Philippe and Henriette composed a quartet at the very pinnacle of court society. They entertained each other constantly in a succession of receptions, banquets, balls, comedies, operas, ballets, and suppers that seemingly lost none of their charm despite the continual repetition of diversions, persons, and places. The *Gazette de France* and the *Muse Historique* must have strained the limits of their vocabularies as they attempted to describe the sumptuous elegance and profusion of marvels displayed by the hosts and their guests.

The social round was very nearly continuous, broken only by religious observances, childbirth, death, and war, and even then never for long. In the spring of 1662, shortly after they moved into the Palais Royal and after Henriette gave birth to their first child, the couple entered on their first social season in their new establishments and as the second couple of the kingdom. This was the year in which the king staged his famous Grand Carrousel, a pageant and elaborate "horse show"[61] that took place at the Place de Carrousel, just west of the palace of the Tuileries. While the king, Monsieur, and the princes of the blood, representing "Romans" (Louis), "Persians" (Philippe), and other "nations" displayed their equestrian skills, Maria Theresa as queen of the carrousel, with Henriette at her side, gave out prizes to the victorious "knights." For nearly a month, while the show went on, most of the court watched the spectacle by day and partied by night either at the royal residences or at the Palais Royal.

Even after the carrousel's conclusion the merrymaking continued, moving out from the city in the summer weather to Fontainebleau, Versailles, and Saint-Cloud. Late in May, after a ball at the Palais Royal, the court followed the king to Fontainebleau only to return once again to the hospitality of Monsieur, this time at Saint-Cloud, where the "delicious house" was the site of a "most splendid collation."[62] Of another of these parties at Saint-Cloud during the same season, the *Muse Historique* describes the "charming palace where hundreds of fountains jetting water and thousands of other wonderful things" were seen. It was a magnificent gala complete with violins, comedy, and ball, for Monsieur "produced such things wonderfully."[63]

By the mid-1660s a long and spectacular carnival season featuring musical and dramatic entertainments and followed by late spring and summer extravaganzas was the accepted and expected thing. In 1664 the year began with a series of comedies and musical spectacles performed either at Versailles or at the Palais Royal. After Lent the gaiety resumed in garden parties at Saint-Cloud and climaxed at the three-day festival of the famous Fete of the Enchanted Island at Versailles.

Preceding this, even though Madame was again in an advanced state of pregnancy, she and Monsieur frequently received the court at Saint-Cloud. Philippe had ordered the construction of an elegant boat, a kind of barge, on the Seine, on which Henriette and the queens could embark from a point near the royal palaces in Paris and float downriver in fine weather to a landing dock at the château of Saint-Cloud. There they would be met by open carriages in which they could promenade in the gardens and growing park. Later, of course, they would enjoy the usual comedy, ballet, supper, and ball. "In such manner," wrote the *Gazette de France* of one such occasion, "nothing was missing from this gala, where the king was also present."[64]

The following years, 1665 and 1666, were darkened by grave illness and death: a stillborn infant born to Henriette in July 1665; the suffering of Henriette's mother, who had returned from England in an advanced stage of tuberculosis; the last agonies and death of Anne, who died of breast cancer in January 1666; and finally the death of Philippe and Henriette's only son, Philippe Charles, duke of Valois, at two and one-half years old, in December of the same year. Even so, the social life of the court was not permitted to be disrupted seriously or for long. Perhaps they were all so accustomed to its rhythm that they could not in fact live without it; and for Louis the spectacles often served a political purpose as well. The desire or need for society was especially true for Henriette. In any case, although she and Philippe had gone to Villers-Cotterêts in the country, where the princess could supposedly rest and regain her strength after the ill-fated childbirth, the same frenetic round continued. Mademoiselle, returning from a visit to her country estates, found all the ladies "dressed magnificently." "They hunted every day, and in the evening they danced or there was a comedy."[65] This pattern was to be repeated in the late summer of 1667 after Henriette had suffered still another, very dangerous miscarriage.[66]

During Anne's last illness, which was further saddened by the death of her brother Philip IV in September 1665, both Louis and Philippe continued to give parties. On January 5, 1666, only a fortnight before the queen mother's death, Philippe hosted an especially elaborate affair at the Palais Royal. Molière's *Médecin malgré lui* was presented, after which came a supper and a ball. Dancing continued far into the night. Even though Louis was in mourning for his uncle and fellow king, he as well as Philippe and Henriette were lavishly bejeweled.[67] A few days later, even though Anne had taken a turn for the worse and was clearly on her deathbed, the brothers again attended a comedy at the Palais Royal. Meanwhile, Henriette threw a celebrated party to fete the betrothal of one of her ladies-in-waiting, Mlle d'Artigny,[68] a lady with a well-earned reputation for intrigue and dubious morals.

Not even the death of the little duke de Valois seriously interrupted the social season of his parents. Even making full allowance for the resignation with which sixteenth- and seventeenth-century parents accepted the deaths of their children, in contrast to the growing sensibility of subsequent centuries, the speed with which Philippe and Henriette seemingly recovered from the loss of their only son and heir is astonishing.[69] Taken ill in November while at Saint-Cloud, the child was brought to the Palais Royal in December, where Monsieur and Madame were to celebrate the Christmas and carnival seasons. On December 2 Henriette danced in the *Ballet des muses*, which she had been rehearsing since October. The following day the child's condition became so alarming that Philippe quickly arranged for his baptism.[70] On December 8 he died. Nonetheless, the new year opened with a whirlwind of social activity. After joining the king at Saint-Germain, where Maria Theresa gave birth to a daughter on January 2, Philippe and Henriette went to Versailles for several days of festivities—balls, ballets, comedies— presented with an "extraordinary magnificence." January 9 found them again at the Palais Royal, where Henriette gave a great ball in which "the jewels of the seigneurs and dames vied with the chandeliers in brilliance." The fourteenth saw them back at Versailles, where Henriette again appeared in the *Ballet des muses*, after which there were the usual collation and ball. And so on through the carnival season, which climaxed on February 19 at Versailles with a Spanish comedy, still another ballet, and finally an elaborate *Course de bague*. This affair, staged in front of the orangerie, where were seated Maria Theresa, Mademoiselle, and other ladies, began with a fanfare and the entrance of troops of knights. They were followed by "the principal beauties of the court," notably Madame, mounted on a white horse hooded with brocade, pearls, and jewels. Then came the king, costumed *à la hongroise* (Hungarian), Monsieur, "richly garbed *à la Turque*," and the princes of the blood, each dressed in the fashion of a different nation. They all formed quadrilles and, after saluting the queen, began a succession of races and displays of horsemanship "following the example of His Majesty, who has always excelled in these fashionable exercises of the nobility."

The social life of the court was a reflection not only of Louis's, and to some extent Philippe's, desire for entertainment but also of their tastes and discernment in the arts. Since childhood, under the tutelage of Anne, Mazarin, and even Gaston, the brothers had learned to enjoy the theater and the dance, both of which figured prominently in these early decades of Louis's personal rule. They were fortunate indeed to have had at their command some of France's greatest musicians and playwrights, among them Lully, Corneille, Molière, and Racine. But perhaps no less important than the availability of these artists was the discriminating ability of the royal brothers to recognize unusual talent and their willingness not only to bestow their patronage on its possessors, but to attend and even participate in their performances. By making the dance and the theater a continuing and prominent feature of their social life, Louis and Philippe not only supported the careers of the artists concerned, but ensured the high quality of the arts in the French court.

Philippe was especially influential in the career of Molière, who in fact owed to the prince his introduction to Louis and his opportunity to perform before the court. This turning point had taken place in 1658 in circumstances that are far from clear. In the spring of that year the playwright, then head of a prosperous troupe with a growing reputation, had been touring the provinces and was in Rouen. According to one of the members of the group, who left a journal of its movements, Molière made several secret trips to Paris during which he met the prince and received his patronage for the troupe in an annual pension of three hundred livres.[71] Who was the unnamed intermediary between the two? A fair guess might be Gaston, who had patronized Molière in an earlier, less successful stage of his career and who, understandably, would have seen Philippe rather than Louis as more receptive to his influence. Although the duke was then living on his estates in Blois, he might well have provided the letter of introduction that opened the door to his nephew. If so, the overture was completely successful. True, the pension seemingly was never paid. But no matter; it was the honor of the thing and the opportunities it afforded that counted. Henceforth the troupe styled itself "Troupe de Monsieur, frère unique du roi." The following October, after the court had returned to Paris from Compiègne, Philippe introduced Molière to Louis and to Anne, who invited him to present *Nicomède* and *Le docteur amoureux* before them at the Louvre late in October. Louis was so pleased with the performance that he placed the hall of the Petit Bourbon, adjoining the palace, at the playwright's disposal. Two years later, when that theater was torn down, on the request of Philippe he permitted the troupe to move its operations to the *salle de théâtre*, built by Richelieu in the Palais Royal. There the playwright continued, playing frequently before the royal brothers and the court, until his death in 1673.

In the summer of 1661 Molière expressed his gratitude to Monsieur by dedicating to him the first play published by his express will, *L'école des maris*. "This [play] is not a present that I offer [to His Royal Highness]; rather, it is a duty that I perform," ran the humble dedication, "and because the act of homage is never judged by that quality of the offering, I have dared to dedicate this bauble to Your Royal Highness . . . and, if I refrain from elaborating on the fair and glorious truths that could be said of him, it is only from the apprehension that these lofty sentiments would contrast too strongly with the meanness of my gift."[72]

As Molière's reputation grew, it was the king, of course, and to some extent Henriette, also an ardent lover of theater, who displaced and even effaced Philippe as principal patron. When Molière produced the highly controversial *L'école des femmes* in 1662, whose theme was the jealousy of a husband who could never be sure of his wife, Louis sided with the playwright and to prove it placed him on his list of annual pensions for the sum of 1,000 livres. The following year, after the play had become an enormous success, and despite the theme, which might be supposed offensive to a husband with a flirtatious wife, Henriette accepted its fulsomely worded dedication. In February 1664 the king and Madame served as godparents to the playwright's second son. In 1665 the king saw his protection officially recognized when he obliged Philippe to relinquish the troupe to him. Henceforth it was known as the Comédiens du Roi and received an annual subsidy of 6,000 livres.[73]

In the case of Racine, younger than Molière, Henriette rather than Philippe was often seen as the influence behind the playwright's early success. True, the prince ordered the performance of *La Thébaïde* at Villers-Cotterêts in 1664 when Racine was still in his early twenties;[74] but it was the approval and influence of the princess that allegedly lay behind his growing fame and his acceptance by Louis and the court. When Racine suddenly removed the presentation of his successful tragedy, *Alexandre le Grand*, from Molière's troupe in 1665, gave it to the theater at the Hôtel de Bourgogne, and broke with the older man, the gazetteers gossiped not only of a rupture between the two playwrights but of a division in the household of Monsieur as well. While Madame became *racienne*, so it was said, Monsieur remained faithful to his former protégé, Molière. Henriette's acceptance of the dedication of *Andromaque* in 1667, in which Racine hinted broadly at her influence and hailed her as "the arbiter of taste" in the court, increased the rumors.[75] She was even supposed to have suggested to Racine, and to Corneille as well, the theme of *Bérénice*, which, according to later legend, represented the king's early love for Mazarin's niece, Marie Mancini, and his heroic renunciation of it.

Many of these rumors have been discounted. Philippe's second wife, for example, who attended many performances of *Bérénice*, could not believe and never heard it suggested that the Mancini affair was the subject of the comedy.[76] And if it were true that Philippe had taken a dislike to Racine, nothing in his subsequent enjoyment of the theater substantiates it. For the rest of his life, and long after the death of Henriette, he attended presentations of Racine's plays and frequently ordered their performance, as well as those of Corneille and Molière, at Saint-Cloud and at Villers-Cotterêts.

In the art of the dance, the king and Monsieur were not only appreciative spectators but also, during the decade of the 1660s, enthusiastic participants. In 1663 Louis created an academy of the dance, which institutionalized the ballet performances at court. During the winter months there were several ballets put on every week in which all the dames and seigneurs, Louis and Philippe at their head, took part. Their quality was much enhanced by the collaboration of Lully and Molière, beginning in 1664, in which ballet entrées were interspersed in the scenes of the playwright's comedies. Probably the year 1665 was the high point of entertainment of this genre. Three new comedy-ballets were introduced: *Le favory*, performed at Versailles in June in honor of Maria Theresa; *L'amour médecin*, given at Versailles in September; and *Ballet de la naissance de Vénus*, staged at the Palais Royal in January. This last, in which both Louis and Philippe danced, was written in honor of the marriage of Monsieur and Madame, and of it the poet Jean Loret wrote:

I have seen thirty ballets in France,
But among those of the greatest importance,
(May I die if I do not tell you the truth),
I have seen none
More rich, superb, and smart.
Beyond the majesty of the king
Who danced the best, believe me,
And Monsieur, his only brother,
On whom the just heavens confer
All the beautiful virtues
Which are desired in princedoms.[77]

BEHIND THE FACADE: FAMILY STRIFE

Behind the ordered facade of graciousness, opulence, and festivity shown to the public, the private lives of the royal family were a confused welter of love and hate, trust and hypocrisy, affection and betrayal. In the middle years of the 1660s Louis's triumphs in love left a stream of misery in their wake: the despair of Maria Theresa, the distressed disapproval of Anne, and the heartbreak of Louise de La Vallière, who saw herself displaced by the dazzling Françoise Athénaïs de Rochechouart de Mortemart, marquise de Montespan, in 1667. Philippe, caught in a loveless marriage to an irrepressible coquette, struggled helplessly with the humiliations of his position at court and of his relations with his brother. If in these years the waves were for a moment to part to reveal a distant shore of honor and self-respect, they closed once again to sink him even deeper in degradation. For both brothers the death of their mother early in 1666 was not only a time of genuine sorrow but also a subtle turning point in the direction of their lives.

Anne's last illness was prolonged and agonizing. Previously enjoying robust good health, she was taken dangerously ill in the spring of 1663 with an unidentified malady. Although she seemed slowly to recover, she began experiencing pain in her left breast a year later. By the end of 1664 the diagnosis was cancer, for which no treatment existed beyond local applications of ointments or caustics. During the summer of 1665 her end was judged near. As the tumor spread its tentacles into the putrescent flesh and her suffer-

ings intensified, Anne prepared herself for death with Christian resignation. It came at last on January 20, 1666, and she must unques-
tionably have welcomed it.

Although Louis and Philippe had been capable of continuing
their round of entertainments throughout the many months of
Anne's agony, they had by no means been unaffected by her impending death or inattentive to her sufferings. As sovereign, Louis
ordered public prayers and vigils throughout the kingdom and saw
to it that the best doctors and medicines were provided. As a loving
and dutiful son, he visited her bedside frequently and was obviously
genuinely and profoundly moved by her death. But of the two, contemporary accounts leave the distinct impression that it was Philippe whose grief was the keener. During the crises that punctuated
her suffering in its last years he remained fast at her side while
Louis, seemingly finding the sight of her pain too much to endure,
would seek relief elsewhere. There are touching vignettes of mother
and son in their last months together: of Philippe, seeing that Anne
was falling and unable to prevent it, slipping his body quickly beneath hers to break the impact of her fall; of Philippe wishing he
could lighten his mother's pain by sharing it with her; and of Philippe begging his mother to intercede for him when she was with
God in heaven. In her last hours, as she gave her blessing to both
sons and their wives, they all burst into copious tears. Louis, who
was fainting, then withdrew, ordering his brother to follow. Philippe, remaining where he was, sent word that he could not obey,
but that it would be the sole act of disobedience of his life. Present
when she drew her last breath, "Philippe embraced her tenderly in
a flood of tears that revealed the depths of his affliction."[78]

One plainly senses in all this the presence of the perpetual but
one-sided rivalry between the two brothers as well as Philippe's
guilty but unconscious intuition that he might for once displace
Louis in their mother's affections. In the last years of Anne's life,
mother and younger son had moved closer together, while the king
had remained to some degree estranged from them both. For Anne
had been seriously upset by the king's extramarital affairs, which
involved him not only with Mlle de La Vallière but with other ladies
of the court as well, and she had let him know it. For weeks during
1664 the two did not speak to each other except on public occasions.
Louis had eventually begged her pardon, but without changing his
ways, and indeed he had obliged his mother to admit Mlle de La
Vallière to her circle. There had been additional unpleasantness
with Louis in 1665 when Anne remade her will and wished to leave
her jewelry to Philippe's daughter, Marie Louise. The king wanted

her pearls for the crown jewels; and Maria Theresa, too, wanted a share. As a compromise, the queen mother left her jewelry, valued at more than 1,300,000 livres, to be divided between her sons, while the bulk of her remaining fortune, 1,000,000 livres, went to her granddaughter.[79]

Philippe too was on distant terms with the king, and he offered his mother a sympathetic shoulder when Louis turned a deaf ear to her reproaches. "You see how he treats me," she had sobbed.[80] Philippe could neither forget the humiliation of his brother's flirtation with Henriette nor forgive the continuing favor she found in his court. Anne sided with her son in his incessant battles with his wife and, viewing Henriette's flouting of the conventions and disrespectful conduct, came to regret the match that she had helped to arrange. If only Philippe had married Mademoiselle, she confided one day to her niece, "you [Mademoiselle] would have lived on better terms with me, and my son would have been fortunate indeed to have a wife as reasonable as you."[81] By the time Anne died, mother and younger son were on such tender terms as to give Philippe the reputation of being a mother's boy, sheltering behind her skirts and leaning on her for support.

The emotions of the bedside scenes and their common sorrow served briefly to reconcile the brothers. In the crises of her long illness the queen mother had repeatedly admonished Louis to love Philippe and Philippe to love and to obey the king. In their first meeting after her death the two fell into each other's arms and professed their mutual devotion. Louis, in a tender mood and as proof of his affection, went so far as to promise to raise the prince's baby son, the duke of Valois, in the company of the young dauphin. Philippe, naively seeing in the king's pledge a simple act of fraternal love, was deeply grateful. For his part, he resolved to turn over a new leaf and to show everyone he lacked neither heart nor ambition.[82]

As could easily be anticipated, these tender emotions and noble resolves were of short duration. In the long term the death of Anne worsened rather than ameliorated the brothers' relationship. Their mother's passing from the scene deprived the prince of his only source of solace and protection. As the perceptive Motteville observed: "He was right [to grieve. With her death he lost not only a mother but] his friend . . . his confidante, and finally she who could always best relieve his troubles."[83] Her death further served Philippe ill by its effect—subtle but not the less real—on Louis and on the court, for whom it was a liberation. Anne had been far from controlling Louis's conduct, but her presence and her appeals to his conscience reminded him of his better nature and of his trespasses. Henceforward he was free from her restraining influence. He could bring his mistresses into full view; he could legitimize the children they bore him. No longer need he listen to her preaching about his duty to his brother. Observers noted an increased laxity of manners and vulgarity of speech in the court.[84] Henriette too was freer to live as she wished. Philippe had lost his only ally in censoring her conduct, for her own mother, in poor health, usually lived away from court.

Louis himself realized—if not at the time, then later— that nothing had changed in his relationship with Philippe and that he was more than ever in control. "Although the moment I said those things [his profession of love and promise to raise Valois with the dauphin] to him [Philippe], and the emotional state I was in leaves no doubt that they were motivated by a sincere feeling of affection," he wrote subsequently, "it is nevertheless certain that if I had figured it all out in advance I could have hit on no better means to place my brother in my debt and to take as hostage for his conduct the most precious thing that he could give me."[85]

Given these circumstances, Philippe's resolution to reform was going to be difficult indeed to fulfill, as he himself must have been aware. He knew that the early influence of Mazarin on his youth and his subsequent devotion to his mother had denigrated him in the eyes of the court.[86] Louis was clearly contemptuous of the style of life he led.[87] He had openly confirmed his low opinion of Philippe in 1663 when, taken ill with measles and obliged to consider the governance of the kingdom in the event of his death, he had declined to designate Philippe as regent. Monsieur should have been the obvious choice. He was the only brother of the king, of appropriate age, and in excellent health. Nonetheless, after thinking first of his mother, whom he ruled out owing to her deteriorating health, and second of his wife, whom he considered too young, the king had settled on his cousin Conti.[88] Considering that prince's past as a Frondeur, the choice was scarcely flattering to Philippe.

Philippe possessed an ally, however, in his chaplain, Daniel Cosnac, bishop of Valence—he who had joined the prince's service in 1658 on the strength of the bowl of bouillon thrown in the king's face. Since then, although he had been disappointed in his earlier hopes, he had continued to believe that the prince possessed both the intelligence and the spirit to distinguish himself, given the proper encouragement. Ambitious and with a talent for intrigue, the young prelate saw the path to his own success in that of his patron. After the death of the queen mother, seeing the change of heart of the prince, Cosnac began to counsel him on ways to fulfill his resolve. "You must acquire the reputation of a prudent, wise, and discreet prince," he advised. Philippe should embark on a program of reading and study or, if that proved too heroic an undertaking, he should at least appear to do so. He should attempt to ingratiate himself with the king, but without descending to flattery. With the members of the court, the better to throw into contrast the formal coldness of the king, he should adopt an open and welcoming manner, taking an interest in all and inviting their confidence and support.

The prince and his adviser were soon provided the opportunity to move from declarations of intent to action. The death of Conti in February 1666 once again opened up the post of governor of the province of Languedoc. At the same time Henriette, eager for visible proof of her new status as second lady of the court, desired the right to a chair with arms (*fauteuil*) instead of a mere stool (*tabouret*) when seated in the presence of the queen. Thus, within a month following Anne's death, Louis was presented with two requests from his brother.

The king promptly and decisively denied them both. In the case of the governorship, even though circumstances and precedent seem to have favored the prince—the province was not on a frontier and Gaston had held the post—Louis held to the resolution he had taken in 1660 under the guidance of Mazarin. The mere reminder of Gaston and the use he had made of the resources of the post during the Fronde sufficed to doom Philippe's petition. "I did not think it right to grant this request," he explained later, "persuaded as I was that it was neither prudent nor reasonable to place the large governances in the hands of the sons of France." He continued, "the example of my uncle, which my brother cited, was a confirmation of my thought." He concluded with his celebrated dictum that the sons of France "must never have any other shelter than the court nor any other refuge than in the heart of their brother."[89] To emphasize the firmness of his decision and his displeasure with the petition, he dismissed Cosnac, who had presented it, with casual coldness and awarded the coveted post to another (M. de Verneuil, a legitimized offspring of Henry IV and titular bishop of Metz) in the very presence of Philippe.[90]

The petition for a chair with arms for Henriette was a question of mere etiquette but was nevertheless of more import than modern readers might suppose. Contemporaries took such marks of distinction very seriously, since they clearly indicated the pecking order of those at court and often translated themselves into more tangible evidences of power and prestige. The right to be seated in the presence of the queen was in itself a very great honor, bestowed only on the wives of dukes and peers of France. All other French subjects had to stand. But to Henriette and Philippe, even the company of those with the right to stools was too crowded, since it included not only the wives of the princes of the blood, inferior to Henriette in rank, but even the wives of mere gentlemen who in the past had been elevated by sovereigns for political reasons.[91] On the other hand, should Henriette have the right to an armchair, she would enjoy a privilege possessed only by the wives of foreign monarchs—that is queens, not princesses. Henriette would in effect be raised to the rank to which her royal brother would be entitled should he visit the French court and in the process would elevate both Monsieur and Madame to a position nearly indistinguishable from that of the king.

All this was too much for Louis. He would have liked nothing better than to agree, he explained to his brother in seeming sadness, "but I did not believe, out of consideration for the dignity of my rank and for the lack of precedent of his petition, that I could permit him to lessen the distinction between us." "And," he concluded, "I made it clear how useless it would be for him to persist."[92]

So much for Philippe's resolutions. Helpless but resentful, the prince gathered up Henriette and retired from court to Villers-Cotterêts in his appanage at Valois. In the past, a similar act by a Gaston or a Condé might have announced the onset of civil war. Louis was not impressed. After the king had denied the requests he wrote, "My brother adopted a line of conduct toward me that might have given me cause for alarm, had I not known well both his character and mine."[93]

Despite these rebuffs, one arena of activity still remained in which the prince might show his worth: the army. In the spring of 1667 the king entered on the so-called War of Devolution of 1667–68, the first of the four wars of his adult reign. Claiming to exercise the right of Queen Maria Theresa to the throne of Spain (her earlier renunciation of it was conditional on a dowry that had not been paid), Louis intended to partition the Spanish inheritance and occupy the Spanish Netherlands, which, he pronounced, were rightfully hers. He had been preparing for a year and had brought together an army of 70,000 that was thought to be the finest Europe had ever seen. The ensuing hostilities involved a war of sieges in the Low Countries in which the French were commanded chiefly by Turenne in 1667, and in the following year a rapid conquest of Franche-Comté by troops under Condé, recalled to service for the first time since the *Fronde*. Little serious fighting took place. The preparations had been so thorough, the French army was so superb, and supplies were so plentiful that the problems were primarily the logistic ones of moving men and horses across the land. The cities surrendered almost at the sight of the assembled besiegers.

Philippe apparently saw the war as an opportunity to learn the arts of war, in which both he and his brother were apprentices, and to earn the esteem of his contemporaries. Cosnac, who advised him in detail on how to conduct himself while with the army, had warned that this campaign might well be his last chance for personal glory. "Follow me to Flanders," Philippe had replied; "You will be well satisfied." In fact, the prince had prepared carefully for his role. Having ordered his treasurer to advance him 150,000 livres for his equipment, which was of "the most magnificent," he carried off his departure from the capital late in May with considerable éclat.[94] Inevitably, he drew criticism for the reported assiduity with which he filled his tent with mirrors and crystal chandeliers. Such critics, however, seem to have found no fault with Louis, whose quarters were sumptuous to the last degree—equal, it was said, to those of a king of Persia.[95] Once at the front, though a simple volunteer without command, the prince joined the king at the siege of Tournay and earned admiration and praise for his willingness to visit the trenches, to expose his person to fire, and to reward the troops (with money, it appears, that he had borrowed from his chaplain). Cosnac, for his part, made sure that his patron's exploits were reported at length in the *Gazette de France*. "People began to take the view," wrote the chaplain, "that he [Philippe] had indeed the strength to withstand exertion and the courage to surmount danger; it was as if he had become another man."[96]

This promising beginning counted for little at the time. The war was both too short and too easy to afford much in the way of serious military instruction or continuous service. Early in July after Tournay fell, Philippe left the army to return in haste to Saint-Cloud, where Madame had suffered a miscarriage and almost died.[97] August found him again with the king, much of the court, and the army as it made a triumphal procession of their conquests; and he was present at the siege of Lille in August. But by early September both brothers were back home again. For Philippe this was the end of his active participation in the war. Although he was supposedly to be given command of an army to invade Catalonia in the spring of 1668, the project did not materialize.[98] The prince did not accompany Louis and Condé on the swift and final campaign of the war in Franche-Comté.

Nor did the war improve Philippe's relations with the king, who seemingly was not among those impressed by the prince's martial capacities. One especially galling incident was reported in 1667 when Louis, who commanded one of the three invading armies under the guidance of Turenne, wished to consult his officers. Noting the presence of Philippe in his tent, he ordered, "Brother, you may go amuse yourself elsewhere, we are going to take counsel." The prince left the royal presence in rage and humiliation. Again he betook himself to the trenches but, it appears, without appreciable effect upon the king.[99]

From Philippe himself we have only one piece of evidence during his time with the army: a letter in his hand that he wrote to Mme de Sablé, saloniste and intellectual, who had taken an interest in the prince's efforts to make something of himself and with whom he corresponded frequently.[100] Written from Lille during the siege, it affords little in the way of information but leaves no doubt that its author, despite his modesty in his subordinate position, did not fear the prospect of combat.

In the manner of the protective male shielding the little woman from the realities of war, he wrote:

> I shall not describe in detail what is going on here, for I should have to speak of things that you do not like, so I shall content myself with saying that all your friends are well and that the city [Lille] will not hold out much longer unless they receive the reinforcements expected any day. The last news is that the enemy is gathering forces to come here; if that is true, we shall do them great honor, as we are preparing . . . to receive them warmly. To tell you the truth, I do not think they will try to force our lines. . . . But, being still a novice, I should not speak of such things without knowing them well.[101]

The letter seems to indicate that Monsieur, still a mere apprentice in the army, was developing a taste for the art of war. It makes more comprehensible the events of ten years later when, experienced in combat, he routed the prince of Orange in battle at Cassel and established a reputation for skill and valor on the battlefield.

FIVE
·

Madame Is Dying! Madame Is Dead!

A House Divided

The storm center of Philippe's private life continued to be his unhappy marriage with Henriette. Neither her frequent pregnancies
nor parenthood served to bring them closer. The months of waiting
were difficult, the deliveries, often resulting in stillbirths, agonizing.
Only two of their children survived to adulthood, the first and the
last born, both daughters, and their only son died before the age of
three. How much effect the births and deaths of these children had
upon Philippe and Henriette is, for want of trustworthy evidence,
difficult to say. Certainly the prince was proud when he became the
father of a son. "Your sister ... [was delivered] of a fine fat boy
who appears to be very healthy," he had written to Charles II in
July 1664.[1] But when that son died two and one-half years later, if
the report may be believed he experienced little grief and was principally pained by the loss of the 150,000 livres a year that the little
prince had brought him from the Crown for his upbringing.[2] Of
Henriette there is even less evidence. "Throw her in the river!" she
reportedly cried out in despair on learning that her firstborn was a
girl.[3] And later, she no more than Philippe would long interrupt the
social calendar for the illnesses or even the deaths of her children.
Even so, not too much can be read into one cry emitted in the throes
of childbirth, especially given the pressures of society for a male
heir. In any case, both father and mother were so immature, and the

98

distance, filled by a plethora of household attendants, between them and their children was so great, that it is small wonder if Henriette and Philippe paid them little attention.

Meanwhile the battles between the spouses were incessant. Usually the flirtations of Madame and the jealousy of Monsieur were the casus belli. The list of men who were allegedly in her coils at one time or another was an extended one. The affair with Guiche had gone on for the better part of four years until in 1665, having offended the king, the young man was obliged to leave court for good. Even then the damage it had done was not finished. The next year Henriette was horrified to learn that a pamphlet with the titillating title *Amours de Madame et du comte de Guiche* was circulating in Holland. It was only a matter of time before it would reach the French court. Cosnac leaped into the breach and seemingly saved the situation by sending an agent to the Netherlands to buy out the edition from the printers. Not, however, before a copy reached the eyes of Monsieur, with the effect that might be expected.[4]

Others who then and subsequently vied for Henriette's favors included some of the greatest names in court. At their head, of course, had been Louis himself. If he were subsequently cured of his early infatuation and had gone on to other romantic adventures, he could and did continue to stimulate Philippe's suspicions by the special favor he reserved for Madame. Then there was François VII, prince of Marcillac, soldier and governor of Berry, who enjoyed the good graces of the king. Or M. Le Grand, count of Armagnac, *grand écuyer*, whose attentions to Henriette nearly broke up his own marriage as well as that of Monsieur and Madame. Or again the young gallant the marquis of Vardes, captain of the Swiss guards and governor of Aigues-Mortes, who sought to take Guiche's place during the latter's absences from court. There was even the archbishop of Sens, a worldly prelate, Louis-Henri de Pardaillan de Gondrin, uncle of Mme de Montespan, who did not conceal his passion for the princess. More briefly mentioned were Louis de Rohan-Montbazon and the count of Puyguilhem. Earlier, even before Henriette's marriage, there had been Buckingham and Admiral Montague. And last, at least chronologically, was the handsome James, duke of Monmouth, who was no less than the illegitimate son of Charles II and thus the nephew of the very lady whose favor he sought.

Every glance of Madame and every sulk of Monsieur were noted assiduously by the many attentive gossips of the court, who did not fail to record them in their memoirs. Today these amorous escapades read like scenes from low comedy replete with bedroom farce. A lover hides behind the fire screen when Monsieur arrives unexpectedly in his wife's chamber. Or the suitor dresses as a woman to win entrance to her dressing room and escape the detection of her household. Masked balls offered especially useful occasions to whisper professions of devotion into the ear of *la divine*. Theatrical compositions came uncomfortably close to the mark in publicly pointing the finger of ridicule at the deceived and helpless husband. In July 1668 during a summer festival at Versailles, when the bold attentions of the beau Monmouth to Madame were entertaining the court, Molière's *George Dandin, ou le mari confondu* was performed. Everyone laughed uproariously at the poor cuckold, who was only too transparent a cover for Monsieur (and also, no doubt, for the equally unfortunate husband of Mme de Montespan).[5] Monmouth left the court the following day.

The accumulation of these humiliations at the hands of his wife and brother continued the erosion of Philippe's self-confidence and the demoralization of his personality. The brief resolve to recapture his self-worth after the death of his mother and the seeming reconciliation with Louis had broken down before the relentless dominance of his brother and the continuing misbehavior of his wife. Although during these years he must have occupied Henriette's bed not infrequently, judging from the results, he apparently found no satisfaction in heterosexuality. The rage over his humiliating life that he could not outwardly express was turned inward in the form of self-destructive homosexuality. Again, as before in his relationship with Guiche, he sought abasement before a male lover. Unhappily for Monsieur, another young man was present at court who was only too willing to fulfill the prince's need for self-punishment, seeing in it a means to serve his own ambitions and make his fortune.

Philippe of the house of Guise-Lorraine, known in court as the chevalier de Lorraine, came into Monsieur's life during the War of Devolution. On the request of the prince and with the permission of the king (who perhaps anticipated and desired the resulting relationship), the young man attached himself to Monsieur's entourage. By the time the war ended they were inseparable. Proud of name, the chevalier was penniless of purse, the younger son of the count of Harcourt, who had been grand écuyer of France but had died a ruined man. The chevalier's intelligence, athletic grace and beauty, and single-minded determination to make his way were more than sufficient assets for the role to which he aspired. Ever conscious of his high birth and haughty in manner, he was to rule Monsieur, *bâton haut*,[6] for much of the remainder of his life. Like Guiche before him, his resemblance to the king was uncanny. Soon in possession of luxurious apartments in the Palais Royal and Saint-Cloud, enriched by gifts of jewels, money, and objets d'art, as the acknowledged favorite of Monsieur he came close to controlling his household as well. Although the true preference of the chevalier was for women (with whom he continued to be very successful), he had no qualms in gratifying the most demeaning weaknesses of his patron.

Dominated by the chevalier as the 1660s drew to a close, Philippe entered upon perhaps the most degrading years of his life. The Palais Royal became the focus of intrigue and scenes of notorious pleasures. L'archimignon, as Lorraine was known (a sobriquet recalling the court of Henri III), and his epigones, male and female, hoping that the favors he enjoyed might extend to them, formed a bloated cabal within the house of Orléans. The prince appeared to glory in his subjugation. On occasion he even appeared publicly, at least in the Palais Royal, in female attire.[7] During Mardi Gras balls, disguised only by a mask, wearing a low-cut gown and earrings, he gave his hand to the chevalier to be led out in the minuet. Later he took his seat amid the ladies. Little urging was required to induce him to remove the mask. "He seemed to wish nothing more than to be seen," wrote an observer of this scene. "Il ne cherchait pas le mystère."[8]

With the entrance of the chevalier de Lorraine into the life of Monsieur, relations between the spouses reached a stage of active and vindictive animosity. Jealous of the young man's influence over the prince and fearful of being eclipsed in her own court by his cabal, Madame began to assemble her own forces and plans to combat the enemy. The Palais Royal soon came to resemble a battlefield with the household ranged in two warring camps.

Superficially, at least, the contest appeared to be an extremely uneven one, with all the high ground held by Philippe. As brother of the king and head of his household, he had immense patronage at his disposal. He could count on the support not only of Lorraine but, among others, of Joachim Seiglière Boisfranc, his treasurer, the père Zoccoli, his confessor, and the maréchal du Plessis-Praslin, his former governor, all of whom owed their high station at court to the prince. In his role as husband he was master of Henriette's person, purse, and household. A word from him could dismiss any member of her service, even the governess of her children. As his wife, Henriette was obliged to follow him wherever and whenever he might command, nor could she make any journey without him except with his express consent. Therefore in the camp of Madame, instead of the influential male figures supportive of Monsieur, there were found only one man, Cosnac, bishop of Valence, who had defected—or rather been evicted—from the cabal of Monsieur, and a cluster of women: Mme de Saint Chaumont, daughter of the maréchal de Gramont and the children's governess; Mlle de Fiennes, one of Madame's favorite ladies-in-waiting, with whom she danced ballets; and Mme de Monaco, with whom the chevalier was supposedly in love. Henriette's mother, who might once have been a force to be reckoned with, was living at Colombes apart from the court, was mortally ill, and could be of small help to her daughter.

And in fact the opening rounds were won by Philippe and company, with Cosnac the first casualty. Ever since the bishop had failed to secure the governorship of Languedoc for the prince, his credit had begun to fall. Then he had made the mistake of saving Madame's reputation in the affair of the libelous pamphlets. Lorraine, who had immediately understood that Cosnac was his enemy, had little difficulty in finishing him off. With the aid of supposedly secret letters of dubious authenticity, he persuaded Philippe that Cosnac had been plotting to come between them and to drive Lorraine from his court. Despite the excited protests of Madame, Cosnac was stripped of his office of chaplain to Monsieur and ordered to retire to his diocese in Valence.

The exile of Cosnac was a heavy blow to the princess, since she knew that he had in his possession three letters of a most compromising nature written in the hand of the chevalier, for whom she was lying in wait. Refusing to despair, she maintained contact with the bishop using Mme de Saint Chaumont as her habitual intermediary. In the autumn of 1669, judging the time right to strike, she prevailed upon the bishop, fearful of arrest, to meet her secretly at Saint-Denis, where she was to attend a religious service in memory of her mother, who had recently died. Cosnac was to bring her the chevalier's letters, which she would use to discredit him with the king and secure his banishment from court.

The upshot of this planned venture was another disaster for Henriette and her troops. Recognized and seized before he could meet with the princess, Cosnac was again sent away, this time far to the south to a small town in the Midi. Nor was that the extent of the damage. One of the letters found on his person (he had managed to save those of the chevalier through a device worthy of Rabelais) had exposed the role of Mme de Saint Chaumont. She too was ordered from court, dismissed as governess of Monsieur's children, and obliged to retire to a house of the Carmelites. Stung by her defeat and outraged at the disgrace of her friend, Henriette poured out her grief and wrath in letter after letter to her brother.

If Henriette had lost a battle, she had by no means lost the war. For despite all appearances, the two camps in the Palais Royal were much more evenly matched than they appeared. What Madame lacked in independence of will and freedom of movement she more than made up for by the extraordinary assistance she might invoke on high. Merely for reasons of family if nothing else, the kings of France and England would have taken her side. True, Louis had so far permitted Philippe to have his way in the cases of Cosnac and Mme de Saint Chaumont and had even put the force of his police behind him, for the king had his own reasons for wanting to be rid of both of them.[9] In the long run, however, Madame was too useful as an instrument for controlling his brother for him to allow her to fall into disgrace. Charles, moreover, was constantly attempting to lend his aid to a beloved sister who was wronged, so he believed, by a prince for whom he had a strong and growing aversion.

The two kings also had other, far more compelling motives having nothing to do with domestic quarrels for extending their support to the princess. Ever since the conclusion of the War of Devolution, Louis had been laying his plans to make war on the Dutch in order to unite the Spanish Netherlands to the kingdom of France. For this purpose he needed to break up the Triple Alliance of England, Holland, and Sweden so that he could strangle the Dutch without interference from Europe. Charles had little liking for the alliance but, engaged in a prolonged struggle with Parliament, on whom he was dependent for money, so far had little choice in the matter. Louis needed an English alliance; Charles needed a French subsidy. Both kings needed Henriette to help them advance toward their goals. Thus the domestic war in the Palais Royal became inextricably intertwined with the high policies of the two sovereigns and the negotiation of the Anglo-French alliance.

DISTAFF DIPLOMACY

"People were aware," wrote Mme de La Fayette, memoirist and confidante of the princess, "that the negotiation in which she was involved was on the point of completion; at the age of twenty-six she had become the link between two of the greatest kings of this century; in her hands lay a treaty that would affect the fate of . . . Europe." Despite this and other positive declarations by contemporaries, the idea that a dilettante like Henriette could conceivably play a major part in the diplomacy of the kingdoms of England and France would still be received with utter incredulity were it not corroborated by letters of unquestionable authenticity preserved in the French Foreign Ministry.[10] Their authors include such personages as Louis himself, Colbert, Colbert's brother Colbert de Croissy, assigned to a special mission at the Court of Saint James, the ambassadors of England and France, and above all Charles, whose letters in his own hand to his cherished Minette from 1660 to 1669 make up an entire volume in the Mémoires et Documents series devoted to English affairs.[11] Nearly every week (not all the letters are present) the king wrote to his sister in English lest, he said, she forget that language altogether (her letters of reply were in French). They are gossipy and affectionate. They teased her about her admirers, consoled her in times of illness, and commiserated with her efforts to combat the "fantastical humours" of Monsieur (Charles's term for Philippe's jealous anger).[12] When he believed he had a messenger he could trust, he discussed his diplomatic relations with Louis with total frankness. Throughout the checkered course of Anglo-French relations in the 1660s he insisted that he would not "have this business passe through other hands than yours [Henriette's]" and on the "most principle part therin" she should play in his diplomacy. By December 1669 when the negotiation of the Anglo-French alliance was in a critical stage, he was declaring flatly to Colbert de Croissy that "the intermediacy of Madame was absolutely essential" to its success and that she must come to England for its consummation.

Madame was anything but reluctant to accept the proffered role of ambassador. Perhaps she saw herself following in the footsteps of her mother, Henrietta Maria, who as wife of Charles I had schemed actively (if disastrously) to introduce foreign armies into England to defend the Catholic recusants. Now the daughter also could show that a highly placed woman could influence affairs of state. After the death of Henrietta Maria in September 1669 the princess saw that she had become the sole link between the royal houses of England and France and realized that she could exploit the position to her advantage. Having become indispensable to the success of the negotiation, her stock at the French court soared. Moreover, what a splendid new way to humiliate Philippe, who was excluded from public affairs as usual and was tormented anew by the extended tête-à-têtes between his brother and his wife. And finally and most important, she could, through Charles, make demands on Louis regarding her domestic war that he could not refuse without endangering the success of the negotiation. Lorraine should be banished; Cosnac would be returned (and with a cardinal's hat

to boot); and she would be the victor of the Palais Royal and uncrowned queen of the court.

Charles readily helped her realize this scenario. He had long
sympathized with her desire to be rid of the chevalier. "I thinke you
have taken a very good resolution, not to live so with [Lorraine],"
he had written, "but that when there offers a good occasion, you
may ease yourselfe of such a rival, and by the carrecter I have of
him there is hopes he will find out the occasion for himselfe."
Quickly Charles came to her defense after her aborted interview
with Cosnac and the dismissal of Mme de Saint Chaumont. Repeatedly he and his ministers bearded Colbert de Croissy, who reported
directly to Louis, to express their dismay over the treatment accorded Henriette's friends. Cosnac, argued the king, had left his
place of exile only for urgent reasons of health and in search of
medical treatment. And as for Mme de Saint Chaumont, whom, he
said, he had always considered a very circumspect lady, he was
convinced that her role in the adventure was all the result of an
intrigue by the chevalier de Lorraine. Madame was very upset, he
and the ministers emphasized. After all, Charles reminded Croissy,
his sister had suffered this humiliation only because she had refused
to reveal to Monsieur the secret of the treaty she was negotiating
on behalf of the king of France. Her extreme distress over the incident, he added in a thinly veiled threat, "could very well change the
whole fact of the affairs under negotiation." Could not, therefore,
Madame be extended some kind of "striking satisfaction" in compensation for the humiliation she had suffered?

Of course the king of England could not tell the king of France
how to order affairs in his own family and court. But if Charles
could not in so many words ask Louis to banish the chevalier, by
January 1670 he was, according to Colbert de Croissy, making himself unmistakably clear. Charles had told him, reported the special
ambassador, that he was still disappointed that the king of France
had done nothing for Madame that could compensate her in the
eyes of the court. The king was also aware, he continued, that Monsieur was treating Madame badly, but since he attributed that abuse
to the intrigues of Lorraine, he was less concerned about it than he
was when the source of ill treatment came from the French king
himself. "The interests of this Princess," Charles had told Croissy,
"were dearer to him than those of his own kingdom, and . . . he
would be more grateful for any grace that he might extend to Madame than as if they had been destined for Charles himself."

Louis, of course, had no difficulty getting the message. Even though at times he suspected Madame of being more favorable to her brother's interests than to his,[13] given Charles's continued insistence on her intermediacy, he felt compelled to accede to his wishes. Later in the same month, January 29, he wrote Colbert de Croissy that he was sure the English king would be "satisfied."[14] The very next day, January 30, while Philippe and the chevalier were conversing in the prince's apartment in the *château neuf* at Saint-Germain, Louis's captain of the guards and a contingent of soldiers burst in. Unceremoniously, they seized and arrested the young man and on orders of the king escorted him to the prison of Pierre-Encise near Lyons.

The prince reacted with a burst of temper reminiscent of those in his earlier youth when, out of control, he had struck out against the sovereign. Outraged at this act of lordliness perpetrated within his own chambers and in the presence of officers and servants of his own household, he rushed to confront his brother. Receiving no satisfaction, he gathered up Madame, hastened to the Palais Royal to order the removal of his furnishings, and even though it was the dead of winter, betook himself and his household to his draughty and isolated château at Villers-Cotterêts in his appanage. There on February 2 he poured out his grief in a bitter letter to Jean Baptiste Colbert, arguably Louis's most influential minister:

Monsieur Colbert, as for some time I have regarded you as among my friends, and as of them you are the only one having the honor of approaching the king since the frightful misfortune that has just befallen me, I believe you will not be angry if I ask you to inform the king that I came here in an extremity of grief that required me either to leave his presence or to remain in his court in shame. I beg him to consider what the world would think of me if it saw me merrily enjoying the pleasures of carnival while an innocent prince and the best friend that I have on earth for the love of me languishes in a wretched prison far away. Furthermore, the manner in which he was seized could not have been more insulting to me, since for some time no one knew for sure if in fact it were I that was to be taken, for my rooms were surrounded with guards at doors and windows, and frightened servants would come to me saying they could not say if it was my person that was wanted. And worse, the king went so far as to ask my wife what she intended to do, thus making clear that he wanted to authorize her not to follow me, as her duty required. Even so, if I believed I might be useful to the service of the king, I should not have left him, but the manner in which he has treated me all his life makes me think just the contrary.[15]

The two brothers appeared to have reached a standoff. Philippe continued to declare roundly to Colbert, and to others sent by the king to persuade him to rejoin the court, that he would not set foot in Saint-Germain until Lorraine was liberated. Louis, refusing to be blackmailed, raised the ante by transferring the chevalier from Pierre-Encise to an even worse prison, the dreaded Château d'If, in the roadstead at Marseilles. Still the prince held out while the court and foreign diplomats buzzed. The scandal assumed such proportions that Louis felt obliged to make reassuring explanations for the benefit of foreign governments and the French public. Because so few were privy to the treaty negotiations under way with England, those at court could only guess at the reasons for the chevalier's arrest, which indeed were far from clear. Then and thereafter in their memoirs they speculated freely.[16] Most, however, had no doubt that in some way or other Madame was at the bottom of it. Mademoiselle, even though she was totally ignorant of Henriette's diplomatic activity, was not at all taken in by the anger the princess feigned over the king's action. Meeting the couple in the Palais Royal during the few hours they were there before departing for Villers-Cotterêts, she wrote: "In the depths of her heart she [Henriette] was really very pleased. . . . No one doubts that she was behind [Lorraine's] disgrace.[17]

Only at the end of twenty-five days did the prince yield and agree to return to Paris with his wife. His reappearance at court on the evening of February 24 was announced abroad[18] and in the *Gazette de France*. The precise terms of the deal cut between the brothers cannot be known with any certainty (the official version was that Monsieur had returned without any condition whatever),[19] but undoubtedly its principal stipulation was that the chevalier should be released from prison but should not be permitted to return to Paris. Freed from the dank fortress, the young man traveled to Italy and settled in Rome.

Was the prince's submission merely another example of a deplorable weakness of will and a lack of tenacity? Did he in effect have any other choice? What leverage, if any, did he possess in a contest with his redoubtable brother? According to law, the duke of Orléans was as much subject to Louis's authority as the meanest pauper in the land. His financial dependence on the king, save for the paltry (for an enfant de France) income from his appanage, was total. He had no governorship in the provinces that might have afforded him a base of support such as had in fact sustained his uncle Gaston. Nor did the adult Philippe resemble Gaston in character. As the king well knew, his brother was no Frondeur. The unconscious desire to destroy Louis was buried deep within him and found expression only in a guilty need for self-punishment, not in conspiracy or overt rebellion. Little of real significance had changed in the relationship between the brothers since that day over ten years before when the seventeen-year old prince had thrown a bowl of bouillon in the sovereign's face.

There were probably only one or two good cards at most in Philippe's hand, and all things considered, he seems to have played them adroitly. These were the public embarrassment he could cause Louis by his continued self-imposed exile from court and the authority he possessed over his wife, who was crucial to the negotiation of an Anglo-French alliance (of which by this time he had been privately informed). While at Villers-Cotterêts he wrote to Charles expressing extreme irritation with Madame, whom he held responsible for Louis's action. As he no doubt intended, the English king now became alarmed lest the continued imprisonment of the chevalier cause Monsieur to forbid Madame's departure for England and the conclusion of the alliance. Could not, he asked Louis, a remedy be found?[20] Either of Monsieur's cards could, of course, have been trumped by a direct order from the king. But after all, there are limits that even kings are reluctant to exceed with the entire court and diplomatic corps looking on. Rather than play the autocrat, Louis yielded to his brother's pressure at least to the extent of releasing the chevalier from prison.

This minor concession should not conceal the enormity of Philippe's defeat. Present again in court and unable to strike back at the king, he vented his wrath on his wife. "The absence of the chevalier de Lorraine," wrote Mademoiselle, who was a close observer of the Orléans ménage, "was a new source of discord between Monsieur and Madame. Every day they had another row."[21] She was aghast at the violence of her cousin's rage, and more than once felt obliged to remind him of the existence of the children from their marriage. Wounds from former battles were reopened as the prince returned to accusations of Henriette's past infidelities. One especially painful scene elicited from Madame the singular protest: "So if in the past I made some mistake, why did he not go ahead and strangle me then when he claimed I was deceiving him? To suffer like this now, and for nothing, I cannot stand it."[22]

Nor can these marital battles obscure the fact that the true object of Philippe's hate and source of his resentment was the king, ever the rival he could not defeat. By this time the prince was aware of the negotiation his brother and his wife were involved in, having learned of it from Lorraine, who had been able to penetrate the secret shortly before his arrest.[23] It soothed him not at all to know that Louis and Henriette could legitimately claim to be engaged in the work of diplomacy rather than of Cupid. How could he be expected to forget or to forgive their flagrant dalliance when Henriette and he were bride and groom? In any case, his exclusion from their affairs was one more reminder of Louis's domination and an especially galling one at that, since over the years he had frequently attempted to act as go-between for the two kings, only to be rebuffed.

From the time he became betrothed to Henriette the prince had been at pains to establish and maintain cordial relations with the English king. On file in the State Papers, France, of the Public Record Office in London are dozens of Philippe's letters to Charles in his own hand.[24] For the most part they contain little of substance, having been prompted by events within the two families: births, deaths, weddings, anniversaries, and such, that called for congratulations or condolences. They were replete with protestations of friendship and devotion and, a reflection of Philippe's close attention to etiquette, unfailingly closed with a deft touch of deference implicitly acknowledging the superior rank of the English king. Charles, in turn, replied in an equally cordial vein; superficially, at least, the brothers-in-law were on the best of terms. In reality the English king disliked Philippe intensely, having absorbed Henriette's antipathy for her husband and having accepted her version of the marriage as the true one. Thus, whenever the prince mentioned affairs of state, Charles brushed him off disdainfully.

In the second half of the 1660s Philippe tried repeatedly to entertain Anglo-French relations with the English king. In 1665 when France was at least ostensibly the ally of Holland, with whom England was at war, Philippe unreservedly expressed his hopes for an English victory. Apprised of the success of the English fleet in a battle with the Dutch in the English Channel, Philippe wrote excitedly to Charles:

> The three days in which I have been in a mortal impatience to know the results of the engagement have made me realize as never before how much friendship I bear Your Majesty and how keenly I am interested in all things that concern him. I cannot doubt that the end will be favorable, since it began so well; having learned just now [of the English victory] I hasten to express my joy [and my pleasure] that the

duke of York [Charles's brother, who commanded the English forces] is in good health. . . . If my wishes are fulfilled, Your Majesty will have all kinds of good fortune, for no one wishes it more than I.[25]

Over and over he expressed his desire to work for friendship and understanding between the two sovereigns. In January 1666, efforts to mediate Anglo-French differences having failed, Louis was on the point of declaring war on England. A few days before he did so, Philippe wrote to his brother-in-law at length offering his services "to continue the good understanding that for so long has prevailed between France and England." He should think himself fortunate indeed, continued the prince, were he able to contribute to this work. "I agree that one should never abandon one's allies [a reference to the French alliance with Holland], but affairs are in that state that an accommodation can be reached on the part of one or of the other. . . . I can assure Your Majesty that excepting only the interests of France there are no others for whom I have greater . . . attachment than those affecting Your Majesty, for whom I have much respect and friendship."[26]

To these and other offers Charles remained deaf. Throughout the difficult year of 1665 he was firm in his conviction that it must be Henriette who played the go-between for the two courts. In July of that year he wrote to his sister: "It must be your part to keepe your selfe still in a state of contributing the events, and having a most principle part therin, which will not be a hard taske to your discretion and good talent."[27] The princess too, knowing well that neither king would admit her husband to his confidence, had nothing but contempt for his attempts to play the diplomat. Knowing also, as Philippe did not, that Louis was committed to at least a show of force against England, she belittled his efforts to stave off a declaration of war. "Monsieur is writing you a great letter to speak to you still of an understanding," she wrote Charles. "As for me, I confess that I do not like to be party to useless things."[28]

And sure enough, useless it was. On January 26, 1666, Louis declared war on England. Charles, like his sister, refused to take Philippe's offer seriously and denied him even the courtesy of a response and word of thanks for his goodwill. To Henriette he commented: "Last week I had intended to answer your letter and that of Monsieur on the subject of his good offices proffered between France and me; but, in a letter from the Queen [Henrietta Maria] of a more recent date, I have seen that such mediation is now out of the question . . . and so I content myself now with writing Monsieur a simple letter of condolence on the death of his mother."[29]

Louis's declaration of war against England had been merely a temporary expedient in his maneuvers toward his real goal, the conquest of the Spanish Netherlands. It provided him with a screen behind which he could build up his forces for a test against the Dutch. Because the English alliance was a virtual necessity for the success of that venture, Louis and Charles soon resumed their parleys through Henriette. By the time the chevalier de Lorraine had been arrested, the main outline of the treaty had been agreed upon: the English alliance against the Dutch, including the participation of an Anglo-French fleet under the command of the duke of York, in return for a French subsidy that would enable Charles to escape financial dependence on Parliament.[30] Corollaries were Charles's public conversion to Catholicism and the signing of a commercial treaty. Only the exact amount of the subsidy and a few minor details remained to be negotiated.

The affair was in this state in February 1670 while Philippe and Henriette were at Villers-Cotterêts. At midmonth two English agents arrived in France with letters from Charles officially requesting that during the coming spring, on the occasion of a programmed visit of the French court to Flanders, Madame pass from Dunkirk or Calais to England to visit her relatives and, of course, to consummate the secret treaty. Proceeding to Valois in the company of the English ambassador, the agents learned from Madame herself that despite the ill will of her husband she did not despair of her ability to meet her brother either in Dover or in Canterbury.

The snag, of course, was that for Henriette to make such a voyage, Philippe's permission must be obtained, and the prince was seemingly adamant in his opposition to her departure. Apparently Madame's voyage had not been a part of the agreement between Louis and Philippe that had brought the prince reluctantly back to the court in February. Late in March Louis informed Colbert de Croissy in London that his brother was still so carried away with anger whenever the subject was broached as to wish to deny her permission even to accompany the court to Flanders in May.[31]

Yet in this resolve too, as in his earlier determination not to return to Saint-Germain until the chevalier was again at his side, the prince was gradually overborne. Another humiliation at the hands of his brother and, as its corollary, another triumph for Madame were in the offing. As Louis and his ministers set to work on him, Philippe softened to the point of offering his consent on a variety of conditions, among which were that the prince should accompany his wife and thus participate in the negotiations; that the visit should last no longer than three days and be limited to Dover (on

no account should Madame be received in London); that the duchess of York should yield to Madame the honors of etiquette; that
the duke of York should pay a simultaneous visit to France—and
so on.[32] The first of these conditions never had the smallest chance
of acceptance, the king and Madame having determined not to grant
the prince the slightest role in the negotiations. The others too,
except for the exclusion of London from the itinerary, were one by
one eliminated as the prince, grumbling but defenseless before his
brother's implacable will, gave way. The voyage was to take place,
and there was nothing Philippe could do to prevent it.

The royal party that set out from Paris for a tour of Flanders at
the end of April was sumptuous to the last degree. Louis always
traveled in style, and this trip, with the publicly announced purpose
of showing Maria Theresa her Spanish heritage, acquired in the
War of Devolution, was designed to dazzle the king's new subjects
with his magnificence. "The brilliance of the turnout in this voyage
can not be exaggerated," wrote a contemporary. "The troops were
superbly uniformed; the court never appeared more grand: the king,
his hands full of gold pieces, distributed money freely in all the
towns of his new conquests."[33]

Inside the splendid royal carriage, however, the mood was anything but festive. First of all, owing to the execrable weather, they
were physically uncomfortable, constantly cold and wet (Louis
liked the windows open at all times). Once when their passage was
barred by a swollen river, they were all obliged to bed down for the
night in a barn, where dinner was a thin soup served without benefit
of cutlery. Such hardships, however, could be laughed off by the
hardier ones, among them Mademoiselle, who was of the party.
More difficult to ignore must have been the emotional tension filling
the air. The presence of Mme de Montespan in the royal carriage,
then in the flower of her beauty and clearly in possession of the
king's affections, would in itself have ensured the misery of the
queen. Mademoiselle too was, if not exactly unhappy, far from se-
rene, with her eyes fixed on a young captain of the king's guard, a
world below her socially and financially, to whom she was actually
contemplating marriage. But above all it was the ill humor emanat-
ing from the duke of Orléans that befouled the atmosphere. Sullen
and resentful at his forced participation in a journey that was bringing Henriette ever closer to her port of embarkation, he carped at
his wife incessantly. At Courtray, where a message from Charles
informed them of his imminent arrival off Dover, where he would
receive his sister, the prince's renewed protests were quelled by
Louis, who declared that "he willed it absolutely."[34] One evening

when the prince and Mademoiselle found themselves alone, she came to realize by the depth of his anger that he could never be reconciled with Henriette. On another occasion, when the conversation in the carriage turned to astrology, the prince remarked brutally: "I have been told that I should have several wives; and given the condition Madame is in, I can well believe it."[35]

Indeed, the health of Madame appeared frail, a fact that did not escape Louis's attention. Listless and tired throughout the journey, she took no nourishment except milk; on alighting from the carriage in the evening she retired immediately to her quarters, generally to take to her bed. Concerned at the weakness of his ambassador (and one suspects with an eye to the effect on his brother), he visited her frequently and overwhelmed her with attentions. These in turn served to exacerbate the misery of Philippe.[36]

In this contentious humor the royal party arrived on May 24 at Dunkirk, where Madame and a retinue of over 230 embarked on an English warship. Arriving off the coast of England on May 26, she was met by her brother and other relatives (among them Monmouth) who had come out to meet her in a bark. From all accounts[37] the ensuing visit, which lasted nearly three weeks, passed off brilliantly. Madame reportedly had returned to good health. The Secret Treaty of Dover, whose details had been for the most part agreed upon before her departure, was promptly concluded. Charles, who had wished to receive his sister in London, made up for his disappointment by hosting a series of gala banquets, arranging a side trip to Canterbury to attend a ballet and comedy and ordering a sea excursion to visit the neighboring coasts. As an expression of his gratitude he presented Henriette the handsome sum of 6,000 pistoles (the equivalent of 60,000 livres)[38] to help defray the expenses of her voyage. Triumphantly, Madame embarked at Dover on June 12 and arrived at the château of Saint-Germain on June 18.

Oh, Disastrous Night! Oh, Dreadful Night!

Once back in the French court the princess found conditions little changed. Still in a rancorous mood, Philippe had refused to go out with his household to greet his wife and escort her to the château as etiquette required, and he had urged Louis to remain within as well. The king compromised to the extent of advancing only a short distance to meet her cortege, but then he overwhelmed the returning victor with embraces, compliments, honors, and a gift of money matching that of his English brother-in-law. A few days later the sovereign and his ambassador repaired to Louis's apartments in the old château (Philippe's were in the new) to talk over the details of negotiation and the events of the voyage, conversations from which Philippe was pointedly excluded. Seemingly in good health, Henriette radiated happiness and contentment as all the court flocked to do her honor.

Madame was given but a short time to bask in her glory. The following day, June 19, Louis left for Versailles and Philippe, "in order to spite Madame,"[39] refused to follow. Instead the couple repaired to Paris and from there, on June 24, to Saint-Cloud. The princess, now in a state of irritable excitement, began to complain of pains in her side and stomach; yet since the weather was warm and she was unable to sleep, she bathed in the river and took to promenading in the gardens late in the evening. Mme de La Fayette, arriving at the château during this time, found her dispirited and moody. She noted, too, that when Madame napped after dinner on June 29 her face changed almost beyond recognition. On awakening, she looked so ill that even Monsieur remarked on it.[40] Even so, no one suspected that anything was seriously amiss. Henriette, as was her custom late each afternoon, drank a cup of chicory water brought by one of her ladies. Philippe, who was planning to spend the evening in Paris, came to his wife's apartment to take his leave.

The scene changed with horrifying swiftness. Still holding cup and saucer, the princess clutched her side and cried out: "Oh, what a cramp in my side! What pain!"[41] Pale and nearly in a faint, she was helped to her bed. While her ladies undressed her, scurrying about for doctors and medicines, she called despairingly for her confessor. Fixing her eyes upon the cup from which she had drunk, she pronounced that one bottle had been substituted for another, that she had been poisoned and was going to die.

What was the demeanor of Philippe as he heard the charge of poison from the lips of his wife and observed her agonies? Not surprisingly, he was closely observed by those present.[42] He appeared deeply touched when she reached out to embrace him and declared with tenderness: "Alas! Monsieur, it is long since you have loved me; but that is unjust: I have never been unfaithful to you." According to Mme de La Fayette, who was on the scene throughout, the prince showed no signs of guilty confusion. Instead he agreed that poison remedies should be brought to Henriette and ordered that the remainder of the chicory water be given to a dog as a test of its contents. At first he seemed not to believe she was in any danger, but as the broths, drugs, powders, oils, purges, and bleedings failed to relieve the patient's sufferings, he became frightened and angry at the calmness of the physicians. To one, who assured him he could answer for her recovery, he replied angrily that he had heard that before. The doctor had once answered to him for the health of his son, he declared, and look what had happened to him. Judging that the time had come for the sacraments, he permitted the entrance of Henriette's confessor, the vicar of Saint-Cloud; but ever conscious of appearances and the niceties of etiquette, he bethought himself of someone more distinguished, a bishop, the esteemed Bossuet, to speak to her of death and to administer the sacraments.[43]

As the night wore on and word of the princess's illness spread, family, courtiers, and officials gathered to say farewell. Louis, Mademoiselle, Mlle de La Vallière, Mme de Montespan, and others all left her bedside in tears. Among the last to arrive was Lord Montagu, the ambassador from England, with whom Henriette exchanged a few words in English. Those in the room could make out the word poison, although they could not say for sure if the princess was professing herself a victim of it.[44] Philippe, by this time in tears himself, remained with Henriette almost to the end. After a last embrace she begged him to retire "and told him she was greatly moved by his tenderness."[45] At three o'clock on the morning of June 30,[46] nine hours after the onset of her sufferings, Henriette of England was dead. She was twenty-six years of age.

The death of one so young, so charming and gracious, so highly placed, and so manifestly favored by the king set off powerful reverberations. The eloquent eulogy of Bishop Bossuet well articulated the shock of the court: "Oh, disastrous night, oh, dreadful night, in which resounded like a clap of thunder the unbelievable words: "Madame is dying! Madame is dead!" . . . Like the flower of the field in the morning she was gone from us by night. . . . What haste! Within nine hours His work was done."[47] From the pen of Mme de Sévigné, whose friends were Henriette's friends, flowed the graceful tribute: "She was taken ill and died within the space of eight hours, taking with her all the joy, all the grace, and all the pleasures of the court."[48]

But it was the cause of this death that immediately riveted the attention of the court. "No one was talking of anything but the death of Madame, of the suspicion that she had been poisoned, and of the terms on which she and Monsieur had long since lived."[49] Poison was the first thing anyone thought of in the seventeenth century when even slightly unusual circumstances surrounded a death.[50] Although knowledge of toxicology was then slight, people had no difficulty believing in the lethal properties of a variety of repellent, perhaps nauseating, but otherwise relatively harmless substances. Their readiness to impute this crime to persons they encountered in their daily life and with whom they were on polite terms is nothing less than astounding to the twentieth-century mind. Moreover, in the case of Madame their predisposition was magnified by the association of criminality and homosexuality in the public mind.[51] Because Madame's known principal enemies, over whom she had recently scored a signal victory—Monsieur, the chevalier de Lorraine, and his epigones—were guilty of the "Italian vice," they could the more easily be identified as killers. Any one of them could easily be supposed to have arranged the introduction of poison into the draught of chicory water that Madame herself had believed was the cause of her death. The English, chief among them Charles himself, were also ready to believe the worst. "The king of England is inconsolable," wrote Colbert de Croissy. "And what adds to his grief are the rumors running all over the city that the princess died by poison."[52] It was even believed that Charles had been so horrified and outraged by his sister's death that he had refused even to receive the special messenger sent by Monsieur to announce Madame's death and extend his condolences.[53]

Louis, of course, made haste to assure the public, English and French alike, that the death was a natural one. Not only the honor of his family and court was at stake, but his English alliance as well. On his orders an autopsy was conducted by France's most eminent physicians in the presence of the ambassador from England and an English surgeon, and its results were published in the *Gazette de France*.[54] The stomach, it was reported, was found flooded with a "fermented bile," and the organs of the abdominal cavity were in an advanced state of gangrene. The verdict put out was that the princess had died of a colic to which they put the name *cholera-morbus*.[55]

The official pronouncement did little to shut down the rumor factory at court, which turned out a variety of scenarios showing by whom, how, and where the crime had been conceived and executed. In them, perhaps not surprisingly, it was the chevalier rather than Monsieur who usually played the villain's role, even though the former was in Italy and the latter was not only on the scene but, with the access of a husband to the victim's private apartments, could most easily have done the deed. Yet who at court could wish to be overheard accusing the brother of the King of the murder of his wife? But beyond such considerations of prudence was the undeniably innocent demeanor of Monsieur during the hours of his wife's agonies, a demeanor that had placed him above suspicion even by those, like Mme de La Fayette, most likely to have suspected him. Henriette herself, although convinced she was poisoned, clearly had not held her husband responsible for the act. In effect, those at court who knew the prince best simply could not believe that he was capable of such a crime.

Consequently other scripts were devised in which the chevalier, seeking revenge for his banishment from court, sent the poison to one of his henchmen in Paris, who managed to rub it on the rim of the cup from which Madame drank the chicory water. Monsieur knew nothing of the deed (although implicit, at least in some of the accounts, is his approval, or at least his consent, had he known). The perpetrators, knowing the prince's weakness under pressure from the king and fearing he would be unable to keep the secret, deliberately excluded him from their plans. "No, let's not tell him," they allegedly decided. "He will not be able to keep quiet. If he doesn't talk the first year, he will get us hanged ten years later."[56] This theme, with variations and embellishments, has come down to subsequent generations chiefly through the widely read memoirs of Saint-Simon and the published correspondence of Liselotte, Monsieur's second wife.[57] That the one had not even been born and the other had not yet left her native Palatinate when Henriette died in 1670 seemingly did not diminish their credence in the eyes of their eighteenth- and nineteenth-century readers. From Voltaire to Michelet and beyond, the poisoning of Henriette of England has been the subject of sensational histories, dramas, and novels. In her dramatic and pathetic end, Madame was transfigured and Monsieur debased. To no small degree the legend attaching to her death has been responsible for the low esteem in which Philippe has been held ever since.

Today that legend has lost much of its credibility. We are much less inclined to see a poisoner in every closet, poison no longer being the murderer's preferred medium (advances in technology have provided much surer, swifter instruments of death). With more knowledge of toxicity and its history, we are skeptical of the availability to the chevalier of a poison so lethal that even a trace of it on the rim of a cup sufficed to kill. We remember, too, the precariousness of Madame's health throughout much of her adult life and the obvious symptoms of illness she evinced in the weeks and days preceding her death. We are aware of the seventeenth-century proclivity to confound criminality with vice. But above all, the attitude and reactions of Louis XIV render the poison thesis impossible to sustain. Reasons of state, certainly, required him to assert that his brother and his close associates were innocent of any crime. But they did not require him, only two years later, to return the chevalier de Lorraine to court, to reward him liberally and publicly,[58] and even after the death of Monsieur and long after the English alliance had passed into history, to continue to extend his favor to him.[59] It is beyond belief that a prince such as Louis XIV, who never forgot an injury, could have behaved in such a fashion toward one who had murdered a princess within his own family, whom he had honored with his confidence and his favor.

Knowledgeable authorities of the twentieth century have usually attributed Madame's death to peritonitis engendered by a perforated duodenal ulcer.[60] In an acute form resulting from perforation, it can carry off its victim within hours. This diagnosis is consistent with Henriette's entire known medical history. It is also consistent with more recently acquired knowledge of anorexia nervosa, which not uncommonly afflicts girls and young women of high intelligence and whose manifest symptoms include hyperactivity.[61] The princess had always been thin to the point of emaciation, and in her last years, as contemporaries frequently noted, she was exceedingly frail. Even so, she did not slow her frenetic pace. Gui Patin, one of the doctors near to the court, had also long believed that Madame suffered from tuberculosis,[62] a disease that can attack the peritoneum as well as the lungs and persist in chronic form. Louis himself had told another of her physicians that for over three years Henriette had experienced pain in her side so severe that she was obliged to lie on the floor for hours at a time, and even then failed to find relief. These symptoms in turn might well have been exacerbated by gastrointestinal disorders, including duodenal dilatation, arising from anorectic eating habits.[63] All things considered, one can only agree with another of Madame's doctors, Vallot, who thought it nothing short of a miracle that she had lived as long as she did.

In the days following Henriette's death Philippe continued, at least in public, to behave impeccably. Leaving Saint-Cloud, he went immediately to the Palais Royal to receive the formal visits of condolence from members of the family and dignitaries of the court. He paid assiduous attention to each detail of the many elaborate funeral ceremonies appropriate to burial of one of royal birth: the embalming and laying out of the body in the chamber of death; the conveyance of the heart to Val-de-Grâce; the deposit of the entrails in the Church of the Celestins; and on July 4, the bearing of the body of the princess to Saint-Denis, where it lay in state until the final obsequies, carried out with great pomp on August 21.[64] During this last interval detachments of the prince's guards stood vigil night and day over the sarcophagus. All in all, it amounted to a sterling example of what the French would call *un bel enterrement*. Not even the prince's small daughters were exempted from participation in the observances of mourning. When Mademoiselle paid her respects at the Palais Royal she found the older child, age eight, decked out in a long black habit that trailed on the floor. The younger, who had not yet attained her first birthday and was still in the nursery with her wet nurse, had likewise, at the prince's request, to receive a visit of condolence in due form. Mademoiselle found her cousin's insistence on pomp and ceremony ridiculous to the last degree for, she observed naively: "[Monsieur] did not appear to be grieving at all."[65]

In all probability Mademoiselle's observation was a remarkable understatement of the sense of satisfaction, even of elation, that the prince, consciously or unconsciously, was experiencing. But then the princess was never a keen observer of human nature. True, Philippe had been moved to the point of tears during Henriette's last hours. Illness and suffering had always brought out the tender side of his nature. He had revealed it much earlier when Louis had nearly died in 1658 and again during the last agonies of Anne of Austria. But no sooner had Henriette drawn her last breath than his mood and behavior altered abruptly. Immediately he had gone to Henriette's dressing room, seized the keys to her cabinets, and taken into his possession not only a casket containing the last dispatches from Charles on the subject of the Anglo-French treaty, but also the 6,000 pistoles he had given her for her role in the negotiations. Only on the outraged protests of the English ambassador Montagu, who claimed that Madame had charged him with distributing the pistoles among her servants, did Philippe reluctantly relinquish half the sum with a promise to return the rest at a later date. The ambassador was still greatly dissatisfied and predicted darkly to Charles's secretary of state that if those to whom he gave the money were not careful to conceal their identity, Monsieur would not fail to take it away from them.[66]

Why did the prince behave in so brutish a fashion? On the conscious level, the act was clearly one of revenge and retaliation, an obvious manifestation of his resentment at having been excluded from the negotiations in which his wife was involved. Having possessed himself of the letters, which were in English, he ordered them translated and deciphered so that he could read the details for himself. By pocketing the gold pieces, he was taking for himself the reward that had been destined for Henriette.

What else may the action have denoted? It was most certainly a

greedy, grasping act, one that in the eyes of his world was unbecoming to a gentleman, let alone a prince of his high station. Yet it
was by no means the first time the prince displayed a desire
amounting to passion for acquisition and collecting, a drive that was
to become an obsession with the passing years. Long ago Mazarin
had learned that gifts, large or small, were most effective as a means
of controlling the prince's behavior. The château of Saint-Cloud
was visible evidence of the cardinal's gratification of the prince's
desires. Much more recently, when Henriette's mother died in 1669,
Philippe had again displayed this facet of his character by claiming,
in the name of his wife and over her objections and those of her
brother, the right of total possession of his mother-in-law's estate.[67]

On the unconscious level, such a passion is far from simple. It
might simply be absolute; it might be functional, merely a means to
attain power. From a psychoanalytic perspective, it could signify
any number of conditions ranging from anal-retentive fixations to a
delayed oedipal triumph.[68] In Philippe's case it seems to betoken, if
nothing more, passions closely linked to wishes and hatreds that he
could never satisfy or exorcise. Seen in that light, the prince's act
could have been a substitute or compensation for the power and
authority of which he had always been deprived.

In any circumstance, Philippe was interested in and enjoyed ceremony. It would be surprising if he did not take a special, mean
pleasure in this one. He had outlived his tormentress and had won
a victory of sorts over his brother, whose agent she had been. No
longer could she revel in her diplomatic triumph and her favor with
the king. Not even Louis's sovereign authority could save her from
death. The score between Monsieur and Madame was even at last.

Plates

ONE Anonymous engraving commemorating the accession of the child
Louis XIV. Philippe, le Petit Monsieur, stands at his mother's left. Louvre Museum. The Chalcography.

TWO Philippe as a boy. Painting by Nocret. Bibliothèque Nationale. Manuscripts.

SERENISS. PRINCEPS. GASTON. DE FRANCIA. CHRISTIANIS.
REGIS FRATER, DVX. AVRELIANENSIS.
Vosterman sculp.   Ant. Van Dyck pinxit   cum priuilegio

THREE   Gaston, duke of Orléans, scapegrace brother of Louis XIII, whom
Philippe greatly loved and admired as a child. Engraving after a painting by
Van Dyck. Louvre Museum. The Chalcography.

FOUR   Monsieur as he appeared as the "king of Persia," in the carrousel of 1662. His love of extravagant dress and jewelry is evident. Engraving by I. Silvestre after painting by J. Bailly. Versailles Museum.

FIVE The coronation of Louis XIV. Philippe, age thirteen, stands at the right of the bishop and assists. Louvre Museum. The Chalcography.

SIX Philippe's handwriting near his tenth birthday. The letter is to his uncle Gaston, whom he addresses as "Sir my good-for-nothing rascal" (*Monsieur mon Pendart*). He signs himself "your very affectionate servant and good-for-nothing rascal." Bibliothèque Nationale. Manuscripts.

SEVEN Monsieur's nearly illegible handwriting as an adult. The letter is addressed to Colbert. Bibliothèque Nationale. Manuscripts.

EIGHT   Henriette of England, Philippe's first wife. She displays a portrait of the prince, her husband. Versailles Museum.

NINE Mlle de Montpensier, "Mademoiselle," or "la Grande Mademoiselle,"
Philippe's cousin and fellow "underdog" at court. She is depicted as the warlike
Frondeuse and displays a portrait of her father, Gaston. Versailles Museum.

TEN The adult Louis XIV. Giraudon/Art Resource.

Monsieur le Chevalier de Lorraine

ELEVEN The chevalier de Lorraine, the most cherished of Monsieur's favorites and to whom he was deeply attached for much of his adult life. Bibliothèque Nationale. Engravings.

TWELVE Battle of Cassel, April 11, 1677. Monsieur, sword upraise
foreground at right. Mount Cassel is in the background. Versailles M

THIRTEEN   Monsieur as a young adult in the 1670s near the time of the Battle of Cassel. Bibliothèque Nationale. Manuscripts.

FOURTEEN Elizabeth Charlotte, "la Palatine," Monsieur's second wife. She is
depicted as a young girl. Portrait by Pierre Mignard (?). By permission of Histo-
risches Museum der Pflaz Speyer.

Veuë des Jardin, et Parterre

I.sruel siluestre inuen. et fecit.

FIFTEEN The Maison Gondi at Saint-Cloud. Monsieur received it as a gift from the Crown in 1659. Bibliothèque Nationale.

ôn de Gondy a sainct Cloud.

Israel Henriet ex. cum priuil. Regis

LE CHASTEAV DE S.ᵗ CLOV du costé que l'on arrive, achevé en 1680. es M.ʳ Mignard en a peint la gallerie qui est a main droite, et le Salon ordinaire de Son Altesse Royalle.

SIXTEEN The court of honor of the château of Saint-Cloud as it appeared in the 1680s. The Maison Gondi has been incorporated within the south (left) wing. Bibliothèque Nationale. Engravings.

onsieur frere vnique du Roy. le sieur Girard en a esté l'Architecte;
ages de Peinture qui sont de l'autre costé, sont de M.ʳ Nocret Peintre

a Paris chez I Mariette Ruë S.ᵗ Iacques aux Colonnes d'Hercules

N. Poilly ex. C.P.R.

Veüe et Perspectiue du C

SEVENTEEN The park and château of Saint-Cloud in the 1680s seen from the bank of the Seine. Only the upper waterfall (at left) is in place. Bibliothèque Nationale. Engravings.

e la Caseade de S.t Clou.

A. Perelle del. et scul.

Veüe et perspectiue des no...

EIGHTEEN   The waterfalls at Saint-Cloud as perfected by Monsieur late in his life. The lower waterfall was completed in 1699. Bibliothèque Nationale. Engravings.

scades de St. Cloud   fait par Aueline Auec Pruilege du Roy

Veuë d

NINETEEN   The Palais Royal, Monsieur's residence in the center of Paris, as it appeared in 1679. Bibliothèque Nationale. Maps and Drawings.

Royal

Dessigné et gravé par la Boissiere en 1679.

TWENTY Monsieur as he appeared at the time of his death. Bibliothèque Nationale. Manuscripts.

Gravé par C. Desrochers et se vend à Paris chez luï rüe S.t Jacques au Moecenas

Il est bon, puis qu'on voit mon visage et mes yeux,
Que l'on apprenne aussy quel est mon caractere:
Quand il s'agit des droits de mon rang glorieux
J'ay l'ame délicate, et quelques fois altiere,
Et mon Cœur en revenche au foible, au malheureux
Ne se montre jamais que tendre, et debonnaire.

TWENTY-ONE Elizabeth Charlotte as the dowager duchess of Orléans after the death of Monsieur. Bibliothèque Nationale. Manuscripts.

SIX

·

Liselotte

A Vacant Place

In contrast to Philippe, Louis sincerely mourned the death of Madame, albeit after his fashion. When Mademoiselle called at Saint-Germain early on the morning of Henriette's death, she found the king in tears. But whatever the depth of his grief over his loss and the extent of his fears for his diplomacy, they did not long test the limits of his self-control. Having taken his medicine, dressed, and dined, he was ready for business as usual.

"Cousin," he addressed the princess, "here is a vacant place. Do you want to fill it?"

At these words Mademoiselle turned "pale as death." From the very moment she had learned that Madame had been taken ill, she had been dreading just this contingency. "I had not closed my eyes all night [the night Henriette lay dying]; I was thinking that should she die and should Monsieur take it into his head to marry me, I should be in a terrible fix."

All atremble, she stammered: "You are the master; I shall never have any will but yours."

"But are you opposed to it?" persisted the king.

Silence.

"Well, I shall think more about it and talk to you later," he dismissed her.[1]

The princess's quandary was brought about by her infatuation with a young guardsman in the service of the king whom she had privately resolved to marry. The hero in question was the marquis de Puyguilhem (Péguilin), later duke of Lauzun, the name by which he is usually known. He was an ambitious adventurer some eight years younger than the princess, who had made his way by his sword and his wits. Péguilin was not without assets: his valor in war had won him the notice of the king and his post as captain of the guard; his prowess in the drawing room and the bedroom had earned him a long list of conquests with the ladies. Poor Mademoiselle! At the age of forty-three, a novice in love, inexperienced and naive as a schoolgirl, she was caught up in the passion of her life.

What happened next was neither very dignified nor entirely honorable. The principals involved, with the exception of Péguilin, seem not to have been entirely sure of what they wanted. The princess, even though far gone in love, was still sufficiently conscious of her *gloire* not to forgo the title of Madame, second lady of the court, without a twinge. Louis too, despite the offer he had just made, must have been of several minds over the prospect of a match between his brother and his cousin. Mademoiselle was the richest heiress in the land. Enjoying an annual revenue of at least 330,000 livres, she possessed, in addition to the Luxembourg Palace in Paris, principalities, duchies, domains, and châteaus across the land.[2] Certainly the king must have wished to keep this inheritance within the family. But did he truly desire to bestow such a bonanza upon his brother, whom he had always denied any source of independent income, sufficient to free him from financial dependence on the Crown? And what of the princess's age? At forty-three, nearly thirteen years older than Philippe, she would soon be, if she were not already, too old to bear children.

What were Philippe's inclinations in the matter? Considering the timing of the king's proposal, coming within hours of Henriette's death and while the prince was at the Palais Royal receiving visits of condolence, it had been made without his knowledge (unless, of course, which was possible, the two brothers had laid down contingency plans at some earlier date). He could not have had any kind of romantic feeling for this cousin, nearly thirteen years his senior, whom he had known since childhood. The bond between them had always been one of shared misfortune, not the attraction of man to woman. He seems, however, to have fallen in with Louis's proposition without difficulty. "My brother has spoken to me like a man who ardently desires to marry you," the king told Mademoiselle not long after their first conversation.[3]

If not precisely ardent, the prince was not averse to the prospect of marriage to the princess. Many a man much less avaricious than Philippe would have been tempted by that vast fortune. He had come quickly to realize how it could serve his interests during her lifetime and those of his house after her death. Consequently, he was ready to propose matrimony on certain remarkable and specific conditions: that should the union prove childless—an eventuality he hoped and expected would be the case—the princess would leave her entire inheritance to Philippe's older daughter, who in turn would become the bride of the dauphin and presumably, in due course, queen of France. Too embarrassed to present so crass a proposal in person, he tried it out on Louis who, although inwardly amused and contemptuous, reported the scenario to the princess.[4]

Philippe's proposition had no chance of acceptance by either Mademoiselle or the king and put an end to all talk of the match. Her vanity offended by the kind of union the prince implied, she summoned the courage to state her objections. Louis did not insist. He too had thought better of the marriage. Among other things, he was strongly opposed to committing the dauphin, for whom he already had other projects in mind, to Philippe's daughter.[5] The choice of his son's future wife was one of his better diplomatic bargaining chips. He was certainly not going to throw it away this early in the game, and on a niece, even a rich one, when so much more might be gained by it later.

With Mademoiselle out of the picture and the "place" still "vacant," Louis cast farther afield. His choice in due time fell upon a young German princess, Elizabeth Charlotte von der Pfalz, daughter of Karl Ludwig, elector of the Palatinate; she was subsequently known in the French court either as La Palatine, Madame, or, within the family, Liselotte. At first glance her selection from among so many other aspirants (the brother of the king being no mean match) appears surprising. In contrast to Mademoiselle, she was poorly endowed with worldly goods, belonged to a princely family of only minor importance (although her maternal grandmother was a Stuart), was Protestant, and was reputed to be no beauty.

These drawbacks might have prevented her entrance into the competition had it not been for the presence in the French court of a relative of the princess who not only was a friend of Monsieur but had a passion for matchmaking and politics. This was Anne of Gonzaga, princess Palatine, widow of Edward von der Pfalz, brother of Liselotte's father, the elector, and as would be the case with her niece, also known as La Palatine. She had long been a supporter of

Philippe and had been part of the cabal that formed around him in 1658 in expectation of Louis's death. From the moment this lady learned of Monsieur's widowhood (she was visiting relatives in Germany at the time), she envisioned her niece as the second Madame. From Frankfurt on July 12, 1670, in a letter to the elector she sounded the ground: "I arrived in this city to learn the astonishing news of the death of Madame the duchess of Orléans. . . . This unfortunate event is going to make many a change in a variety of ways. . . . I confess that I am greatly affected by this death and, being what I am to Monsieur, could wish to be in France at a time of such bizarre misfortune." There followed protestations of devotion and an offer to stop in Heidelberg on her return to learn the wishes of the elector "in all things."[6]

The response must have been encouraging, since two days later she was prepared to be more explicit: "I have received two letters from Monsieur, who is much afflicted by his loss. People must be abominable indeed to dare to say he had a hand in it. . . . Now they are beginning to say that Monsieur is a good match, already letters have come to me about it, but it is a bit too soon. Even so, I wish I were in Paris. . . . I shall do everything in my power to see you in Heidelberg; two days' delay will make little difference, and perhaps we shall find enough to say about present possibilities and how best to take advantage of them."

Indefatigably, the matchmaking princess pursued her vision. At first resistance did not come from the elector, ruler of a small and poor land only slowly recovering from the ravages of the Thirty Years War. Believing the Habsburg emperor Leopold a weak reed on which to lean, he was more than willing to look for protection to his powerful neighbor across the Rhine. The marriage of his daughter to the brother of the king of France should be sound insurance for the future.[7] Also, he counted not a little on the supposed wealth the new Madame would command to ease his financial problems exacerbated by a rapidly growing family. Rather, it was Louis and Philippe who needed to be won over, reluctant as they were to settle for a bride who would be virtually without dowry. With Mademoiselle out of the running, however, the going was smoother. Louis could see the benefits to be derived from a friend on the throne of Heidelberg in the event of war with the emperor. Just possibly, although it is unlikely, he may also have seen in the marriage a means of establishing a claim somewhere down the line to a share of the Palatinate inheritance, a claim that he did later assert.[8] The religious objection, too, proved easy to overcome. For reasons of state the elector could not publicly permit his daughter to convert to Catholicism; but privately neither of them—both were utterly indifferent to questions of theology and religious orthodoxy—had any objection. A stratagem was devised by which the bride would abjure the Reformed (i.e., Calvinist) faith after she had left her father's house and then, once on French soil in Metz, by letter announce to him the fait accompli. The elector would consequently be able to express his surprise and disapproval without inconveniencing any of the parties concerned in the slightest.[9]

Undoubtedly the highest card in the hand of Anne of Gonzaga was the youth of Elizabeth Charlotte, who had turned eighteen only one month before Henriette's death. Hence she was eminently nubile in a manner that Mademoiselle was not. The expectation of progeny was a primary consideration in the negotiation of any princely marriage, and in this one it was critical, given the pressing need of both brothers for male heirs.[10] Philippe had lost his only son in 1664; Louis's legitimate children were dying off one by one at an alarming rate. At the time of Madame's death two sons survived, but in July 1671 the younger prince succumbed, leaving only the dauphin. The existence of a single heir was far from adequate insurance for the continuation of the dynasty in that age when death was no stranger. The child's premature end may in fact have been the event that tipped the balance in favor of Liselotte. Only a few weeks after his death La Palatine could write to the elector that "the marriage of Liselotte with the duke of Orléans is absolutely assured, if you wish it. Monsieur desires it, and the king of France has given his full consent."

It was one thing to want the marriage, as the elector indubitably did; it was another to pay for it. The paltriness of the revenues Karl Ludwig could draw from his impoverished lands and people combined with his natural avarice to throw up the last hurdle in the way of the marriage: the contract of marriage stipulating the amount of the dowry. In vain did La Palatine urge the elector to name a figure, even an insignificant one, arguing that the king and Monsieur had already resigned themselves to accepting the contract regardless of its financial terms. Perhaps she knew, as did Louis and Philippe, that the astronomical figures gracing the marriage contracts of many a bride were often worth little more than the paper they were written on. The 500,000 écu[11] dowry of Maria Theresa remained unpaid, as did much of the 840,000 livres constituted in favor of Henriette.[12] In any case, Karl Ludwig held firm and in the end got off very lightly. The document as finally signed and sealed pledged the elector to provide for his daughter merely "the same amount that the princesses of the Palatine House have been accustomed to receive" and specified that it would be delivered in the form of money, rings, gold and silver vessels, and other precious articles one year after the consummation of the marriage.[13] When the appraisal of these items was made in due form, their value came to a total of 10,400 livres.[14] As one of Liselotte's biographers has observed: "Even for a German princess, it was a modest sum."[15]

The remaining clauses of the contract, which concerned the bride's renunciation of her claims of inheritance and the financial provisions made on her behalf, presented no problems. Most of them were identical to the contract of 1661 signed between Philippe and Henriette.[16] Specifically, Elizabeth Charlotte renounced all rights to lands and goods, whether sovereign or feudal, paternal or maternal, within Germany and reserved only her rights to those of the same quality outside Germany and to the allodial lands of her house. In return, if she outlived her husband she was to receive as widow's jointure the right to reside in the château of Montargis for the remainder of her life as well as an income of 40,000 livres each year. All assets of any kind accumulated during the years of the marriage (but excluding the previously held property of Monsieur) were to be held between husband and wife as community property.

Liselotte later was to complain bitterly about the terms of this contract, which, she said, could not have been worse had she been the daughter of a tradesman.[17] To the end of her life she moaned over the "poverty" in which she was obliged to live and at her father's supposed error in giving her away so cheaply. But the princess was completely mistaken. From a financial point of view, it was Louis and Philippe, not Liselotte and her father, who had come off the losers. Even the exclusion from their community property of Monsieur's assets at the time of the marriage, a clause that had not appeared in Henriette's contract, was not as discriminatory as it first appeared. Except for his appanage and Saint-Cloud, at the time of his second marriage the prince possessed little real property of much value. Of those two properties, the first was reserved by law for the brother of the king and his male descendants, and hence was untouchable by a wife, and the second, at least in comparison with its later glory, was still a relatively modest country château.[18] The major assets that eventually constituted the great fortune of the house of Orléans were acquired by Monsieur at a later date, after his marriage to Liselotte.

As a bride of nineteen the princess knew nothing of these financial arrangements and never came to understand them fully. Finance was never her forte.[19] But her ignorance in no way mitigated her later complaints. Like father, like daughter. Once in the role of Madame, Liselotte was not slow to develop a high regard for money and no mean ability to pinch a penny.

What was the prince's reaction to his impending remarriage and to the German princess who would be his wife? Of the bride herself he knew virtually nothing and could have had no strong feeling one way or another. But was he despondent over the continued absence of the chevalier? Did he resent the obligation imposed upon him of reentering the marital bed and resuming his métier d'époux? The memoirists and diarists afford no answer to these questions. The only clue we have to his state of mind is the record of his movements during the interval when he was between wives. These in fact appear to have been very much his habitual ones and in no way reveal any serious distress of mind or body. The opening months of 1671 saw him enjoying the diversions of the carnival season. Once more he was hosting balls and suppers, attending the theater, and following the peregrinations of the court from one royal residence to another.[20] In the last days of March he devoted nearly an entire week to religious observances in Paris, making the stations of the cross on foot at no fewer than six churches, including Notre Dame and finishing at his parish church of Saint-Eustache on Resurrection Day.[21] Late spring and early summer found him with Louis, the queen, and much of the court in Flanders, where the two brothers inspected the military installations, reviewed the troops, and attended the obligatory receptions and dinners attendant on a royal progression. While in the area, he made a short side trip with Mademoiselle to visit the gardens at Enghien, which were renowned for their beauty.[22] He was still traveling on the first anniversary of Henriette's death, which he commemorated by ordering a service in her honor at the church of Val-de-Grâce in Paris and attending mass in a religious house in the city of Athe. By the end of July he was again at Saint-Cloud, where he regaled the king and queen with the delights of his gardens and the bounties of a rich table.[23]

Clearly, if the prince were depressed or unhappy by the prospect of the marriage before him, he had become neither recluse nor rebel. And perhaps he could even derive some satisfaction from it. This time, in contrast to his former quiet wedding with Henriette, he would celebrate his nuptials with all the pomp and ceremony owed to the brother of the king.

"What do you think about the marriage of Monsieur?" Mme de Sévigné asked her daughter soon after the prince's betrothal was announced. "You will easily understand the joy of Monsieur to see himself married in style."[24]

TO MARRY IN STYLE

According to the custom by which a princess of quality must wed before leaving her land, or at least as soon as possible thereafter, while a French prince could not marry on foreign soil, the first ceremony was by procuration. On November 16, 1671, in the cathedral at Metz, just inside the French border, the marshal Plessis-Praslin wed Elizabeth Charlotte in the name of Monsieur. By the time the couple met for the first time, they were already husband and wife.

Emerging from the cathedral as Madame, Liselotte found her modest world transformed. She who had traveled to Metz in her father's plain coach, with a cot and a single tapestry as her only accommodations for the nights en route (the great of those days took the precaution of taking with them the necessary furnishings for lodging), now found at her disposal a magnificent carriage, squads of foot pages and valets, and baggage trains bulging with furniture and goods. Greeted by cannon salutes and hedged by double rows of soldiers, she was conducted in state to the city hall to dine in solitary splendor. Around her gathered the members of Parlement and city dignitaries, waiting their turn to present their respects and congratulations.

According to the official account, at least, the new Madame kept her composure and did credit to her position, making her responses "with a marvelous presence of mind."[25] Only at the invitation to a ball in her honor did she demur, pleading that such a diversion would contrast too strongly with the solemnity of the ceremonies she had just gone through. In fact she must have been fatigued and under considerable strain. Within the space of twenty-four hours she had become not only a French subject and a bride, but a Catholic as well. In the hours preceding her marriage, in accordance with the previously agreed religious arrangements, she had abjured her Protestant faith, confessed her new one, taken first communion, and received confirmation. "What a lot of sacraments in a single day!" she was later to exclaim.

While Elizabeth Charlotte was undergoing this transformation, Monsieur, richly attired and blazing with gems, went forth from Paris with his entire household to greet his bride. His progress from city to city was a royal one as he accepted the greetings of dignitaries, acknowledged the cheers of the people with that affability so endearing to them, distributed alms to the poor, listened to harangues and sermons, and dined to the sound of violins.

The meeting of bride and groom took place by prearrangement on the road between Châlons and Bellay. Leaving his carriage and approaching hers, Monsieur for the first time laid eyes on Madame. Before him was a blond girl of nineteen, fresh with the bloom of youth but "rustic as a Swiss." Inappropriately turned out in dowdy taffeta, she was short and dumpy, her small eyes set in a broad face with flat cheeks and heavy jaw. Rumors of her homeliness had not been exaggerated.

"Oh," the prince is said to have groaned, "how shall I ever be able to sleep with her?"[26]

This was not the time for getting acquainted. After the exchange of greetings, the couple proceeded immediately to Châlons. There they received the nuptial blessing, attended mass, and returned thanks in a solemn Te Deum. The religious ceremonies complete, the city fathers did their best to rise to the occasion. Only after the now-familiar feasting, fireworks, harangues, and salutes were the couple able to retire to the privacy of their apartments for the night. The following morning the duke and his new duchess took the road for Villers-Cotterêts and for the world in which they would live.

These incessant festivities attendant on their marriage were merely curtain raisers to the galas and spectacles that ensued. The bride had to be shown the marvels of all the châteaus, palaces, and hunting lodges of Monsieur and of the king, each of which in turn became the site of banquets and balls. Madame's entrance to Paris was especially impressive. She was introduced not only to the municipal dignitaries, who feted her, and to the people of Paris, who acclaimed her, but to the diplomatic corps as well. Her husband, it was observed, received the compliments of the Venetian ambassador together with his expectation of a "progeny of heroes" with "extreme satisfaction." The merrymaking went on without interruption throughout the carnival season until Lent. "Every day there are balls, comedies, and masquerades at Saint-Germain," wrote Mme de Sévigné. "The king exerts himself to please Madame in a way that he has never done for anyone else."[27]

La Sévigné was not the only one to observe the success the new Madame had scored on high, which became the talk of the court. After the king met his new sister-in-law for the first time at Villers-Cotterêts, he came away with the most favorable impression. "He told us that she is very intelligent and that as for build, the late Madame could not hold a candle to her."[28] Sic transit gloria! Madame is dead; long live Madame! But unlike Louis's former attraction to the coquettish Henriette, his admiration of Liselotte had nothing whatever in it of gallantry. Instead, he was completely charmed by the bride's utter candor and total absence of guile. For Liselotte, it was soon apparent, was as plainspoken as she was plain looking. It was an unprecedented experience for the king to speak with a subject who said exactly what was on her mind without circumlocution. He was as taken with her as a child with a new plaything, and to watch her reactions to her new surroundings and hear her pronouncements on them was for him a continuous source of diversion and amusement.

The sovereign soon developed another reason to enjoy the company of his sister-in-law. Like Louis, Liselotte became addicted to hunting wild game in the royal forests.[29] The sturdy physique that he had admired proved admirably adapted to active sport. When Madame arrived in the French court she did not know how to ride a horse, though, tomboy that she was, she had always spent much time in outdoor exercise. Introduced to equestrian skills by the king, she soon became a bold and avid huntress. Soon he could count on her, alone among the ladies, to join the chase no matter what the weather and no matter how dangerous the prey. Rude falls and broken bones did not diminish her enthusiasm. Her stamina as an Amazon and her love of horses and dogs in time became legendary. Long after Louis was obliged to give up the sport for reasons of health, Madame—then usually in the company of the grand dauphin, as tireless in the chase as his father had been, and in opposition to the counsel of her physicians—continued her habit of nearly daily hunts on horseback.

In his pleasure over his brother's marriage the king proved himself generous. When Liselotte arrived at court she received as bridal presents from Louis and Maria Theresa a diamond rose whose value was estimated at 40,000 écus (between 120,000 and 240,000 livres) and three money caskets that contained a total of 30,000 pistoles (300,000 livres). The latter, stipulated the king, were for Madame's *menus plaisirs* ("little luxuries").[30] Since this sum equaled approximately half the revenue Karl Ludwig collected in the Palatinate over the course of an entire year[31] and five times the amount Louis had awarded Henriette for her role in negotiating the Treaty of Dover, the king could scarcely be accused of being niggardly toward his new sister-in-law. At the same time, as he had done when Philippe married Henriette, he awarded his brother an annual brevet, or gift, of 252,000 livres "for the maintenance of the household of Madame," with the understanding that the birth of sons would bring him an additional 150,000 livres each year of each child's life.[32] This largess was followed in April 1672 by a supplementary grant of lands to the prince's appanage. Yielding an annual income of some 55,000 livres, it brought the total yearly revenue from the appanage to slightly more than 200,000 livres.[33] True, this sum was but a small fraction of the income Philippe received in the form of pensions from the Crown, and it was also, in a manner of speaking, long overdue, the king having stated at the time of the first grant of 1661 that the appanage should have that value. Nonetheless, it was a welcome sign of grace on high that augured well for the future.

Much to the surprise of all, the little German rustic seemed neither intimidated nor dazzled by her newly acquired riches, the elegance of the company, and the munificence of her surroundings. "Everyone is saying that the new Madame is not at all overwhelmed by the grandeur of her rank," wrote Mme de Sévigné. Liselotte was far from convinced of the superiority of all things French and to the end of her days retained a preference for the customs, habits, and especially the cuisine of her native Germany. She was especially disgusted by the indolence and effeteness of those around her. Except for the king and one or two others, she wrote, "there is not a soul here who can do more than twenty steps without sweating and puffing."[34] But no matter what she did or said, having won the approval of the sovereign, her favorable reception at court was assured. And so, for a time, was her enjoyment. Even her unfashionable dress and disheveled coiffure, ridiculed at first by the sophisticates at court, became objects of emulation rather than derision. "I am now very much à la mode," she wrote to her Aunt Sophie. "Whatever I say or do, whether it be good or awry, is greatly admired by the courtiers, to the point that when I decided to wear my old sable in this cold weather . . . , everyone had one made from the same pattern, and sables have become quite the rage."[35]

Probably Liselotte was as surprised as everyone else at her contentment, since she had married against her will and had expected to be utterly miserable in France. She had parted with her German relatives in a flood of tears. In a letter to her Aunt Sophie soon after her marriage she confessed: "It is true that I cried so much that I made myself sick. From Strasbourg all the way to Châlons I did nothing but bawl all night."[36] But if the princess were as honest with herself, or at least as perceptive, about her background and family life as she was about the shortcomings of things French, she would have admitted, or at least partly understood, why her grief in parting was not prolonged. She would also have come to comprehend, as no one else seemed to do, why she and Monsieur, seemingly so totally different from each other in every way, were for some years able to find happiness and contentment in their marriage.

The "family" in which she had grown up was indeed singular. Except in a biological sense, Liselotte really had no mother, and she also felt herself rejected by her father. Karl Ludwig had taken as his first wife Charlotte of Hesse-Kassel, of whom little is known but who was, at least in the opinion of her husband, of shrewish temperament and given to coquetry and lavish expenditure. The elector could not abide her, and after several years of marriage during which Liselotte and an older brother were born, he determined to get rid of her and take as a second wife one of Charlotte's ladies, a charming young blond, Luise von Degenfeld, who had meanwhile become the object of his affections. But this was easier said than done. Charlotte appeared in no way of dying, and she refused to leave her husband's house. The solution hit upon by Karl Ludwig was to exercise the Erastian formula accepted in the states of the Germanies by which the supremacy of the lay ruler is recognized in ecclesiastical affairs. In January 1658 he married Luise in civil and religious ceremonies and bullied his pastor into accepting their validity.[37] So far so good. Luise moved into his château in Heidelberg and in her wifely capacity began uncomplainingly to bear one child after another until she died in childbirth with number fourteen. Still, a slight problem remained: because Charlotte persisted in her refusal to depart, the elector now had two wives living under the same roof. It was not a situation conducive to family peace.

Liselotte, six years of age at the time of Karl Ludwig's remarriage, saw her little world destroyed. Instinctively, no doubt from a sense that she was being rejected as well as Charlotte, Liselotte took her mother's part. Yet in Charlotte she could find no refuge. Embittered and probably unbalanced by the turn of events, the scorned wife seemed unable to return the child's devotion. Perhaps the child reminded her too much of her father. Mother and daughter were permanently estranged. In later years, long after her marriage, Liselotte turned a deaf ear to Charlotte's continuing complaints and, despite the urging of Monsieur, refused to consider making a place for her in the French court.[38] On the other hand, by siding with her mother she had earned the lasting hostility of her father, who, stung by the public criticism his irregular action had provoked, judged one and all by the attitude they took toward his new "treasure," Luise.

All but stranded in the war between her parents, Liselotte was rescued, temporarily at least, by her aunt, Duchess Sophie of Braunschweig-Lüneburg, sister of Karl Ludwig and later electress of Hanover. An intelligent, compassionate woman of great good sense, she took pity on the lonely child and from 1659 until 1663, slightly over four years, took her into her family and little court at Hanover where her husband's brother, George William, was then elector. For Liselotte, "Ma Tante" was the only mother she was ever to know, and whatever sense of identity as woman and mother that she ever acquired was derived from her.

What could Liselotte learn from Aunt Sophie and from the new surroundings in which she was placed? Certainly not the refinements of the great world, at least as they would be defined at the court of Louis XIV. "We live here almost like bourgeois," wrote Sophie, "and see almost no one."[39] Plain and rustic, the little court gave itself over to simple pleasures of its own making. George William and his several brothers loved women and hearty fare and deprived themselves of neither. Nor did they *ménager* their manners. A Rabelaisian sense of humor combined with a coarseness of language set the conversational tone of the salon. The courtiers in France were doing and saying the same things, of course, only less openly and by innuendo. The difference was one of style. It is doubtful that the young girl was shocked; her father's house had been no school of virtue. And in her day she was to become famous for her earthy speech and her love of ribald jokes.

She must also, to judge by her later views, have absorbed many of her aunt's ideas about marriage, which were realistic to the extreme. It is impossible to analyze the personality of the duchess Sophie in any depth from this distance, given the scantiness of the evidence. But very probably she entertained a low regard for men in general and none at all for romance. Coquetry was seemingly not in her, nor did she desire it for her niece, who would, she told her brother, never learn it at her court. Certainly Sophie had no illusions about her husband, Ernest August, and on the occasions, seemingly not infrequent, when he stepped outside the marital bond she accepted his behavior with indifference and may even have abetted it. She could never understand why Karl Ludwig became so worked up over his wife (or wives). "I am sorry to see that you are taking everything so to heart," she wrote him. "We only come this way once, so why make yourself so unhappy when, after all, one can always eat, sleep, and drink, sleep, drink, and eat?"[40] Her philosophy, which she was to preach more than once to Liselotte in later years, was to look at the material compensations attendant on matches arranged in high places and to ignore the rest. "After all," she was later to advise, "one can get used to anything."[41] Men were simply not worth getting upset over. In later years one of Madame's favorite maxims was "What can't be cured must be endured,"[42] although she was not always as successful as her aunt had been at practicing what she preached.

Yet the court at Hanover was not without its lights, among which were learning. The duchess supervised a program of instruction for her niece that included languages, literature, music, and dancing accompanied by strict discipline and much exercise in the open air. When Liselotte married, French was no problem for her. She could speak it fluently and write it much more correctly than most in court (including her predecessor and her husband). She had also been introduced to the principal works of literature of her day as well as to some of the classics (in German or French translation). Thus, once married she could immediately appreciate and enjoy the great dramatic works of Corneille, Molière, and Racine. A love of theater, in fact, was one of the few tastes Monsieur and Madame were to have in common.

The Hanover interval in Liselotte's girlhood came to an end when her mother at last returned to her home in Kassel and Karl Ludwig sent for his daughter, then just turned twelve, to return to Heidelberg. From that time until her marriage she lived with her father's second, young family. It was neither a happy period of her life nor one designed to improve her views of men and marriage. Even without the presence of Charlotte the atmosphere was turbulent. Karl Ludwig alternately tyrannized over and petted his "angel" and "treasure" Luise. She in turn was continuously either in ailing health owing to the frequency of her pregnancies or in mourning over the deaths of her children, only five of whom survived to adulthood. Liselotte remained on terms of barely concealed hostility with both, though she got on well with her half-brothers and half-sisters. Perhaps in self-defense, she seems to have stayed away from the house as much as possible. Exploring the streets and byways of Heidelberg and roaming the adjacent vineyards and forests, she acquired that knowledge and love of the Palatinate revealed in her later letters from France.

What kind of young woman had this combination of heredity and upbringing produced? Observers would note first and foremost the striking absence of beauty and feminine grace. Liselotte, too, was always very conscious of her homeliness, which she did not hesitate to describe in great detail. And if she had not been aware of it herself, she would have learned it from her father and brother, who did not fail to bring it to her attention during her youth. "All my life I have made fun of my ugliness," she wrote late in life. "I just laughed. My father and our late brother often told me how unattractive I was; I laughed it off and never cared one bit. My brother called me *badger nose*; and I laughed even harder."[43] A certain hollowness can be sensed behind this laughter. The frequency with which Liselotte alluded to her grotesque appearance in her correspondence and her refusal either to look in a mirror or to attempt to conceal or improve on her looks by artifices of the toilette leave the impression that she cared much more deeply than she let on. Left to herself, she said, she would have worn nothing other than a riding habit. When forced to endure the torture of formal dress, she would have appeared in court with the weather-beaten complexion of a sergeant at arms had not Monsieur in person sat her down to apply rouge and powder.[44] "I am hideously ugly," she wrote on another occasion, "but fortunately for me I do not care one whit. For I do not desire anyone to be in love with me and know that those who love me as friends are interested in my character and not in my appearance."[45] Her best defense was the pretense of indifference and the deprecation of the importance of external beauty.

But if not comely, she was most certainly robust, with the strength of body that derived from heredity reinforced by the healthful habits of her daily life. She was rarely sick, and on those few occasions when she was, she attempted as much as possible to avoid the ministrations of physicians whom she suspected, very sensibly, of generally doing much more harm than good.[46] As a rule her prescription for any illness was a five-league walk in the forest, a rule that indeed served her well for most of her long life. Only in the matter of her diet did she violate the principles of good health, at least as they are known and practiced in the twentieth century. All that exercise in the open air lent her a ravenous appetite, which she gratified freely, especially when her German relatives provided her with good sauerkraut and sausages to be washed down with warm beer. In middle and old age she became enormously fat. This condition, in turn, did nothing to improve her appearance. "[All] my fat is in all the wrong places, which is bound to be unbecoming," she wrote as a woman of forty-seven. "I have a horrendous, begging your leave, behind, big belly and hips, and very broad shoulders."[47]

Observers would also have not been long in recognizing the lively intelligence of Elizabeth Charlotte. This endowment too she had improved upon and developed by her wide, if eclectic reading, her interest in numismatics, and her practice of daily correspondence with her German relatives. These tastes and habits served her well later in life when, having lost favor in court (mostly through her own doing), she retired to her apartments to work on her coin collection—especially remarkable for its series of Roman emperors—and to put down on paper her impressions of the day and recollections of the past. She became in time one of the great letter writers of her century. If her correspondence lacked the elegance and finesse of that of Mme de Sévigné, its sheer volume (often ten or twelve letters per day each running twenty to thirty pages), its spontaneity and vigor of expression, and the irrepressible impishness of its author compensated for the absence of literary grace. No wonder her letters have become one of the principal, if not always reliable, sources of information on the court of Louis XIV in particular and the life and the ways of the seventeenth-century "great" in general.

The experiences she had lived through at the courts of her father and aunt had also, of course, done much to mold the young woman's personality and character. Lacking a mother in any real sense except for the few years with Sophie, she was deprived of a role model and was probably never very sure of her sexual identity. She displayed a strong aversion to the feminine role. Marriage and motherhood certainly had no charms for her. As she was later to declare many times, she would never have married if she could have avoided it and much preferred a celibate life.[48] When she became pregnant in due course, she complained incessantly because she was forbidden to ride to the hunt and had to be carried about.[49] She regarded the whole process of reproduction "from the beginning to the end, [as] a very nasty business, dangerous and filthy, that I have never liked."[50] This attitude is certainly not surprising given the disastrous marriage (or marriages) of her father and the incessant childbearing of Luise von Degenfeld that she had observed as a child. Even the happier atmosphere of her aunt's home, given Sophie's disillusionment with the male sex, was not designed to engender much taste for the role of wife. The plainness of her appearance also disinclined her to adopt the usual feminine attitudes and habits. She sensed early on that she would never achieve much success as a woman and as a coquette would have absolutely none. A personality theorist might see in her background an unresolved oedipal complex and a sublimated lesbianism. When the little girl turned to her father as an object for love, she felt herself rejected. At the same time, she was denied a mother. Thus she had been unable to transfer to another male that love that was never developed for her father and unable to reconcile herself to the feminine role.

It will not have gone unremarked that in almost every respect Liselotte was the opposite of Henriette: the one the quintessential Eve, the other the tomboy who behaved as much like a man as possible. Whereas the one was delicate, coquettish, and full of a grace that served as well as beauty, the other was robust, awkward, and homely. The one was thin to the point of emaciation, the other fat, at least in later life, to the point of obesity. Henriette throve in the ballroom and the salon; Liselotte yearned for the open air and a spirited horse to ride to the hunt. Only perhaps in their intelligence and in their love of the theater did the two Madames resemble each other.

It was also very obvious, and much remarked upon, that the second Madame differed from her husband in nearly every respect: appearance, tastes, and enjoyments. He was graceful, diminutive, and feminine; she was mannish, bulky, and tactless. A more ill-assorted couple, or so it appeared at first glance, could scarcely have been brought together as a result of the matchmaking success of Anne of Gonzaga. After the birth of Liselotte's second child, Philippe II, the wits of the court were saying that the future regent owed his very existence to the masculine appearance of his mother.[51] The observation may have hit closer to the mark than they realized. A mannish wife like Liselotte could not threaten Philippe and undermine his always frail sense of self-esteem. Her success with Louis, based on camaraderie, not coquetry, could not arouse his jealousy. In many ways it was a good match, perhaps the only one that could have worked for either party. His femininity and her masculinity complemented each other. What a relief for Philippe to have a wife who was neither rival nor coquette, one he could treat as a friend and even as a confidante. The prince soon regained his natural gaiety, became the life of the court, and played the affectionate husband in public.

No Better Marriage since the World Began

Undoubtedly to the surprise of all, the first years of the marriage were very happy ones in which both husband and wife experienced the period of greatest fulfillment and contentment in their lives. Circumstances were auspicious from the beginning. Louis's generosity and the elaborate festivities staged in honor of the newlyweds must have been deeply gratifying, especially to Philippe. He who usually ran a very distant second to his brother was now, with his wife, the focus of all eyes. The absence of the chevalier de Lorraine, still in exile in Italy, freed the ménage from divisive competition. Both partners had occupations and duties that proved demanding and rewarding. The nineteen-year-old bride was in that blooming stage of youth and health when she could most easily and quickly satisfy the expectations of progeny to continue the line. As for the groom, in addition to his métier d'époux, there was in the near future the prospect, for the only time in his life, of honorable service to the Crown. The Dutch War, which broke out almost immediately after Monsieur's marriage, and in which he was granted command appropriate to his rank as brother of the king, would reveal his undeniable talents as a field captain and his valor in battle. These exploits in war, followed with mounting pride and anxiety by Liselotte, afforded her reason not only to love but to respect the man who had become her husband.

Both spouses seem quickly to have overcome the surprise and discomfiture of their original meeting. By the time she had arrived in court early in December Liselotte could write Aunt Sophie: "I will tell you one thing about Monsieur: he is the best man in the world, and we get on very well together. He does not resemble any of his portraits in the least."[52] Nine months later the honeymoon was still going on. Sophie, who had her own sources of information on her niece's household, wrote to Karl Ludwig: "I am assured that there is a very perfect love and friendship between Monsieur and Madame."[53] And three months later came the best and most desired news of all: "Madame is doing marvelously, for she is still pregnant and unhappy only because she is not allowed to ride a horse."[54]

Philippe had found an answer to the question that had come into his head on first laying eyes on his wife and had devised a unique formula for success. For many years Liselotte kept his secret until, as an old lady with nothing better to do than regale her relatives with anecdotes of bygone days, she succumbed at last to the temptation of a story too good to suppress. How much of it may have been made up is anyone's guess. But whatever it may or may not tell us of what went on in the marital bed, it is charming proof of the lively and merry companion Liselotte must have been.

> Monsieur always acted very devout [began Elizabeth Charlotte in her letter]. Once he gave me a really good laugh. He always used to take to bed with him a chaplet from which dangled a quantity of medals, and he used them to say his prayers before he went to sleep. When that was over, I would hear a great jingling of metal as if he were moving them about underneath the covers.

I said to him: "May God forgive me, Monsieur, but I suspect that you are moving your relics and images of the Virgin into a land where they have never been before."

Monsieur answered: "Be quiet and go to sleep; you do not know what you are saying."

One night, I got up very quietly, and I placed the light so that it lit up the entire bed, and at the moment he began to promenade his medals under the cover, I seized his arm and said, laughing: "Caught in the act; now you can no longer deny it."

Monsieur began to laugh too and said: "You who have been a Huguenot, you do not know the power of relics and images of the Holy Virgin. They guarantee the success of anything they touch."

I answered: "Forgive me, Monsieur, but you will never convince me that you do honor to the Virgin by parading her image over those parts made to destroy her virginity."

Monsieur could not help but laugh and said: "I beg of you, do not ever tell a soul."[55]

In the ensuing years husband, wife, and growing family formed a nuclear unit of almost classic form. Between the spring of 1673 and the autumn of 1676 Liselotte gave birth to three children, two sons and a daughter. Philippe, caught up in the demands of the Dutch War, spent the better part of the spring and summer of three of those years with the army in Flanders and the Netherlands. As had not been the case in Philippe's previous marriage, both parents became deeply attached to their children. Liselotte again probably surprised herself. She who had been so reluctant to give birth found that once the child was born she could be the tenderest of mothers. Her letters to her German relatives were replete with details of weaning, cutting of teeth, and first steps. Philippe too established strong relationships with all of his children, even his two daughters by Henriette. Although he followed them less closely day-to-day than Liselotte and was never the slightest use as a disciplinarian (he complained that they refused to listen to him and did not fear him),[56] he won their love by his genuine tenderness.

Not even the unexpected return of the chevalier de Lorraine in the spring of 1672 was able to disrupt, at least for some time, the unity of the close-knit family. His recall from exile came as a total surprise, since the king had previously declared he would never permit him to appear again in his brother's court.[57] Perhaps at this time Louis was thinking of the impending war with Holland, in which the already proved military capacities of the chevalier would be useful. Perhaps, too, he was unwilling to permit Philippe to es-

cape permanently the ignominy of his former life of subjection to
Lorraine and his association with the disreputable cronies of his
cabal. In any case, and for whatever reason, in a conversation with
Philippe in February 1672 that has become famous through the pen
of Mme de Sévigné, the king announced his intention of recalling
the chevalier.

> "But do you still think of this chevalier de Lorraine? Do you still care
> for him? Would you like to see him returned to you?"
>
> "Truly, Monsieur," replied Monsieur, "that would be the greatest
> joy that I could know in my life."
>
> "Very well," said the king, "I wish to make you this present; in fact
> the courier left two days ago. [The chevalier] will return; I give him
> back to you and want you to remember all your life that I have done
> this for you, and that you love him for the love of me. And I shall do
> more, for I shall make him camp marshal in my army."
>
> On these words Monsieur threw himself at the king's feet, embraced
> him about his knees and kissed his hand with an unsurpassed joy.
>
> "Brother, that is not how brothers should embrace," said the king,
> raising him and kissing him in fraternal fashion.[58]

But despite the fervor of Philippe's gratitude, the return of the
chevalier did not at the time interrupt the tenor of his life with his
wife. He did not, in fact, slip back into his former life and allow the
young man to dictate. Lorraine, kept at a distance and, surprised
that his former relationship was not resumed, turned his attention
to the ladies instead. For the time, at least, Monsieur, otherwise
occupied, had taken up another life. Liselotte still had some years
before her in which to be happy with the devotion of her husband,
the care of her young family, and the favor of the king.

Not only the chevalier de Lorraine but also, and to a much
greater degree, Karl Ludwig, Liselotte's father, was discomfited by
the solidity of his daughter's marriage. He who had such high hopes
of the protection of France and of a shower of gold on his young
raugraves, what had he so far received? Absolutely nothing. True,
Liselotte had received Karl Lutz, his oldest son by his second marriage, in Paris and had showered him with caresses and fond words.
But no material bounty had followed. His second and third sons
were to be no more fortunate.[59] She who could gamble away in an
evening more than his whole brood of raugraves saw in a year
could not possibly be without the means of assistance.

Much worse was to follow. In July 1674 he saw his land invaded
by the army of Marshal Turenne and some twenty-seven of his

villages put to the torch. Overlooking the fact that he had himself invited this destruction by signing a treaty the previous January with Emperor Leopold giving over to him the city of Germersheim on the Rhine, from which post the imperials could threaten the French position in Alsace and Lorraine,[60] he had appealed to Monsieur and Madame to intercede for him with Louis in an effort to stave off French retaliation. And what was the result? For some time Philippe did not even deign to answer the elector, which caused him to fume incoherently: "I am not surprised that [Liselotte's] dear other half [Philippe] has not answered my letter, for all he thinks of is conquering, just like his brother, who would like nothing so much as peace, but all on one side, like neutrality, that is to say that I put up with anything and shut up."[61] And when at length the answer did arrive, it was cold comfort. Despite its assurances of goodwill and of the happiness of Philippe's life with Madame, it amounted to a stark warning: either accept Louis's terms of friendship or expect the worst. "For bethink you," wrote the prince, "it is not pleasant to have an enemy army as large as that of M. de Turenne in the midst of one's country. If I speak too frankly, excuse me; it is only from my desire to serve you."[62]

And what was the reaction of the elector's daughter to this lecture from her better half and to the "martyrdom" of her father? Despite her protests of filial respect and devotion, she was going about her business of having babies and enjoying herself. A few weeks after receiving Philippe's letter he learned that Liselotte, having given birth to a son in July, was up and about again "and that she is extremely gay and happy, having put on weight and growing more handsome."[63] And so it continued in the coming years. "[Liselotte] does me the honor to write me the most entertaining letters," reported Sophie to the elector, "all of which proves that she is very happy. She goes to the hunt and attends the theater with as much zest as the late queen our mother used to do."[64]

The elector was extremely vexed with his daughter's seeming indifference to his plight. He could not understand that Liselotte, having none of the ambitions of her predecessor and understanding nothing whatever of high policy, had no intention of disrupting the harmony of her household and the favor she enjoyed with the king with unwelcome importunities on behalf of her father. And if this attitude were heartless and callous, she was for the time, at least, too contented to care. Even Sophie, usually so eager to plead her niece's cause, could not pretend that Madame was of any help and was reduced to making excuses in her behalf.

For Monsieur and Madame these years were not untouched by

care and sorrow, but they were such as to bring husband and wife together rather than drive them apart. Each of Elizabeth Charlotte's confinements was painful, but she recovered without complications. Monsieur, she reported, sat with her on these occasions (her appreciation of his attentiveness attenuated by the highly offensive odors generated by his perfumed Spanish gloves).[65] By far the worst was the death of their firstborn, the little duke of Valois, not yet three years old, in the spring of 1676. Liselotte was inconsolable over the "unexpected disaster God Almighty has visited upon me."[66] She could never, she wrote, recover from it. Pregnant at the time with her third and last child and in a state of morbid depression, she brooded pessimistically over the baby's chances of survival. Worst of all, she had no one to comfort her, she confessed, since Monsieur had just left for the army with the king.

These absences of her husband while he went to war were an added source of grief and foreboding. Soon after the child's death Liselotte wrote to her former governess: "[Philippe] has already made me suffer a thousand frights by exposing himself to terrible dangers, as I am told in letters from all sides, in Condé's two sieges and then in that of Bouchain. . . . And now I have even more worries, for we are told that many people in the army are falling ill, and since Monsieur fatigues himself no less than the others, often staying on horseback for twenty-four hours and going without sleep, I am afraid that he will end up getting sick too."[67] But fortunately for both her fears proved groundless, and her anxiety and loneliness only intensified the happiness of their reunion. "Madame is in ecstasies over the return of Monsieur," wrote Mme de Sévigné in July when the prince arrived again in court in his usual health and spirits.[68] And the following autumn, after the birth of her child, a little girl they named after her mother, Liselotte had shaken off her depression and wrote contentedly: "Now there is one more Liselotte in the world; if God grant that she is no more unlucky than her mother, she will have little enough to complain about."[69]

In fact it was the health of Madame and not that of Monsieur that was, at least on one occasion, the cause of greatest alarm during this decade of the 1670s. Her illness was the source of the greatest outpouring of love and affection between husband and wife, fortunately preserved for posterity in letters that testify irrefutably to the strength and tenderness of the bond between them. While living at the Palais Royal in March 1675, Liselotte contracted one of those mysterious and violent infections of the day that brought her to death's door. Her doctors diagnosed it as *fièvre tierce*,[70] and for several days her life was in doubt. Philippe, always good in times of sickness, spared neither his household nor himself in combating the fever. Mustering the physicians in his household and in that of the king and scouring Paris for specialists, he sent an army of doctors into the sickroom. As the court marveled, the prince himself followed to wait on his wife as bedside nurse and self-appointed guardian. As the crisis of Liselotte's illness approached and as he judged the treatment of the doctors too heroic, he countermanded their orders for still another purge and threw the offending medicinal powders into the fireplace. Well informed as usual, Aunt Sophie wrote with admiration of Philippe's attentive care: "Monsieur never leaves her side, puts her himself on the pierced chair, serves her better than any servant could do, [and] with a passion and a tenderness beyond expression."[71]

Whether because of or in spite of these medical ministrations, Liselotte's strong young body pulled through. When recovered sufficiently to reassure her relatives, she gave the credit to husband and family rather than to the doctors for her return from death. "It is Monsieur, Papa, Your Grace [Sophie], and uncle who have saved me," she wrote, "and not the seventy-two purgations those gentlemen [the physicians] prescribed for me."[72] Philippe too, never the most articulate of men, for once found words to express the depth of his joy and relief. To Karl Ludwig he wrote:

I begin my letter by telling you how great is my happiness that Madame is now entirely out of danger and almost free of fever, as for some twenty hours she was all but dead. . . . She has demonstrated in this illness a devotion, a firmness and a tenderness for you, for me, and for the king (who spent three hours in tears at her bedside) that make everyone here admire and love her, for from the king down to the least bourgeois in Paris, everyone was in such a state of affliction that I should not have believed it had I not seen it. Finally, thanks to God, she has been cured, her rise in fever today has been much less. Nonetheless, in two hours she should be bled lightly in the arm, because she has a little cough. . . . I was forgetting to tell you that she was bled in the arm last Wednesday at ten in the evening. . . . Finally she was so ill that the Holy Sacrament was brought into the house with Extreme Unction. Knowing that you would want them, I am writing you all these details. She strongly recommended to the king that he recollect what he had said to her in your regard and that he retain you in his friendship. And as for myself, I was more dead than she, *for I do not think that since the world began, there has been a better marriage than ours.* I pray that it may long endure and that I shall have occasion to be able to come to your service and to let you know how much I honor you.[73]

SEVEN

Long Live Monsieur, Who Has Won the Battle!

SOLDIER-PRINCE

Louis's War of Devolution of 1667–68 to enforce Maria Theresa's claim to certain districts in the Spanish Netherlands led him to the Dutch War of 1672–78. Having broken up the Triple Alliance of England, Holland, and Sweden by signing the Treaty of Dover with Charles II, and having made judicious use of French money to secure the benevolence, or at least the neutrality, of most of the German princes, including even the emperor, and of the Swedish regency, he was in a position to act on his plan to unite the provinces of Flanders to the French kingdom and at the same time to crush the commercial power of the Dutch empire. By the spring of 1672, after supervising the assembling and equipping of a magnificent army, the king was ready to undertake an offensive campaign deep into the heart of enemy territory.

The war has often been interpreted as a gratuitous act of aggrandizement or revenge on the part of a young and arrogant king in his search for glory,[1] although given the political morals and standards of the seventeenth century its outbreak was nearly inevitable. Certainly the acquisition of the Spanish Netherlands was as advantageous to French interests of state as it was to the personal honor of Louis, whereas the Dutch, fearing the dangerous military and economic consequences of such an act, would resist it with all the force they could command. Certainly the war was far longer and much more destructive than the earlier and easy War of Devolution, though not to the degree of Louis's subsequent wars. Yet while the Dutch War was to bring suffering, ruin, and death to those in its path, especially the poor, for a favored few it spelled fame, fortune, wealth, and glory. Philippe was one of the fortunate ones. The co-incidence of this war, in which for once in his life he was permitted honorable service to the Crown, with the first years of his second marriage is no small reason why the decade of the 1670s was the happiest and most fulfilling of his life.

Philippe's skills as a soldier have usually been denigrated. While contemporaries and subsequent historians might give the prince the benefit of an instinctive valor—legacy no doubt of an illustrious Bourbon ancestry—they would note that "the spirit of Monsieur was far from martial"[2] and that as a rule he was far more interested in his toilette and the luxurious appointments of his quarters than in fighting the enemy. His astonishing success in routing Prince William of Orange in 1677 at Cassel has usually been attributed either to the professional generals who served under him or to a sort of fluke or lucky chance. Thus ran the rumor that Marshal Humières, who commanded the prince's right wing in that battle, had himself begun the attack while his commander-in-chief was still engaged in adjusting his wig before the mirror in his tent.[3] A half-century later Voltaire was echoing this refrain when, after noting the general astonishment at Monsieur's victory, he decided that after all "courage is not incompatible with effeminacy."[4]

Those close to the prince knew how erroneous these judgments were. On those few occasions when he had experienced life on campaign and exposed his person to enemy fire, he had manifested enjoyment and even enthusiasm for the arts of war. Even as a child of seven when, for once, he was permitted to accompany Louis to the army and had observed the siege of Montmédy, he had elicited the admiring approval of his governor. While cannon and muskets thundered about him, the child "remained so calm and sustained this first test of fire with such fine grace" that Plessis-Praslin was completely satisfied with his "intrepid" demeanor.[5] Such an experience, which no doubt had taken place in very carefully controlled circumstances and was fairly routine in the lives of princes, would have meant nothing in itself. But as a young adult in the War of Devolution he had again drawn attention to himself by his visits to the trenches under hazardous conditions. Moreover, his letter to Mme de Sablé during the siege of Lille had evinced an undeniable eagerness for the test of arms, a test he was to pass with full honors in the Dutch War. Liselotte too, whatever other criticisms she may have later heaped upon Philippe, never wavered in her admiration of her husband's courage in arms and skill in battle. When her son, the future regent, made his first appearance with the army in the War of the League of Augsburg, she held up his father as the connoisseur of war to emulate and expressed her joy that the son carried on the bravery of his race.[6] Nor did she hesitate to compare Monsieur with the king in their bravery under fire and to declare uncompromisingly in favor of her husband. The late king "was no poltroon," she wrote in her old age, "but he was not as brave as Monsieur."[7]

Today Philippe's attraction to the military life seems by no means as astonishing as it was to his contemporaries. A number of very obvious reasons come immediately to mind. First of all, it was an aspect of his existence that remained unsullied and through which he could gain esteem and respect. It was in fact the only arena in which the king ever permitted him to perform honorable service to the state. It was also an area in which he could exercise his old rivalry with his brother. As the Dutch War progressed, the sense grows that to some degree the brothers were in a kind of contest to prove their valor under fire. And it was a game where the stakes were high, given that in the seventeenth century combat was still held to be the highest calling of the nobleman. Finally, personality theorists would be aware of a whole complex of interconnections between the military life and the homosexual experience. As Freud has reminded us, in the army "there is no room for woman as a sexual object."[8] Homosexual love is far more compatible with group ties. Groups of males acting together in a highly structured system are afforded the opportunity to exercise leadership denied them elsewhere in their existence. Philippe, though always subordinate to his brother and never displaying the characteristics of an authoritarian personality, was still in a position to command and could express his sublimated homosexuality, at least briefly, as a lieutenant general.

It is true, of course, that Philippe was not a soldier by profession. Nor was Louis. With them both on campaign there were always experienced commanders who had made war their career and on whose expert knowledge they could rely. But just as Louis's presence in the army served a real purpose, so did that of Philippe. Whoever takes the trouble to peruse the documents in the French War Ministry perceives at once that the prince was not a commander in name only. When in the company of the king and his army, Philippe probably had little to do. Louis was strong on detail, and his orders for the placement of camps and for the opening of the trenches were usually very precise. But when detached on a special assignment beyond the purview of the king, as he frequently was, Monsieur bore the final responsibility for all orders given and for the mission's ultimate success or failure. Always, of course, he was required to defer to Louis, who, as the supreme commander, retained the last word. But often the king's orders gave Philippe considerable freedom to maneuver and to decide for himself what was best in a given situation. "His Majesty permits Monsieur to open the trench either in front of the high bridge or before the city of Saint-Omer, according to which he thinks best,"[9] ran a typical instruction of the campaign of 1677. Or another: "Since His Majesty has no specific knowledge of the situation, he leaves it to Monsieur to decide the best course to take after having thoroughly examined the site."[10] We learn of marches at dawn and of entire nights spent in the trenches. Reports of exposure of his person to fire are too numerous and too diverse in their origins to be written off as flattery of the court. Philippe was no armchair general. In fact he may well have, at least in Louis's opinion, begun to take his métier as soldier too seriously for his own good. After the Battle of Cassel Marshal Luxembourg, who had commanded Philippe's left wing on that occasion, expressed fear lest Monsieur become too absorbed in military affairs. "So important a success may make him want to do nothing else. Better that Madame should have married a clerk than a man like that who thinks only of war."[11]

THE CAMPAIGNS OF 1672 AND 1673

The Dutch War went through three successive phases in which the aims and strategies of the French army changed significantly. The first constituted the offensives of 1672 and 1673, whose object was to destroy Dutch commerce and invade the United Netherlands. Then followed the indecisive years of 1674 and 1675 in which the French evacuated the lower Rhine, successfully invaded the Spanish province of Franche-Comté, and maneuvered freely in the Spanish Netherlands, though without capturing a major city or fortress. In the last stage, in the years 1676 to 1678, the French reduced their aims to straightening out and rectifying their northern border at the expense of the Spanish Netherlands. Philippe's victory over William of Orange at Cassel in 1677 and Louis's capture of Ghent in 1678 were sufficient to attain these modified objectives and brought the enemy to make peace.

Monsieur's participation in the Dutch War marked both the culmination and the effective termination of his career as a soldier. His significant and active service took place during the offensive campaigns of the first two years and in the mostly siege warfare in Flanders in 1676 and 1677. In those four years he enjoyed the rank of *généralissime*—lieutenant general second in command to Louis with all of the other princes of the royal family, including the prince of Condé, and the marshals subordinate to him.[12] During the other three years of the war, for reasons that are not entirely clear and that seem to have arisen either from his relationship with Liselotte and the king or from political strains within the army and war office, he either accompanied Louis as a simple volunteer (1674 and 1678) or (1675) did not go to the army at all.

In his capacity as lieutenant general he performed a number of independent missions in command of independent armies that laid successful siege to important cities and fortifications. Not once did he fail to perform as ordered. And in 1677 he far exceeded the expectations and even the orders of the king in engaging the prince of Orange in battle and routing him from the field. That victory brought him to the moment of his greatest glory and perhaps of his greatest despair. Never again did Louis permit him to command an army on the field. The battle was a major turning point in Philippe's life and in the relationship between the two brothers as well and thus has an interest and significance beyond the scope of military history.

The war could scarcely have begun more auspiciously for France, for Louis, and for Philippe. Louvois, minister of war, presented the king with a magnificent and well-provisioned army. To aid him in its command Louis could count not only on his brother but on famous soldiers such as Condé and Marshal Turenne, veteran of the Thirty Years War and the War of Devolution, as well as on an outstanding roster of other marshals and lieutenant generals.

For a brief time, at least, it appeared as if the war would be a repetition of the easy victories of the War of Devolution, with cities and fortresses surrendering almost on the appearance of the besieging French forces. Striking through the Netherlands and pushing to the Rhine at the head of an army of 40,000, and provided with the finest equipment and furnishings money could buy (Louis, in fact, contributed 172,000 livres annually toward the expenses of Philippe's campaigns), the two brothers began the campaign with éclat. The king decided to lay siege to four cities simultaneously. Assuming command personally at Rheinberg, he charged Philippe, Turenne, and Condé with the operations respectively at Orsoy, Burick, and Wesel. At Orsoy, the prince had only to summon the governor of the place with his trumpet to receive the Dutchman's surrender. Victory came no less easily to his colleagues.[13] A few days later, early in June, Louis and Philippe heard mass in great ceremony in the church at Rheinberg and afterward dined in state with the archbishop of Cologne.[14]

Eager to follow up his early success, Louis decided to cross the Rhine and to invade the heart of the Dutch Netherlands. The crossing, on the whole carried out successfully and with skill, later came to assume an almost mythical character in the annals of Louis's wars. Yet because it was not unattended by loss of life, which could have been avoided in the king's view, it was proof both of the cautious approach he always favored in the conduct of military operations and of the critical attitude he would henceforth adopt toward those marshals and generals, not excluding his brother, who were more adventurous than he.

While Louis, with Philippe at his side, supervised the passage of the infantry and cavalry across the carefully prepared bridge of boats, a few young hotheads that included Condé's son and nephew, eager to distinguish themselves under the eye of the king, got themselves in trouble by crossing independently either in a small boat or by swimming their horses. On the other side, encountering a small body of Dutch infantry that would have been totally ineffective against the regular forces crossing in orderly fashion, they charged impetuously. Condé, seeing his young relatives in danger, impulsively went to their aid. In the ensuing melee the nephew and several others were killed, and Condé himself was wounded. Louis, profoundly mortified,[15] was disgusted at the uncalled-for action and the resulting casualties. He could see nothing heroic either in the charge of the young nobles or in the attempted rescue staged by Condé. A general had no business behaving like an amateur; nor were spontaneous sorties, whose outcome could not be anticipated, any substitute for careful planning and methodical organization. As one of Louis's biographers has remarked: "[The king] had never favored the impetuous school strategy [and] henceforth he was even more suspicious of it."[16]

Once across the Rhine, the king decided to continue the offensive by detaching Monsieur at the head of an independent force with orders to strike deep into enemy territory and to attack and besiege the fortification of Zutphen on the Ijssel River. The city was protected by high walls with half-moon fortresses, was circled by two moats, and was defended by a garrison of 2,500 infantry and four squadrons of cavalry.[17] Its reduction would be a much more difficult and dangerous feat than any that had preceded it and was the first

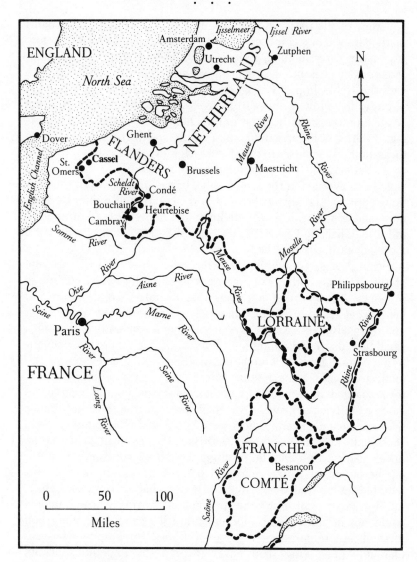

MAP ONE.   The Dutch War

in which the prince would be called upon to exercise in earnest any martial skills he might possess. Fortunately for the historian, the documentation is sufficient to follow the prince and his command closely in this his first test of arms.

Philippe broke camp at dawn on June 21 at the head of 2,500 infantry and four squadrons of cavalry and arrived before Zutphen after a march of fourteen hours. His general officers were the chevalier de Lorraine, the count de Gadagne, and the marquis de la Freselière, an artillery specialist. Reconnoitering the formidable defenses and feeling the weight of command, he wrote immediately to Louvois to ask the king for additional artillery and supplies. "I hope [the reinforcements and supplies] will not be long in coming, for it would be no pleasure to fall short all of a sudden; think also of bread, for there are . . . some regiments who are without."[18]

The prince and his officers were then in a position to organize the siege. Receiving reinforcements of 4,000 infantry and 1,500 cavalry, Monsieur opened the trench the following day. By June 23 the French artillery was within firing range of the city's ramparts and began to destroy them.

With French forces now greatly outnumbering those of the city, Monsieur and his officers must have expected a repetition of his easy victory at Orsoy. The besieged, however, refused to surrender without a fight. Making a determined sortie on June 24, they frightened numbers of the French infantry into fleeing the trenches. The day was saved for the French when the chevalier de Lorraine, intrepid under fire as usual, repulsed the Dutch with his cavalry, while Philippe betook himself to the trenches to raise the morale of his men by his presence and by the judicious distribution of food, drink, and money.

With the failure of the sortie, the Dutch realized the hopelessness of their position. Fearing the consequences of further resistance— pillage or worse—the defenders ceased fire and the following day, June 25, sent a delegation to Philippe offering to surrender and pleading for quarter.

Monsieur showed himself magnanimous in victory. By the "Articles and Conditions"[19] signed by his hand he took prisoner only the officers and specifically guaranteed the security of the citizens in their homes. The inhabitants were granted all their customary privileges, even including freedom of conscience. On June 26, astride a prancing war-horse, sporting polished steel armor and an enormous black wig, adorned with feathers, plumes, and laces, victor's baton in hand, the little man made his triumphal entry into the city. With Father Zoccoli, his confessor, he proceeded to the center of the town to celebrate mass under a pavilion and to render thanks for his victory. Two days later, having granted his army a day of rest, and in possession of twenty-nine flags and two standards of the enemy as laurels of his victory, he marched out to rejoin the main army of the king.

The prince was riding the crest of a personal triumph. True, considering the superiority of the forces he commanded and the advanced state of the French art of siege warfare, he could scarcely be said to have brought off an extraordinary feat of generalship. Yet he had demonstrated irrefutably that he was capable of leading an army numbering in the thousands, of operating independently beyond the limits of the king's protective supervision, and of carrying to successful conclusion a mission requiring both determination and considerable organizational skill. The *Gazette de France* wrote long, flattering accounts of the siege in which Philippe's "heroic" and "generous" actions received lavish praise. Louis himself was heard to express his satisfaction both with the accomplishment of his brother and with the excellence of his report relating the action. Insiders at court, no doubt taking their cue from the king, outdid themselves describing the valor of the prince in visiting the trenches and the futility of the attempts of his subordinates to bring him back to the relative safety of his quarters.[20]

The fruits of his victory were still sweet when, with Louis, he left the army and returned home in August. Observers noted the animation and radiance of his countenance as he attended the numerous ceremonies at Notre Dame de Paris and elsewhere dedicated to the success of French arms. The climax of the celebrations was achieved by the hero himself in a twenty-four-hour outdoor party staged in the park and gardens of Saint-Cloud on August 15. A profusion of flowers perfumed the air while Louis and the court promenaded, feasted under a gigantic pavilion, watched a display of fireworks, danced, and attended a ballet.[21] Ostensibly offered in honor of the king, the brilliance and splendor of the event, outstanding even among Philippe's fetes, redounded as much to the reputation of the host as to the glory of its august guest.

JUDGING ONLY FROM the festivities at court and at Saint-Cloud, one might conclude that the Dutch Republic had been destroyed and the war brought to a successful close. The reality was quite different. Even while the French army was occupying the right bank of the Rhine and while Monsieur was laying successful siege to Zutphen, the Dutch, rather than surrendering meekly and unconditionally, had cut their dikes, flooded their polders, and so placed Amsterdam and The Hague, their key cities, out of reach of the invaders. At the same time they had offered to make peace on terms that now, with the benefit of hindsight, appear remarkably favorable to the French. Perhaps unaware of the extent to which the flooding would cripple his operations, Louis had scorned the Dutch offer and resolved to continue the attack. In fact, the Dutch action and Louis's decision marked a real turning point of the war. Its first phase, which had begun with promise of total success, had ended in a virtual standoff. Because the Dutch, safe behind their flooded fields, would not consent to their own destruction, and because Louis was insisting on nothing less, the war could not end.[22]

In the campaign of 1673, despite the ambiguity of his position, the king was determined to continue the offensive and to remain in the center of the action. While Condé and Turenne led diversionary forces into Holland (to keep the enemy guessing) and into Germany (to observe the imperials), Louis, at the head of the principal army and with Philippe as his second-in-command, decided to attack the fortified city of Maastricht. Situated on the Meuse River at the confluence of the Jaar, it commanded communications with the Rhine and, once captured, would protect France from attack from the north.[23]

For Monsieur the campaign of 1673 was a time of fulfillment in both his public and his private life. The renewal of hostilities and his service in his brother's army afforded further opportunity to win experience in siege warfare and acclaim for his valor under fire. The birth of a son, the first child of his second marriage, while he was away on campaign brought deep personal happiness and the promise of the continuation of the house of Orléans.

Leaving Liselotte, then in an advanced state of pregnancy, at Saint-Cloud, Philippe departed for the army in mid-May. Joining the king at Maastricht, he received orders to cross the Meuse with an independent force to attack the fortress of Wick, which composed part of the overall defenses of the place. The fortress was a formidable target. Heavily fortified by half-moon bastions and surrounded by a deep moat, it had steep approaches covered with nearly impenetrable thickets. His duty was not to capture the fortress but rather to serve as a decoy, carrying out a diversionary attack and dividing the enemy forces while Louis assaulted Maastricht on the other side of the river.[24]

As in the campaign of 1672, Philippe was completely successful in executing his orders. Under cover of darkness, the prince ordered his men to cross the moat and climb the escarpment. Despite the

"furious resistance" of some two thousand defenders, the French—
to the later surprise of Louis, who had not anticipated their success—
were able to make their way to the very walls of the fortress.[25] Only
the lack of ladders prevented them from scaling the walls and actually capturing the place. Retreating in good order, at least they had
the satisfaction of knowing that the simultaneous attack launched at
Maastricht had succeeded and that their diversionary attack had
served its purpose.

This time Louis was less free in his praise of Philippe's performance and more insistent on his own responsibility for the victory.
Although he admitted that "the decoy attack had been more successful than anticipated" and that "my brother gave the necessary
orders very well," he observed that the prince had done nothing
more than carry out the king's explicit orders. Louis had visited his
brother's headquarters at Wick, had reconnoitered the site, and had
demonstrated to him exactly where to place his forces and begin the
attack.[26] Moreover, refuting what he doubtless viewed as an implied
criticism of his own leadership, the king denied that the want of
scaling ladders had prevented the capture of the city, holding instead that had the attackers attempted to climb the walls they would
have been slaughtered by the men within.

However it may precisely have been, by the time Maastricht fell
on June 30, Philippe had more to celebrate than his military success.
On June 2 at Saint-Cloud Liselotte had given birth to the much-
desired male heir. Congratulations poured in from all sides. A Te
Deum was ordered at the Church of the Urselines at Saint-Cloud.
Displays of fireworks and the distribution of alms delighted the
cheering crowds in the garden. Conscious of the prince's image in
Paris, Boisfranc, Philippe's treasurer, ordered the illumination of the
Palais Royal and an open house for the public. Violins played while
a fountain of wine (literally) flowed over the main portal into the
cups of the Parisians, eager to drink the health of Alexander-Louis,
the little duke of Valois. The major cities of the prince's appanage
followed suit with Te Deums in the churches and fetes in the public
squares.[27] Philippe's arrival in Paris in mid-July set off a new round
of festivities as princes of the blood and other great seigneurs presented their compliments. By August Liselotte was sufficiently recovered to take part in the rejoicing. Early in the month Louis
hosted a memorable *combat des bêtes* and royal hunt at the château
of Vincennes, where Madame distinguished herself mounted *en
amazone* (sidesaddle).[28]

DESPITE PHILIPPE'S TWO years of honorable and successful service, he did not resume significant military activity until the campaign of 1676. In 1674 the prince briefly accompanied the king into Franche-Comté as a simple volunteer, while the duke of Enghien, Condé's son, served as Louis's second-in-command. The *Gazette de France* merely noted Philippe's arrival and departure dates from the army, observing that as usual Monsieur had "shared the illustrious fatigues" of his brother.[29] Other accounts of the campaign of 1674, including that of Louis, make no mention of him whatever. The following year he did not join the campaign in any capacity.

Surely the reason for his absence or low profile was not that the war was going so successfully for France that no need for his services existed. Quite the contrary. By the end of 1673, even while the two brothers had been celebrating their successes, the position of the French army in the Netherlands had become precarious, while the war itself was broadening into a European conflict, with the Empire, Spain, and the duke of Lorraine in league against France. Humiliating reverses suffered by Condé and Turenne had forced the French to abandon the offensive in the United Netherlands and to evacuate the lower Rhine. Only the easy conquest of Franche-Comté in 1674 could be viewed with entire satisfaction.[30] Even a succession of pitched battles fought by Turenne that temporarily forced the Germans out of Alsace failed to destroy the enemy armies and caused heavy casualties in the French army. Worse still, the campaign of 1675 ended with the death of Turenne (shot by a stray cannonball), with the Imperials back in Alsace, and with a French defeat on the Moselle.

How else to account for the two-year hiatus in his military career? His absence in 1675 is probably sufficiently explained by the fever that felled Liselotte and threatened for a time to remove her from life. True, she was out of danger by April, and the king did not leave for the army until the beginning of May. Nonetheless, her convalescence seems to have been protracted. The couple remained quietly in Paris until mid-July and neither entertained guests nor attended social functions. The sole extent of Philippe's reported public appearances was attending church or receiving ambassadors.[31]

How to explain Philippe's presence in the army in 1674 as a volunteer instead of second-in-command? Liselotte, who never adjusted easily to Monsieur's absence, was again pregnant and carrying the child, born early the following August, with difficulty. Just possibly he might have declined the responsibility of command in order to be able to return to his wife's side on short notice should the need arise. But it seems unlikely. In the spring of 1673 he had not hesitated to accept command and to leave his wife when her pregnancy was even more advanced. And he would do the same in 1676, even though the little duke of Valois had then just died and Liselotte, deeply depressed and feeling unwell,[32] was again pregnant. Another possibility, but equally unlikely, or at least incapable of substantiation, is the existence of a quarrel between Louis and Philippe, for which the historian has no record, that caused the king to deny his brother command as punishment. Yet so far as is known the two brothers appeared on unusually friendly terms.[33] Shortly before leaving for the army in April, Louis came with Maria Theresa to the Palais Royal so they could serve as godparents at the baptismal ceremony of the prince's son.[34] They had stayed on into the evening to enjoy music, a banquet, and a performance of *Alcide* that Philippe had arranged for their pleasure. The following June, when the king returned from the campaign, Philippe showed no sign of resentment and instead rode out to Fontainebleau to greet his brother affably in public.[35]

A more likely explanation, though admittedly still a hypothesis, is that Philippe was sacrificed to the political strains within the king's administration. In 1673 a near war had broken out between the two veteran generals, Condé and Turenne, and Louvois, minister of war, whom they regarded as an arrogant young upstart. When the campaign went sour in its last months the two blamed the war office and nearly effected Louvois's disgrace. He had been saved by his father, Le Tellier, who had astutely "bought" the favor, or at least the neutrality, of Condé with the promise of an important independent army in the next campaign. Louvois, whom the king regarded as indispensable to his war machine, was saved, since Turenne by himself lacked the clout to sink him.[36] In the spring of 1674 when the time came to make good on the promise, Condé was placed at the head of a fine army to lead into Flanders against William of Orange. At the same time Enghien, his son, received the post of lieutenant general and second-in-command of Louis's army. Very likely this appointment was part of the same bargain made to reconcile Condé with Louvois. Enghien, it may be remembered, was one of the young hotheads who had caused all the trouble at the crossing of the Rhine. The king must have had some very special reason to choose him instead of his brother, whose military record was spotless. This line of reasoning is the more convincing in that once Turenne was dead and Louvois again secure in the war ministry, Philippe reappeared at his brother's side in the campaign of 1676 in what might be called his normal position as second-in-command.[37] It is also one more proof, if such were needed, of Louis's willingness to subordinate Philippe to the interests of state and to the needs of his administration.

HEURTEBISE AND CASSEL, 1676 AND 1677

French prospects were unpromising in the spring of 1676. France was now nearly alone against the united forces of Spain, the Netherlands, and the empire. England had signed a separate peace with the Dutch in 1674; Sweden, the only remaining ally, was expending most of its energy in a futile effort to defend Pomerania from the invading Brandenburgers.

Given these harsh realities, the French reduced their war aims to rectifying of their northern frontier in the Spanish Netherlands: specifically, eliminating a deep pocket of enemy territory stretching from the Schelde River to the Somme. The campaign of 1676 was designed to besiege Condé and Bouchain on the Schelde and to mop up the remaining isolated fortresses the following year.

Although the campaign can be said to have been successful in that both Condé and Bouchain were captured, it may have been more important, at least in the lives of Louis and Philippe, for what did not take place than for what did. The circumstances were these. After the successful attack on Condé, Louis ordered Philippe to march south with an army to undertake the siege of Bouchain while he, with the remainder of the army, acted as a screening force to prevent William of Orange and the Dutch army from coming to the rescue of the besieged. Both brothers were keenly aware of the possibility of a battle between the French army and the combined Spanish and Dutch forces. Louis even promised Philippe that if such an opportunity presented itself he would notify him in time for him to leave the siege at Bouchain and join the king's army for the encounter.[38] Both brothers were eager for battle. Not only was combat still thought to be the highest calling of the nobleman, but it was a proud part of the Bourbon heritage. The valor of Henry IV was legendary; Louis XIII, despite his morose temperament and sickly body, had galloped boldly at the head of his troops. Condé, first prince of the blood, had won a great victory at Rocroi only a few weeks after Louis became king. Both Louis and Philippe had by now commanded numerous sieges. Neither had met steel with steel. Here was the king's first opportunity to command on the battlefield and to win a military reputation.

William of Orange duly appeared at the head of his army, but no battle ensued. Arranged in battle formation, the two armies faced each other for an entire day and night at Heurtebise, east of Bouchain and near Valenciennes. Louis took command of the right wing and on the arrival of Philippe, whom he had summoned from Bouchain according to his promise, placed him in command of the left. But in the end neither Louis nor William attacked.[39] The armies moved away from each other. "Because you have more experience than I, I yield, but with regret," the king was reported to have remarked to Louvois and his generals, who had advised him not to give battle.[40] All could agree that the French outnumbered the enemy and the outcome was not in doubt; but the risks of battle were nonetheless real. The death of Turenne was fresh in everyone's memory. Many believed, and with them Louis probably instinctively agreed, that a king had no business fighting a battle.

For the rest of his life Louis regretted his decision.[41] Inevitably some had interpreted his caution and prudence as cowardice. For Philippe, too, the experience was frustrating. For several days he had been in high spirits, elated at the idea of clashing swords with the enemy. "I am so pleased with the king and with all his army," he had written Mme de Sablé from Bouchain, "that I am . . . feeling better than ever."[42] Then, having hastened to Heurtebise "full of joy at the prospect of battle," he had immediately taken his position at the head of the left wing. Only at that time, while still rallying the men about him, did he learn "with anger equaled only by surprise" of the council of war earlier in the day in which Louvois and others had talked Louis out of attacking.[43] Whether he expressed these feelings to his brother we do not know. But for Louis, especially in light of what happened the following year at Cassel, the knowledge that Philippe had watched as he let William of Orange slip from his grasp much have rankled in his soul.

At least Monsieur had the satisfaction of ending the campaign with the capture of Bouchain. Leaving Heurtebise and returning to the siege, he ordered a frontal assault "sword in hand." "In the presence of Monsieur," the troops attacked "with such valor as to put the besieged to flight." The governor of the city surrendered the following day. In ordering this attack we do not know if Philippe was acting on the king's orders (as one account would have it) or if he was independently acting out his frustration at the nonbattle at Heurtebise.[44] No matter. Once again the prince proved his worth as a commander and fully executed his orders to capture the city.

WHEN THE WAR resumed in the spring of 1677, Louis quite inadvertently dressed the stage for the greatest triumph in his brother's life: victory over William of Orange at Cassel—inadvertently, because the principal goal of the campaign was not the defeat of the Spanish-Dutch army on the battlefield but rather the completion of the unfinished business of the previous year. Neither Louis nor Louvois had any intention of permitting Philippe to risk the loss of a French army in an event as chancy as a battle. The plan called first for the capture of the now isolated fortresses of Valenciennes and Cambray, after which the army would march north to besiege the small but strongly fortified town of Saint-Omer in Flanders, which dominated a pocket of enemy territory between Lille and Dunkirk. As in the previous year Louis assumed the overall command with Philippe as his lieutenant general. Under them were Sébastien Vauban, famous specialist of siege warfare, and a strong cast of marshals and generals.

At first all went in accordance with the plan of the campaign. Joining the king early in March at the siege of Valenciennes, Philippe watched while Vauban's trenches rapidly closed in upon the city walls and permitted the French to take the place by storm. William of Orange was nowhere to be seen. Three days later, still according to schedule, Louis moved his army southward toward Cambray and ordered Philippe to lead a smaller force to the north to besiege Saint-Omer.

The scenario changed after the king and Monsieur had taken up their respective sieges. Louis began to receive intelligence that the Dutch commander was in the area and might move to the relief of Saint-Omer. At first there was little cause for alarm. According to this same intelligence the Spanish-Dutch forces were badly equipped, had little or no cavalry, and were small in numbers. As a precaution, the king and Louvois began sending Monsieur substantial reinforcements of infantry and cavalry.[45] Their purpose was not to instigate a battle between Philippe and William of Orange but, on the contrary, to avoid one. They counted on the supposedly enormous numerical advantage of the French army to deter the enemy from attacking and to permit Monsieur to continue the siege of Saint-Omer uninterrupted. Louvois was most explicit in his instructions to Philippe's adviser, Marshal d'Humières, and to his *maréchal du camp*. "An army trying to prevent a relief of Saint-Omer [Philippe's army]," he wrote, "must not march against another army [the army of the prince of Orange]."[46] Most of all, he did not want Monsieur "to make a bad mistake" [fight a battle], which could be almost as disastrous as one committed by the king. He even conveyed contingency plans to Humières for the evacuation and retreat of Philippe's army if the prince of Orange managed to bring his army up to the fortification.[47] Louis's instructions to his brother were less precise, "leaving Monsieur at liberty to conform so far as he thinks practical," but their purport was clear: Philippe should remain on the defensive and should stay close to the trenches of Saint-Omer.[48]

Meanwhile, at Saint-Omer Monsieur viewed the arriving reinforcements from the king in an entirely different light. To him they represented an offensive weapon that enabled him, as he wrote, "to await the arrival of the enemy with joy."[49] Early in April he began to move the bulk of his forces away from Saint-Omer out to the plain of Cassel, dominated by a nearby hill of that name, twelve miles to the northeast. An important crossing of roads, the site had seen important battles in the past: in 1071 when Robert, Count of Flanders, vanquished his rival Arnulf, and in 1328 when Philippe of Valois, a distant ancestor of Monsieur, defeated the Flemish. With Humières and with Luxembourg, who had arrived with the reinforcements, he placed their forces so that the prince of Orange could neither relieve Saint-Omer without first fighting a battle nor retreat without exposing his rear guard. When the Spanish-Dutch army came in view on April 10, the French were prepared for battle.

Louis and Louvois no doubt had been right in not wishing to entrust the fate of the prince's army to the gods of the battlefield. Although the French forces outnumbered those of the enemy (40,000–45,000 to some 31,000),[50] the ensuing encounter was a stiff one that at one moment could have gone either way. French eyewitnesses and official accounts all agreed that it was the actions of Monsieur that tipped the balance.[51]

Far from sticking to his tent to arrange his coiffure, Philippe was on the field at dawn. Throughout the day he acted as both field commander and captain leading the charge. Placing Humières in command of his right wing and Luxembourg in command of the left, he took up a position in the center of the line. With him were the chevalier de Lorraine and the marquis d'Effiat. Soon after the fighting began on the extreme left of the French line, the prince of Orange, intending to attack in force at this point, began to reinforce his own right wing with troops borrowed from his left. Perceiving the maneuver and comprehending its intent (with the "clairvoyance of the born soldier," according to one account),[52] Monsieur swiftly ordered Humières to charge the exposed enemy flank. The result was a completely successful attack that routed the weak cavalry Orange had left to conceal his movement and cover his flank.

Meanwhile, however, the French center was in trouble, the infantry floundering in a small creek and in danger of crumbling before the charging Dutch cavalry. The problem may have been a failure of morale as much as anything else. Wishing to inspire his men, Philippe ordered up the second line of French infantry. Placing himself at its head he repeatedly charged "like a grenadier" into the enemy line. "Because he was always in the thick of the fighting," ran one eyewitness account, he saw dozens of persons around him killed. The chevalier, at his side, was seriously wounded in the temple. Philippe himself took a musket ball in his armor and had his horse shot out from beneath him. "Emboldened by the presence of Monsieur," concluded this same reporter, "all the troops performed miracles."[53] As Philippe and the French center pressed through, the enemy gave way in a movement that changed into a rout. William of Orange, also in the center of the action and outraged at the sight of his fleeing soldiers, shouted helplessly at his men and slashed at their faces with his sword.[54] In vain. Luxembourg and the French left completed the sweep of the field.

What assessment can be made of the extent of Monsieur's victory? The verdict of Luxembourg was that "Monsieur has won one of the most complete battles of our day."[55] Enemy losses amounted to 3,000 dead, 4,000 to 5,000 wounded, several thousand prisoners, and all of the army's artillery, baggage, and supplies. The French bore forty flags and fourteen standards off the field. They had lost some 2,000 dead and 2,400 wounded. Yet if numbers of combatants and casualties are the criterion, and placed in the larger context of the major battles of French history or even of those of the four wars of Louis XIV, the Battle of Cassel does not figure prominently. Many battles in the War of the League of Augsburg and in the War of the Spanish Succession involved much larger numbers of soldiers and higher losses, though nowhere near as large as those of the wars of the French Revolution, of the First Empire, and of subsequent modern warfare.

Nonetheless, Cassel was arguably one of the major victories of the Dutch War, perhaps the most decisive. The Battle of Seneffe fought by Condé against William of Orange in 1674 had been far bloodier than Cassel on both sides, but it gave neither combatant a significant advantage. At Turkheim in Alsace the same year, where Turenne commanded some 35,000 men against an enemy force of some 50,000, his victory enabled the French to evict the Germans and temporarily hold the province. Philippe's victory at Cassel sealed the fate of both Saint-Omer and Cambray and made it possible for Louis to rationalize—that is, straighten out—his northern frontier into a defensible line. Neither Turkheim nor Cassel, of course, brought the war to an end. But the French seizure of Alsace after Turkheim proved brief; the province fell again to the imperials the following year. Cassel, on the other hand, enabled France to occupy permanently those pockets of land in Flanders dangerously close to the French capital and accomplished the principal goal of the campaign of 1677.

From the point of view of the biographer, the most interesting aspect of the battle scene is the abandon and valor with which Monsieur risked his life in charging into the thick of the enemy. The performance baffled his contemporaries, except for his intimates, and has bemused historians ever since. And indeed it must have been a bizarre sight: the little man with his ribbons, rouge, and wig—for reportedly he was as meticulous in his toilette on campaign as in court[56]—astride a great horse, sword drawn, furiously engaged in hand-to-hand combat with the stubborn Dutch cavalry. But perhaps his behavior is not after all so difficult to explain. On the conscious level, he may well have been trying to outperform his brother. He knew what had not happened at Heurtebise. Very likely he was remembering it and burning to demonstrate that he could do what the king had not: defeat William of Orange and the Spanish-Dutch army in battle. On the unconscious level, group psychology may have been at play. As is well known to students of group behavior, the individual in a group undergoes a radical alteration in his mental processes. His emotions are intensified, his intellectual abilities reduced. He may take risks from which on other occasions he would prudently abstain. Furthermore, acting as in a group, the individual throws off the repressions of his unconscious instincts. His conscience or sense of responsibility may disappear.[57] If the group is an army and is engaged in a battle, the individual will be free to act out his aggressions against others. In Freudian terminology, these destructive drives make up the "death instinct," which originally is turned inward upon the individual.[58] In striking out at the Dutch, Philippe could find a legitimate, viable outlet for the displacement of those powerful destructive drives that he usually channeled inward against himself. It was probably no accident that this externalization of aggression took place at a time when his love for a woman, Liselotte, was no doubt the most satisfactory sexual relationship of his life. When the erotic or libidinal impulses are ascendant, Freud theorized, destructive impulses are more "bound" —that is, more controlled or directable. With Philippe it appears that the apex of his heterosexual phase occurred simultaneously with the apex of his externally aggressive behavior.

Immediately following the battle, Philippe dispatched Effiat to report to the king (Lorraine, who otherwise would have had this honor, was incapacitated by his wound) and another messenger to Liselotte in Paris, where she and her ten-year-old stepdaughter, Mademoiselle, had been keeping vigil, running to the staircase each time a visitor approached. "[The joy] of Madame, who for two days had been in a state of nervous emotion, was so great that it was indescribable," wrote the *Mercure Galant*.[59] "She wept with happiness even while her fears continued to torment her." Paris erupted with joy at the news of victory, "for the city of Paris loved [Monsieur] very much."[60]

What was the king's reaction to the personal triumph of his brother? Publicly and officially it was gracious and generous. A witness reported that when Louis received the report of the battle he twice exclaimed "from the fullness of his heart" that "on his honor he was happier for his brother than for himself."[61] He immediately sent off congratulations to the prince and to Madame. Louis was equally gracious in a letter to Condé, to whom he wrote: "Cousin, you are right to congratulate me on the Battle of Cassel. If I had won it in person I could not be more moved by the grandeur of the action, by the importance of the event, and especially by the honor for my brother."[62] He celebrated the victory with éclat. Te Deums were ordered in every major city in France, and the flags taken from the enemy were placed at the altar of Notre Dame de Paris.

Yet Louis's subsequent actions belie his public affirmations of pleasure and satisfaction with his brother's performance. Rather than continuing to avail himself of Philippe's talents and abetting his military career, he removed him from command and in effect terminated his active service. Never again did Monsieur lead an army into the field. In the future when he went to war he either accompanied the king as a simple volunteer or held honorific posts far removed from any likely enemy action.

Privately the king may well have been displeased by Monsieur's conduct at Cassel. Of course there was no arguing with success, and he could not openly reprimand the victorious hero. But when the prince had moved his forces away from Saint-Omer and out to the plain of Cassel and had invited battle, if he had not disobeyed a specific order, he had certainly violated the spirit if not the letter of his instructions. A letter from Louvois to Humières written before the engagement informs us that the king had been "pained" by Monsieur's maneuver.[63] Moreover, neither Louis nor Louvois entirely trusted Philippe's judgment, and they had privately ordered Humières to ride close herd on him to counter the bad advice he might well receive from his favorites.[64] There is also evidence that at the last minute both Luxembourg and Humières had tried to talk the prince out of giving battle and had urged on him the priority of the siege at Saint-Omer. Their arguments having been rejected by Monsieur, they had allegedly replied "*that they could only obey.*"[65]

The historian cannot be certain that this conversation took place, but it is not implausible. Humières was under orders to prevent Monsieur "from making a bad mistake"[66] and to shield him from the influence of Lorraine and other hotheads in his entourage. Luxembourg is on record as having opposed the presence of kings in battle.[67] Philippe was not king, but he was, after all, only once removed from the throne. Moreover, consider Monsieur's conduct when he charged into the Dutch cavalry. He had risked, perhaps even invited, injury or death. His action must have appalled Louis, who had a horror of impulsive behavior and unnecessary risk. The battle, which had been a near thing at one point, was just the kind of affair the king liked least.

Then there was the question of Louis's jealousy. The king would not have been human had he not at least envied Philippe's success. He himself had never led his army into battle and had let slip the opportunity when it presented itself the previous year at Heurtebise. Many in court noted cracks in what they saw as a veneer of royal graciousness. When the two brothers met for the first time after Cassel, Louis asked few questions and did not even have the curiosity to inspect the site of the battle.[68] He was thought to have displayed signs of irritation when the crowds along their path cried out: "Long live the king and Monsieur, who has won the battle!"[69] Moreover, the official account, although it praised Philippe for his "presence of mind" and his "energy," gave principal credit for the victory to Louis for having had the foresight to supply the essential reinforcements for the prince's army.[70] Contemporaries took it for granted that the king's jealousy was at the root of Monsieur's demotion.

That Louis's self-esteem had suffered a blow is clear from his management of the campaign of 1678 in which he closed out the war by the conquest of Ghent. It was another siege, not a battle; but while Philippe looked on as an observer or volunteer, the king did it all: planning the strategy, fooling the enemy by a clever feint, leading the forced marches, and descending on the unprepared city. And why had he decided to attack a fortification that, in his own words, had resisted the attempts of "the greatest captains of our century"? Because, he confessed in his memoirs, "of the jealousy that I felt . . . of those who were the most esteemed. . . . I aspired to surpass them."[71]

For Philippe the army had been the last and only avenue of honorable service to the Crown. Now that too was closed to him. When France entered upon the War of the League of Augsburg a decade later, Monsieur pleaded with the king for an active command. In vain. In the words of one of Philippe's eulogists after his death, no matter how often the prince "looked sadly but avidly" toward Flanders and Germany, the answer was always the same: "It was necessary to shelter so precious a life . . . , a life more important to the state than the most celebrated victories."[72]

In terminating Philippe's military career, Louis could have had no real fear that the prince might exploit his popularity in the army to mount a revolt against the throne. Nearly thirty-seven years of age, Monsieur had by now served the king too long and too faithfully to be suspected of disloyalty. In any case, his financial dependence and his fatal lack of self-confidence ruled out any possibility of rebellion. But it appears, the king could not tolerate even a hint of rivalry from this brother he had been trained to fear and to subordinate. Personality theorists tell us that the older child in any family will tend to be of a dominating disposition, ambitious and authoritarian. During his adult life he will strive, no doubt unconsciously, to retain or to recapture the privileged status he once enjoyed, first as the only child with no sibling competition, and second, as the older child superior in every way to the younger, weaker brother or sister.[73] Viewed in this light, Louis may have unconsciously seen Philippe as a threat to his status as first warlord of the state. Or to state the case differently and more simply, as did Ernest Lavisse many years ago, "Louis XIV took it ill if someone stole something of his glory."[74] His cruel act in once more effacing Monsieur may reveal as much about his own personality as it does about his brother's life. Perhaps Philippe was not the only one lacking in self-confidence.

EIGHT

·

Service to Mammon

THE PALACES AND THEIR TREASURES

The effective termination of Philippe's military career at Cassel in 1677 closed the prince's last avenue of honorable public service and threw him back on his own devices. What was left for Monsieur to do? In addition to his life with Liselotte (which was to undergo a rapid and radical alteration), to his favorites, to the social pleasures of the court (gambling, the table, the theater, etc.), there were, notably, the building and decoration of his palaces, his collections of paintings, jewels, and objets d'art, and the accumulation of personal wealth. These pastimes were not new, of course. From his early youth Monsieur had taken evident pleasure in material possessions. Now that he had time to spare and more abundant resources at his command, gratifying this mounting passion for possessing and collecting became the principal occupation of his remaining years. In the exercise of his innate aesthetic gifts and love of beauty he could, at least to a certain degree, compensate for the outlets denied him and manifest his independence from his brother. In the process he would form the core of that great fortune of the house of Orléans that one day would liberate his heirs from financial servitude to the Crown.

In the case of the Palais Royal, the work of Monsieur took place in two stages: the restoration and redecoration of the 1660s and the more substantive embellishments and additions of the 1690s after he became the proprietor of the palace instead of its lodger. During his marriage to Henriette, as a result of the couple's handiwork and the effects of their social presence, the dilapidated old palace had come alive as the center of their brilliant court and theatrical presentations. After Henriette's death and for many years after his marriage to Liselotte, the palace played a less prominent part in his life. Although the prince continued to reside periodically in the city and ordered the redesigning of the interior garden, he made relatively few changes. He played no part in the introduction of opera in the theater of the Palais Royal in the 1670s, first under the authorization of Abbé Perrin, and subsequently under that of Jean-Baptiste Lully.[1] In the reorganization of the theater after the death of Molière in 1673 he suffered a rebuff at the hands of Louis and Lully, who was on his way to becoming the "pope" of music at the French court. When Monsieur obtained royal authorization for one of his officials to present spectacles in the theater, Lully objected, and the king abrogated his brother's permission.[2] For the remainder of the decade of the 1670s and much of the 1680s the prince focused his attention as an architect on the transformation of the château and park of Saint-Cloud. Probably, too, he was influenced by the aversion of the second Madame for urban life. Although popular with the Parisians, she found the filth and smells of the city intolerable and claimed that she always felt unwell there. Both, moreover, must have experienced a sense of transience in the Palais Royal, which belonged to the king, not to Philippe, and which they occupied on royal sufferance.

The turn of the palace came in 1692 when Philippe acquired it from his brother as an addition to his appanage as part of a bargain between them. When Cardinal Richelieu had donated the palace to the king, his will had designated it specifically as the residence either of future kings or of their direct descendants. Monsieur, as head of a collateral line, was legally barred from ownership. But such technicalities were as nothing when the will of the master was at stake. Louis had wished to marry one of his illegitimate daughters by Mme de Montespan, Mlle de Blois, to Monsieur's only son, duke of Chartres, the future regent. Not unexpectedly, he had no small difficulty in obtaining his brother's consent to this mésalliance between the only male heir of the house of Orléans, who was a petit fils de France, and the offspring of a double adultery. The donation of the Palais Royal was at least a portion of the grease on the palm that did the job.[3] After the young Philippe and Mlle de Blois were married in February 1692, a royal edict accorded the palace and its dependencies "to our very dear and beloved Philippe, fils de France, duke of Orléans ... under the title and quality of appanage ... so that our said brother and his masculine posterity may possess lodging appropriate to the grandeur of their birth." The prince was authorized to make such additions, improvements, and embellishments "as he saw best"—of course, at his own expense.[4] Henceforward the house of Orléans was legally as well as sentimentally linked to the city of Paris.

As soon as he became the proprietor of the Palais Royal, or perhaps even earlier, in anticipation of the event, Monsieur began extensive renovations and redecoration of the existing buildings, especially a lavish suite of rooms destined for his daughter-in-law, the young duchess of Chartres. He then undertook the reconstruction of the halls where Richelieu had once housed his library and that had been the location of the royal academies from 1661 to 1691. These rooms, which ran east and west and terminated on the rue de Richelieu, were destined for Monsieur's collection of paintings, for his audiences with ambassadors, and for his banquets. The plans were probably entrusted to Jules Hardouin-Mansart, by then the most famous architect of his day, who had established his reputation in work on Versailles, Marly, the Trianon, and the Hôtel des Invalides. The decoration of the new gallery was entrusted to Antoine Coypel, later the preferred painter of the regent, whose father, Noël Coypel, had worked on the Palais Royal in the past.[5] The overall expenditure for this work exceeded 400,000 livres: nearly 300,000 livres for building, close to 12,000 livres for mirrors, some 12,000 livres for repair and maintenance, 36,000 livres (paid in yearly installments of 1,800 livres) for the purchase of an adjacent small building, and 60,000 livres to Coypel for decoration.[6]

In the last decade of Monsieur's life the Palais Royal regained its social éclat. As the young Saint-Simon, who joined the court in the last years of the seventeenth century, observed: "There was always a crowd at the Palais Royal." "[Monsieur] loved the social whirl; he had an affability and an honesty that drew the crowds. . . . He allowed everyone an entire liberty without diminishing in the least the respect in which he was held and the high tone of the court. He had learned from his mother and well remembered the art of holding court."[7] But if there were more freedom at the Palais Royal than at Versailles, there was no less, or at least, very little less, prodigality and extravagant luxury. Like Louis, Philippe not infrequently made "lotteries" the theme of his parties, in which every lady among the guests drew a winning ticket. At one such in 1689 at the Palais Royal the *Mercure Galant* listed thirty-seven fair winners of jewelry and other choice items, including diamond pendant earrings, diamond and emerald buttons, a Chinese escritoire, porcelain objets d'art, and a ruby and diamond cross.[8]

By the end of the century the edifice had metamorphosed, both externally and internally, from the dilapidated mansion in the semi-deserted quarter it had been in 1660 into a regal palace in a bustling center of urban life. The garden, which was open to the public, was already much frequented. An English visitor, the zoologist Martin Lister, wrote of it in 1698: "The garden of the Palais Royal . . . is very large, has two or three great bassins with their jet d'eaux, but not well kept; nor hath anything elegant in it, but the good order and disposition of its shady walks and parterres. It is ever full of good company."[9] Cafés and restaurants had begun to appear around the square in front of the building and on the rue de Riche-lieu. By the end of the century *nouvellistes* found these establish-ments convenient sites in which to hawk their newspapers and read them to the public.[10] Together with its theater, its opera, and the elegance of the company within, the palace drew crowds from all levels of society. Its genial host, who frequently visited the city, often for several weeks at a stretch,[11] continued to be much more beloved than the king, who kept to his distant palace at Versailles.[12] It was almost as if the head of the house of Orléans and the old Palais Royal were anticipating the historic role they would play throughout the eighteenth century, first during the regency, subse-quently in the years before and during the French Revolution.

The great work of Monsieur's life, and the sole manifestation of independence of his mature years, was without doubt the château of Saint-Cloud. Its design, building, and decoration, to which he devoted much time and care, were endeavors that Philippe most enjoyed and for which he was innately gifted. His principal advisor was Louis de Béchameil, who was alternately the prince's superin-tendent of finances or treasurer and his superintendent of buildings. A man who liked the good life, who knew how to accumulate wealth and how to enjoy it, he had excellent taste in architecture, paintings, and jewelry and also in cuisine (the sauce today usually known as béchamel was reportedly his creation).[13] The final result of their efforts at Saint-Cloud provided an exquisite framework for Monsieur's vast collections of paintings and objets d'art and for the lavish fetes for which he was celebrated. Undoubtedly the château must have helped shore up the prince's battered self-esteem. Alto-gether, it was the consummate synthesis of his talents, drives, and style of life.

The château of Saint-Cloud with its vast park, gardens, water-falls, and orangerie as completed by Monsieur at the end of his life bore almost no resemblance to the relatively modest Gondi Maison (which had been slightly enlarged by Barthelemy d'Hervart, its former owner) that he had received as a gift of the Crown in 1658. Although its site overlooking the Seine was magnificent, he had from the very first regarded its grounds as insufficient for his purposes and had begun to purchase adjacent land in small lots as his finances permitted and as the properties came on the market. He continued to add to the park well into the 1690s. One of his last acquisitions, made in 1695, was a picturesque little island not far from the bank of the river that he named the Ile de Monsieur. The completed ensemble of property extended over some 1,200 acres and had been acquired at a cost of more than 450,000 livres.[14] The gardens of the park, very irregular of terrain, were designed by André Le Nôtre and executed with such skill that they appeared perfectly regular to the human eye.[15]

Although the exact date is in doubt, Monsieur seems to have decided in 1675 or 1676 to begin the transformation of the relatively modest château of the 1660s into a veritable palace on a grand scale.[16] During the lifetime of Henriette he had incorporated the Gondi Maison into a larger structure that in the new designs was to become much of the south wing and part of the central corps. On the north he erected an entirely new wing that would contain the château's most famous feature, the gallery of Apollo. In the rear of the central corps stretched a vast orangerie containing exotic fruits and other delicate plants. The whole would blend and harmonize with the surrounding landscape, including the park and gardens that he had already embellished with a waterfall, one of the wonders of his day. The result would be a dwelling that could rival and even surpass Versailles (then under construction), if not in size and expense, then at least in natural beauty and grace.

Unlike the king, who as a rule simply chose among the plans and projects submitted to him, Monsieur preferred to rely upon his own inspiration and on the advice of Béchameil and of his chancellor and sometime superintendent of finances, Boisfranc. Consulting neither Colbert nor Charles le Brun, who was patronized by the king and was considered the official arbiter of taste of his day, he confided the enterprise to the architects Le Pautre and Thomas Gobert. A certain Girard, sometimes thought to have been the architect of the central corps, was more of a financial entrepreneur than a designer. Hardouin-Mansart, then in an early stage of his career, was later called on to harmonize the exterior of the south wing with the new edifices and to amplify them. For the interior decoration, again eschewing the talents of Le Brun, who was at work on the salons of

Versailles, Monsieur turned to Jean Nocret, first painter in his household, and—a surprising choice—to Pierre Mignard. The latter, although he had worked on the frescoes at Val-de-Grâce and had completed a pleasing portrait of Louis XIV, had the reputation of being a nonconformist, having earned the wrath of Colbert by refusing to work under Le Brun at Versailles. Monsieur had visited Mignard's workshop on the eve of his departure for Flanders in the spring of 1677[17] and had been delighted with the graceful curved lines and light colors of the artist's frescoes (later they would be recognized as having anticipated the "Regency style" of the early eighteenth century). It was his artistry that decorated the gallery of Apollo, which occupied almost the entire north wing.

Construction of the palace, its exterior embellishments, the gardens and waterfall went on from the late 1670s to nearly the end of the century. The central corps of the building and at least a part of its decoration by Mignard were partially completed by October 1678 when Monsieur, with Madame at his side, is said to have invited the king to inspect the handiwork of his workmen and to have aroused his jealous admiration. After completing the tour of the grounds, Louis came inside to view the great gallery where Mignard was at work on the ceiling and walls. There followed an interminable, strained silence. "I very much hope, Madame," the king is said to have pronounced at last, "that the paintings in my gallery in Versailles will be the equal of these in beauty."[18]

By 1681 the palace was sufficiently finished to enable Philippe to authorize published descriptions of its principal features. Monsieur's recent victories in the Dutch War provided a theme for much of the decor. In the bedroom of Madame was a representation of the prince as Mars returning from battle. And in the central corps in the hall Monsieur used for audiences was the "Salle de Cassel" with a painting by Nocret representing the scene of the battle. The great staircase and especially the completed waterfall, which Philippe transformed by adding cascades, fountains, and basins (designed by Mansart) on the lower level, were not in place until late in the 1690s.[19]

Once they were on the road to completion, Monsieur filled his two great palaces (and to a lesser extent his residences at Villers-Cotterêts and Montargis) with his collections of paintings, jewels, and objets d'art. A collector of discerning taste, he especially appreciated the Dutch painters, for whom his brother had nothing but scorn. Owing in large part to the faultiness of the inventories made after his death, no accurate and complete register of his paintings has ever been made.[20] Some four hundred canvases, there is no doubt that they became the core of one of the great collections of Europe in the Old Regime.

A notable part of his collection of objets d'art reflected the taste for orientalism in seventeenth-century France. Mazarin and Anne of Austria had collected Chinese porcelains and lacquers. Philippe followed their example, accumulating a vast and varied assortment of pieces and ordering the decoration of rooms in Saint-Cloud appropriate for the proper display. Of one such room Lister, the English visitor, wrote in the 1690s: "At the end of the apartments of Monsieur, are a fine set of closets: the first you enter is furnished with a great variety of rock chrystals, cups, agates upon small stands, and the sides of the rooms are lined with large panes of looking-glass from top to bottom, with Japan varnish and paintings of equal breadth intermixt; which had a marvellous pretty effect. The other room had in it a vast quantity of bijous, and many of very great price; but the Siam pagods [sic], and other things from thence, were very odd."[21]

Monsieur's love of jewelry and precious stones was conspicuous even in that day and society, in which the importance of men as well as women could be judged by the size and number of gems adorning their persons when they appeared at court. It was taken for granted that on ceremonial or festive occasions the jewels on the king's raiment would be so closely set as to totally conceal the fabric beneath. With Philippe, however, the passion for jewelry seemed to reflect an avidity that went deeper than a desire to impress. Fortunately for him he had a wife who took no interest in adornment; otherwise, wrote Liselotte, they would have had a constant battle over who was wearing the best gems. When Aunt Sophie visited the French court in 1679, although she was charmed by the prince and thought him the perfect host, she left no doubt that his interest in gems was peculiar to say the least. During her very first evening at the Palais Royal and in Paris the prince could think of nothing better to do than to take her on a tour of inspection of his collection of jewels as well as of the bejeweled trousseau of his oldest daughter, Marie Louise, who was soon to marry the king of Spain. After admiring all—the fantastic diamonds, rubies, and sapphires and the bridal dress, which was seemingly made entirely of cloth of gold—the duchess found her own toilette attracting the critical eye of her host. "And as he is especially knowledgeable about such things," she wrote, "he took pains to rearrange all my jewelry with the desire of rendering them more fashionable."[22] A few days later, when Monsieur escorted her to be presented to Maria Theresa, the introduction made, he immediately played the light of his candle over the queen's jewels, inviting the visitor to admire their richness. "I can scarcely look at the precious stones for the pleasure I take in being able to see the queen herself," demurred Sophie diplomatically, taking the candle from the prince's hand.[23] Imperturbable to the end, when the duchess left the court Monsieur made a gift to her young daughter of a dozen diamond buttons and as many diamond-studded boutonnieres together with precise instructions on their proper positioning on dress or sleeve.[24]

Nowhere, of course, was the prince's passion for jewels better reflected than in his personal collection. It is described in detail in the inventory after his death, impeccable in this regard, where their total value is estimated at 1,623,922 livres. Set in rings, brooches, earrings, studs, and buttons and imbedded in sword handles, crosses, snuffboxes and all manner of bric-a-brac, the stones tested the limits of the jeweler's art and provided a nearly inexhaustible arsenal from which the prince could choose according to the occasion. Some of the pieces he had inherited—from his mother or from Mademoiselle, for example; some he had received as gifts— such as a diamond-studded snuffbox from the king of Spain; and some he had bought for himself.[25] In the words of the *Mercure Galant*, in describing one of those ceremonies in which Monsieur had appeared in blinding radiance of gems: "The words do not exist that can do justice to its magnificence."

During his life Monsieur derived great satisfaction and much recognition from his contemporaries for his artistry, most especially for his building of Saint-Cloud. The *Gazette* and the *Muse Historique* were insatiable on the subject of the *délicieuse maison* and its charms. The young Saint-Simon, who saw it in its years of final glory, wrote: "The pleasures of every sort of play, the singular beauty of the site . . . , [and] the fine table made of [Saint-Cloud] a house of pure delight with much grandeur and magnificence."[26] Lister, visiting near the end of the century when the work of Monsieur was nearly complete, was especially impressed by the manner in which the prince had taken advantage of the natural beauty of the site. Whereas the king's palace at Versailles was set "in a very ungrateful soil," that of Monsieur, he wrote, with its view from the balustrade in the upper garden of the river Seine and the "plain bounded by Paris . . . makes a most delightful prospect." The vast park was arranged not for hunting, as at Versailles, but for promenades on horseback or by carriage through well-shaded alleys interspersed with basins and fountains. Wildlife flourished in the protected preserve. "These vast riding gardens are unknown to us in England," he commented. "I saw in some of the quarters not only partridges and hares plentifully, but ... five biches or female red-deer feed-ing."[27] The impressions of Aunt Sophie, although from an earlier date and from a woman's perspective, were not dissimilar. "I greatly admired his splendid gallery, his handsome salon, and the cleanli-ness of all things," she wrote in her memoirs, "for [Monsieur] has a marvelous understanding of how to keep a house. I was assigned a chamber from which I could enter the garden, which is the most beautiful in the world both for its site and for its waterfall."[28] Even after seeing Versailles her enthusiasm did not diminish. There at Versailles she continued, "expense has wrought more marvels than nature. I should prefer Saint-Cloud, if I had to choose."[29] In the published descriptions of Versailles and Saint-Cloud specifically ap-proved by both the king and Monsieur in 1681, the author com-pared the châteaus to "two sisters whose beauty is different and of whom it might be said that while the older sister [Versailles] is the more beautiful, the younger [Saint-Cloud] has a better bearing [air]."[30]

In his late years Philippe took special pride in his last major embellishment, the lower waterfall, the creation of Mansart. A de-scription of both cascades published on Monsieur's orders informs us that the two, upper and lower, were designed to be "regarded as an object of magnificence by the [French] people as well as a source of astonishment for foreigners." After detailing the number of ba-sins, pools, fountains, and pyramids, to say nothing of the (orna-mental) tortoises, frogs, and crayfish, the author concluded grandly that "these waterfalls have no equal elsewhere in the world."[31] And impress they did. Dangeau, diarist of the court in the 1690s, tells us in 1699 that the grand dauphin thought the falls "très-magnifique," while the king himself found them "perfectly beautiful."[32] Mon-sieur, proud of his success, permitted the falls and fountains to play for the public even in his absence. The Parisians who thronged the garden each evening "had nothing but praise for the goodness of His Royal Highness."[33]

Unfortunately for the memory of Monsieur, little of his architec-tural and collector's work remains to be admired today. Within a year of his death Madame auctioned off those of his jewels that he had not specifically bequeathed to his wife and daughters.[34] During the French Revolution, Louis Philippe Joseph, duke of Orléans, bet-ter known as Philippe Egalité, then close to bankruptcy, sold almost the entire collection of oil paintings of the house of Orléans, many of which had been acquired by his great-great-grandfather.[35] The Palais Royal still stands, but being the place of business of the Council of State, the Ministry of Culture, and the Constitutional

Council, it may not be visited. Although its facades and garden are familiar landmarks in the center of Paris, they are far more reminiscent of the eighteenth- and nineteenth-century alterations and additions of Monsieur's descendants than of his own work on the palace. Of the château and park of Saint-Cloud, his crowning artistic achievement, little remains. The palace itself was burned during the Franco-Prussian War, and for political reasons the ruins were razed in 1891. (Having been one of the preferred residences of Napoleon I and Napoleon III, it had become a symbol of Bonapartism as well as of the old monarchy.) Only a small marble dais and rows of yew trees mark its former placement. The great waterfall and the park may still be enjoyed. They hold the status of a national domain and are well maintained by the state and by a small group of dedicated enthusiasts organized as Les Amis du Parc de Saint-Cloud. But the shape and composition of the cascade, especially the lower one, are very different from Monsieur's designs, while the park is reduced in size and devoid of much of its once elaborate gardens and statuary. Together they are pallid reminders of their former glory.

FINANCIAL MANAGEMENT

The cost of Monsieur's palaces, collections, and style of life was obviously enormous. How did he pay for it all? "With money from the king" has always been the ready answer, which, if it is largely the truth, is not quite the whole truth, and which certainly leaves many questions unanswered. Why did Louis place such extravagant funds at his brother's disposition? Did not this generosity conflict with his determination never to permit the prince to enjoy the means to oppose the royal will? How precisely did he allocate the subsidies? Were in fact these sums adequate to support both the prince's lavish projects and his flamboyant style of life, which included heavy gambling and the support of favorites without number? How did the prince and his financial administration make use of the royal bounty? Was there any rational plan of investment, or did the prince, fast on the road to debt and ruin, as Liselotte persisted in thinking, simply squander it all as quickly as it came in?

Of all these unresolved questions the first two are probably the most easily answered. The king's pensions and gifts to his brother did not contravene his policy of subordinating him to the Crown; they complemented it instead. They were entirely consonant with his method of domesticating the greater nobility in general. Louis wanted his great nobles and his brother to live extravagantly so that they would reflect his glory as the Sun King. The key to his success was his ability to reduce them to financial dependence on him at the same time. As a result of his patronage, a noble might enjoy immense wealth, but it would be the wealth of a courtier, not that of a landed proprietor of independent means.[36] To use academic jargon, the pensions were "soft money" that rendered the recipient dependent on the donor. He had no "tenure," or vested right, to the funds and could lose them if he stepped out of line. In the case of Monsieur, the king had been able to apply this method with effortless ease: the young prince, as a fils de France, possessed nothing that had not emanated from the Crown. Until 1693, when he inherited the remains of the fortune of la Grande Mademoiselle, excepting only the relatively small income from his appanage, his financial dependence on his brother was almost total.

Thanks to the recent availability to scholars of the archives of the house of Orléans, the remaining questions may be answered more completely and precisely than was possible even a decade or so ago. Buried in the private papers of the family are records of what Philippe and his council were doing with the wealth at their disposal. Although many lacunae and gray areas remain, the documents yield new evidence of Monsieur's investments and estate management that were to have an influence on the future of his house of which his contemporaries (and no doubt Monsieur himself) could have had no comprehension.

A review of Monsieur's principal sources of income between 1661, the time of his first marriage, and 1693, when he inherited the Montpensier succession, reveals that they were primarily of two kinds: pensions and grants of various sorts from the Crown and revenue from his appanage. Of the two the first was by far the more important. According to the "Inventaire des titres du duc d'Orléans [Monsieur]" in the family archives,[37] he received from the king each year a Crown pension of 560,000 livres for life; another pension of 150,000 livres from stipulated tax receipts; a grant of 100,000 livres for "extraordinary expenses of his household"; in 1661 (and again in 1671 on the occasion of his second marriage) a brevet or gift of 252,000 livres "for the maintenance of the household of Madame"; and an additional 150,000 livres on the birth of a son, to be paid during the child's life. (One son, born in 1664, died two years later; another, born in 1673, died in 1676; the third, the future regent, was born in 1674 and outlived Monsieur.) Thus, for most of these years between 1661 and 1693, Monsieur received an annual income from the Crown of 1,212,000 livres. Beyond this bounty, the prince received grants from the king for special expenses: dowries for his daughters, war chests for his military campaigns, and in 1680, a brevet of 600,000 livres to be paid from the royal treasury over a three-year period that probably went to furnishing and decorating the château of Saint-Cloud. Moreover, it should not be forgotten that Monsieur had received the property of Saint-Cloud as a gift in 1658 and that after his first marriage in 1661 he also enjoyed the right to occupy the Palais Royal, with most maintenance costs paid by the Bâtiments du Roi until he received it as an addition to his appanage in 1692.

Most of the remainder of his income until 1693 came from his appanage, which was granted him by royal edicts of March 1661 and April 1672. According to the language of the first edict,[38] the appanage was to be of a "grandeur and size" that would enable Philippe "to maintain his house more honorably, to sustain with brilliance any [marriage] alliance he may contract," and "to provide for the male descendants of that marriage." There followed several closely printed pages listing the lands of the appanage with their accompanying "Villes, Cités, Châteaux, Châtellenies, Placet, Maisons, Forteresses, Fruits, Profits, Cens, Rentes, Revenus, Emolumens, Honneurs, Hommages, Vasseaux, Vasselages; Sujets, Bois, Forêts, Etangs, Rivières, Fours, Moulins, Prez, Pâturages, Fiefs," and so on. Yet when the revenues were added up, despite the impressive array of rights and dues, the bottom line showed that the duchies d'Orléans, Valois, and Chartres with the seigneurie of Montargis (the lands comprising the first grant) yielded an annual net income of only 85,640 livres, with an additional 60,384 livres from the aydes of Orléans, Montargis, and Pithiviers—that is, a total annual income of 146,024 livres. The supplementary grant of 1672[39] added to the appanage the duché of Nemours, the comtés of Dourdan and Romorantin, and the marquisat of Coucy and Folembray. These yielded net revenues of approximately 55,000 livres and brought the total income of the appanage to slightly over 200,000 livres. True, these returns made Philippe's duché-pairie the most remunerative in France at the time[40] and would of themselves have admitted him to the ranks of "the great."[41] But in the financial stratosphere inhabited by a fils de France, whose style of life was considered a reflection of the glory of the king, they counted for much less and in fact composed only 16.5 percent of the subsidies regularly received from the Crown and only 14 percent of his total regular income at the time.

Indeed, if the yield of the appanage had been more substantial it might have spelled a degree of real financial independence from the Crown. For although he received it from the king, once his, his right of continuous possession was surer than his claim to royal gifts and pensions. According to the jurisprudence of the day, an appanage was an indemnity to cadet branches for the sovereignty of which they were deprived.[42] Even though it remained part of the king's domain, which in theory was indivisible, it could revert to the Crown only in the absence of a male heir. To resort once more to academic parlance, it came very close to amounting to tenure and effectively sheltered its possessor from the whim or will of the administration (in this case the king).

In 1693 the fortune of the prince was augmented when la Grande Mademoiselle (Mlle de Montpensier, "Mademoiselle," was known as "la Grande Mademoiselle" after the birth of Philippe's first daughter, Marie Louise, who also had the right to the title "Mademoiselle") died after a long illness and designated Monsieur heir to the Montpensier succession (from Marie de Bourbon, duchesse de Montpensier, first wife of Gaston d'Orléans).[43] It was a windfall that has generally been thought to have turned the prince into a Croesus. The inheritance was indeed vast by any normal standards of the day, comprising as it did domains and seigneuries, many held from the Crown and possessing the royal offices, in Auvergne, Normandy, Poitou, Burgundy, Champagne, and Flanders and, in addition, of a collection of rentes on gabelles and on the finances of cities and provinces. Best of all, these lands and rentes became proprietary possessions of the house of Orléans for which Philippe and his heirs were accountable to no one.

Despite Monsieur's pleasure in receiving this fortune, which he had long coveted, his emotions on receiving it must have been mixed. With the death of his cousin he lost the oldest and probably the best friend he had ever had at court. During her long illness the prince and Madame hovered constantly at her bedside (Saint-Simon was so unkind as to say that Monsieur was paying court to her fortune).[44] And from a strictly financial point of view he had reason for disappointment, since owing to Mademoiselle's tragic-comic involvement with Lauzun, the succession had already lost some of its choicest morsels. After the princess had declined to become the second Madame in 1670, she had arranged to marry her guardsman, only to be blocked by the king, who not only forbade the marriage but clapped the lover in prison. After ten years of martyrdom at court while Lauzun languished in the dreaded fortress at Pignerol, Mademoiselle had consented to the extortion the king demanded of her as the price of his liberation: the donation of the principality of Dombes, the county of Eu, and the duchy of Aumale to the eleven-year-old duc de Maine, the idolized oldest son of the king and Mme de Montespan, who thereby became the prince of Dombes and the count of Eu.[45] La Grande Mademoiselle's remaining assets yielded an annual income in the range of 140,000 livres: 60,271 livres from rentes and some 80,000 livres from the domaines and seigneuries (precision is impossible, given the condition of the records).[46] The duc de Maine had been made a gift of approximately one-third of the former income of the princess. Greatly embittered by the experience and unhappy in her last years (her brief "idyll" with Lauzun ended, as might have been expected, in disenchantment, quarrels, and separation), the princess had been obliged to reduce her retinue and to scale down her style of living.[47]

Not only had the Montpensier succession been "plucked" by the king, but its remainder was heavily encumbered by debt. "My father [Gaston, duke of Orléans] had left [many] debts and very little to pay them with," la Grande Mademoiselle had written in her memoirs. She knew whereof she spoke. When Monsieur died a few years later, the Orléans succession was still 2,193,023 livres in debt and required an outlay of over 100,000 livres annually merely to service it.[48] As a result of this debt, the net revenue from the legacy during the prince's lifetime amounted only to some 40,000 livres and composed less than 3 percent of his total income.

The question now to be addressed is what use Monsieur made of his income (chiefly from the Crown, the appanage, and after 1693, the inheritance from la Grande Mademoiselle). Did he manage to balance the annual budget? Did he give important sums to the church or to the poor? How did he manage his appanage and other properties? Did he invest part of his income in land or other assets that augmented the revenues of the appanage and his proprietary holdings in his later life and benefited his descendants in the eighteenth century? Or did he, like many of his noble contemporaries, simply squander his assets and end up saddling his heirs with crushing debt?

Unfortunately, the documentary evidence does not enable us to answer the first of these questions for any given period. No tables of annual expenditures or budgets, if such ever existed, have come down to us in the family archives. We cannot determine methodically how Monsieur spent his money from day to day or even year to year. Some expenses that were reputedly heavy—losses at the gaming table and gifts to his favorites, for example—may not even be guessed at. Although the number of servants and officers in the combined households of Monsieur and Madame increased steadily over the three decades of their marriage—from approximately 850 persons in 1672 to 1,226 in 1698—their toll on the family finances is unclear inasmuch as the king usually, though not invariably, paid their salaries.[49] Nor, as we have seen, can the costs of the building of the palaces and the accumulation of paintings, jewels, and objets d'art be estimated with any precision.

On the other hand, the existing evidence deals considerably better with the remainder of the questions and gives us a fair picture of how, if not always exactly when, the prince made use of the financial resources at his disposal. By an analysis principally of the legacy of Monsieur as set forth in his inventory after death, of his testament, and of financial statements of the house of Orléans in the mid-eighteenth century, his principal investments, donations, and other important financial activities become clear.

The records disclose that Monsieur dispensed relatively little of his fortune in formal charity. Although orthodox in his religious beliefs and assiduous in observance of external forms, he cared nothing for theology, was indifferent toward "the poor," and had no inclination whatever toward "enthusiasm."[50] Like most of his contemporaries, he was little troubled by a social conscience. Such donations as he made began late in life (none is recorded before 1688) and were apparently the result of the warnings of his confessor and a growing awareness of human mortality. The most substantial allocations were for the establishment of a hospital for the poor and a chapel at Saint-Cloud that, after 1690, received annual rentes totaling 5,350 livres. In the 1690s he and Liselotte donated 6,000 livres in cash and 2,800 livres in rentes for another hospital in Normandy. In his last will and testament, after allocating 6,000 livres for masses for the repose of his soul, he donated an additional 10,000 livres to the hospital at Saint-Cloud and another 10,000 livres for the establishment of a similar institution at Villers-Cotterêts.[51] His total recorded charities, including those recognized by his son after his death, could not have exceeded a principal of more than 84,000 livres.[52]

For a fils de France drawing more than one million livres from the royal treasury each year, these figures are not impressive. La Grande Mademoiselle, for example, left some 200,000 livres in charitable donations although she possessed a much smaller annual income.[53] Another contemporary for whom such information is available, Louis II, Phélypeaux, comte de Pontchartrain, the king's chancellor (1699–1714), committed at least 51,000 livres to charity from an estate whose total value in 1714 was no more than one million livres.[54] Perhaps, as his funeral orators affirmed, Monsieur gave generously to an "infinite number of poor" upon occasion and informally.[55] The inventory of the minutes of his council records sporadic gifts of firewood to religious houses during severe weather.[56] Contemporaries noted the liberality with which the prince distributed coins to soldiers while on campaign. At Saint-Cloud the park was always open, and tables of food and wine were set out for the public when the prince received guests in the château.[57] And during the famine of 1693–94 Monsieur was to be seen on the highways and byways from Paris to Brittany flinging money to crowds of eager peasants through the windows of his carriage from a sack between his knees.[58] Such gestures were certainly in keeping with the image of liberality and generosity that the prince (and other "greats" of the day) liked to cultivate. But they did not require parting with any substantial percentage of his assets. The instincts of Monsieur were to accumulate and to acquire, not to give away and distribute. These spontaneous offerings could not have amounted to more than a bagatelle compared with his financial worth.

Although Monsieur gave the impression that he cared little for money and finances, the management of his assets was no casual or slipshod affair. By the 1680s and 1690s the prince's council entrusted with overseeing the administration of the appanage and the proprietary holdings of the house numbered between sixty and seventy men. Its two chief officers were the chancellor and guardian of the seals and the superintendent of the domains and finances. There was also a grand master of waters and forests, a controller general of finances, a general treasurer, and to handle burgeoning legal problems, a *procureur général* (state's attorney), a half-dozen *maîtres de requêtes* (venal officers who handled the Crown's legal affairs), and a staff of lawyers. A historiographer, an interpreter of foreign languages, and a host of secretaries filled in the ranks. Together they are evidence of the complexity of managing the assets of the brother of the king.[59]

The Appanage

The imprint of Monsieur and his council on the appanage can be perceived very clearly even if it cannot always be measured precisely in monetary return. The circumstances in which the prince received the appanage in 1661 and 1672 could scarcely have been less auspicious. Generally across France rentes from land were entering a period of decline that continued to the end of the century.[60] Before the Colbertian reforms of the 1660s the forests of the realm were rapidly being depleted, the result of corrupt and neglectful administration of the *grand maîtres des eaux et forêts*.[61] The appanage itself was in the most appalling disorder, the former appanagiste, Gaston, having neglected it almost totally. Many of the seigneurial dues had gone uncollected for decades; records of feudal dependence of one fief on another had often been lost. The great forest of Orléans—which extended over thirty-five square leagues, or approximately eighty-five square miles—and the smaller forests of the appanage yielded scarcely enough wood to cover the costs of their administration and showed no profit whatever. Finally, although this was not Gaston's fault, the greater part of the appanage had been mortgaged—that is, pawned (*engagé*)—in the past by the Crown and brought in little or no revenue.[62]

The work of Monsieur and/or his council to increase the profitability of the appanage took three principal forms: rationalizing and reforming its administration, buying back or redeeming mortgaged lands, and, above all, constructing canals for transporting wood to Paris. To some extent all these efforts began as early as the 1660s, but with the augmentation of the prince's revenues in later years they increased dramatically in the 1680s and 1690s.

Reform and rationalization meant in large part verifying the prince's seigneurial rights, searching for those that had fallen into disuse, measuring and surveying parts of the forests, repossessing lands and rights that had been usurped, and systematically collecting the myriad fees, dues, *cens*, *banalités*, *rentes foncières*, and so on, with which the lands of the appanage were encumbered. These aims were accomplished chiefly by stimulating the zeal of the contractors (*fermiers*) who leased the land (and who therefore stood always between the prince and the cultivators), by appointing *vérificateurs* charged with examining records of parishes, notaries, and special tribunals, and by requiring residents to present proof of their claimed rights to fish in the Loire or to pasture their beasts on the commons. These efforts culminated in 1676 in the drawing up of a monumental *terrier général*, which served the family administrators until the middle of the eighteenth century, when it was revised on the order of Monsieur's grandson. All of the tactics above reflected an advance or improvement in the science of measurement, classification, and general policing of seigneurial holdings and, moreover, were not unlike similar administrative reforms taking place elsewhere in the kingdom. Often labeled a seigneurial reaction, this activity was, in the case of Philippe's council at least, simply a practical attempt to make up for years of neglect and to avail itself of better techniques of estate administration.[63]

THE NUMEROUS FORESTS of the appanage presented an even greater challenge to Monsieur's administration owing to their virtually limitless but unexploited potential for revenue. In the seventeenth century wood was the principal source of energy. Forests were thus the rough equivalent, financially, of oil wells in the twentieth century. Chief among them were the two largest forests of the realm, the vast forest of Orléans bordering the Loire River and the forest of Retz (locally known as the forest of Villers-Cotterêts) in Valois, renowned for its venerable stands of oaks.[64] Their condition in the early 1660s can best be described as chaotic. That they yielded no revenue was bad enough; even worse was the threat to their very existence. Gaston, habitually short of funds, had recklessly cut and sold the prized *haute futaie*, trees between fifty and one hundred years of age.[65] Alienation of land by previous appanagists, encroachments of neighboring seigneurs, religious houses, and peasant communes, ravages of herds of unauthorized livestock, poaching of peasants claiming the right of *chauffage*, and the irrational and often indiscriminate cutting of timber were diminishing their acreage and destroying the trees at a rate that, if continued, would result in their total destruction within 150 years.

The solutions of the council to these problems may have been neither enlightened nor entirely productive, but at least they brought a semblance of order to the administration and halted the destruction. For the most part they complied with the general reform of the forests of the realm undertaken by Colbert in the 1660s that culminated in a comprehensive forest ordinance of 1669.[66] Monsieur, however, retained his own officers within the forests of the appanage and did not replace the *grands maîtres*, possessors of venal offices, with *commissaires*, salaried officials, in the forest of Orléans as was done elsewhere in the kingdom.[67] Attempting to repossess lands alienated in the past and to halt poaching and other abuses, the council revoked all old rights and provided monetary compensation to their possessors. The forests were then closed as places of pasture except on payment of a fee, and as sources of heating and cooking fuel (with exceptions made for certain religious communities). To preserve existing timber, the council forbade harvesting trees younger than sixty years, a policy later deplored but in line with the best-known forest practices of the day.

How much these administrative reforms and innovations may have cost Monsieur and what may have been their exact monetary return cannot be known. The geographic dispersion of the appanage, its mixture of farms and forests, and the complexity of its revenues rendered the work long and arduous. A memoir written in 1790 or 1791 reviewing the history of the appanage informs us merely that the terrier général of 1676 was drawn up *à grands frais* (at great expense) and that the good administration of the family was "in very large part" responsible for the large increases in its revenues. The memoirist concluded that it would be no exaggeration to put at twenty million livres the amount that the house of Orléans spent on management of the appanage from 1661 to 1790.[68] From these generalizations and other evidence the only thing that may be said with confidence is that Monsieur and his council were willing to invest substantial rather than trifling sums on rationalizing the appanage and that, to judge by subsequent developments, they were successful to no small degree.

Another important contribution to the profitability of the appanage was the buying back or redemption of domains that had been mortgaged in the past and consequently had brought no revenue to the appanagist. Monsieur's first acquisition was the châtellenie of Beaugency in the duchy of Orléans, only one of whose ten châtellenies had been free in 1661. Redeemed in 1665 for the sum of 152,975 livres, it lay downriver from the city of Orléans with a *domaine utile* of approximately twenty-one square miles composed of islands, meadows, and most important of all, some nine acres of forest (the buisson de Briou). From its much larger *domaine directe*, Monsieur henceforth had the right to collect myriad dues and fees as well as the *cens*, quitrent, and *lods et ventes*. With an estimated annual revenue of approximately 5,100 livres, it was second in size and monetary return in the appanage only to the châtellenie of Orléans.[69]

His second important acquisition was the seigneurie of La Ferté-Milon in Valois, which was redeemed in 1694 for the sum of 90,000 livres. With a *domaine utile* consisting of a crumbling château and the usual mixture of seigneurial rights and dues, it had an estimated annual revenue of not more than 3,000 livres. However, included in the price of redemption was the right to a percentage of the returns from the sale of wood from the 176 acres of the magnificent oaks of the forest of Retz; hence its value in the future could be expected to increase appreciably. By these acquisitions alone Monsieur had immediately raised the annual estimated revenues of the appanage by some 8,100 livres, a figure not impressive compared with his total income, to be sure, but that nonetheless represented an increase of nearly 10 percent of the total annual revenue of 1661 from the duchies of Orléans, Valois, and Chartres (85,640 livres) and of 4 percent

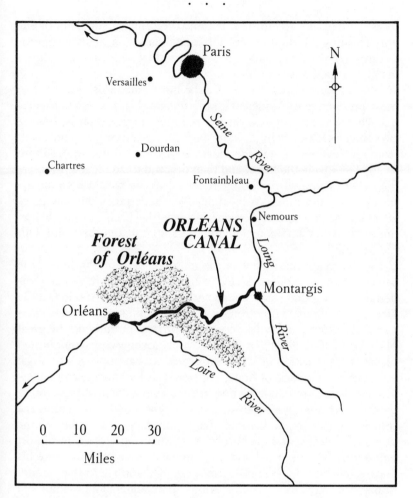

MAP TWO. Orléans Canal

of the estimated income (200,000 livres) of the appanage as a whole
after the supplementary grant of 1672.[70]

However, by far the most important contributions of Monsieur
to the increase of the profitability of the appanage were the construction of the Orléans Canal linking the Loire with the Loing
River and, to a much less extent, the canalization of the Ourcq River
in Valois. These waterways made possible for the first time the
cheap and efficient transport of wood from the forests of Orléans
and Retz to the city of Paris. By the eighteenth century the two

forests, especially the former, became the primary suppliers of energy (heating and lighting) of the capital and with the rise of price of timber in the latter half of the century they yielded over half the income of the house of Orléans.

The Orléans Canal was by far the most ambitious and also the most productive of Monsieur's investments. It involved constructing what was known as a canal *à point de partage*—that is, linking two rivers separated by a watershed. The waterway would climb from an elevation of 321 feet upstream from Orléans on the Loire to 407 feet inside the forest and then descend to 262 feet at Montargis, where it joined the Loing River. Its route would be approximately forty-five miles. At the time it was undertaken the only precedent for such a feat of engineering was the Briare Canal, begun under Henry IV and completed in 1642, that linked the Loire with the Seine.[71]

Involving an investment in the range of two million livres, the canal, if built in modern times, would undoubtedly have been undertaken by the state and funded with public money. And in fact the king and Colbert, who strongly favored facilitating internal navigation by canals, and who were in the process of building the great Midi Canal (1666–81), watched closely over every complicated phase of construction of Monsieur's canal. It was approved by royal edicts of the Council of State, registered in Parlement, and supervised and brought to completion in 1692 by Jean de Creil, the intendant of Orléans. Nonetheless, although the canal was within the prince's appanage, it became the proprietary possession of the house of Orléans, and the burden of its financing was borne almost entirely by Monsieur, who at one time was forced to mortgage his appanage (with the express permission of the king) to the amount of 600,000 livres to buy out previous shareholders and assume full ownership of the completed waterway.[72] Moreover, from the very time of its inception the purpose of the canal was not the promotion of general commerce and the prosperity of the realm but rather the more narrow aim of transporting wood from the forest of Orléans to Paris. When the project originated in the latter half of the 1670s it was designed simply as a small channel originating within the forest to carry timber northeast to the Loing River. Monsieur received the right to build a canal between the two rivers only in 1679.[73] If in time the completed canal was used for shipping grain and other goods to the capital, it little benefited the city of Orléans and may have, at least at times, actually have done it harm. Its point of departure was not within the city, for the convenience of local merchants, but rather five miles upstream. Moreover, in times of famine, when the king desired to provision the capital from the fertile soil of the Beauce, north of the Loire, the canal proved all too effective a conduit for draining the countryside of requisitioned grain and depriving the local people of their food supply. Neither Monsieur himself nor his council ever gave the slightest indication of interest in the general prosperity of the region. Their concern was solely with the profits to be realized from the sale of timber. Consequently, in 1694 the new intendant of Orléans would conclude that while the Orléans Canal was "a very fine work" that was useful to the city of Paris, "it was in effect very detrimental to the city of Orléans and to all the parishes on the main road from Orléans to Paris."[74]

The administration of Monsieur also undertook the canalization of the Ourcq, a small river flowing into the Marne. A much less ambitious project than the Orléans Canal, it called for introducing weirs to raise the water level at low stages so that wood might be floated downstream to the Marne and ultimately to Paris. Even so, it amounted to an outlay of nearly 300,000 livres for construction, procurement of the *droit de péage*, and indemnities to residents with riparian rights.[75] This canal, unlike the Orléans Canal, remained within the appanage and was not a proprietary possession of the house.

Increasing the Revenues of the Appanage

The significance of the work of Monsieur and/or his council in the appanage can be better appreciated by a glance at its income in the mid-eighteenth century as compiled by the superintendant of finances of Monsieur's grandson, Louis, then duke of Orléans (see table 1). The totals listed represent the averages of the yearly income the family received from the appanage for the years 1734–43.

Most impressive of all these figures is the enormous increase in the total revenues of the appanage since Philippe received it. The bottom line reveals that by the mid-eighteenth century it was yielding an income of well over one million livres compared with the approximately 200,000 livres it had produced in 1672. In other words, in a period of sixty to seventy years the monetary return of the appanage had increased nearly 600 percent. Equally impressive, even astonishing, is that the proceeds from the sale of timber were then close to 600,000 livres and thus constituted over half of the total income of the appanage in the 1740s. In the 1660s and 1670s, it will be remembered, wood from the forests had yielded the family no income whatever. In harvesting timber and delivering it for sale to Parisians, the house of Orléans had indeed "struck oil." The other, slightly smaller half of the income, 587,295 livres, came from the traditional sources of seigneurial and feudal dues, including fees paid by holders of venal offices, and represented an increase of nearly three times the income of 1672 (when there was no income from wood).

To what extent can the investments and management of Monsieur and/or his council have contributed to this dramatic growth? First of all, the acquisitions and the construction of the Ourcq Canal were yielding an annual revenue of 41,085 livres in the 1740s: 8,085 from Beaugency; 30,000 livres from the canal (which was leased); and at least 3,000 livres from La Ferté-Milon. Thus Philippe's investments during his lifetime were yielding a revenue of more than 20 percent of the 200,000 livres the appanage produced when he received it. They also accounted for nearly 11 percent of the increase in profitability experienced between 1672 and the 1740s. Such returns on his investments were surely solid if not spectacular.

These acquisitions, however, constituted but a small part of his effective contribution to the enhancement of the estate. The administrative reforms that culminated in the terrier général of 1676 must

TABLE ONE
Average Annual Revenue of the Appanage, 1734–43, in Livres

Donation of 1661		
Duché d'Orléans	447,621	14.1
Duché de Chartres	11,886	11.1
Duché de Valois	28,073	16.1
Seigneurie de Montargis	11,076	14.7
Supplement of 1672		
Duché de Nemours (see Montargis)		
Comté de Dourdan (see Chartres)		
Comté de Romorentin	9,344	
Marquis de Coucy and Folembray (see Valois)		
Appanage in General		
Parties casuelles des offices	69,291	13
Sale of timber	596,453	
Messageries	10,000	
TOTAL	1,183,748	7.7
Recapitulation		
Sale of timber	596,453	
All other revenue	587,295	7.7
TOTAL	1,183,748	7.7

Source: "Etat des biens de la maison d'Orléans, 1748," AN 300 AP I 826.

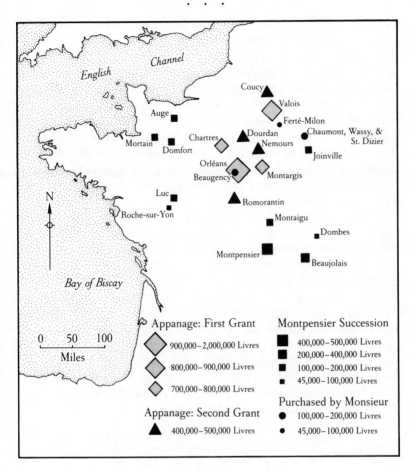

MAP THREE. Lands of Monsieur in France

have borne their fruit, even though they cannot be measured precisely in monetary returns. Nothing in the record of either the regent or Monsieur's grandson Louis can explain the dramatic rise in profits in their time. Philippe II enlarged the appanage only slightly, his acquisitions yielding a mere 7,178 livres annually. The redemptions Louis effected took place after the financial statement of 1748 had been compiled. Neither instituted administrative changes of any importance, although it is true that the regent was able to exploit his official position to obtain favorable leases from the fermiers. Until the latter half of the eighteenth century both continued to rely on the work of Monsieur's *vérificateurs* and their resulting register of property assessments.

It was in the forests, of course, that Monsieur's administration had been most effective. It had not only halted their destruction and reformed their governance and harvesting, but had increased their extent by additions to the forests of Orléans and Retz and, above all, had constructed canals to provide economical transport of the timber to Paris. In Gaston's time the administrators of the forests had been lucky if they broke even; Monsieur's council, availing itself of the enlightened zeal of Colbert, understood the immense potential of the forests of the appanage and made possible its realization. The administrators of the regent and Louis continued the intelligent work of their ancestor, continuing to build on his practices, but their investments would have availed them little without the innovations and vast expenditures of Monsieur.

*Proprietary Possession and Orleanist Wealth
in the Mid-Eighteenth Century*

Not content with the legacy of la Grande Mademoiselle, Monsieur and/or his council acquired additional lands and assets outside the appanage. Together these became the core of a great landed fortune that by the middle of the eighteenth century exceeded even the appanage in its revenue. Most of these investments came late in Philippe's life, after he had fallen heir to the Montpensier succession, and were designed principally either to round it out or to acquire additional rights within it. They consisted of purchase of the offices of the *controlleurs des actes des notaires* in the comté de Mortain and vicomté d'Auge (lower Normandy) in 1696 for 50,749 livres; redemption of a legacy of 100,000 livres bequeathed by Mlle de Guise to the princess de Harcourt in February for 50,000 livres; and purchase of the domains of Chaumont, Wassy, and Saint-Dizier in Champagne, lands once part of the Montpensier succession and

TABLE TWO
Average Annual Revenue in Livres of
Proprietary Acquisitions of Monsieur, 1734–1743

Actes des notaires	28,000
Legacy of Mlle de Guise	4,166
Chaumont, Wassy, and Saint-Dizier	20,706
Orléans Canal (lease of tolls)	100,793
Carrosses d'Orléans	25,000
TOTAL	178,665

Source: "Etat des biens de la maison d'Orléans, 1748," AN 300 AP I 826.

held from the Crown that had been alienated, for a total of 370,000 livres in July 1699. Other proprietary investments of Monsieur unconnected with the legacy from la Grande Mademoiselle were the Orléans Canal (not part of the appanage although situated within it) discussed earlier and the right to license public stagecoaches traveling between Paris and the towns and cities in the duchy of Orléans (*carrosses d'Orléans*) in April 1701 for 287,917 livres. All told, Monsieur expended a total of 2,758,666 livres in additions to the proprietary holdings of his house.[76]

By the 1740s these proprietary investments were proving their worth by yielding an average annual revenue of 178,665 livres (see table 2). This figure represents not only a respectable 6 percent return on his original investment (even excluding the contribution of the Orléans Canal to the profitability of the appanage, which was its chief purpose) but a startling increase of over 100 percent of the total gross income generated by the Montpensier succession when Philippe received it in 1693. Stated another way, as can be seen from the total income of 1,355,258 livres the family derived from its proprietary possessions in the 1740s (see table 3), the proprietary acquisitions of Monsieur were responsible for 13 percent of the total revenues from those holdings.

These investments by Monsieur began the process of emancipating the house of Orléans from its financial bondage to the Crown. By the mid-eighteenth century, as can be seen from table 3, its in-

TABLE THREE
Average Annual Revenue of the House of Orléans in Livres, 1734–1743

Appanage	1,183,748	7.7
Patrimonial possessions	1,215,080	6.9
Domains held from the king (patrimonial)	140,178	7.10
Personal income of Louis, duke of Orléans	135,000	0.0
TOTAL	2,674,007	2.2

Source: "Etat des biens de la maison d'Orléans, 1748," AN 300 AP I 826,
"Table du présent Etat."

come came primarily from land and other investments to which it had a proprietary or other legal right rather than from pensions or grants from the Crown.

Aside from the spectacular increase in income reflected in the bottom line, the most striking change that emerges from the figures above is the reduction of income the family received as royal largess only some forty years after the death of Monsieur. Whereas Philippe had drawn over one million livres regularly from the Crown each year, his grandson as first prince of the blood received a pension of only 150,000 livres, which, after subjection to the *dixième* tax, yielded him a mere 135,000 livres. Monsieur had depended on his brother for the bulk of his income. Louis drew only some 5 percent of his annual revenue from the Crown. On the death of the regent (who had helped himself generously from the royal treasury) in 1723, Louis XV had abruptly discontinued payment of household expenses, dowries, war chests, and so on, to the duke of Orléans.[77] In part his decision was the natural result of the increased distance of relationship between the families. Whereas Louis XIV had been the brother of Monsieur, Louis XV, his great grandson, was the second cousin once removed of Louis, duke of Orléans. It was also no doubt a reflection of the king's personal dislike of Louis, who, possessed of an unfortunate temperament, had managed early on to alienate himself from most of his relatives.[78]

The members of the house of Orléans were no longer courtiers dependent upon the Crown for their lavish life-style. By the mid-eighteenth century the income from the patrimonial possessions, to which it was accountable to no one, exceeded even that from the appanage. And the appanage itself and its revenues, even though by law they were inseparable from the Crown, could not be touched by the king so long as the dukes did not fail to provide a succession of male heirs.

Evaluation of Monsieur as an Investor and Estate Manager

What do these figures suggest may have been the total value of the investments Monsieur made over the course of his adult life? Acquisitions (including redemptions) of seigneuries and the canalization of the Ourcq River in the appanage amounted to 542,975 livres; the Orléans Canal and acquisitions of land and other income-bearing assets outside the appanage came to a total of 2,758,666 livres. To this should be added 2,193,023 livres for the amount owed on the Orléans succession, an inescapable obligation if Monsieur were to accept the Montpensier legacy for the future enrichment of the house: a total of 5,494,664 livres. This total, however, includes neither the cost of the terrier général and other administrative reforms nor that of his jewels, paintings, and objets d'art and of the park and château of Saint-Cloud. These last were expenditures that, besides affording him immediate gratification, frequently appreciated in value later on. Although we have no means of putting a precise figure on them, they could not have, all told, amounted to less than two million livres and probably cost him much more. Therefore the assumption seems reasonable that his investments of one kind or another that bore fruit in the eighteenth century lay at least in the range of seven and one-half million livres. Averaged over the forty years of Philippe's adult life, they reflect an annual outlay of some 187,500 livres.

Cited in isolation this figure is, of course, meaningless. Although 187,500 livres was more than the total annual income of almost any of "the great" except the princes of the blood, can it be considered a substantial allocation of capital for Philippe, in comparison with the magnitude of wealth at his command? The answer appears to be yes. For though it cannot be related to Monsieur's annual gross income (for which no records exist), it works out to have been over 15 percent of the 1,212,000 livres that he received more or less regularly from the Crown and that throughout his life composed the bulk of his revenue—not a negligible rate of reinvestment even for a fils de France.

The record of the investments and estate management of Monsieur and/or his council was one of the better-kept secrets at court. Hence the persistence at court of Monsieur's image as the wastrel who squandered every sou as quickly as he could lay hands on it in pursuit of his dubious pleasures. Not the least of those perpetuating this myth was Liselotte. To her dying day she believed (or at least said she believed) that Monsieur had left nothing behind but his debts and had failed to make adequate provision for her. Like many a wife before and after her, she apparently knew nothing of the true condition of the family finances. Her knowledge was limited to what she saw every day: her husband's habitual gambling and his lavish presents to his favorites.[79]

The truth, course, was very different but still of a kind, rooted in French law and not in the alleged improvidence of her husband, not likely to quell the complaints of the aggrieved widow. On Monsieur's death his estate passed not to Liselotte but to his son, the future regent. Liselotte was left with the legal provision that had been hers ever since the day of her marriage: a dower house at Montargis and a stipend of 40,000 livres a year.[80] Small wonder if these arrangements spelled impoverishment to a princess accustomed to the splendors of Saint-Cloud and the Palais Royal and to the service of a staff numbering in the hundreds. She was in fact spared this fate by the generosity of the king and, after his death, by that of the regent. Liselotte was able to live out the twenty-one years of her widowhood either at Versailles or in the palaces of Monsieur with every luxury and perquisite of rank she had ever enjoyed. If she ever learned anything of the truth about the financial holdings of the family and their revenues, she did not share it with her German relatives.

One additional aspect of Monsieur's financial legacy remains to be examined before the role of his administration can be clearly defined: his indebtedness. (Liselotte was aware that the prince left debts, although she got the figures wrong.) The inventory of his financial obligations made upon his death, which is fortunately intact, reveals (see table 4) that he had not been able to invest for the future without substantial borrowing.

At first glance a total indebtedness exceeding nine million livres requiring more than 400,000 livres annually to service would seem to undo at a stroke any idea of Monsieur as the founder of the family fortune and instead to cast him as its prodigal prince. If so,

TABLE FOUR
Indebtedness of Monsieur upon His Death, in Livres

Nature and Purpose of Debt	Principal	Debt Service
Rentes perpétuelles	5,521,180	276,059
Construction of Orléans Canal		
Park of Saint-Cloud		
Charitable foundations		
Pensions and *rentes viagères*	480,000	24,000
To retiring members of household		
To individuals for money borrowed		
(purpose unspecified)		
Unspecified instruments	2,193,023	105,177
Owed on Orléans succession		
(includes Montpensier)		
Bills outstanding	1,115,355	Little
Wages to officers of household		or none
Wages for construction of Orléans		
Canal and other construction		
Total	9,309,558	405,236

Source: "Inventaire après décès de Monsieur, AN 300 AP I 746.
Note: Dated June 17, 1701, the section on debts began: "Declarant mon dit Seigneur Duc d'Orléans [Philippe II] qu'ayant pris connaissance depuis la mort de SAR Monsieur de l'Etat des affaires de sa Maison Il a trouvé qu'il étoit deu par Sa ditte AR les sommes cy après mentionnées."

he would have been no different from the princes of the blood and other *grands seigneurs* of his day who generally bequeathed crushing debts to their heirs. Upon analysis, however, the record of Philippe emerges in a more favorable light. Over half of his debts were in *rentes perpétuelles*, whose principal could not be called. Approximately one-fifth were for construction of canals that multiplied revenues from forests and for buildings and land in the park of Saint-Cloud. The latter brought no income, it is true, but they proved eventually to have been a farsighted investment in real estate. Valued at 1,031,740 livres (excluding furnishings) in 1723 after the death of the regent,[81] the château and park of Saint-Cloud were sold to Queen Marie Antoinette in 1784 for six million livres.[82] Moreover, a sizable amount of Monsieur's indebtedness arose out of conditions over which he had little or no control. In 1699, for example, the king, hard pressed for money, abruptly reduced Philippe's annual stipend and obliged him to assume responsibility for part of his household expenses. Monsieur was obliged to alienate 20,000 livres of rente on a principal of 400,000 livres to pay the officers and merchants serving his house.[83] The indebtedness of the Orléans succession was the unavoidable penalty for acceptance of the Montpensier legacy. The pensions paid to retiring personnel of his household were also virtually obligatory. Similar arrangements, even exceeding those of Philippe in liberality, were made by each of the successive dukes of Orléans in the Old Regime, even by the penurious Louis. In fact, only a very small part of Monsieur's indebtedness arose from sumptuary spending and other expenses that would not increase the wealth of the family in the future. Weighed against the enormous returns they were to bring in the eighteenth century, Philippe's investments (and consequent indebtedness) were well worth the "burden" he bequeathed his son.

What conclusions may finally be drawn from this analysis of the administration of Monsieur's assets over his adult life? What were the effects of his work upon his heirs? First of all, it must be admitted that we have no way of determining who was the mastermind of the estate management—whether it was Philippe, his chancellor and superintendent of finances, his council as a whole, or some combination of them. Among his contemporaries, Monsieur had a reputation for childlike insouciance, for wishing to know nothing about his finances while he went about building his châteaus, collecting his jewels and paintings, and rewarding his favorites.[84] And it is true that his signature appears but rarely in the minutes of his council.

Even so, the evidence is too fragmentary to rule him out or to assign the responsibility to others. The council's record in buying properties and amassing wealth was entirely consonant with the acquisitive, even avaricious, instincts of the prince that had manifested themselves ever since his youth.[85] Moreover, despite Louis's unwavering resolution to bar his brother from his administration, the prince had maintained close relations with a number of important ministers, notably Colbert and Louvois, and as possessor of a large appanage he had an acknowledged stake in the realm. The king had long permitted him to attend his Council of Dispatches, which supervised internal affairs of the realm: forests, public works, charitable institutions, and the like. The only government body of which Monsieur was a member, and probably its least important, it nonetheless would have afforded him information indispensable, for example, in constructing the Orléans Canal and implementing reform of the forests.[86] Doubtless Monsieur did not concern himself with detail. Probably like Louis he believed that great projects should be completed regardless of expense. Great kings and their brothers should not be expected to count costs like tradesmen or accountants. Notwithstanding, it was with the prince's authorization that the council made its decisions, and it was on him and his successors that their effects were felt.

Second, the fundamentally conservative and pragmatic nature of the management is striking. Most of the acts of Monsieur's council were designed to increase revenues from traditional forms of wealth, whether woodland or seigneuries. Very little capital was allocated in rentes; speculation in mercantile or colonial ventures was eschewed altogether. Only in the construction of canals was there evidence of a willingness to innovate or of a connection with commerce. Neither Philippe nor his council seems to have had any theoretical interest in economics or any inclination to utilize the immense assets at their disposal for any purpose other than the narrow one of immediate enrichment of the family. The lands of the appanage, the Montpensier succession, and the revenues from the Orléans Canal were placed in their entirety in the hands of fermiers. There is no hint of the physiocratic doctrines of the future, no evidence of plans to increase agricultural production or improve the condition of those who worked the land. Faced with the difficult task of supervising a complex and geographically dispersed empire, the prince and his council contented themselves with establishing up-to-date terriers and with stimulating the zeal of the leaseholders. The possibility of increasing soil fertility through scientific farming seems not to have occurred to them. The administration was not interested in agriculture per se; it saw no further than a profitable return on its leases.

Nor did the prince and the council possess what would today be called a social conscience. They acted in the interests of the house of Orléans—its appanage and its proprietary possessions—without regard for the well-being of the communities in the area and their inhabitants. The Orléans Canal, for example, was built not to promote the prosperity of Orléans and Orléanais (which were probably harmed rather than benefited by its completion) but to augment profits from the forest of Orléans by transporting timber to the capital. It would be a mistake, of course, to judge Monsieur by the more democratic and humanitarian standards of a later era. Philippe was entirely a prince of his century. Although capable of spontaneous gestures of generosity, such as distributing coins to soldiers in the trenches or throwing money to peasants from his carriage, he saw no need whatever to curb his appetite for luxury simply because the people were poor. Probably it never occurred to him, any more than it did to Louis. Monsieur enjoyed cultivating the image of a liberal prince and was especially mindful of his popularity in Paris, no doubt to contrast himself favorably with the king. But most of his acts were mere tokens: permitting the people to promenade in his gardens or to drink his wine on festive occasions. Never did they involve parting with any sizable amount of wealth. At times his behavior could be, at least to modern sensibilities, shockingly callous. In 1693, during the War of the League of Augsburg when harvests had failed, the kingdom was in severe economic difficulties. The government, fearing revolt in the capital, began in October to distribute bread from the steps of the Louvre and Tuileries palaces to the starving and clamoring poor. Seemingly oblivious to these sights and sounds of deprivation only a few steps from his Palais Royal, Monsieur calmly inspected the progress on his new gallery and other innovations, on which he was expending some 400,000 livres, and proceeded to entertain with his usual éclat during the brilliant winter social season.[87] Nothing in the minutes of his council for the years 1693 and 1694 beyond occasional gifts of firewood to religious houses reflects an awareness among the prince's people of the economic distress in the land.

Even more obvious is the fact that the patronage of the Crown formed the foundation on which the edifice of the family fortune was raised. In Monsieur's day his finances can serve as a nearly classic example of the manner in which Louis XIV used the royal power of the purse to domesticate his greater nobility. For Philippe, the royal largess was basically of two kinds: the *dons* and *brevets* allotted him over the course of his life and the appanage granted to him and to his male heirs in perpetuity. The second, if it was paltry in value, relatively speaking, when he received it, contained a magnificent potential. The first, although subject to the king's will and confined to the lifetime of Monsieur, enabled the prince not only to begin transforming his appanage but also to acquire proprietary holdings for his house. Serendipity in the form of the Montpensier succession, of course, came to his aid late in his life. Yet without the huge and more or less regular stipends from his brother he could not have accepted the indebtedness that accompanied Gaston's legacy or gone on to enlarge and develop its estates as he did.

Yet if the king laid the foundation, it was Philippe and his administration that began to build upon it. If Monsieur had devoured the entirety of his pensions by conspicuous consumption or if, like Gaston, he had neglected his appanage and squandered his resources in abortive conspiracy and revolt, he would have, like his uncle, bequeathed his successors little beyond his debts and a tarnished reputation. Philippe's position in society was indeed unique. The riches showered upon him had spelled servitude, as his brother had intended. His submission and loyalty were unbroken. Denied conspicuous and honorable service to the realm, it is small wonder he fell back on those pleasures within his reach and yielded to the appetites of his nature. But while playing out his public role as court buffoon, he had in private begun to convert substantial portions of the royal bounty into a landed empire that would emancipate his successors. Monsieur was not only the biological but also the financial founder of the house of Orléans.

The End of the Tether

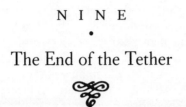

One of the better-known truisms of the late twentieth century is that many males, especially those in socially advantaged positions, experience a "midlife crisis" the manner of whose resolution in large part determines the quality of life of their remaining years. Its onset may be sudden, triggered by an emotionally charged event or series of events, or it may manifest itself gradually as a combined result of the physical changes accompanying middle age and of a mature, sobering realization of the circumscriptions of the life cycle. Individuals who weather it well supposedly adjust to their limitations, realize their potential to the fullest, and secure in their sense of self-worth, live to a rewarding old age. Those who do not are doomed to all manner of unhappiness in their inability to reconcile the realities of their lives with the unrealized drives of their inner nature.

Seventeenth-century males, even those in the highest circles of society, probably experienced nothing of the sort—at least nothing that in that less introspective age was recognized and given a name. The pressures and opportunities of life in the court of the Sun King were so entirely alien to the twentieth-century experience as to rule out relevant comparison. Even so, the process of aging must have taken its toll physically then as later, although owing to the shorter life span its onset must have occurred at an earlier age. And even then there must have been, for some, a sense of frustration or despair at the seeming futility of their lives.

In any case, whatever name one chooses to put to it, Monsieur's behavior and demeanor underwent a marked change in the several years preceding his fortieth birthday. The Battle of Cassel and the events surrounding it marked a decisive turning point in his life. That victory had brought him not only honor and public acclaim but, for the only time in his life in an event of any importance, the knowledge that he had succeeded where his brother had failed. The memoirist Primi Visconti epitomized the public attitude when he wrote: "You must see the joy of the Parisians at the victory of Monsieur, because the city of Paris loved him much. The court, to the contrary, would have much preferred that Monsieur had lost the battle, as all were saying that the king would willingly have given ten million pounds to have offered battle at Heurtebise [in 1676], close to Cassel." The suppressed and unacknowledged fear and hatred the brothers bore each other must have exacerbated the naked emotions accompanying the prince's triumph. For a short time at least the prince's guilty fantasy of outdoing his brother had come true.

Reality, however, was not long in reasserting itself. After the victory celebrations were over, the king punished Philippe rather than rewarding him for his achievement. In the campaign of the following year in which Louis commanded the capture of Ghent, the prince accompanied the army as a mere observer, without benefit of rank. Never again did the king permit him a position where he might lead troops into battle against the enemy. The circumstances of his life controlled as ever by the dictates of his older brother, within a matter of months Philippe had experienced both the greatest success and the profoundest humiliation of his military career. Figuratively, he had suffered a kind of castration.

At the age of thirty-seven Monsieur had reached the end of his service to the Crown. Submissively, for the remainder of his life, he bore the gilded chains that bound him to the prison of his life in court. Revolt seems not to have entered his mind, and not the least hint of it appears in the memoirs of the myriad observers at court. "No child," wrote Elizabeth Charlotte, "could have been more blindly obedient to his parents than Monsieur was to the king."[1] Yet in the euphoria of his victory the unthinkable chimera of surpassing the king, even of destroying him, must once again have risen perilously close to the prince's consciousness. As had been the case in his previous displays of independence, followed inevitably by the royal retribution, the need for self-punishment had returned.

The strong homosexual orientation of his personality brought him again to seek acquittance or discharge of his secret guilt in feminine passivity and personal humiliation. Out of the wings, to which they had been relegated since the prince's second marriage, stepped the chevalier de Lorraine and his epigones to resume their dominance over his life and to destroy the domestic happiness he had briefly known.

The letters of Liselotte inform us that at this period of their lives, probably not long after the Battle of Cassel, husband and wife began to occupy separate bedrooms. "Yes, Monsieur, with all my heart," the princess had allegedly replied to the prince's proposal of the new sleeping arrangements. "So long, that is, as you do not hate me and I continue to have a place in your affections."[2] She had never liked sharing Monsieur's bed, she wrote, since in her efforts not to disturb his slumbers she had clung to the edge of the bed and more than once had fallen like a stone to the floor. Moreover, and much more to the point, she had "never liked the business of making babies," and after the birth of their third child she seemingly considered she had adequately performed her duty. Hence her relief a few years later, in 1682, that she, unlike the dauphin's new wife, was not in an advanced state of pregnancy and on the point of giving birth. "I do not have such worries," she confided to Aunt Sophie, "for it is now four years and more that I am permitted to live in perfect chastity."[3]

Alas for Liselotte's hopes that husband and wife could continue to live in harmony despite the absence of marital relations. The physical separation engendered, or at least was followed by, an emotional estrangement so unmistakable that within a space of several years the turbulence of the prince's ménage, just as in his marriage to Henriette, became the food of court gossip. By 1682 Aunt Sophie in Hanover knew, and so did everyone else, that Monsieur and Madame were living "like cat and dog."[4]

The disintegration of the marriage can best be followed in the voluminous correspondence of Liselotte, who supplied the firsthand evidence otherwise lacking. An unmistakable bitterness crept into her letters as the 1680s approached. Earlier in her married life, during the years of physical closeness with her husband, Liselotte had been able to shrug off or dismiss the chronic irritations inherent in her position at the French court. She could groan over her slavery to etiquette but not miss a night at the theater; she could chafe at the physical restraints incumbent on her during pregnancy only to return to the hunt with renewed vigor; she could bewail her alleged poverty and still enjoy the grandeur of her life in the princely palaces and the services of myriad staff. Even her resentment of the brutal treatment of her father and her homeland could be subordinated to her desire to bask in the company and royal favor of the king. But late in 1678, perhaps a year after husband and wife began sleeping apart, the intrigues of the "cabal," by which she meant the chevalier, his mistress Mme de Grancey, his acolyte Effiat, and their clique, had begun an intrusion on her peace of mind and on her well-being that she could no longer ignore. "As for the hope expressed by Your Grace that the devil may take the entire cabal," she wrote Sophie, "I do not know what will happen, but I can say at the moment they are having a free run of it." All told, their intriguing had caused her no end of care and had taken its toll. "But it is not the hunting that makes me so old and ugly but rather the cabals, which throughout these seven years have given me so many wrinkles that my whole face is covered with them."[5]

The princess soon had numerous additional cares and sorrows with which, in her condition of increasingly chronic unhappiness, she was poorly equipped to cope and over many of which, it is true, she had no control. Not the least was the king's aggressive foreign policy in the Rhineland: his so-called Chambers of Reunion by which he asserted territorial claims and forcibly annexed lands belonging to, among many others, a host of German princes and noblemen. Liselotte's father was one of his victims, and as in the past the elector had completely miscalculated the ability of his daughter and her husband to mitigate his lot. This time, however, Karl Ludwig had little opportunity to express his outrage. In August 1680 he was felled by a heart attack that carried him swiftly to his death.

The reaction of Madame was emotional in the extreme. Given the sad news by a compatriot without warning, Liselotte burst into tears, wailed and moaned inconsolably, and fell into a faint. The outburst was altogether so out of character that Mme de Sévigné, for one, found it exceedingly strange.[6] Madame's letters to her aunt after the event confirmed the intensity of her emotions. With her eyes so swollen she could scarcely see, she wrote, and the pangs of her grief too painful to describe, she prayed God Almighty that he might let her "follow Papa," for henceforth she was sure that her "entire life [was] bound to be wretched." Hardest of all to bear, she groaned, was the obligation "to live with those who without any doubt have caused the death of His late Grace the Elector through all the anguish they have caused him."[7] The king, formerly her "idol," whom she had striven to please, now became a target of her wrath. He and his ministers had persecuted her father until he had "died of grief and sorrow." And Monsieur too was odious in his lack of understanding. Instead of telling His Majesty straight out that France should give back the land unjustly taken and cease to covet what did not belong to her, she wrote, he contented himself with pious vows that did no one any good.[8]

Could the death of this father whom Liselotte had not seen— and had made no effort to see—for nine years and with whom she had strained relations at best have truly been the cause of these laments? It is scarcely credible. For well she knew, and later would admit, that her father's amorous exercises with a "young and robust" Swiss (with whom he had immediately consoled himself on the death of Luise von Degenfeld in 1677) had very likely contributed at least as much to his death as the effects on his spirits of the king's Chambers of Reunion.[9] One senses first of all that Liselotte was experiencing strong pangs of guilt: guilt at her resentment amounting to hatred of the bigamist who had rejected her as a child and who had disgraced her mother (and by implication the children of that mother) by his second marriage to a woman below him in rank. Since coming to France she had earned her father's continual reproaches for failing to exert herself by appeals to the king to ease the precarious position of the Palatinate vis-à-vis its powerful neighbor. And only the previous year she had angered the elector again by protesting his then declared intention of definitively divorcing his first wife, Liselotte's mother.

Second, in addition to the guilt there was also the erosion of the secure and happy position she had enjoyed in her family and at court. With Monsieur the insidious effects of the separate bedrooms and intrigues of the cabal were beginning to tell. Although husband and wife had managed to show a united front during Sophie's visit in 1679 (impressed by the luxury in which her niece was living, she had pronounced Liselotte the happiest of women),[10] they had argued long over Monsieur's desire to bring his mother-in-law to the French court.[11] And in another vein Liselotte had expressed to her aunt in the plainest language (to the point of obscenity) her disdain for her husband's fascination with jewels and their proper display.[12] With the king she was visibly losing favor. He not only had rebuffed or ignored her infrequent and half-hearted protests at his policy in the Palatinate but had rejected her plan, and with it her clumsy efforts at matchmaking, to marry Aunt Sophie's daughter to the dauphin.[13] In January 1680 the prince had married Maria Anna Christine of Bavaria, who thereby became "Madame la Dauphine," and presumably the future queen of France. These failures were perhaps inevitable, given Louis's usual refusal to let his sentiments intrude upon high policy. Far more serious was the infrequency with which the king now sought his sister-in-law's company and the diminution of the camaraderie that had always existed between them.

The principal cause of Madame's loss of favor was the emergence of a new and strong personality at court who came to command the king's affections and to satisfy his need for companionship in the late years of his reign. This was, of course, Mme de Maintenon, née Françoise d'Aubigné, daughter of a disgraced and impoverished nobleman, the young widow of a minor poet, Scarron, and governess of Louis's illegitimate children. As the court watched dumbfounded, this lady of virtuous and modest demeanor converted her humble post as governess into a place as the friend, then the daily companion of the king, and ultimately much more. Louis gave up his "gallantries," and to all outward appearances returned to his wife. Yet by 1682, even though the queen was still living, the position of Mme de Maintenon was recognized as unassailable.

The following July, in 1683, Maria Theresa suddenly and unexpectedly died. "The King is terribly grief-stricken," wrote Liselotte naively,[14] for her years in the French court had not increased her understanding of human nature. Despite his very proper and official display of sorrow, Louis quickly entered into "the marriage of conscience" with Mme de Maintenon. Although the exact date and circumstances of the ceremony have never been ascertained, and although the marriage was never officially acknowledged, its existence cannot be in doubt.[15] Even at the time, although many were at first incredulous (Liselotte among them), the court came (or was obliged) to accept the lady as its uncrowned queen.

As Louis began to spend more of his days with Mme de Maintenon, he found less and less time for his sister-in-law. Liselotte found herself displaced by an intelligent woman who could fulfill the king's need for friendship as well as the desires of his body. Little by little Liselotte was edged out of his presence. The day came when he would dismiss her with a nod of his head. The freedom and vulgarity of her language would irritate him and bring down on her head a reprimand. The grand dauphin became her escort in pursuit of the wolf in the forests of Versailles. Eventually she complained that she would be obliged to request a formal audience to win a few minutes of the great one's attention.[16] In self-defense she retreated to her apartments, emerging from her isolation as infrequently as possible.[17] There she read books, played with the little dogs that were her constant companions, sorted and arranged her collections of coins, and wrote ever more voluminously about the indignities of the life she was forced to endure.

For the woman who displaced her in Louis's company, Madame conceived a violent and uncontrollable hatred. Scorning concealment, she vented her anger over the years in a series of epithets as remarkable for their variety and vulgarity as for their inappropriateness: the "old piece of dung," the "old hag," the "wicked old devil," the "old slut," the "old trollop," or when inspiration failed, simply the "old lady." No deed so foul that she was not at the base of it: "Where the devil cannot go, he sends an old woman." No fate too dreadful to be her just deserts: death by cancer of the womb, "bursting into bits," or burning in hellfire were among the congenial hopes she expressed for the lady's future.

There were some who thought that the fury of Madame was that of a woman scorned, and they derived no little amusement from her supposed misery. Wrote Mme de Sévigné after a gossipy visit with her good friend the princess of Tarente, a sister of Liselotte's mother: "[Madame] has a violent attraction for the older brother of her husband. . . . how we laughed at this affliction whose existence she does not even suspect. A fever has her in a grip. All the pleasure or pain of her being depends on how she is received in that quarter."[18] According to their thinking, only Madame's defeat in love, unrecognized though it was, could explain her very obvious state of agitation and the violence of her hatred of the king's new companion.

Conceivably they were correct. With the disintegration of her marriage and the growing coldness between husband and wife, Elizabeth Charlotte could perhaps, in all innocence, have developed a kind of "crush" on the king who seemed to possess all the strengths and masculine qualities that her husband now lacked. Even so, the explanation is not wholly convincing. Liselotte had never evinced any special aversion for the former mistresses of the king, although it is true they had supposedly not invaded the "realm of friendship" (the term and concept were those of Mme de Sévigné) with the king that she had regarded as peculiarly as her own. But in itself the idea of an alliance between the king of France and a lowborn subject would have struck at the core of Madame's being and could have accounted for her vehemence. Philippe also, to whom the concept of rank was very dear, disliked Mme de Maintenon intensely and disapproved of the marriage. He had not been admitted to his brother's confidence and had been left to find out about the match by accident. Unlike his wife, however, he was careful to keep his opinions to himself.

In the case of Liselotte, her loathing of derogation sprang from the experiences of her childhood. Her father's second marriage to a woman beneath him in rank had spelled rejection for her and for her mother. The ascendence of Mme de Maintenon, governess of Louis's bastards, was a threat to her rank and to the position of her family. Thus Liselotte's spontaneous rage a few years later when she got wind of a plan to marry two of those children—the duc de Maine and Mlle de Blois—to her daughter and son. Products of a double adultery, she wrote, the king's children were misbegotten beings, deformed in body and mind. Her blood boiled over, she wrote, at the very sight of "those bastards." It was only then that she found her full voice against the "chambermaid" and "she-devil" whom she blamed for hatching the plot.

However it may precisely have been, Liselotte's despair, evinced in her continual lamentations in her letters, measured the mounting antipathy between husband and wife. Their quarrels became public in 1682 when the "cabal," always alert for an opportunity to widen the breach, noted Madame's free and easy demeanor with one of the young officers who accompanied her to the hunt and spread the rumor that she was engaged in a flirtation. Given her character and reputation, probably no accusation could have been more ridiculous or less likely to be taken seriously. Neither Monsieur nor the king believed a word of it when Liselotte, hot with indignation at this attack on her honor, demanded that they come to her defense. Philippe, indeed, told his wife that "if she had no other reason to torment herself, she could put herself quite at ease, as well he knew that coquetry was not in her."[19] No doubt he spoke sincerely, and if in fact the squabble had no other cause it would have vanished as quickly as it appeared. Unfortunately, it was merely a surface symptom of the deep rift between them.

Both unburdened themselves to others: Monsieur to the very cabal that had instigated the affair, Madame to one of her ladies, Mlle de Théobon, who had her confidence. These in turn hastened to embroider the details and pass them on for the delectation of others. The Palais Royal reverberated with accusations and rejoinders. Madame was overheard making fun of Monsieur and complaining of his debauches. Aunt Sophie, to her horror, learned that her niece, alluding to the premature death of her predecessor, had even expressed her expectation of being poisoned in turn. "Such speeches could scarcely be agreeable to Monsieur," she knew, and she feared for her niece's mental condition.[20] Philippe, understandably sensitive in the extreme on the subject of poisoning, obtained the king's permission to dismiss the lady-in-waiting and others of her friends he believed were abetting the gossip. All this served only to double the outcries of Madame.

The affair blew itself out or, rather, was quelled by higher authority when Madame, quite beyond reason, again took her case to the king. Declaring that she was surrounded by enemies who turned Monsieur against her, she pleaded to be allowed to leave the court and retire to a convent. How sorry she would have been to be taken at her word! No danger. Louis was unmoved. So long as he lived, he told his sister-in-law, he would never consent to her separation from her husband. "You are Madame, obliged to keep this position. You are the wife of my brother, so that I will not permit you to do him such a turn that would hurt him in the world." Finishing his homily, he proposed a diplomatic settlement among the principals and, bringing husband and wife together, obliged them to embrace. "Above all," he added in closing, "I advise you not to do too much explaining, for that will only lead to further recriminations."

The king's advice was no doubt sound, for as he had well realized, although the quarrel might be at an end, no reconciliation had taken place. Liselotte was unable to regain her peace of mind. In the ensuing years a torrent of complaints continued to spill from her pen, reflecting the misery of the ducal household. Monsieur believed her enemies and suspected her of conspiring against him. He lied about her to the king. In public he was polite to her, "but in fact he cannot stand me." Neglecting his children and refusing to discipline them, he nonetheless took them into bad company and encouraged their corruption. Only her most strenuous protests had prevented the appointment of Effiat, her "worst enemy," "sodomist," and the "most debauched fellow in the world" as her son's governor. To Sophie's defense of Monsieur and her warnings to her niece of what befell wives who alienated the affections of their husbands (the mother of Liselotte was only too egregious an example), she replied that she knew Monsieur too well to expect any improvement but could not resign herself to her lot. All his thoughts were of his "young fellows, with whom he wants to gorge and guzzle all night long," she wrote, and to whom he gave huge sums of money. She saw him but rarely as he passed his days at the gaming table and his nights with his favorites. He gambled away every sou he could lay hands on, to leave Liselotte "begging" for the barest necessities. Although her sole pleasure in life was riding to the hunt, he refused to replenish her stable even when her poor horses were so worn out they could scarcely walk. It was needless to add, she would write (but did so anyway and not infrequently), that her impoverished condition prevented her from giving to charity or helping her young German relatives as she would otherwise have done.[21]

These lamentations must not be taken too literally, of course. Liselotte often took liberties with the truth, the more so when pleading her own case. Other sources of information, many of them reliable, attest to the very real love Monsieur bore his children and they him. And the chronic complaints of poverty were either vastly exaggerated or made up entirely out of whole cloth. Her enjoyment of hunting, for example, was never endangered by the alleged stinginess of Monsieur. The weariness of her horses, we learn from one of her letters to a different correspondent at the same time, was the simple and inevitable result of the increasing girth of their rider (she was "as big as a grenadier," she confessed, "and had well-nigh lost my human shape").[22] Her problem was solved when she found hunters that were up to her weight.[23] Unfortunate it is that Philippe has left us neither letters nor memoirs giving his side of the story. Unlike a modern marriage counselor, the historian in this instance hears only one of the aggrieved parties.

Yet if Madame's catalog of complaints is taken simply as a reflection of the idleness and moral decay of Monsieur's existence, little objection can be made to it. Except for building his palaces and accumulating his wealth, the labor of which was performed by those in his service, the prince was a victim of his otiosity. A man of undeniable gifts, he suffered the frustrations and boredom attendant on the enforced pointlessness and limited opportunities of his life. He could play no part in nor express any opinion on the great affairs of state of the 1680s and 1690s, whether domestic—the revocation of the Edict of Nantes of 1685[24]—or foreign—the entrance of France into the world war known as the War of the League of Augsburg in 1688. By the latter date he had a daughter, the duchess of Savoy, married to a ruler participating in the coalition of Louis's enemies.[25] Moreover, his wife was a relative of the elector of the Palatinate, whose lands were to be ravaged and burned by French armies, and it was in her name that Louis asserted French claims and collected monetary tribute. The devastation of the Palatinate, which included even the burning of the palace at Heidelberg in which Liselotte had spent her childhood, was a keen source of friction between husband and wife. "If Monsieur will not open his eyes to see how we are being taken [by the French], I can nevertheless not refrain from letting my own people see the truth."[26] Monsieur remained a mere spectator while, through his wife's "claims," he passively served Louis's high policy.[27] Perhaps by this time, shut out for so long from the king's deliberations, he was no longer much interested.

Indolence and debauchery began to take their toll on his health. Between 1684 and 1688 Monsieur suffered at least four serious bouts of fever. The 1690s were to prove even worse. Gout became a chronic affliction. Endowed with a prodigious appetite since childhood, he continued to eat voraciously. Once he was seen to consume eighty oysters at a sitting.[28] Eschewing physical exercise, he gained weight and became perceptively red in the face. As he passed his fiftieth birthday he came more and more to resemble the famous and merciless pen portrait sketched by the young Saint-Simon, newly arrived at court: "He was a potbellied little man propped up on heels like stilts; gotten up like a woman with rings, bracelets, and jewels everywhere; a long wig, black and powdered, spread out in front; ribbons wherever he could put them; and exuding perfumes of all kinds. . . . With more vivacity than intelligence and entirely without learning, although with an extensive knowledge of genealogies, births, and marriages, he was capable of nothing. No one so soft of body and mind."[29]

THE PROGENY

While Monsieur was advancing into an undignified old age, his children were growing up about him. Soon they would be ready to marry and take their places in the dynastic network of European royalty. Louis had been well able to dispense with the services of his brother in the operation of his government; but neither he nor his kingdom could do without the offspring of that brother in the conduct of foreign policy and in his arrangements for the future. They were among the most precious resources of the state. No one, of course, could as yet know that before Louis died he would experience the deaths of three eldest sons in the direct line (his son, the grand dauphin; his grandson, the duke of Burgundy; and a great-grandson, the duke of Brittany) and that on his death only the fragile life of a five-year-old would stand between Monsieur's son, Philippe II, regent for the child-king, and the throne of France. Nor could anyone anticipate the fruitfulness and astonishing ramifications of all but one of the matches arranged for Monsieur's daughters, marriages that would in time make him a patriarch of Catholic royalty in Europe. But all were keenly aware in that age of short life expectancy of the critical importance of collateral lines in a system of government in which alliances in war and peace were sealed by dynastic marriages and in which the orderly transfer of power from one generation to the next was effected through succession of a legitimate heir.

The first to be established—that is, married—was the oldest: Marie Louise, the little Mademoiselle, the firstborn of Philippe and Henriette, who was married to Charles II, king of Spain in 1679. It was a diplomatic match of crucial importance for France, from which great things might be expected. If Louis had had a daughter, undoubtedly she instead of his niece would have been the bride. At stake was the eventual disposition of the vast empire of Spain, extending from Belgium to the Strait of Gibraltar and from Milan to Mexico to Manila. The ruler of these lands, at least in name, and the sole male survivor of the direct line of the Spanish Habsburgs (house of Austria), was Charles II, brother of Louis's queen, Maria Theresa. If the new queen of Spain could gain some ascendancy over the mind and policies of her weak husband, she could help solve the problems of succession either by giving birth to an heir, who could be brought up to favor France, or failing that, by arranging for the transfer of the Spanish crowns to a Bourbon prince at the time of Charles's death.

From the point of view of royal dignity, the marriage was also one of the most brilliant to which any princess could aspire. Despite the waning power of the Spanish monarchy in the seventeenth century, the throne of His Most Catholic Majesty was among the oldest and most prestigious in Europe. For nearly a century French kings had served the honor of their dynasty and the foreign policy of their realm through marriage alliances with the Spanish house of Austria. The ceremonies and festivities attendant upon the betrothal and marriage by proxy of Marie Louise would be splendid in every respect. The new queen would be treated with full royal honors by Louis, would dine at his table, would make a formal entrance into the city of Paris, and would take precedence over her father in the French court.[30]

Despite the official rejoicing and exchange of compliments with the Spanish ambassador, everyone knew that the bride was a human sacrifice on the altar of the state. The court of Spain, reportedly peopled by monks, duennas, and dwarfs, enjoyed the most lugubrious reputation in France. Its king, product of a consanguineous marriage between Philip IV and his sister's daughter, was so infirm of body and mind that he took little part in the government of his dominions. Poor Marie Louise, shown a portrait of her future husband, failed to be convinced that the sickliness of his features was the fault of an unskilled painter.[31] Even had the king of Spain been a more acceptable groom, the princess would have been in despair. To the surprise of many, the seventeen-year-old daughter of Henriette, who resembled her mother in vivacity of spirit, had fallen deeply in love with the dauphin and was heartbroken at the prospect of leaving the French court forever. Informed by Louis of her impending marriage and admonished "that he could not have done more for a daughter of his own," the princess, sinking into a deep curtsy, had allegedly replied, "But you could have done better for your niece."

From the time of her betrothal in July and her marriage in the chapel at Fontainebleau until her departure for Spain late in September 1679, Marie Louise spent much of her time weeping. Seeing her on the street, the people were heard to cry out: "Ah! Monsieur is too good. He will not let her leave. She is too grief-stricken."[32] The king left no doubt of the permanence of the union. In the presence of the grand duchess of Tuscany, Gaston's daughter, who had left husband and throne, Louis had admonished: "Madame, I hope never to see you again; the greatest misfortune that could happen would be to see you once more in France."[33] Displays of emotion were de rigueur among the great upon all formal occasions such as that of marriage. But the profusion of tears that were shed by all according even to the official account leaves the impression that the "festivities" were more befitting a funeral than a wedding.[34]

In fact, Monsieur may have been sad at the prospect of parting and at the future in store for his daughter. Urged by Louis to go and console Marie Louise, who had retired in tears to her apartments, he replied that he could not, since on seeing her face "he should be as moved as she."[35] He seems to have gone beyond the dictates of etiquette in attempting to defer and soften the moment of parting. Accompanying her in her carriage as far as Amboise, he diverted her with card games during the voyage and spent much of the night with her before the final separation.[36]

Not too much should be read into this evidence of paternal sympathy. In fact, Monsieur took enormous pride and pleasure in the brilliance of his daughter's marriage. Only a match with the dauphin could have given him greater satisfaction. Sophie, who was in France at the time, found him "as happy as he could be" while he supervised every detail of the elaborate ceremonies, counted the diamonds on his wedding suit, and displayed the bejeweled trousseau of the bride.[37] Madame, too, was very pleased. She was tenderly attached to Marie Louise, with whom she had lived more as a sister than a mother (only ten years separated them in age), but as conscious of rank as Philippe, she looked no further than her stepdaughter's elevated status as queen.[38] Moreover, hoping at the time to see the dauphin married to Aunt Sophie's niece, she was secretly relieved at the removal from the field of a formidable competitor.

The marriage proved more tragic than anyone could have foreseen. No child was born of the union. At Madrid the new queen was surrounded by Francophobe enemies. Even her French-speaking parrot was strangled. Her letters to Monsieur, which seem to have been frequent, detailed the atmosphere of hostility and isolation in which she lived.[39] Even though she achieved some influence over her infirm husband,[40] her ascendancy was cut short by her death in February 1689. Monsieur was devastated by the news. Like her mother at the end of her life, she was twenty-six years of age and had been married nearly ten years. This time the rumors of poison surrounding the death had considerable basis in fact.[41]

The next daughter of Monsieur to serve the king's high policy of state by marriage was Anne Marie, Mlle de Valois, who was married in 1684 to Victor Amadeus, duke of Savoy, king first of Sicily and then of Sardinia. The second, and last, of the surviving children of Philippe and Henriette, born in 1669, she was scarcely fifteen years old at the time of her betrothal. Because the court was still officially in mourning for the queen, the ceremony, performed by procuration on April 10, was a simpler one than her father might have wished. The new duchess departed immediately for Savoy, accompanied by Monsieur only as far as Juvisy, not far from Paris. A self-effacing child who had been raised by Liselotte in place of the mother she had never known,[42] Anne Marie had not yet become a personality in her own right when she left her homeland for good.

This marriage too was to be a desperately unhappy one, although, unlike that of the queen of Spain, it was remarkably fruitful and was not cut short by premature death. The duchess became the mother of eight children whose marriages, and those of their innumerable descendants, would transmit the blood of the house of Orléans into, among others, the dynasties of Spain, Parma, Saxony, and France itself. Through her the Stuart blood of Henriette would pass through kings of Sardinia, through princes of Modena and Bavaria, to the Jacobite heirs of James II in the nineteenth and twentieth centuries.

When the young Victor Amadeus married Marie Louise he had just begun to rule in his own right over a land that had long been dominated by the king of France. His mother, regent during his minority, had been obliged to accept French dictation; soon after his marriage the young duke was forced by Louis to make war on the few Protestants among his subjects, owing to the revocation of toleration in France in 1685. A victim of French persecution, the duke sustained a great hatred for his father-in-law in Versailles. Throughout his reign he was to prove the most reluctant and unreliable of allies, deserting the French whenever he thought he could get away with it to seek better terms with the empire and its coalition. Ultimately his astute changes of alliance were to pay off handsomely in the aggrandizement of the house of Savoy, to which he added the crown of Sicily (later exchanged for that of Sardinia). Meanwhile, as he maneuvered back and forth between the French and imperial camps he vented his rage against Louis XIV through the alternate neglect or mistreatment of his wife.[43]

From the point of view of the subsequent history of France and of life in the court of Louis XIV (and of Monsieur), the most important child of this marriage was their firstborn, Marie Adélaïde, who became duchess of Burgundy in 1697 by marrying Louis, the oldest son of the dauphin.[44] The match had come about as a result of the Treaty of Turin of the previous year, through which the king had been obliged to part with sizable territory in the French Alps in order to bring his wily son-in-law into the French camp.[45] After his first glimpse of the exquisite child (she was only eleven years old at the time of her arrival in France), he as well as the rest of the court agreed that the sacrifice had been well worth making.

Monsieur was transported with joy at the results of his brother's war and diplomacy. One of his descendants—his first grandchild, in fact—would in all probability become queen of France. On greeting the little girl at Montargis, where Marie Adélaïde met her future husband's family for the first time, Philippe, forgetful of etiquette for once in his life, advanced eagerly to kiss and embrace her before Monseigneur (the dauphin, who outranked him) had presented his compliments. The king did not fail to remind him of his error.[46]

The little princess soon had the entire court at her feet, especially its two most important members, Louis and Mme de Maintenon. Whether spontaneously or as the result of careful coaching, Marie Adélaïde had immediately gone to the lady with open arms and paid her the prettiest attentions. Both the king and his wife were captivated by her grace and delicate beauty. Only Madame failed to fall under her spell. You can see "what a politician she already is,"[47] she carped. Monsieur, ignoring his wife's sour humor, soon won a place in his granddaughter's heart. Although finding him "a bit too fat," Marie Adélaïde came to adore him and was a frequent visitor at Saint-Cloud. At the time of his death she was physically overwhelmed by her grief.[48]

Through the marriage of this princess to the grandson of Louis XIV, Monsieur and Henriette became the direct ancestors of the future Bourbon kings of France. Marie Adélaïde and her husband did not themselves become king and queen of France, since they died in 1712 while Louis XIV still lived. But on the death of the old king in 1715 their only surviving son, then a child of five years, assumed the crown as Louis XV.

The third child of Monsieur to be married, and the older of the two surviving children of his second marriage, was Philippe II, duke of Chartres, the future regent. Liselotte had been entirely correct in her earlier suspicion that the king intended to marry this prince, the only male heir of the house of Orléans, to Françoise Marie, Mlle de Blois, one of his daughters by Mme de Montespan. Both Madame and Monsieur were strongly opposed to this match, which they saw as an ineradicable stain on the honor of the family. "Monsieur," reported Saint-Simon, "was infinitely attentive to the preservation of his grandeur," while Madame, with her instinctive horror of illegitimacy and derogation, "was of a disposition never to look favorably on this marriage."[49] Both well knew, as did everyone else, that Louis could not negotiate a dynastic marriage for a royal bastard with any of the ruling families of Europe. No doubt advantages might accrue to a son-in-law of the king of France, but no foreign prince could be expected to pay the price. Louis had previously married two of his illegitimate daughters, one by Louise de La Vallière, one by Mme de Montespan, respectively to the prince de Conti and to Louis III, duke of Bourbon-Condé.[50] Princes of the blood in France could be "induced" to accept as wives, and perhaps even to be grateful for, such daughters of the king as he could not marry off abroad.

The sacrifice was the more bitter for Monsieur and Madame because Chartres, unlike a daughter, would remain in France to inherit his father's appanage and to carry on the name and honor of the house. The prince appeared to possess every grace of body and mind to carry out his destiny with distinction. A precocious and intelligent child and (unlike his father) an eager student, he had become something of a savant with a comprehensive knowledge of foreign languages, mathematics, history, and even chemistry. Having inherited his father's aesthetic sensibilities as well as his mother's taste for belles-lettres, he had achieved near-professional levels of performance and appreciation of music and painting and was later to patronize the greatest writers and thinkers of the early eighteenth century. Even more important for one so close to the throne, he possessed his father's natural courage and talents as a soldier.

His first campaign was carried out at the age of seventeen in Flanders under Luxembourg. In 1692 and 1693 he distinguished himself at the battles of Steenkerke and Neerwinden with displays of valor reminiscent of those of Monsieur at Cassel. Like those of his father, they did not earn him the gratitude of the king. For the remainder of the war he remained on the sidelines.

In many ways the position of Chartres was similar to that of Monsieur. Both were gifted men who could not be permitted to excel. Both were close to the throne but on a lower rung. His father was the perpetual loser in a lifelong rivalry with Louis. Chartres had no brother but inevitably fell into competition with his cousins, legitimate and illegitimate, especially the duke of Maine, natural son of Louis, the Bourbon princes Conti and Condé, and Burgundy, oldest son of the dauphin. It was his misfortune that while he outshone them in every way, he could neither receive the recognition that was his due nor realize his potential in service to the Crown.

Although Monsieur and Madame took immense pride in their son's talents and achievements, they also worried, although in different ways, over his early and unmistakable penchant for debauchery and dissolution, traits of character that in time became so extreme as to tarnish his reputation and make a caricature of the real man. His drinking sprees and his womanizing, like his aversion to religious practice and conventional morality, very likely began as adolescent rebellion and bravado. Certainly they exacerbated the tensions already present in his ambivalent position at court and were ultimately to take Monsieur into his last and unresolved battle with the king.

Philippe and Liselotte had often been in disagreement on how their children should be raised. To Liselotte had fallen the role of disciplinarian. Although she loved her children tenderly and could be fierce as a lioness in their protection, she insisted on a strict code of morality and made free and vigorous use of the rod when they violated it. Monsieur, on the other hand, turned helplessly to his wife when the children needed correction. "They fear only you,"[51] he would reply by way of excuse for his softheartedness. As the children grew older, Madame began to see in Monsieur's indulgence of his children, and especially of his son, a willingness, and perhaps even a desire, to allow them the moral laxity that had made a scandal of his own life. One of their worst quarrels over Chartres arose in 1689 over Monsieur's inclination to appoint the marquis d'Effiat as the boy's governor.[52] Madame, horrified at Effiat's reputation as a sodomist, had protested the harm so close an association might do her son. Monsieur, who had to admit that in the past Effiat had "loved the boys," replied in his defense that the marquis had long since corrected himself of this practice. Liselotte was able to make her objections prevail by an appeal to the king, who, for once attentive to her complaints, appointed a well-qualified governor who was acceptable to both parents.

No evidence whatever exists that Monsieur wished to "corrupt" his only son. Even if indeed such were possible, which is most doubtful, it was clear from a very early age that Chartres's taste was for women, not for men. Philippe I's permissiveness and his willingness to permit his son to go in dubious company undoubtedly reflected an unconscious wish to justify his own conduct, past and present, which had been an affront to the accepted mores of the court. Through his son he could mount a second, vicarious protest against the king. Chartres was his alter ego, a stand-in, even an instrument of revenge, through whom he could make a final attempt to achieve the prerogatives and recognition he had been denied. On a more conscious level, Monsieur wished to spare his son the enforced idleness and humiliations that had been his lot. In springing to the defense of the young man's dissolute habits and his notorious liaisons with women of easy virtue, he would urge his brother to grant him the appointments and responsibilities befitting his talents and his rank. What could the king expect of a young man given nothing better to do than pace the galleries of Versailles?[53]

With this background in mind Monsieur's ultimate acceptance of the marriage of Chartres to Mlle de Blois becomes understandable. Louis, well aware of the resistance he would encounter and wishing to preserve the facade of friendship with his brother, seems to have prepared the ground well in advance and was prepared to pay a high price for Philippe's consent. The chevalier de Lorraine, the dominant force in Monsieur's household, was admitted to the rarefied ranks of the Order of the Holy Spirit in order, it was said, to obtain his support for the match. In 1691 during the months immediately preceding the proposal of marriage Monsieur and Madame found themselves the recipients of unusual favors from on high. They were escorted by Louis to Flanders, where Chartres underwent his first trial by arms. A gift of 2,000 pistoles swelled Madame's purse. And Mme de Maintenon herself was seen to call at the ducal palace and break bread at the table of the chevalier of Lorraine. As a condition of the marriage, the Palais Royal was added to Monsieur's appanage. Moreover, the dowry the bride brought was dazzling: no less than two million livres (the brides of Conti and Condé had done with only one million each), with an additional annual pension of 150,000 livres and jewels valued at 600,000 livres.[54]

These, of course, were the kinds of material inducements, or bribes, that had worked so well with Monsieur in the past. But this time, to judge from the protests and reproaches Philippe later heaped on his brother, there was more. By entering into matrimony with his daughter, the king had argued, Chartres could aspire to a noble career in the service of the king. High command in the army and the governorship of an important province would be his. The future would be in his hands to make. Like the Grand Condé, should his talents prove their worth, he could bring honor and fame to his name.

Monsieur was later to bitterly repent his consent to this marriage and to accuse his brother to his face of breach of promise. At the time, however, these promises, coupled with the monetary incentives, proved irresistible. One afternoon in January 1692 Monsieur entered the apartment of Madame and informed her of the fait accompli. "Madame," he said, "I have a message from the king for you, which will not be too pleasing to you, and you are to give him your answer in person by tonight. The king wishes me to tell you that since he and I and my son are agreed on the marriage of Mademoiselle de Blois to my son, you will not be foolish enough to demur."[55]

The rest of the story is only too well known. The marriage was celebrated with great ceremony at Versailles on February 18, 1692; a less joyous wedding party could scarcely be imagined. At the time of the betrothal Madame, unable to accept with dignity what she had been helpless to prevent, had paced the galleries of Versailles in tears, had turned her back on the king, and had cracked her palm over the face of her son when he approached to present his respects. During the ceremony the groom, crimson faced, and Monsieur, already repentant, were the personification of humiliation. The bride, mortified, had salvaged her pride as best she could. "I don't care if he loves me," Françoise Marie was heard to declare. "I care only that he marries me."[56] Only the king radiated his satisfaction.

Monsieur and Madame were required to drink the bitter cup of humiliation to the dregs.[57] After the marriage ceremony was performed, with the king and royal family they accompanied the young couple to the apartments of the new duchess of Chartres. To Liselotte fell the "honor" of handing the chemise to the bride.[58] A few days later Monsieur and Chartres went to the Palais Royal to receive Louis and permit him to view the magnificent rooms that had been prepared for his daughter. The inspection complete, the king took his departure while the remaining members of the royal family enjoyed the usual lavish hospitality of Monsieur in opera, banquet, and ball.[59]

Little joy was to come of this marriage. Husband and wife were still mere children—he not yet eighteen, she but fifteen years of age. Neither seems to have had either the maturity or the desire to establish a harmonious relationship. Chartres, dubbing his bride "Madame Lucifer," picked up the pace of his already dissolute life and spent as little time as possible in her company. In time his obvious contempt for his wife and the successive births of illegitimate children to his mistresses became the scandal of the court and a major source of grievance of the king. Liselotte, who entertained a truly visceral hatred of her daughter-in-law, was totally unsympathetic to her plight. She deplored her son's habits, she wrote, but whenever she caught sight of his wife all she could think of was "mousedroppings."[60] Monsieur was scarcely more fond of Françoise Marie than Liselotte, though, insistent as always on the precedence of rank of Chartres over the princes of the blood, he demanded that the princess of Conti and the duchess of Bourbon-Condé address his daughter-in-law respectfully as "Madame," while she in turn was free to call them "my sister."[61] (This detail of etiquette duplicated in the feminine form precisely the precedence of the king over Monsieur; they invariably addressed each other respectively as "my brother" and "Monsieur.")

Despite the misery of this union, it was marvelously fruitful. The young duke and duchess became the parents of one son and six daughters, many of whom, like their sisters, married into royal houses across Europe. The only son, Louis, later known as "the Pious" (in perfect contrast to his father), married a princess of Baden and carried on the direct line of male descendants of Monsieur. As generation gave way to generation, this collateral line of Orléans proved ever more prolific, even while the senior line, descended from Louis, saw its ranks increasingly diminish as it was visited by every conceivable misfortune, including revolution and intermittent sterility. By the mid-nineteenth century only the count of Chambord remained to carry the flag of Louis's house of Bourbon. At the same time Louis Philippe, king of the French and duke of Orléans, had ensured the succession of his collateral line of Monsieur by fathering five sons, all of whom lived to adulthood. With the death in 1883 of Chambord, who was childless, the Bourbon line became extinct. The descendants of the oldest son of Louis

Philippe became the legitimate pretenders to the throne of France. If France had adhered to the system of hereditary monarchy, today one of the direct male descendants of Monsieur—the count of Paris (himself the father of eleven children)—would wear the crown.[62]

Only the third daughter and the last of the children of Monsieur remained to be established. This was Elizabeth Charlotte, born in 1676, a "little leaf-rustler"[63] whose pranks and wild ways Liselotte had recounted through the years with a mixture of affection and dismay. Seemingly she resembled her mother in vivacity of spirits and also, unfortunately, in absence of beauty. To her parents' great relief, this daughter was able to escape the duke of Maine, who was married off in 1692 to another daughter of the house of Bourbon-Condé. Even so, they were not precisely enthusiastic over the king's choice for her: Duke Léopold Joseph Charles of Lorraine, whose lands, long occupied by France, had been returned to him by the Treaty of Ryswick of 1697. Wishing to draw the house of Lorraine into the orbit of his high policy, Louis had decided to employ his niece as his diplomatic pawn. The marriage took place by procuration at Fontainebleau on October 13, 1698.

Both Monsieur and Madame could have wished for a prince with more money and more éclat. Compared with the king of Spain and the duke of Savoy, the duke of Lorraine seemed to come off poorly. Liselotte was especially disappointed, since at times in the past she had hoped to bring off a match with the dauphin (following the death of the Bavarian dauphine), with the dauphin's son, the duke of Burgundy, and even with William of Orange, king of England (after the death of Queen Mary). They were partly mollified by the generosity of the king, who provided a dowry of 900,000 livres, to which were added jewels, furniture, and other items valued at 100,000 écus.[64] Only the bride was perfectly content. She was delighted to escape the strict governance of her mother[65] and, residing in the city of Nancy in Lorraine, still remain on the outskirts of France.

Alone of Monsieur's children, this daughter was to be happy in her marriage. The duke was reported to be "horribly keen on his pleasure," a fact the bride found not in the least disconcerting. Not long after her arrival in her new home her mother told Sophie: "She is already quite used to the thing and does not dislike it as much as I did."[66] The couple became the parents of four children, one of whom, their son Francis, born in 1708, was later to marry Maria Theresa of Austria. The genealogical consequences of the founding of the house of Habsburg-Lorraine are only too well known.

Among the many children of the imperial couple were the emperors Joseph II and Leopold of Austria and Marie Antoinette, wife of Louis XVI. By a strange quirk of fate, the last king and queen of France before the Revolution were both to be descendants of the younger brother of Louis XIV.

The Last Years

In the last decade of Monsieur's life his manner of living changed little. His character was formed, his tastes set, his limitations—those imposed from without as well as from within—already well recognized and defined. The homosexual habits that had reappeared in force after his retirement from the army set the pattern of his daily life. The only new, or relatively new, factor in the balance of his days were the bouts of ill health that increased in frequency and duration.

For most of these years he was as assiduous as ever in the pursuit of pleasure and profit. When Sophie inquired in 1691 whether perchance Monsieur had become pious with advancing age, the prince had replied through Liselotte: "Tell your aunt that I am counting my diamonds more than ever before and that I am no more devout than I was when I had the honor to see her."[67] Privately, Monsieur and his council continued to add to the proprietary wealth of the house of Orléans. Publicly, he added to his reputation as a host—most often at Saint-Cloud, sometimes at the Palais Royal, occasionally even at Versailles, where he might sponsor and supervise the staging of a ball[68]—and as a gambler, usually in the company of the grand dauphin, who was his frequent companion in pleasures during the last years of Monsieur's life. An entry in the journal of Dangeau, typical of many in the 1690s, read: "Monseigneur [the grand dauphin] went to Paris to dine at Monsieur's. Afterward there was gambling at high stakes; then they went to the opera; after the opera they resumed gambling. Monseigneur remained for supper . . . and did not return home until three o'clock in the morning."[69]

In itself this virtual addiction to gambling is consistent with Monsieur's psychodynamics at this stage of his life. To some degree it may have been a substitute for the political role that was denied him—that is, a kind of trial with fate to prove his power. A deeper psychoanalytical meaning also attaches to gambling: an appeal to the infantile, to the ritualistic, to the superstitious part of one's nature (which in Monsieur was not inconsiderable) that believes wishes alone will bring satisfaction and fulfillment of desires.[70] In gambling he could seek unconscious compensation for his impotent position in his brother's court.

At Monsieur's parties his guests ranged from visiting royalty, princes of the blood, foreign ministers, and ambassadors of highest rank to gambling cronies of dubious reputation. Invariably present were crowds of ladies who loved to gamble and liked a good time. From childhood on the prince had enjoyed the company of women, and he was never very particular on matters of morals or reputation. "His court was never strong on virtue," admitted Saint-Simon.[71] Nor did he receive the slightest help from Madame, who disapproved of many of the guests, deplored the gambling, and appeared as infrequently as possible.

To the young Saint-Simon, and probably to many others at court, the parties at Monsieur's palaces in those days were far more attractive and lively than those at Versailles. The king still provided diversions such as concerts, opera, theater, buffets and dancing, and the gaming table, but he had lost much of his taste for excitement and had given up gallantry entirely. With his formerly robust health eroding (he had been operated on for an anal fistula in 1686 and suffered chronic digestive illnesses) and increasingly preoccupied with the problems and failures of his high policy, Louis preferred a quiet evening in the sedate company of Mme de Maintenon to the merrymaking of his youth. Philippe, excluded from the king's counsel and no longer on intimate terms with his wife, had little enough to do save seek amusement, and with the completion of the château of Saint-Cloud and the renovation of the Palais Royal, he could now provide the ambiance appropriate to his talent for hospitality. As the Grand Siècle drew to a close, youthful pleasure seekers found in Monsieur's entertainments the élan and easy freedom lacking in the more restrained atmosphere of Versailles. When he died the entire court felt the loss. "It was he who provided all the amusement, its life, and its pleasure, and, when he left, it all seemed lifeless and dull."[72]

The War of the League of Augsburg (1688–97) intruded little on the comfortable tenor of Monsieur's days. During the first months of hostilities he had hoped for active command of one of the king's armies; by the 1690s, perhaps owing to the deterioration of his health or to his vicarious enjoyment of Chartres's military promise, he appeared resigned to a role on the sidelines. In 1691 he accompanied the king to the siege of Mons, where Chartres had met his first trial in arms. Two years later, in the spring of 1693, he accepted an honorific command with the rank of lieutenant general of a force of 60,000, whose duty was to protect the coasts of Normandy and Brittany from the British fleet. No credible threat of invasion existed, and the prince's tour of duty amounted to a promenade through the countryside from late May to early August punctuated with ceremonious receptions, elaborate banquets staged by the governor of Brittany, and overnight stays in the episcopal palace. When time permitted, Monsieur and his entourage made ritual inspections of the coastal fortresses.[73] Even the grand dauphin, whose martial ardor was not outstanding, had declined the post and had preferred to go with the French army to Flanders. Philippe himself seems to have been bored with it all. At times he sought distraction by casting money from his carriage window to the peasants, whose suffering from the great famine of that year was terrible.[74] He is also reported to have amused himself by promoting the careers of young officers who caught his eye[75] and by striking up a friendship with a vivacious local belle who was capable of holding her own at his gaming table.[76]

This sortie into the provinces in 1693 and the earlier brief appearance at the siege of Mons were the only occasions when the war inconvenienced—if such is the appropriate word—Monsieur in his personal life. Not until its conclusion did he figure in the war again, and then briefly and to his profit. Present at the deliberations at Ryswick was a representative of the prince, who maintained his claim over lands within the Palatinate in the name of Elizabeth Charlotte. Both Monsieur and his delegate were of course mere extensions of Louis's negotiations with his enemies. The resulting treaty in 1697 awarded Monsieur 200,000 livres annually, known locally as the *orleanse guelte* to be paid until such time as the claim could be definitively regulated.[77] In effect, the house of Orléans was serving as a face-saving measure in a treaty that was generally unfavorable to France. The provision for monetary compensation helped mask Louis's failure to maintain his hold over Lorraine, whose lands were returned to its duke, and to take over the lands of the Palatinate.

On only one other occasion during the remainder of his life did Monsieur participate, even indirectly, in affairs of state: on the announcement in November 1700 of the accession of Louis's second grandson, duke of Anjou, to the throne of Spain, the momentous event that set off the War of the Spanish Succession. Monsieur had a particular interest in the succession in addition to its broad implications for France and most of Europe. He was intent on preserving the right of the house of Orléans, in certain circumstances, to claim the Spanish inheritance. If not for himself—for he must have known he would never rule in Spain—then for his son, he tried to make the most of the opportunity.

The last testament of Charles II, the infirm king of Spain whose death had long been expected, left the throne of Spain first to Philippe of Anjou and after him to his brother, duke of Berry, both grandsons of Louis XIV. After those princes were named, successively, Archduke Charles, son of Emperor Leopold I, and the duke of Savoy. The objection to this line of succession, so far as Monsieur and Chartres were concerned, was the absence from the testament of any reference to their rights. As son and grandson of Anne of Austria, herself daughter of Philippe III of Spain, they could mount a better claim to the succession than either the Austrian Habsburgs or the house of Savoy.

When Charles II at last died in the autumn of 1700, Louis as usual did not admit his brother to his deliberations.[78] Only after he had decided to accept the succession for Anjou (but before the public announcement) did he inform Philippe that his nephew was to rule in Madrid. Monsieur, obedient as always, duly announced Anjou's elevation to the members of his own court on November 16 and participated in the official rejoicing. Privately, he was indignant at the omission of his house from the line of succession and, with Louis's permission, lodged a formal legal complaint in the Parlement of Paris. No one could know better than he how dynastic considerations governed the loci of power, the great questions of state, and the lives of the princes who were involved. Ambitious for his son, through whom he was now living vicariously, he understood that the claim represented too vital an opportunity to let slip by default. And in fact his protest was not in vain. Chartres never became king of Spain, but after Monsieur's death he took up the claim and was able to obtain recognition by both Philippe V (the former duke of Anjou) and Louis XIV of his place in the line of succession after his cousin Berry and before the Austrian Habsburgs and the house of Savoy.[79]

Within his family in the early years of the 1690s Monsieur lived on rancorous terms with Madame. The marriage of Chartres to Mlle de Blois in 1692, which Liselotte could not forgive and which Philippe soon began to regret, provoked an all but formal rupture between the couple. Occupying separate apartments and seeing little of each other, husband and wife went their separate ways. Monsieur went alone to Normandy in the summer of 1693 even though his tour of duty was by no means hazardous and could well have accommodated the presence of Madame. News of his social rounds that trickled back to court made it clear that he found ready and agreeable substitutes for her company. During his absence Liselotte contracted smallpox and nearly died. Even though informed of her peril, Philippe remained on the coast.[80] The contrast could not have been clearer to his reaction in 1675 when he had rushed to Liselotte's sickbed and personally nursed her back to health.

Monsieur and Madame could never recapture the closeness of the early years of their life together as man and wife. The decompensation of Philippe's personality was complete, leading to his retreat into self-destructive tendencies and into the more abject forms of homosexual behavior. In turn, the increasing bitterness of Liselotte and the rejection of her femininity (probably a sublimated lesbianism) were too pronounced for marital reconciliation in any true sense of the word to be possible.

Even so, the bonds between them were never entirely severed. As the decade progressed they strengthened almost imperceptibly. By the end of the prince's life the two had achieved a modus vivendi and camaraderie based on a certain compatibility of temperament. They also harbored an unconscious need for each other in a world in which they and their children, especially Chartres, were the underdogs. Even when estranged, their personalities complemented rather than destroyed each other. His femininity and her masculinity made a degree of friendship between them possible that came to take the place of marital love. Just as Philippe and la Grande Mademoiselle had once been drawn to each other by their shared misfortunes in court, so Monsieur and Madame lent each other comfort and sympathy as the eternal losers.

Perhaps the two were not themselves quite aware of their growing accommodation to each other. Liselotte, many of whose letters we possess, did not recognize it—or at least if she did, she was unwilling to admit it even to a close relative like Sophie, with whom she corresponded. Only long after Philippe's death did she confess to the serenity she had found with him in his last years. In 1716 she wrote:

[In the last three years of Monsieur's life] I had brought him around to laughing with me over his weaknesses and to take things as a joke and not become angry. No longer did he permit others to lie about me and to attack me in his presence; he had a certain confidence in me; he always took my part. But before that, I had suffered horribly. I was just on the point of becoming truly happy when our Lord God saw fit to remove my poor husband from life and I saw vanish in an instant the result of all the trouble and pains I had taken over thirty years to become happy.[81]

Liselotte naturally attributed to herself all the success of this reconciliation. She had, she wrote, made her peace with the chevalier de Lorraine. She was always obedient to Monsieur and let him govern her household as he pleased. But even while she was tendering these olive branches, a certain mellowness began to appear in her correspondence when she referred to Monsieur in the last years before his death. One suspects that her peacemaking arose as much out of inclination as from calculation. In 1697 Liselotte, who loved money almost as much as Monsieur, was gratified to receive from him a portion of the Orléans tax in the Palatinate imposed on her behalf.[82] Two years later she could write to her aunt: "There is no doubt that if Monsieur were not so weak and did not permit himself to be bamboozled . . . , he would be the best husband in the world; therefore he is to be pitied more than to be hated when he does one a bad turn."[83] Despite their separate living arrangements, she was always informed of his daily activities and his state of health and mind. "Monsieur, thank God, has gotten over his fever," she wrote approximately a year before his death, "but His Grace is still quite languid and melancholy and does not take pleasure in anything. . . . so I am quite worried about Monsieur."[84]

They may in fact have begun to see more of each other than Liselotte's letters indicated. After 1695, although the couple continued to visit Louis regularly and frequently at Versailles or at Marly, they lived uninterrupted for long periods either in the château of Saint-Cloud or in the Palais Royal, where they could escape the irritations (the presence of Mme de Maintenon chief among them) of the court. When in the country at Saint-Cloud they took regular carriage rides through the park together in the afternoon; when in the city at the Palais Royal they both attended the opera and presided over the brilliant festivities Monsieur organized (he by choice, she with reluctance). Enjoyment of the pleasures of the table was another link between them. Even though their tastes in cuisine were different, both devoted much time to thinking about food and satisfying their appetites. Discussions of smoked sausages, sour cabbage, and herring run like a leitmotif through the letters of Liselotte. The tastes of Monsieur ran to pastries, fruits, chocolate, and candies, with which his pockets bulged and the tables in his rooms overflowed. Both became gluttonous and fat in their late years.

Even at the most strained moments in their relationship the Rabelaisian sense of humor they shared could set them laughing. Consider, for example, this excerpt from the princely "conversations" in the intimacy of their ménage as reported by Liselotte:

> I cannot resist telling Your Grace [Sophie] about a fine dialogue that I recently had with Monsieur, and I hope that it will make Your Grace laugh as heartily as it did my two children. One evening the four of us were alone here in this drawing room after supper, namely Monsieur, myself, my son, and my daughter. After a long silence, Monsieur, who did not consider us good enough company to talk to us, made a great loud fart, by your leave, turned toward me, and said, "What is that, Madame?" I turned my behind toward him, let out one of the selfsame tone, and said, "That's what it is, Monsieur." My son said, "If that's all it is, I can do it as well as Monsieur and Madame," and he also let go of a good one. With that, all of us began to laugh and went out of the room.[85]

This domestic scene took place late in 1692 when feelings in the family were still running high over Chartres's marriage—anger at each other for permitting it to happen and anger at the king for the humiliation he had imposed on them. And it reveals, among many things, the obvious freedom from restraint and relaxation husband and wife felt in each other's presence. Even more striking is the sense of unity enjoyed by family, a closeness and affinity for each other as opposed to their hostility toward the outside world. The target of their humor, with its anal sadistic overtones, was not within the family group but without. It was as if, despite their sharp disagreements with each other, they were saying to the world (Louis, Mme de Maintenon, et al.): "Do what you will to us. We of the house of Orléans will still tell you where you can go!"

The children, but especially Chartres, were undoubtedly the strongest link between them. Although a source of dissension, their son was also their idol. They watched over him, agonized over his safety when he went to war, worried about his misbehavior, and tortured themselves over the king's disapproval and the compromising of his career. When Chartres was the object of concern, the lines of communication between husband and wife were always open. During the summer of 1692 when the young prince was with the army, the rumor suddenly spread in court that he had been injured in battle. Monsieur, who was suffering from intermittent attacks of fever and had retired for the night, rushed to his wife's apartments to reassure her. Holding an open letter in his hand, he called out: "Do not be alarmed, your son is wounded, but only slightly; there has been a raging battle [Steenkerke] in Flanders and the King's infantry has defeated that of the Prince of Orange."[86] Later, after an anxious night, Liselotte learned that Chartres, riding an untrained war-horse, had suffered a fall but had come to little harm. A few years later, in 1696, when Liselotte was in highest dudgeon over Monsieur's indulgence of his son, she could neverthe-less discuss with her husband an especially scandalous example of Chartres's behavior that had come to the ears of the king. What it was all about is not entirely clear, but a letter seemingly of the most compromising kind had come to light that made Madame's "hair stand on end" in horror and, she wrote, threatened to ruin Chartres "with all decent people." But she was to some extent consoled by the reaction of Monsieur, who this time had likewise become ex-tremely upset and had scolded the culprit in the strongest terms.[87]

The Final Showdown

As the Grand Siècle passed into history, Monsieur sensed that he had not much longer to live. Weary and heavy of body, tormented by gout and frequent attacks of fever, he lost something of his natu-ral ebullience and became noticeably dispirited. "I think I know what makes him so dejected," wrote Liselotte. "His Grace realizes that his past life cannot go on any longer; yet all his plans and actions used to turn only on his pleasures.... Of course, he does not want to die either, yet he realizes that his wild life and his ac-tivities must come to an end. That makes His Grace very sad, and this sadness prevents him from regaining his strength."[88] His con-fessor, Père de Trévoux, who had held his post only since 1698 and was of sterner stuff than the indulgent and forgiving Père Zoccoli of the prince's earlier years, reinforced Philippe's worst foreboding in the plainest, even brutal, terms. "He was old," the confessor warned, "used up with debauchery, fat, short-necked, and, all signs indicated, he would die of apoplexy, and that very soon."[89] He de-nied him not only his habits of debauchery but also simpler plea-sures that might serve as penitence for the sins of his past life.

Perhaps from fear of the hereafter, perhaps from simple weari-ness, the prince seemingly attempted to mend his ways.[90] Report-edly he cut down on his gambling and reduced his expenditures. The chevalier de Lorraine, although he continued to reside in the prince's household on terms of friendship, and another favorite, La Carte, who had attracted the prince's eye in recent years, may have been held at a distance. No evidence exists, however, that Monsieur's remorse, if such it were, involved any spiritual or moral change of conviction. Nothing suggests an inner torment or religious experience that turned him from worldliness to godliness. He may have feared the devil, as Saint-Simon reported, but not so much as to divest himself of substantial portions of his fortune to buy his way into heaven. His last will and testament, which dated from 1699 and was not subsequently amended, allocated 6,000 livres for daily masses to be recited "for the repose of his soul," not an unusual sum for a prince of such station. Another 20,000 went to the charitable hospitals at Villers-Cotterêts and Saint-Cloud. These were the merest crumbs of Monsieur's vast estate, which, except for a few pieces of jewelry reserved for his daughters, passed intact to his son, Philippe II, whom he named his sole legatee (*légataire universel*).[91] To the last day of his life religion remained for Philippe, as it did for Louis, a matter of external forms and observances. It was the creed their mother had taught them; seemingly they had learned it well.

With the slowing of his life's pace, Monsieur might have found a measure of peace had he not been in continuous torment over his son. Through Chartres he was reliving his old rivalry with Louis and reopening old wounds that could never completely heal. Once again he appeared the perpetual loser. A psychologist might say that Chartres was Philippe's final act of repetition/compulsion. Monsieur was seeking both to win his brother's favor and, at the same time, to reexperience the rejection and castration he had suffered from his powerful sibling/father. With a mounting inner fury Philippe watched his brother refuse the young man the promotions and positions he had been promised at the time of his marriage to Mlle de Blois. Chartres's courageous, even heroic, performances at the battles of Steenkerke in 1692 and Neerwinden in 1693 failed to win him command. Meanwhile the king's illegitimate sons and other royal relatives received one plum after another. The duke of Maine, who was nothing of a soldier, advanced from grand master of artillery in 1694 to lieutenant general in the army of Villeroy in 1695. The duke of Vendôme, great-grandson of Henry IV and Gabrielle d'Estrées, likewise held the rank of general. The governorship of Brittany, which Monsieur had counted on for his son, had gone in 1695 to the count of Toulouse, who gave up the governorship of Guyenne, which he already possessed, to the count of Chevreuse, nephew of the former incumbent.[92] Chartres, feeling himself cheated, had not helped matters by his dissolute and impious conduct and his neglect of his wife. His drunken orgies, his collection of mistresses, many from the most dubious segments of society, and his unconcealed irreverence, among other things, served only to provide the king with ready-made excuses for passing over his son-in-law.

As these insults and injuries occurred, Monsieur had duly protested but, obedient as usual, had been careful to avoid a quarrel with the king. The issue between them was forced by the outbreak of the War of the Spanish Succession in 1701 and the mobilizing of French armies to serve in Flanders, Germany, and Italy. Once again Louis denied Chartres a command, decreeing that he could serve in the army, but only in a subordinate position. Seemingly he counted upon Monsieur's offended pride to make him forbid his son to accept so humiliating an offer. If so, he was caught in his own trap when his brother offered no objection. The king was obliged to reveal what had been his true purpose all along. Chartres, he declared, should not join the army in any circumstances. The situation did not improve when the young man's mistress, Mlle de Séry, countess of Argenton, and possibly the only woman he may have truly loved, bore him a son only days after the birth of his third daughter by his wife.

Monsieur had reached the end of his tether. When Louis, in April, took his brother to task for having so little authority over his son, to his vast surprise he found before him a man who refused to be cowed. The report of the scene between them has come down to us from Saint-Simon,[93] who came to know Philippe II well (who very likely learned the details from his father) and may well have had a fair idea of what was said.

What, retorted Monsieur angrily, did the king expect of a young man who had been married off as he had been and with nothing better to do than pace the galleries of Versailles? Here he was, son-in-law of the king, yet subordinate in rank to the peers with whom he served. Meanwhile his brothers-in-law were showered with governments, commands, and posts of honor of all kinds. Well he knew, continued Monsieur, that the devil finds mischief for idle hands. He was indeed sorry to see his only son given over to debauchery, to bad company, and to all manner of follies. But it seemed the height of cruelty to him to blame the youngster for his misdeeds while excusing the one who had driven him to them!

Amazed, Louis retreated from the attack and tried to bring his brother around with soft words. He could, he said, well understand and excuse a father's love for his son. But Philippe refused to be mollified. And since neither would yield on the essential point of a command for Chartres, they parted in anger.

As the spring advanced the brothers managed a veneer of cordiality. If Monsieur came less frequently to court to visit the king, and if the king inquired less solicitously than usual after the health of Monsieur and his wife at Saint-Cloud, they could appear together as usual in public. Louis even did Philippe the honor of coming to Paris to admire the new gallery in the Palais Royal.[94] The prince as always was the perfect host. In private they nursed their rancor and awaited the moment to renew the attack. For Philippe the weeks passed unhappily. Liselotte struggled with an intermittent fever. He himself felt increasingly unwell. His appetite unabated, he continued to eat voraciously but refused his physicians' pleas to have himself bled. In his melancholy, the presentiment of death returned.[95]

The final test between the brothers took place when Philippe went to dine with the king at Marly on June 8, 1701.[96] No sooner had he entered the royal apartment than Louis launched into a tirade against Chartres and the humiliations he was causing his wife. Philippe, who had been nursing his rage over the weeks, let fly with a well-aimed ball: "Fathers," he remarked, "who have led certain lives are in no position morally or otherwise to reproach their sons."

Stung by the appropriateness of the remark, Louis drew himself up. The battle royal that had been fought below the surface of their lives for most of their existence broke into the open. Face to face, the brothers confronted each other in fury. Louis, stressing the patience of his daughter in the face of Chartres's infidelities, argued that at least she should be spared the sight of the adulterous creatures.

Oh! retorted Philippe, who had thrown off the last vestige of restraint, had the king forgotten how he had behaved toward the queen, how he had obliged her to put up with his mistresses even to the point of riding with them in her carriage?

The quarrel degenerated into a shouting match. The doors of the king's apartment were open; the room adjacent was filled with courtiers waiting to salute the king as he passed to his dinner. All could hear the passion in their voices.

Monsieur, "beside himself with rage," reminded the king of the marvels that had been promised at the time of Chartres's marriage. And now that not one of them had come to pass, it was not for him, his father, to prevent him from consoling himself with his pleasures as he wished. "Now, he added, he saw it only too clearly, the truth that everyone had tried to make him see, that nothing but dishonor and shame would ever come of that marriage, and never anything to his profit."

Resorting to the weapon always in his possession, Louis remarked that the war would soon oblige him to make economies. Since Philippe was proving so resistant to his wishes, he would begin by cutting back Monsieur's pensions rather than reducing his own expenditures.

Only the announcement of dinner halted the hostilities. At table Monsieur, red in the face and eyes glinting with anger, resisted the many suggestions that he permit himself to be bled and attacked his meat with extraordinary vigor.

Early in the evening following the quarrel Monsieur returned to Saint-Cloud. "Hale and hearty," still exhilarated from his clash with Louis, he called on his wife only to find her too ill to leave her chamber. "I am off to supper," he told her gaily, "because, unlike you, I am hungry," and went forthwith to the table.[97] Supping with Chartres and in company as usual, he was pouring a glass of liqueur when he began to stammer, sketched a gesture with his hand, and collapsed in a fit of apoplexy into the arms of his son, seated on his right.

The end was not long in coming. Borne to his apartments, suffering the usual ministrations of the doctors, he passed the night in intermittent unconsciousness. Liselotte, hearing the commotion, rushed to his side. "You are feverish," he murmured, "you must go back to your room." In despair she returned to scrawl a few words to her aunt: "This comes to Your Grace from the most unfortunate of creatures; Monsieur has suffered a stroke last evening at ten o'clock. He is in the throes of death."[98] Louis, persuaded somewhat tardily of the seriousness of his brother's condition, appeared at the palace in tears toward three in the morning. The court fell into a state of undignified confusion. At dawn Monsieur took a turn for the worse and died six hours later, at noon on June 9, 1701. He had not yet completed his sixty-first year.

Louis paid his final respects to his brother in a state funeral service that followed the wishes expressed in Monsieur's testament and was as elaborate as he no doubt would have wished.[99] On June 14 his heart was solemnly transported to Val-de-Grâce; a week later at nine in the evening his body was borne to Saint-Denis accompanied by his Swiss guards, the officers and servants of the ducal household, and crowds of inhabitants of the town of Saint-Cloud. Numerous eulogies and a solemn high mass preceded the lowering of the casket into the Bourbon crypt. There it remained until 1793, when the Revolutionary mobs desecrated the royal tombs, exhumed the bodies, and turned them all into a common grave.

A few weeks after Monsieur's death the *Mercure Galant* published a poem as a tribute to the brother of the king:

> To Monsieur, Duke of Orléans
> Cassel brought him glory in a great battle.
> Fame raised him up; Fate struck him down.[100]

Epilogue: A Prince for Posterity

After the death of Monsieur, Louis and the court quickly returned to their normal routines. "The king does not wish the court to be bored,"[1] became the order of the day, even before the body of the prince was borne to its place of rest. Louis, drying his tears, promenaded in his garden and worked with his ministers at his customary hours. The gaming tables at Marly soon filled with their usual players. The disappearance of the brother of the king neither interrupted nor inconvenienced the business of government, church, or any other public body. Except for his brief (and glorious) military career and his participation in the ceremonies of state, he had played no public role. Not even the mechanism of the court (although certainly its tone) was altered by his death. Monsieur had enacted no laws and ordained no policies. He left no memoirs and inspired no great literature. Even his architectural triumphs have not survived to the present. To judge only by the memoirs of the day, his existence had been a collection of trivia reflecting the purposeless of the life he had been obliged to lead.

Yet for those closest to Monsieur the effects of his death were immediate and dramatic. For Liselotte the trauma was great. She was losing her spouse of nearly thirty years, the father of her children, and the man with whom she had at the end achieved a friendly and easy camaraderie. She was also in dread of losing her position and even her identity at court. Without Monsieur, who would protect her? Well she knew that she was now at the mercy of the lady she despised and had insulted with abandon throughout the years. "No convent! Don't mention the word convent! I'll have no convent!" she is said to have cried despairingly in fear of eviction from court.[2] Such a destiny seems never to have been a possibility. What in fact she had to dread was what her marriage contract provided for her in case of widowhood: retirement to the château of Montargis with an income of a mere 40,000 livres each year. To Madame, second lady of the court (she was outranked only by the young duchess of Burgundy), such a fate amounted to exile. She need not have feared. The lady she had so maligned showed herself magnanimous in her triumph. Although she had long been aware of the epithets cast her way in Liselotte's letters and conversations, she exerted her influence on Louis to be generous.

To be sure, Mme de Maintenon was only human. In an interview that must have been humiliating in the extreme to the proud Palatine, the lady produced a sample of Madame's offensive correspondence (intercepted by the postal authorities) and forced Madame to eat a large slice of humble pie before offering her mediation. All ended well for Madame. Not only did she avoid retirement from court, but she continued to receive a pension of 250,000 livres annually from the king, to which were added New Year gifts, as during the lifetime of Monsieur. Philippe II promised an additional 200,000 livres each year. Consequently, with an income of over 450,000 livres Madame was enabled to keep up her rank and live as before in the palaces of her husband and in Versailles and other royal residences. After the death of Louis in 1715, her son, regent for the child Louis XV, treated her with unfailing generosity. Until her death in December 1722 she led a peaceful and luxurious existence. Ever more diligent as a correspondent, she reminisced to her relatives about her past, writing often of Monsieur in terms of increasing mellowness and tenderness. "Monsieur was basically a good man," she wrote in 1719. "His weaknesses grieved me more than they irritated me. Sometimes I lost patience, but when he came to beg my pardon I always forgave him."[3] Seventeen years after his death she was still reliving the last hours of his life. "I cannot think of that night without shuddering; I stayed with him from ten o'clock in the evening until five in the morning, when he lost all consciousness."[4]

For Chartres the death of Monsieur was a devastating blow. Father and son had loved each other deeply. Moreover, only Monsieur stood between Chartres and the terrible anger of the king. Even as his father lay dying, the young man knelt before Louis, embraced his knees, and exclaimed: "Ah! Sire, what will become of me? I am losing Monsieur, and I know that you do not love me."[5] The king, surprised and touched, raised him up tenderly and answered gently.

Perhaps Louis was genuinely moved by the grief of his son-in-law. Perhaps, too, he was feeling pangs of remorse and guilt over the angry quarrel he had provoked with his brother only hours before, which might well have precipitated his death.[6] In any case, Louis moved rapidly to make peace with his son-in-law, using the material means only he could command. In the words of Saint-Simon, "the duke of Chartres was, and the term is not too strong, prodigiously well treated."[7] In addition to the vast wealth he inherited as his father's his sole legatee, the new duke of Orléans received from the king the same pensions his father had enjoyed during his life, all the rights of patronage within the appanage, the Swiss guards and regiments of cavalry and infantry, and payment from the royal treasury of the officers of his household. Henceforward he would enjoy an annual income in the range of 1,800,000 livres.[8] To the immense satisfaction of his mother, the black sheep had become a "great seigneur."[9] The mortification of the princes of the blood was correspondingly profound.

In his good fortune Philippe II showed himself generous. Not only did he contribute to his mother's household and provide pensions for those who had served Monsieur, he bethought himself of his father's great "friend," the chevalier de Lorraine. Now bereft of the patron who had made his wealth and position in court, his fate was uncertain. Offering the chevalier continued possession of his apartments in the Palais Royal, he pressed him to accept an annual subvention of some 30,000 livres. "You would have been happy to have received a pension from Monsieur," he urged him. "I have inherited his estate: thus it is still he who gives it to you."[10] Although accepting the first, the chevalier proudly declined the second. He had in fact been more than liberally endowed by Monsieur through the years with a large variety of rentes and charges. But little time remained for him to enjoy them. In December 1702 while at the gaming table, like Monsieur his former patron he died of apoplexy. Seemingly an indifferent manager, he was, wrote Madame, "so poor that his friends had to bury him."[11]

Philippe II went on to carve out his own place in history as the brilliant regent for the child Louis XV. With him always went the legacy of his father: the material possessions that he had inherited from him, of course, but also, and at least as important, the unarticulated but ever present rivalry with the king and the Bourbon line. Like Monsieur, the regent was a loyal and dutiful subject. With the young king he established relations of affection and respect, and he willingly resigned the supreme power when Louis reached his majority. Yet much of the regent's life and government—from his dissolute and self-indulgent habits, the *goût moderne* of his taste in art, to the unorthodoxies of his financial policies—can be (and have been) seen as a protest against the classicism and rigid conformity of Louis XIV's reign. Under him the special relationship of Paris with the house of Orléans was strengthened, and he bequeathed it in turn to his heirs. During the Regency the Palais Royal became the center of government and of the social life of the court (as well as of the regent's debauches). Paris regained the distinction lost to Versailles under the old king. Its Parisian base established and its independence secured, the house of Orléans went on in the eighteenth century to construct an image that contrasted strongly with the spirit of Versailles. Always in the vanguard of their times, the princes attracted to them men and ideas that transcended the narrow question of the succession and flowed over into areas of political ideology, economics, and social progress. By the nineteenth century in the person of Louis Philippe, king of the French, the role of Orleanism was to propose to the French people a more liberal, more modern alternative to the traditional monarchy.

THE MAN AND POSTERITY

"He was a good enough prince, who did neither good nor evil," ran a pen portrait of Monsieur written not long after his death.[12] Subsequent writers were to treat Monsieur even less gently. A half-century later Voltaire, in his history of the age of Louis XIV, noted the general astonishment when the ridiculous little prince led the charge at the Battle of Cassel and defeated William of Orange. The grudging lesson he drew was that after all "courage is not incompatible with effeminacy."[13] A recent American biographer of Louis XIV has judged Monsieur even more harshly: "An unfortunate man . . . at best never more than a grotesque decoration of the court, [who was] at worst a burden, perhaps a disgrace to his brother, the king."[14] Even more recently a French biographer of the regent has concluded: "Monsieur was perfectly odious."[15]

These harsh verdicts are comprehensible enough given the deliberate arresting of his development in childhood and the obstacles placed in his path throughout his life. He was the victim of history and of the state: a younger brother of the king whose potential to challenge the authority of the Crown had to be destroyed. Although intelligent, gifted, and even precocious in his youth, he could not be permitted to excel. While he was still a small child his uncle Gaston, whom he greatly loved and with whom he identified, was a leader of the Fronde. This example was a forceful reminder for Anne and Mazarin of the dangers of a cadet. Louis could never be a great king with another Gaston at his side. As a child and adult Philippe was drilled in his duty of submission and absolute obedience to his brother. Though direct heir to the throne for eighteen years, he was not groomed to succeed Louis. As further insurance against potential revolt, he was systematically estranged from affairs of state and denied any position, such as a governorship, that might serve as a rallying point of support. Financially he was kept in a state of dependence on the Crown, which continued even when his loyalty could no longer have been questioned. On the one occasion when his natural bravery and his talents as a soldier at the Battle of Cassel brought him public acclaim and popularity in the army, Louis moved quickly to terminate his military career.

The demoralizing effects of these experiences of a lifetime on the prince's personality are neither surprising nor difficult to perceive. A fatal lack of self-confidence was evident throughout. As a child he preferred to turn away from competition and retreat into puerile behavior unbecoming to his age. As an adult, rather than revolting, he occupied himself with his palaces, his favorites, and his amusements and was satisfied to hold no position of responsibility. Meanwhile the avaricious side of his nature fed on amassing material possessions and wealth in all forms as a compensation for the authority denied him.

The key to his character, of course, lay in his relationship with Louis, who was both brother and, owing to the premature death of Louis XIII, surrogate father. From Philippe's earliest memories he was engaged in a rivalry with him—for the affections of his mother and for his place in society, among other things. From the fisticuffs of boyhood through the adult humiliations of life at his brother's court, to the final hours of his life when he engaged Louis in a shouting match over the future of his son, his existence was bound up in the unequal contest. His aggressive drives, those of an individual of high intelligence and healthy physique, were turned inward to destroy his confidence in himself.

His demoralization most certainly exacerbated, if it did not engender, his homosexuality. The feminine side of his character with its consequent flagrant homosexual behavior always emerged most strongly after a particularly humiliating defeat at the hands of his brother. The pattern can be seen throughout his life: the first "coming out of the closet" with Guiche after the king's near death and Philippe's abortive conspiracy in 1658; the blatant domination by male lovers, especially the chevalier de Lorraine, in the 1660s after Louis's flirtation with Henriette and the king's continued use of the first Madame as a tool to arouse Philippe's anger and jealousy; and finally, Philippe's return to homosexual behavior following the termination of his military career in 1677 after some six years of heterosexual relations with Liselotte. It certainly could have been no accident that the sole truly satisfying, self-fulfilling years of his life—the early years of his second marriage, in which he fathered three children, began the building of the château of Saint-Cloud, and pursued an active life in the army—were lived in the company of a woman who possessed no power to attract the sexual favors of the king, a woman who had a strong aversion for the feminine role and could not undermine the prince's self-confidence. The ambivalent feelings that he entertained toward the king were a mixture of love and hatred, of admiration and destructive jealousy that engendered feelings of guilt and desire for self-abasement and punishment. The resemblance of Guiche, Lorraine, and others who ruled him with a high hand, to the king was unmistakable.

In a court and society that abhorred homosexuality, the very conspicuousness of the prince's behavior contributed powerfully to the low esteem in which he was held. Even the symbolic definition of his relationship to Louis reinforced (albeit unwittingly) the image of feminine submissiveness of the cadet. Symbolically, the king was the sun, which was masculine. Monsieur was the moon, which was feminine. In the carrousel of 1662 the prince rode into the lists bearing a shield on which was a representation of the moon with the motto: *Uno sole minor*—"second only to the sun."[16] This imagery of inferiority followed Monsieur until his death, when it became the central theme of his many funeral eulogies. If Louis were the sun, ran a typical homily, Philippe was the moon, which could shine only in the reflected light of the king. "Never was a brother more sincerely submissive to his King," pronounced one orator. "Never did a king more tenderly love a brother."[17]

After the court of the Sun King passed into history, Philippe was often identified in the public mind with the Man in the Iron Mask. During Louis's lifetime rumors had circulated about a mysterious prisoner who had died in the Bastille and who allegedly had worn a mask. His identity became a famous historical mystery that Voltaire did much to transform into a legend. In the most popular of its many versions this man, often named Philippe, was a uterine

brother of the king—perhaps the son of Anne and Mazarin—whom
Louis perceived as a threat to his crown and whom he incarcerated,
his face concealed by a mask of iron. The romantic tale formed the
plot of Dumas's celebrated novel the *Vicomte de Bragelonne*.

This legend has, of course, no factual connection with Monsieur,
duke of Orléans. Philippe was never in prison, and he never wore
an iron mask. But if not literally, then figuratively the prince could
be seen as personifying this famous victim. Like the Man in the Iron
Mask, his liberty was sacrificed to his brother. The court of the Sun
King, not the Bastille, was his prison. Lest he pose a threat to the
sovereign, his person and style of life were bound and confined
within the limits of the royal pleasure.

Thus told, the case of Monsieur serves as merely another, if perhaps the most famous and tragic, example of the success of Louis
XIV's policy of subordinating the greater nobility to his royal will.
But this public side of Philippe as the subservient prince was only
one of the many roles he played in history. Had he not played others, the history of the house of Orléans and of France herself would
have followed a much different course. The impact of his personality on his contemporaries, especially the king, the results of his
(or his council's) investments and estate management, and his
popularity with the Parisians, among other things, were to influence
the future in a manner of which his contemporaries (and no doubt
Monsieur himself) could have had no comprehension.

When Monsieur died, the king was most certainly not among
those closest to him. Yet he had known Philippe longer than anyone
else. Their lives had been intertwined since their earliest memories.
What impact during his life and in his death might Monsieur have
had upon the character and the court of the Sun King? For just as
we could not know Philippe without his brother, so we cannot understand Louis without taking into account the existence of the cadet. The court was an elemental world in which the rivalry of the
two brothers, the clashes of their personalities, and the crises of
family life molded their personalities and provided the mainsprings
of their actions.

The contest was entirely one-sided, of course. Behind Louis,
even before he had attained his fifth year, was the full force of law
of the divine monarchy and the weight of the adult world. Philippe
could not hope to win. Yet so long as he existed, especially during
the formative years of childhood and youth when he was the direct
heir to the throne, the prince posed a threat to the king: a threat to
his position as older and preferred son of his mother, a threat to his
life and to his crown. If Louis should falter or should disappear from

the scene, Philippe would take his place. "The king is dead; long live the king." That Louis loved Philippe can not be doubted, just as Philippe loved him. But the king's emotions, also like those of Monsieur, were ambivalent. Fear of displacement and hatred of a potential rival struggled with the feelings of tenderness he entertained for his younger brother.

In defense against the cadet, and with the full support of Anne and Mazarin, he must unconsciously have shored up his position. Always he had to be obeyed. In adulthood the constant deference of everyone around him must inevitably have contributed to his unchecked habits of self-indulgence and selfishness and to his well-known callousness toward the discomfort and suffering of others. While the unequal sibling rivalry demoralized and decompensated the younger brother, it brutalized the older and rendered him insensible. Fearing a challenge, he moved to dominate. Yet always there was the inner absence of security and the need for constant reassurance noted by his many biographers. Perhaps it was this lack of self-confidence that helped turn the king into a kind of moral monster and his courtiers into sycophants. Certainly it would be much too simplistic to consider Louis's psychological dynamics as the only driving force behind the major policies of his adult reign: his wars of conquest, the suppression of the Huguenots, and the development to the extreme of the prerogatives of divine right. Yet in all of them can be seen an extension of the circumstances of childhood in which he had vanquished his brother, the most immediate threat to his self-esteem and to his throne.

In addition to the impact of his personality on his son and on the king, Monsieur influenced the future course of events in at least two other ways. First of all, the vast fortune that Monsieur and his council had put together primarily from the largess of the Crown shaped the political role of the house of Orléans in the eighteenth and nineteenth centuries. Continuing to build on his wealth, the family achieved financial independence by the middle of the eighteenth century. Two generations later, Louis Philippe Joseph, better known as Philippe Egalité, the last duke of Orléans in the Old Regime, was the greatest landlord in France except the king himself. Possessed of a net annual revenue of over seven million livres,[18] he far outdistanced in wealth even Louis XVI's brothers, the counts of Provence and Artois. His fortune enabled him to indulge his taste for politics, to subsidize a "party" in opposition to the Crown, and to attempt to play a leading role in the early Revolution. Eventually he was brought to vote in the Convention for the death of his cousin the king.[19] Nor did the impact of Orleanist wealth cease there. Although the holdings of the family were sequestered and put on the market by the Republic, the unsold remainder, including much of the woodland of the appanage, was restored to Philippe Egalité's son, Louis Philippe, under the Bourbon restoration. Because the appanage had been suppressed early in the Revolution, the returned forests became the proprietary possession of the house.[20] With it, as an indemnity for those lands that had been sold, the prince received an award of 12,704,000 francs of bonds, the largest compensation settled upon any of the émigrés.[21] The head of the house of Orléans was thus once again among the richest subjects of the realm when, profiting by the Revolution of 1830, he ascended the throne from which his Bourbon relative had been evicted. Certainly it is not one of the lesser ironies of history that Louis XIV, who had been frightened by the revolt of Gaston d'Orléans and who had been strong in his determination to keep Monsieur in submission, should himself have laid the cornerstone of the Orléans fortune and with it that of Orleanism, the liberal alternative to Bourbon monarchy, which was to oppose, to supplant, and eventually to outlive the senior branch of the family.

And finally there was that vast progeny, the fruit of Monsieur's two marriages, which multiplied and spread across the face of the Continent. Surely it is another irony of history that he whose taste was not for women should in time have become a veritable patriarch, the *souche de sa race* (founder of his family). Collateral lines such as that founded by Philippe, or the absence thereof, have frequently played enormous roles in shaping historical events. In a monarchical system of government the continuation of the dynasty is entirely dependent upon the existence of legitimate heirs. Consider, for example, how the perilous lack of dynastic safety in Spain affected its fortunes: one heir for Philip II, born late; one heir for Philip III, and one for Philip IV—his born very late; and none at all for Charles II, whose throne in consequence passed to the Bourbon dynasty in the person of the duke of Anjou, grandson of Louis XIV. In France one need only recall the upheavals following the failure of succession of the fourteenth century and the wars of religion of the sixteenth when the Valois line died out with Henry III. Small wonder that Anne and Mazarin, even while declining to initiate Philippe into affairs of state, made haste to arrange his marriage. After that marriage terminated, even though it had been a disaster, the prince was required to marry again almost immediately. Well they, and later Louis, understood the need for children—especially male children, and the more the better. History has proved the soundness of their judgment. Although in time an heir

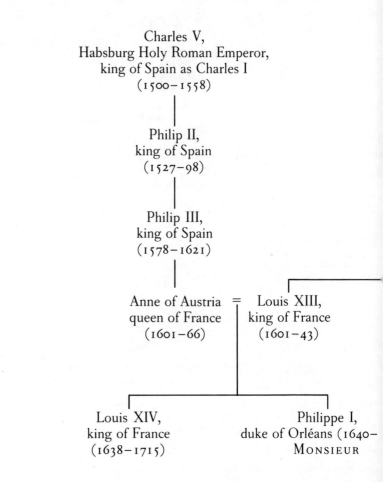

Charles V,
Habsburg Holy Roman Emperor,
king of Spain as Charles I
(1500–1558)

Philip II,
king of Spain
(1527–98)

Philip III,
king of Spain
(1578–1621)

Anne of Austria = Louis XIII,
queen of France   king of France
(1601–66)   (1601–43)

Louis XIV,   Philippe I,
king of France   duke of Orléans (1640–
(1638–1715)   MONSIEUR

Cosimo ("the Great") de' Medici,
grand duke of Tuscany
(1519–74)

y of Bourbon,   =   Jeanne d' Albret,   Francis de' Medici
·of Vendôme   queen of Navarre   grand duke of
518–62)   Tuscany
                                      (1541–87)

Henry IV,   =   Marie de' Medici
king of France   (1573–1642)
(1553–1610)

Gaston, duke = Marie of Bourbon,
of Orléans   duchess of
(1608–60)   Montpensier

Anne Marie Louise,
la Grande Mademoiselle
(1627–93)

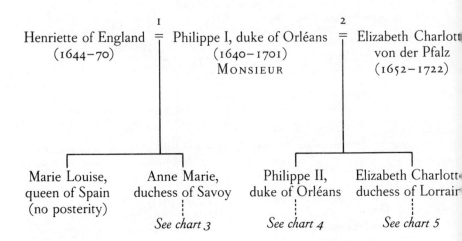

1

Henriette of England = Philippe I, duke of Orléans = Elizabeth Charlott
(1644–70)   (1640–1701)   von der Pfalz
                                    Monsieur   (1652–1722)

2

Marie Louise,   Anne Marie,   Philippe II,   Elizabeth Charlott
queen of Spain   duchess of Savoy   duke of Orléans   duchess of Lorrair
(no posterity)

See chart 3   *See chart 4*   *See chart 5*

Chart Three

Monsieur's Descendants by Henriette of England

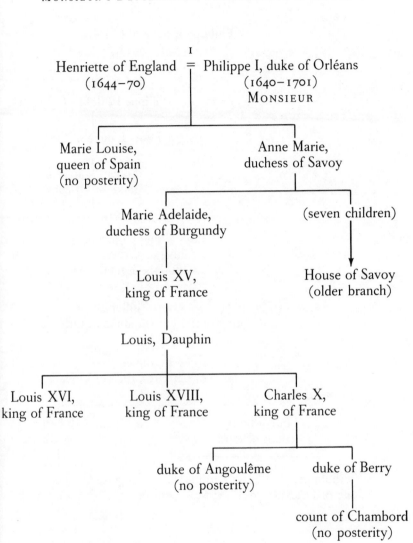

I

Henriette of England = Philippe I, duke of Orléans
(1644–70)   (1640–1701)
           Monsieur

Marie Louise,   Anne Marie,
queen of Spain   duchess of Savoy
(no posterity)

Marie Adelaide,   (seven children)
duchess of Burgundy

Louis XV,   House of Savoy
king of France   (older branch)

Louis, Dauphin

Louis XVI,   Louis XVIII,   Charles X,
king of France   king of France   king of France

duke of Angoulême   duke of Berry
(no posterity)

count of Chambord
(no posterity)

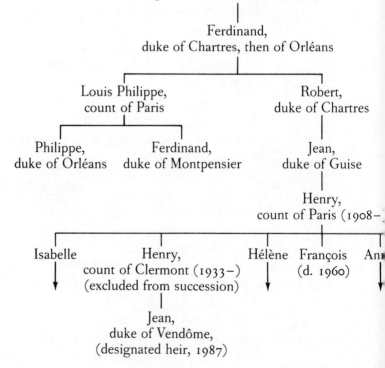

Philippe I, duke of Orléans
(1640–1701)
MONSIEUR

Philippe II, duke of Orléans

Louis I, duke of Orléans

Louis Philippe I,
duke of Orléans

Louis Philippe Joseph,
duke of Orléans
(Philippe Egalité)

Louis Philippe,
king of the French, duke of Orléans

Ferdinand,
duke of Chartres, then of Orléans

Louis Philippe,
count of Paris

Robert,
duke of Chartres

Philippe,
duke of Orléans

Ferdinand,
duke of Montpensier

Jean,
duke of Guise

Henry,
count of Paris (1908–

Isabelle

Henry,
count of Clermont (1933–)
(excluded from succession)

Hélène

François
(d. 1960)

An

Jean,
duke of Vendôme,
(designated heir, 1987)

lizabeth Charlotte von der Pfalz
(1652–1722)

Elizabeth Charlotte,
duchess of Lorraine

See chart 5

Louise Marie Thérèse,
duchess of Bourbon

Louis,
duke of Enghien,
(shot at Vincennes, 1804)

Diane Michel Jacques, Claude Chantal Thibaut
duke of
Orléans

MONSIEUR'S DESCENDANTS
BY ELIZABETH CHARLOTTE VON DER PFALZ:
ELIZABETH CHARLOTTE, DUCHESS OF LORRAINE

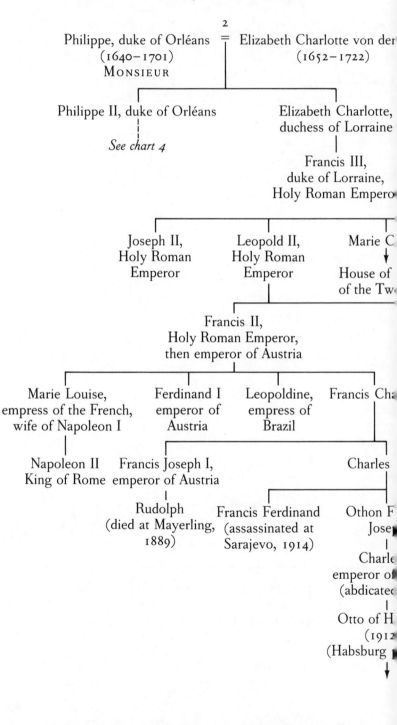

2

Philippe, duke of Orléans = Elizabeth Charlotte von der
(1640–1701)   (1652–1722)
MONSIEUR

Philippe II, duke of Orléans   Elizabeth Charlotte,
                                        duchess of Lorraine
See chart 4
                                        Francis III,
                                        duke of Lorraine,
                                        Holy Roman Emperor

Joseph II,   Leopold II,   Marie C
Holy Roman   Holy Roman
Emperor   Emperor   House of
                                    of the Tw

Francis II,
Holy Roman Emperor,
then emperor of Austria

Marie Louise,   Ferdinand I   Leopoldine,   Francis Cha
empress of the French, emperor of   empress of
wife of Napoleon I   Austria   Brazil

Napoleon II   Francis Joseph I,   Charles
King of Rome   emperor of Austria

Rudolph   Francis Ferdinand   Othon F
(died at Mayerling, (assassinated at   Jose
1889)   Sarajevo, 1914)

Charle
emperor of
(abdicated

Otto of H
(1912
(Habsburg

Theresa of Austria,
Bohemia and Hungary

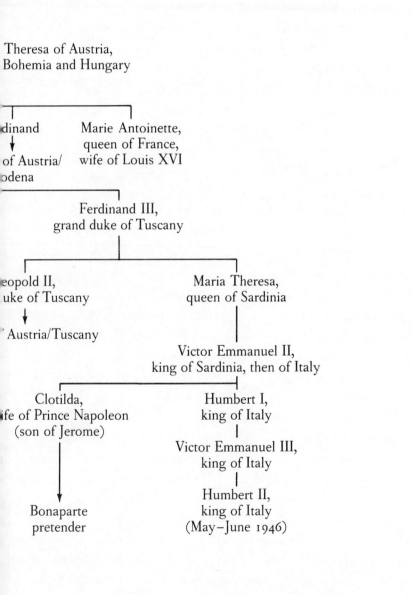

dinand
↓
of Austria/
odena

Marie Antoinette,
queen of France,
wife of Louis XVI

Ferdinand III,
grand duke of Tuscany

eopold II,
uke of Tuscany
↓
Austria/Tuscany

Maria Theresa,
queen of Sardinia

Victor Emmanuel II,
king of Sardinia, then of Italy

Clotilda,
fe of Prince Napoleon
(son of Jerome)

Humbert I,
king of Italy

Victor Emmanuel III,
king of Italy

Bonaparte
pretender

Humbert II,
king of Italy
(May–June 1946)

Notes

ABBREVIATIONS USED IN NOTES

AMAE Archives du Ministère des Affaires Etrangères
        (CP, Correspondance politique; MD, Mémoires et documents)
AMG   Archives du Ministère de la Guerre
AN   Archives Nationales
BA   Bibliothèque d'Arsenal
BN   Bibliothèque Nationale
PRO   Public Record Office
        (SP, State Papers)

PREFACE

1. Philippe Erlanger, *Monsieur: Frère de Louis XIV* (Paris, 1953). There is also in French Guy de La Batut's *La cour de Monsieur, frère de Louis XIV* (Paris, 1927). Less a biography than a chronology of Monsieur's life, it focuses on the court around him.

ONE   BROTHER OF LE DIEUDONNÉ

1. Mme de Motteville, *Mémoires*, ed. C. B. Petitot, Collection des mémoires relatifs à l'histoire de France, vols. 36–39 (Paris, 1824), 1:398. For the public celebration of the birth of the prince see *Gazette de France*, September 24, 1640.

2. Ruth Kleinman, *Anne of Austria: Queen of France* (Columbus, Ohio, 1985), pp. 70–85.

3. Georges Dethan, *Gaston d'Orléans: Conspirateur et prince charmant* (Paris, 1959), pp. 352–53. He received the governorship of Languedoc from the Crown in September 1644. He also had at his disposal the enormous fortune of Anne Marie Louise, duchess of Montpensier, only child of his first marriage, although as a rule he refused to touch it except to pay the expenses of her household.

4. Motteville, *Mémoires*, 1:326, "Portrait de la reine Anne d'Autriche."

5. John B. Wolf, *Louis XIV* (New York, 1968), p. 5.

6. Estat des gouvernant . . . de Monseigneur le dauphin et Monseigneur le duc d'Anjou pendant l'année 1640, Bibliothèque Nationale (hereafter BN), Clairamboult, vol. 816, fol. 213; Kleinman, *Anne of Austria*, p. 113.

7. H. Druon, *Histoire de l'éducation des princes dans la maison des Bourbons de France*, 2 vols. (Paris, 1897), 1:xxxv.

8. One of Anne's attendants, Mlle Andrieu, in a letter to an exiled lady of honor, Mme de Sénécey, cited in Kleinman, *Anne of Austria*, pp. 112–13.

9. See, for example, Druon, *Éducation des princes*, p. 148; and La Batut, *Cour de Monsieur*, p. 5.

10. "Maximes d'éducation et direction puerile. Des dévotions, moeurs, actions et petite étude de Monseigneur le dauphin jusqu'à l'âge de sept ans . . . , BN, Fonds Français 19043.

11. Philippe Ariès, *Centuries of Childhood: A Social History of Family Life*, trans. Robert Baldick (New York, 1965), pp. 364–404, esp. 403–4.

12. One of Louis XIII's valets, Dubois, wrote that when Anne rushed to the bedside of her dying husband, Philippe was passed from hand to hand and ended up crying piteously in the arms of a lady of the court he did not know. Dubois calmed him down by telling him stories (Dubois, l'un des valets de chambre de Sa Majesté, *Mémoire fidèle des choses qui se sont passées à la mort de Louis XIII*, ed. MM. Michaud et Poujoulat, Nouvelle collection des mémoires pour servir à l'histoire de France, vol. 11 [Paris, 1838], p. 525. See also Claude Dulong, *Anne d'Autriche: Mère de Louis XIV* (Paris, 1980), p. 199.

13. Parish records of the city of Saint-Germain, La Batut, *Cour de Monsieur*, p. 4.

14. *Gazette de France*, May 23, 1643, p. 425.

15. It has been argued that absolutism is a "constant struggle" that never ends "by the sovereign power to free itself [from opposition from nobles, institutional bodies and other combinations of social or legal forces restraining it]." See G. Durand, "What Is Absolutism?" in *Louis XIV and Absolutism*, ed. Ragnhild Hatton (London, 1976), p. 18.

16. Ariès, *Centuries of Childhood*, pp. 369–70.

17. Motteville, *Mémoires*, 2:297.

18. Ibid., p. 348; *Gazette de France*, April 4, 1648.

19. Report of Contarini, envoyé extraordinaire from the Republic of Venice, September 5, 1643, quoted in Henri Carré, *L'enfance et la première jeunesse de Louis XIV, 1638–1661* (Paris, 1944), p. 27.

20. Louis to Philippe, Amiens, July 1, 1647, quoted in Carré, *Enfance*, p. 117.

21. Mlle de Montpensier, *Mémoires*, ed. A. Petitot and L. J. N. Monmerqué, Collection des mémoires relatifs à l'histoire de France, vols. 39–43 (Paris, 1825), 1:58.

22. Motteville, *Mémoires*, 2:267.

23. Ibid., 2:266.

24. P. Henri Chérot, *La première jeunesse de Louis XIV (1649–1653) d'après la correspondance inédite du P. Charles Paulin, son premier confesseur* (Lille, 1892), p. 75.

TWO THE "EDUCATION" OF A PRINCE

1. *Gazette de France*, May 2, 1648; Motteville, *Mémoires*, 2:356; Gui Patin to Charles Spon, Paris, May 29, 1648, Gui Patin, *Lettres de Gui Patin à Charles Spon, médecin à Lyon*, ed. J. B. Ballière, 3 vols. (Paris, 1846), 1:396.

2. *Gazette de France*, May 11, 1648; Motteville, *Mémoires*, 2:356.

3. *Gazette de France*, April 24, 1643.

4. Ibid., December 24, 1649, p. 1200; Montpensier, *Mémoires*, 2:76.

5. Chérot, *Jeunesse*, pp. 54–63; *Gazette de France*, December 24, 1649, p. 1272; extra no. 160, pp. 121737–80; Kleinman, *Anne of Austria*, pp. 190–91.

6. Chérot, *Jeunesse*, p. 88.

7. *Gazette de France*, April 27, 1647.

8. Ibid., March 10, 1646; Archives du Ministère des Affaires Etrangères (hereafter AMAE), Mémoires et documents (hereafter MD); France, 855, fols. 55–56.

9. Ellery Schalk, *From Valor to Pedigree: Ideas of Nobility in France in the Sixteenth and Seventeenth Centuries* (Princeton, 1986), esp. pp. 174–201.

10. Kleinman, *Anne of Austria*, p. 198; Wolf, *Louis XIV*, p. 24.

11. Druon, *Education des princes*, 1:197–98.

12. Motteville, *Mémoires*, 2:267; César de Choiseul, comte du Plessis-Praslin, *Mémoires des divers emplois et des principales actions du maréchal du Plessis*, ed. A. Petitot et L. J. N. de Monmerqué, Collection des mémoires relatifs à l'histoire de France, vol. 52 (Paris, 1827), pp. 299–300.

13. Wolf, *Louis XIV*, p. 57.

14. Erlanger, *Monsieur*, p. 35; La Batut, *Cour de Monsieur*, pp. 9–11; Druon, *Education des princes*, 1:197.

15. Colbert to Mazarin, Paris, September 30, 1651, Jean Baptiste Colbert, *Lettres, instructions et mémoires de Colbert*, ed. Pierre Clément, 7 vols. (Paris, 1861), 1:135; see also same to same, October 13, 1651, ibid., p. 144.

16. Plessis-Praslin, *Mémoires*, pp. 419–20.

17. Ibid., pp. 299–300. Emphasis mine.

18. Ibid., p. 422.

19. Quoted in Wolf, *Louis XIV*, p. 68.

20. Wolf, *Louis XIV*, pp. 84–86; Kleinman, *Anne of Austria*, p. 232.

21. Elizabeth Charlotte to Countess Louise, [Paris], July 2, 1717, Elizabeth Charlotte, duchesse d'Orléans, *Correspondance complète de Madame duchesse d'Orléans née Princesse Palatine, mère du régent*, trans. and ed. M. G. Brunet, 2 vols. (Paris, n.d.), 1:304–5. A similar letter is attributed to Elizabeth Charlotte by Jean Vatout, *Souvenirs historiques des résidences royales: Le Palais-Royal* (Paris, 1838), p. 94.

22. Montpensier, *Mémoires*, 3:300, 4:58; Daniel de Cosnac, *Mémoires publiés pour la Société de l'histoire de France par le Comte Jules de Cosnac*, 2 vols. (Paris, 1852), 1:271–72.

23. Motteville, *Mémoires*, 2:198–99.

24. Mazarin to plenipotentiaries Gramont and Lionne, September 2, 1657, *Lettres du cardinal Mazarin pendant son ministère*, ed. M. A. Chéruel, 9 vols. (Paris, 1872–1906), 8:140–41.

25. Alfred Adler, *The Practice and Theory of Individual Psychology*, trans. P. Radin (London, 1955), p. 344.

26. Louis de Rouvroy, duc de Saint-Simon, *Mémoires*, ed. A. de Boislisle, 41 vols. (Paris, 1879–1928), 8:340.

27. Philippe, duke of Anjou, to Gaston, duke of Orléans, undated but ca. September 1650, BN, Baluze, 349, fol. 55.

28. Elizabeth Charlotte to the Countess Louise, [Paris], July 21, 1716, *Correspondance*, 1:257. Samples of the prince's handwriting may be found in the publication of the *Musée des Archives*, no. 899, Archives Nationales. Others of his letters are scattered haphazardly throughout manuscript collections in the Bibliothèque Nationale, the Bibliothèque Mazarin, and the archives of the Foreign Ministry and are cited elsewhere herein. In London the Public Record Office, State Papers 78, France, 1577–1780, contains a series of letters from the prince to his brother-in-law, Charles II, king of England.

29. Père Révérend, *Les dits notables de Monsieur Philippe de France, duc d'Anjou, frère unique du roy* (Paris, 1655), pp. 3–4.

30. Abbé de Choisy, *Mémoires pour servir à l'histoire de Louis XIV*, ed. A. Petitot and L. J. N. Monmerqué, Collection des mémoires relatifs à l'histoire de France, vol. 63, (Paris, 1828), p. 497.

31. Motteville, *Mémoires*, 5:57–61.

32. Cosnac, *Mémoires*, 2:55–56.

33. Peter Gay, *Freud for Historians* (New York, 1985), p. 110.

34. For Philippe's training in physical skills, games, and sports, see Carré, *Enfance*, p. 124; La Batut, *Cour de Monsieur*, p. 12; Motteville, *Mémoires*, 3:281; Druon, *Education des princes*, 1:lxviii; Kleinman, *Anne of Austria*, p. 191; Wolf, *Louis XIV*, pp. 23, 27; Chérot, *Jeunesse*, passim.

35. *Gazette de France*, August 5, 1651.

36. Robert M. Isherwood, *Music in the Service of the King: France in the Seventeenth Century* (Ithaca, 1973), pp. 128–30; *Gazette de France*, passim, 1650s and 1660s.

37. Elizabeth Charlotte to the Countess Louise, [Paris], January 27, 1720, *Correspondance*, 2:216.

38. Elizabeth Charlotte to Countess Louise, [Paris], July 21, 1716, ibid., p. 257.

39. Alfred Adler's theory of the sense of inferiority included the concept of demoralization, according to which a demoralized child, even one gifted intellectually and physically, will run away from life and its demands: "A lazy child can always fall back upon laziness as an excuse. If he fails in an examination it is the fault of his laziness, and such a child prefers to attribute his failure to laziness rather than to inability" (Adler, *Practice and Theory of Individual Psychology*, p. 345).

40. Philippe Ariès, *Centuries of Childhood*, p. 71.

41. Montpensier, *Mémoires*, 3:398.

42. *Gazette de France*, January 1655, passim; Carré, *Enfance*, pp. 270–71.

43. The best general account of the Fronde is probably E. H. Kossman, *La Fronde* (Leiden, 1954). For a bibliography of works in English on the Fronde since 1970 see Albert Hamscher, "Ouvrages sur la fronde parus en anglais depuis 1970," *XVIIe Siècle* 36(1984): 380–83.

44. For some historians the Fronde was more a squabble among elites than a conflict of ideologies or material interests. Denis Richet, *La France moderne: L'esprit des institutions* (Paris, 1973), pp. 112–14.

45. Pierre Adolphe Chéruel, "Les carnets de Mazarin pendant la Fronde, septembre–octobre 1648," *Revue Historique* 4(1877): 103–16.

46. Motteville, *Mémoires*, 3:60.

47. Ibid., 3:135–42; Montpensier, *Mémoires*, 2:40–53.

48. Dethan, *Gaston d'Orléans*, p. 365.

49. Ibid., p. 382.

50. Philippe, duke of Anjou, to Gaston, duke of Orléans, no date but circa September 1650, BN, Baluze, 349, fol. 55.

51. Wolf, *Louis XIV*, p. 42.

52. Dethan, *Gaston d'Orléans*, p. 349.

53. Philippe, duke of Anjou, to Gaston, duke of Orléans, La Fère, August 25, 1657, BN, Baluze, 349, fol. 57.

54. Patronage has been the subject of much recent research. For example, Robert R. Harding, *Anatomy of a Power Elite: The Provincial Governors of Early Modern France* (New Haven, 1978), pp. 21–37, and a recent book by Sharon Kettering, *Patrons, Brokers, and Clients in Seventeenth-Century France* (Oxford: Oxford University Press, 1986). For a good overview of patronage and power during the Fronde see Kettering, "Patronage and Politics during the Fronde," *French Historical Review* 14, no. 3(1986): 409–41.

55. Motteville, *Mémoires*, 3:416–58; see also Dethan, *Gaston d'Orléans*, pp. 390–91.

56. La Grande Mademoiselle to Mme de Choisy, quoted in Bernadine Melchior-Bonnet, *La Grande Mademoiselle: Héroine et amoureuse* (Paris, 1985), pp. 94–95.

57. Increasingly the view of recent scholarship. See, for example, Richet, *France moderne*, pp. 112–14; Christian Jouhaud, *Mazarinades: La*

Fronde des mots (Paris, 1985), p. 237; Ellery Schalk, "Clientage, Elites, and Absolutism in Seventeenth-Century France," *French Historical Studies* 14, no. 3 (1986): 444–45.

58. Louis XIV, *Mémoires pour les années 1661 et 1666 suivis des réflexions sur le métier de roi; des instructions au duc d'Anjou, et d'un projet de harangue*, ed. Jean Longnon (Paris, 1923), pp. 54–56.

59. Ibid., p. 143. Emphasis mine.

60. Ibid., p. 136.

61. Ibid., p. 18.

62. Pierre Goubert, *Louis XIV et vingt millions de Français* (Paris, 1966), p. 47.

63. *Gazette de France*, September 7, 1651; Motteville, *Mémoires*, 4:278–93, has a detailed account.

THREE   LE ROI MANQUÉ

1. Mazarin to the duc de Richelieu, Rueil, September 17, 1648; and Mazarin to M. Servien, Rueil, September 18, 1648, *Lettres du Cardinal Mazarin*, ed. M. A. Chéruel, 3:208, 210.

2. Wolf, *Louis XIV*, p. 84.

3. Mazarin to Anne, Riblemont, July 26, 1653, *Lettres du Cardinal Mazarin*, ed. Chéruel, 5:650.

4. Mazarin to Anne, du camp de Marolles, July 31, 1655, *Lettres du Cardinal Mazarin*, ed. Chéruel, 7:29.

5. Mazarin to Anne, Bergues, July 29, 1658, *Lettres du Cardinal Mazarin*, ed. Chéruel, 8:544.

6. Mazarin to Anne, Stenay, July 17, 1657, and same to same, August 6, 1657, *Lettres du Cardinal Mazarin*, ed. Chéruel, 8:47, 89; Plessis-Praslin, *Mémoires*, pp. 423–24.

7. *Gazette de France*, December 23, 1656.

8. There are many accounts of the consecration. *Gazette de France*, June 20, 1654, is readily accessible. See also the many contemporary accounts in the BN under the call numbers L b 37, 3211–20.

9. For a discussion of the traditional role of princes of the blood and peers of France in French coronations, see Richard A. Jackson, *Vive le Roi: A History of the French Coronations from Charles V to Charles X* (Chapel Hill, N.C., 1984), pp. 155–71.

10. Many authorities place the conceptual origins of adolescence in the nineteenth century and maintain that the idea did not exist in preindustrial times. Philippe Ariès, for example, believes the first youth to portray the qualities of a modern adolescent was Wagner's Siegfried (*Centuries of Childhood*, p. 30). Historians are ever aware that social conditions with their attendant pressures vary greatly over time and across cultures. Nonetheless, most authorities would agree that human biological development (the onset of puberty) and the conflict of sexual urges with adult values are more or less timeless and that the teen years may be seen as a period of

transition from childhood to adulthood with recognizable behavior problems. For a discussion of the controversy over the concept of adolescence see Vivian C. Fox, "Is Adolescence a Phenomenon of Modern Times?" *Journal of Psychohistory* 5, no. 2 (1977): 271–90.

11. Montpensier, *Mémoires*, 3:300.

12. Paulin to Mazarin, Paris, December 25, 1652, Chérot, *Jeunesse*, p. 125. Emphasis in original.

13. Pierre de La Porte, *Mémoires*, ed. A. Petitot and L. J. N. Monmerqué, Collection des mémoires relatifs à l'histoire de France, vol. 59 (Paris, 1827), p. 428. Owing to La Porte's uncontrollable hatred of Mazarin, his memoirs cannot always be accepted as reliable. This incident, however, because it in no way involved the cardinal, may well have taken place as described.

14. Gui Patin to Charles Spon, Paris, June 19, 1657, *Lettres*, vol. 2, no. 310, pp. 320–321.

15. Choisy, *Mémoires*, pp. 382–83; Cosnac, *Mémoires*, 1:271–72.

16. Montpensier, *Mémoires*, 2:25.

17. Sigmund Freud, "Fragment of an Analysis of Hysteria," in *The Standard Edition of the Complete Psychological Works of Sigmund Freud*, trans. and ed. James Strachey et al., 24 vols. (1953–75), 7:55.

18. Sigmund Freud, "Dostoevsky and Parricide," in *Collected Papers*, ed. James Strachey (New York, 1959), 5:229–30.

19. Cited in Ernst Kantorowicz, *The King's Two Bodies* (Princeton, 1957), p. 409, from a sermon of Bossuet, "Sur les devoirs des rois," preached April 2, either 1662 or 1666.

20. Plessis-Praslin, *Mémoires*, pp. 424–25.

21. Mazarin to Anne, Mardyck, May 29, 1658, AMAE, MD, France, vol. 277, fols. 119–20.

22. Mazarin to Anne, Mardyck, May 31, 1658, *Lettres du Cardinal Mazarin*, ed. Chéruel, 8:385; Anne to Mazarin, Compiegne, August 3, 1658, BN, Clairamboult, vol. 1144.

23. Gui Patin to Charles Spon, Paris, July 16, 1658, *Lettres*, vol. 2, no. 332, pp. 407–8.

24. Motteville, *Mémoires*, 4:430.

25. Mazarin to Lockart, Calais, July 5, 1658, *Lettres du Cardinal Mazarin*, ed. Chéruel, 8:489.

26. Mazarin to Turenne, Calais, July 8, 1658, ibid., 8:499.

27. Mazarin to the duke of Modena, Calais, July 8, 1658, AMAE, MD, France, vol. 277, fols. 184–85.

28. Mazarin to Turenne, Calais, July 8, 1658, *Lettres du Cardinal Mazarin*, ed. Chéruel, 8:499.

29. Mazarin to Turenne, Calais, July 7, 1658, ibid., 8:492.

30. Colbert to Mazarin, Paris, July 14, 1658, *Lettres* (of Colbert), 1:303.

31. Gui Patin to Charles Spon, Paris, July 26, 1658, *Lettres*, vol. 2, no. 333, p. 412; same to same, August 13, 1658, ibid., no. 334, 2:414. See also Montpensier, *Mémoires*, 3:324–30; Mazarin to the bishop of Fréjus, Calais, August 12, 1658, *Lettres du Cardinal Mazarin*, ed. Chéruel, 9:7.

32. Mazarin to Anne, Mardyck, May 31, 1658, *Lettres du Cardinal Mazarin*, ed. Chéruel, 8:385.

33. Plessis-Praslin, *Mémoires*, p. 425; Montpensier, *Mémoires*, 3:341; *Lettres du Cardinal Mazarin*, ed. Chéruel, 8:500, n. 1.

34. Mazarin to the bishop of Fréjus, Calais, August 12, 1658, *Lettres du Cardinal Mazarin*, ed. Chéruel, 9:7.

35. Madame de Motteville, always hostile to Mazarin, believed that even he played a double game, taking care to get in the good graces of those who would presumably have great influence over Philippe were Louis to die (Motteville, *Mémoires*, 4:431). On the other hand, Chéruel, the learned editor of Mazarin's correspondence, exonerates him from dishonorable behavior (*Lettres du Cardinal Mazarin*, 8:499−500, n. 1).

36. Motteville, *Mémoires*, 4:430−31.

37. Mazarin to Anne, Calais, August 7, 1658, *Lettres du Cardinal Mazarin*, ed. Chéruel, 8:561.

38. Mazarin to Anne, Calais, August 10, 1658, AMAE, MD, France, vol. 279, fols. 25−26. Some of the guilty attempted to insinuate themselves into the cardinal's good graces. His contemptuous rejection of their declarations of innocence can be seen in a letter to Anne of August 11 and in another of the same day to the duke de Brissac (ibid., vol. 279, fols. 34−35).

39. Anne to Mazarin, Compiegne, August 3, 1658, BN, Clairamboult, vol. 1144. The letter is reproduced in Victor Cousin, *Madame de Hautefort*, 2d ed. (Paris, 1868), pp. 401−2.

40. Mazarin to Anne, August 26, 1658, *Lettres du Cardinal Mazarin*, ed. Chéruel, 9:40.

41. Mazarin to Philippe, Calais, August 25, 1658, AMAE, MD, France, vol. 277, fols. 283−84.

42. *Portraits de la cour*, Saint-Simon, *Mémoires*, vol. 8, appendix 25, pp. 624−25.

43. Louis Hautecoeur, *Histoire de l'architecture classique en France*, 7 vols. (Paris, 1943−55), vol. 2, part 1, pp. 154−55; for the purchase contract see M. de Grouchy, *Bulletin de la Société de l'Histoire de Paris et de l'Ile-de-France*, vol. 18, (1891); Erlanger, *Monsieur*, pp. 52−53.

44. Mazarin to Philippe, Amboise, July 2, 1659, AMAE, MD, France, vol. 279, fols. 315−16.

45. Mazarin to Philippe, Saint-Jean-de-Luz, July 29, 1659, AMAE, MD, vol. 2193, fols. 30−31.

46. Ibid.

47. Mazarin to Philippe, Saint-Jean-de-Luz, September 26, 1659, AMAE, MD, France, vol. 283, fol. 170.

48. Philippe to Mazarin, Bordeaux, September 8, 1659, AMAE, MD, France, vol. 908, fols. 59−60.

49. Montpensier, *Mémoires*, 3:404−5. Mademoiselle reported this exchange as having taken place in January 1659.

50. Ibid., 3:329.

51. Ibid., 3:317.

52. Ibid., 3:344.

53. For a few recent and brief overviews see Alan P. Bell, Martin S. Weinberg, and Sue Kiefer Hammersmith, *Sexual Preference, Its Development in Men and Women* (Bloomington, Ind., 1981); Irving Bieber et al., *Homosexuality: A Psychoanalytic Study* (New York, 1962); D. J. West, *Homosexuality Re-examined* (Minneapolis, 1977).

54. Gay, *Freud for Historians*, p. 6. Gay provides a convenient summary and bibliography of the debate between the proponents and critics of psychohistory.

55. Wolf, *Louis XIV*, p. 88.

56. Virtually all the contemporary memoirs contain some version of this thesis. Erlanger, *Monsieur*, accepts it completely (pp. 38–40, 43–49), as did La Batut, *Cour de Monsieur*, p. 11.

57. Abbé de Choisy, *Mémoires pour servir à l'histoire de Louis XIV* and *Mémoires de l'abbé de Choisy habillé en femme*, ed. Georges Mongrédien (Paris, 1966), p. 219.

58. Primi Visconti [San Maiolo], *Mémoires sur la cour de Louis XIV*, trans. from Italian and ed. Jean Lemoine (Paris, 1905), p. 5.

59. Montpensier, *Mémoires*, 3:41.

60. La Porte, *Mémoires*, p. 433.

61. Vern L. Bullough, *Homosexuality: A History* (New York, 1979), pp. 17–45; Michael Goodich, *The Unmentionable Vice: Homosexuality in the Later Medieval Period* (Santa Barbara, Calif., 1979), p. ix.

62. Emmanuel Le Roy Ladurie, "Auprès du roi, la cour," *Annales: Economies, Sociétés, Civilisations* 38 (January 1983): 28–30.

63. Ibid., 31–32. For these insights Le Roy Ladurie relied on, in addition to his own vast knowledge of the period, the memoirs of Saint-Simon and the letters of Philippe's second wife, Elizabeth Charlotte of the Palatinate. The two expressed absolutely identical views on the hierarchy of the court and on what constituted the pure as opposed to the impure, yet they could not have influenced each other. Socially the position of Madame was so very much higher than that of Saint-Simon that they were almost never in each other's company, and their writings were not published until long after their deaths. Consequently, he concluded that the two must have articulated views generally accepted throughout the court "Du moins dans ses portions les plus portées vers l'auto-réflexion sociologique," p. 32).

64. West, *Homosexuality Re-examined*, p. 7.

65. Ibid., p. 8.

66. Sigmund Freud, *Three Contributions to the Theory of Sex*, trans. A. A. Brill (New York, 1920), pp. 7, 10–12.

67. Motteville, *Mémoires*, 2:267.

68. Choisy, *Mémoires*, ed. Mongrédien, p. 219.

69. Norman L. Thompson, et al., "Parent-Child Relationships and Sexual Identity in Male and Female Homosexuals and Heterosexuals," *Journal of Consulting and Clinical Psychology* 41, no. 1 (1973): 121.

70. The lady in question was Henriette de Gordon-Huntley, subsequently Mme de Gourdan. See Saint-Simon, *Mémoires*, vol. 8, *Portraits de*

la cour, appendix 25, p. 625, and p. 625, n. 1. See also Loret's, *Muse histo-rique*, 1:99, 113, 143, 158, 184, 282, 345; 2:10, 164, 3:252. Erlanger, *Mon-sieur*, refers briefly to the convent episode (pp. 43–44).

71. Mazarin to Anne, Guise, September 26, 1656, *Lettres du Cardinal Mazarin*, ed. Chéruel, 7:387; and editorial notes on same page.

72. Mazarin to the Maréchal de Gramont, Abbéville, May 18, 1658, *Lettres du Cardinal Mazarin*, ed. Chéruel, 8:359; Montpensier, *Mémoires*, 3:330.

73. Montpensier, *Mémoires*, 3:330.

74. Louis-Henri de Loménie de Brienne, *Mémoires inédits*, 2 vols. (Paris, 1828), 1:238.

75. Ibid., pp. 298–99. This anecdote is given in Latin, although the rest of the text is in French.

76. Philippe d'Anjou to the duke of Candale, BN, Fonds Français, vol. 20479, fol. 29.

77. Ibid., fols. 37–39.

78. Montpensier, *Mémoires*, 3:388–90.

79. Saint-Simon, *Mémoires*, 8:348–40.

80. "I was a very pretty boy / And I had all the means / That royal peo-ple have / Who are close to the crown, / When, by dint of getting close / To that fair sex so dear to me / And dressing as they dress, / Finally I became a girl."

81. The opinion of Freud himself, in *Three Contributions to the Theory of Sex*, p. 10.

82. The central concept was developed by Freud, "Dostoevsky and Parricide," pp. 222–42. See also West, *Homosexuality Re-examined*, pp. 97–98.

83. Some theorists have emphasized the importance of the preoedipal phase in the etiology of male homosexuality (Ruth Mack Brunswick, "The Preoedipal Phase of the Libido Development," *Psychoanalytic Quarterly* 9[1940]: 293–319; Jeanne Lampl de Groot, "The Pre-oedipal Phase in the Development of the Male Child," *Psychoanalytic Study of the Child* 2[1947]: 75–83).

84. Heinz Kohut, "Forms and Transformations of Narcissism," in *The Search for the Self: Selected Writings of Heinz Kohut, 1950–1978*, ed. Paul H. Ornstein, 2 vols. (New York, 1978), 1:438.

85. Mme de La Fayette, *Histoire de Madame Henriette d'Angleterre suivie de mémoires de la cour de France pour les années 1688 et 1689*, ed. Gilbert Sigaux (Paris, 1965), p. 36.

86. Ibid.

87. William McKinley Runyan, *Life Histories and Psychobiography: Explo-rations in Theory and Method* (New York, 1982), p. 212; P. Wachtel, "Psy-chodynamics, Behavior Therapy, and the Implacable Experimenter: An In-quiry into the Consistency of Personality," *Journal of Abnormal Psychology* 82(1973): 323–34; O. G. Brim, Jr., and J. Kagan, eds., *Constancy and Change in Human Development* (Cambridge, Mass., 1980); M. Rutter, *Maternal De-privation Reassessed*, 2d ed. (New York, 1981).

FOUR   MINETTE

1. Philippe, duke of Anjou, to Gaston, duke of Orléans, als, Toulouse, December 10, 1659, BN, Baluze, vol. 349, fol. 59.

2. Montpensier, *Mémoires*, 3:466.

3. Ibid.

4. Motteville, *Mémoires*, 8:37.

5. For definitions of an appanage and its jurisprudence see L. A. Maffert, *Les apanages en France du XVIe au XIXe siècle* (Paris, 1900), p. 27; and Beatrice Fry Hyslop, *L'apanage de Philippe-Egalité duc d'Orléans* (Paris, 1965), pp. 1–10. See also "Arret du conseil d'etat du roy [September 16, 1766]" and "du 7 décembre 1766," *Apanage de la maison d'Orléans*, pp. 1–15, Archives Nationales (hereafter AN), 300 AP I 100.

6. For an explanation of the implications of the revenues of the appanage and its significance, see Nancy N. Barker, "Philippe d'Orléans, Frère Unique du Roi: Founder of the Family Fortune," *French Historical Studies* 13, no. 2 (1983): 148–50.

7. Jean-Pierre Labatut, *Les ducs et pairs de France au XVIIe siècle: Etude sociale* (Paris, 1972), p. 285.

8. Dethan, *Gaston d'Orléans*, pp. 351–53.

9. Mazarin to procureur général, Marseilles, March 6, 1660, *Lettres du Cardinal Mazarin*, ed. Chéruel, 9:533; Saint-Simon, *Mémoires*, 8:357, n. 2.

10. *Apanage de la maison d'Orléans*, 1762, p. 12, AN 300 AP I 199.

11. Mazarin to procureur général, Marseilles, March 6, 1660, *Lettres du Cardinal Mazarin*, ed. Chéruel, 9:533.

12. Dethan, *Gaston d'Orléans*, p. 352; Harding, *Anatomy of a Power Elite*, pp. 135–36.

13. Cosnac, *Mémoires*, 1:281.

14. Ibid.

15. Marquis de La Fare, *Mémoires et réflexions sur les principaux événements du règne de Louis XIV et sur le caractère de ceux qui y ont eu la principale part*, ed. A. Petitot and L. J. N. Monmerqué, Collection des mémoires relatifs à l'histoire de France, vol. 65 (Paris, 1828), p. 149.

16. Montpensier, *Mémoires*, 5:40–41; Motteville, *Mémoires*, p. 109; La Fayette, *Henriette d'Angleterre*, p. 34.

17. Louis XIV, *Mémoires*, p. 97. For Louis's diplomacy see also Goubert, *Louis XIV et vingt millions de Français*, pp. 53–54.

18. According to the French ambassador at the Court of Saint James, "The king [Charles] well knows that in giving [his sister] to Monsieur, he is making her happy." Letter of November 8, 1660, quoted by comte de Baillon, *Henriette-Anne d'Angleterre, duchesse d'Orléans: Sa vie et sa correspondance avec son frère Charles II* (Paris, 1886), p. 48.

19. Henrietta Maria of France to Charles II, August 1660, quoted in Baillon, *Henriette-Anne*, p. 40.

20. Henrietta Maria to her son, Charles II (n.d.), quoted in Baillon, *Henriette-Anne*, p. 40.

21. Excerpt from the correspondence of the count of Soissons, French

ambassador to the Court of Saint James, quoted in Baillon, *Henriette-Anne*, p. 48.

22. Henriette of England to Charles II, August 1660, Public Record Office, State Papers (hereafter PRO, SP), quoted in Baillon, *Henriette-Anne*, p. 40.

23. Cyril Hughes Hartmann, *The King My Brother* (London, 1954), p. 21; Baillon, *Henriette-Anne*, p. 47. Over Henriette's protests, Charles wrote to his sister in English, lest she forget that language entirely (Hartmann, *The King My Brother*, pp. 9–10). A letter from Charles of February 7, 1659?) to Henriette notes the princess's protest (ibid).

24. Baillon, *Henriette-Anne*, p. 40. Loret's *Muse Historique*, 2:251, describes the banquet.

25. Montpensier, *Mémoires*, 3:463.

26. Secretary of the French ambassador, Bartet, to Mazarin, November 16, 1660, AMAE, Angleterre, 1660, supplement. See also Baillon, *Henriette-Anne*, p. 47.

27. La Fayette, *Henriette d'Angleterre*, p. 36.

28. Montpensier, *Mémoires*, 5:40–41; Wolf, *Louis XIV*, p. 92; Baillon, *Henriette-Anne*, p. 52; La Fayette, *Henriette d'Angleterre*, pp. 35–36.

29. Montpensier, *Mémoires*, 5:192.

30. Ibid., 3:279.

31. *Apanage de la maison d'Orléans*, AN 300 AP I 199, p. 4.

32. Hartmann, *The King My Brother*, p. 26.

33. Motteville, *Mémoires*, 6:111; Montpensier, *Mémoires*, 4:8–9; *Gazette de France*, April 2, 1661; La Fayette, *Henriette d'Angleterre*, p. 38.

34. Choisy, *Mémoires*, ed. Montgrédien, p. 188.

35. See introduction, La Fayette, *Henriette d'Angleterre*, pp. 12–13, for the editor's summary of and excerpts from contemporary descriptions of Henriette.

36. La Fayette, *Henriette d'Angleterre*, p. 39.

37. Hilde Bruch, *Eating Disorders: Obesity, Anorexia Nervosa, and the Person Within* (New York, 1973), p. 223.

38. The view of Gui Patin, a physician close to the court. Gui Patin to André Falconet, Paris, September 26, 1664, *Lettres*, vol. 3, no. 643, pp. 484–85.

39. La Fayette, *Henriette d'Angleterre*, p. 40.

40. Helene Deutsch, *The Psychology of Women: A Psychoanalytic Interpretation* (New York, 1944), pp. 54–56, 96. Freud placed great emphasis on the narcissistic source of feminine seductive behavior and believed that female charm to a large degree derived from this quality of "wanting to be loved" (Freud, "On Narcissism: An Introduction," in *Collected Papers*, trans. and ed. James Strachey [New York, 1959], vol. 4, quoted by Deutsch, p. 187).

41. The dalliance of Louis and Henriette is described in many memoirs. See La Fayette, *Henriette d'Angleterre*, pp. 39–41; Motteville, *Mémoires*, 5:111–38; La Fare, *Mémoires*, pp. 158–59.

42. La Fayette, *Henriette d'Angleterre*, p. 41.

43. La Fare, *Mémoires*, p. 158.

44. Ibid., p. 44.

45. This glimpse into the bedroom is afforded by a letter from Charles to Henriette that describes his own wedding night and alludes to specific complaints about Philippe as a husband that Henriette had made to him in a letter that has been lost. Charles wrote: "I was married the day before yesterday, but the fortune that follows our family is fallen upon me, *car Monsieur le Cardinal m'a fermé la porte au nez*, and though I am not so furious as Monsieur was, but am content to let those pass over before I go to bed to my wife, yet I hope I shall entertain her at least better the first night than he did you" (Charles to Henriette, Portsmouth, May 23, 1662, Hartmann, *The King My Brother*, p. 39). Later on in the letter Charles explained in an oblique fashion that his bride's menstrual cycle had been disrupted by her long sea voyage from Portugal.

46. Henriette gave birth to her first child in the Palais Royal on March 27, 1662, where, according to the *Gazette de France* (April 1, 1662), "she at present resides." As late as February 11, 1662, however, Philippe, Louis, and the queen were reported to have danced a ballet in the Tuileries Palace (*Gazette de France*, February 18, 1662).

47. Ezéchiel Spanheim, *Relation de la cour de France en 1690*, ed. Charles Schefer (Paris, 1882), p. 67.

48. On the facade of the palace was the inscription "Palais Cardinal." When Anne and her children took up residence this inscription was erased, but out of consideration for the duchess of Aiguillon, niece of Richelieu, who had protested, Anne put it back. Only after 1672 was the palace known as the Palais Royal (E. Dupezard, *Le Palais-Royal de Paris* [Paris, 1911], p. 8).

49. Orest Ranum, *Paris in the Age of Absolutism* (Bloomington, Ind., 1968), pp. 92–96; Pierre d'Espezel, *Le Palais-Royal* (Paris, 1936), pp. 6–13, 86–88.

50. Victor Champier and G. Roger Sandoz, *Le Palais-Royal d'après des documents inédits (1629–1900)*, 2 vols. (Paris, 1900), 1:158.

51. AN 300 AP I 130, "Notes et observations sur la formation des officiers de la chancellerie et du conseil de l'apanage," 1825. These notes were written by the officers of Louis Philippe, duke of Orléans, during prolonged research on the origin and organization of the house of Orléans after the restoration of the French monarchy in 1814 and the duke's return from exile. In 1825 the duke was still in the process of settling the financial affairs of his estate.

52. 'L'èstat général de la maison de Monsieur, duc d'Orléans," in *L'èstat de la France . . . dédié au roy*, 2 vols. (Paris, 1662–1701), 1:355–71.

53. "Maison de Madame," in *'Estat de la France*, 1:372–74.

54. "Maison de Monsieur," pp. 397–432; "Maison de Madame," pp. 433–48.

55. For this period of Philippe's and Henriette's marriage figures are

available for 1664 through 1670. M. Jules Guiffrey, *Comptes des bâtiments du roi sous le règne de Louis XIV*, 5 vols. (Paris, 1881–91), 1:16–17, 74–75, 131–32, 189–99, 250, 329, 411–12. See also Leon Bernard, *The Emerging City: Paris in the Age of Louis XIV* (Durham, N.C., 1970), p. 11. After the death of Monsieur the *Comptes du trésorier de Monsieur* show a total of 417,449 livres expended on the Palais Royal for maintenance, repair, and decoration. Very likely, however, this work was done after 1692, when the palace became a part of Monsieur's appanage. Of this sum 96,000 livres was still outstanding at the time of the prince's death (AN R 4 1066, fols. 231–32).

56. Champier found the king's expenditures insufficient and maintained that Monsieur must have spent considerable sums (Champier and Sandoz, *Palais-Royal*, 1:152). Tony Sauvel ("Le Palais-Royal de la mort de Richelieu à l'incendie en 1763," *Bulletin Monumental* 120 [1962]: 178–79), who has done the best recent work on the Palais Royal, argues the contrary. He notes that Champier fails to specify which things Monsieur paid for and concludes that lacking other evidence the *Comptes des bâtiments du roi* are the most reliable source of information.

57. Espezel, *Palais-Royal*, pp. 66–70; Vatout, *Souvenirs historiques des résidences royales*, p. 82–83; Hautecoeur, *Histoire de l'architecture classique en France*, vol. 2, part 2, pp. 587–88; Sauvel, "Palais-Royal," pp. 176–79; Dupezard, *Palais-Royal*, p. 8; for more or less contemporary descriptions (often imprecise), see Jean-Aymar Piganiol de la Force, *Description historique de la ville de Paris et ses environs*, 10 vols. (Paris, 1742), 2:223, and Germain Brice, *Description nouvelle de la ville de Paris*, 4 vols. (Paris, 1752), 1:194.

58. Cosnac, *Mémoires*, 1:328.

59. Spanheim, *Relation de la cour*, p. 67.

60. Elizabeth Charlotte to Countess Luise, [Paris], September 30, 1718, *Correspondance*, 2:8; same to same, July 27, 1719, ibid., 2:137.

61. Wolf, *Louis XIV*, 277; Motteville, *Mémoires*, 5:166–67; *Muse Historique*, and *Gazette de France* for the month of May 1662; Jean-Marie Apostolidès, *Le roi-machine: Spectacle et politique au temps de Louis XIV* (Paris, 1981), pp. 41–46.

62. *Gazette de France*, June 3, 1662.

63. *Muse Historique*, June 1662.

64. *Gazette de France*, April 26, 1664.

65. Montpensier, *Mémoires*, 4:89.

66. Philippe to Charles II, Saint-Cloud, July 12, 1667, PRO, SP 78/123m, fols. 140–41; Baillon, *Henriette-Anne*, pp. 292–93; *Gazette de France*, July 9, 1667.

67. Motteville, *Mémoires*, 5:279; Baillon, *Henriette-Anne*, pp. 254–55.

68. *Gazette de France*, January 1666.

69. Jacques Gélis, Mireille Laget, and Marie-France Morel, *Entrer dans la vie: Naissances et enfances dans la France traditionnelle* (Paris, 1978), p. 194.

70. Cosnac, *Mémoires*, 1:323; La Batut, *Cour de Monsieur*, p. 78. The godparents were Maria Theresa and the duke of Enghien.

71. Georges Montgrédien, "Molière et Louis XIV," in *Molière*, by Jean-

Louis Barrault, Georges Mongrédien, et al. (Paris, 1976), p. 100; Georges Lafenestre, *Les grands écrivains français: Molière* (Paris, 1909), p. 23.

72. Dedication of Molière, *L'école des maris*, in *Oeuvres complètes*, ed. Louis Moland, 2d ed. (Paris, 1881), 4:63.

73. Molière, *Oeuvres complètes*, 4:235, 370; Lafenestre, *Molière*, pp. 50, 62.

74. Raymond Picard, *La carrière de Jean Racine: Bibliothèque des idées*, 4th ed. (Paris, 1956), p. 105.

75. Jean Racine, "Epitre à Madame," *Andromaque*, in *Oeuvres complètes*, 5 vols. (Paris, 1922), 1:429–32.

76. Picard, *Carrière de Racine*, pp. 156–57.

77. *Muse Historique*, February 7, 1665; Isherwood, *Music in the Service of the King*, p. 144. The poem cited is Isherwood's translation. Wolf, *Louis XIV*, has a good description of Louis's enthusiasm for the dance, pp. 273–74.

78. Motteville, *Mémoires*, 5:304.

79. Jean Cordey, "L'inventaire après décès d'Anne d'Autriche et le mobilier du Louvre," *Bulletin de la Société de l'Histoire de l'Art Français*, 1930, pp. 209–75. For Anne's testament see BN, nouvelles acquisitions françaises 4385, fols. 270–76. See also Kleinman, *Anne of Austria*, p. 286.

80. Motteville, *Mémoires*, 5:202–3.

81. Montpensier, *Mémoires*, 2:217.

82. Plessis-Praslin, *Mémoires*, pp. 437–38; Cosnac, *Mémoires*, 1:300–301.

83. Motteville, *Mémoires*, 5:304.

84. La Fare, *Mémoires*, pp. 162–63.

85. Louis XIV, *Mémoires*, p. 139.

86. Cosnac, *Mémoires*, 1:300–301.

87. Louis XIV, *Mémoires*, 2:64.

88. La Fayette, *Henriette d'Angleterre*, p. 63; Motteville, *Mémoires*, 5:187.

89. Louis XIV, *Mémoires*, p. 141.

90. Cosnac, *Mémoires*, 1:309. See also Choisy, *Mémoires*, ed. Montgrédien, pp. 188–89.

91. Labatut, *Ducs et pairs de France au XVIIe siècle*, pp. 67–73, 82–84.

92. Louis XIV, *Mémoires*, p. 140.

93. Ibid.; Cosnac, *Mémoires*, 1:309.

94. *Inventaire des minutes de Conseil*, AN 300 AP I 814; According to the *Gazette de France* of May 28, 1667, Philippe left Paris on May 26. Gui Patin placed the departure on 30 May (Gui Patin to André Falconte, Paris, May 31, 1667, *Lettres*, vol. 3, no. 752, p. 655.

95. Wolf, *Louis XIV*, p. 204.

96. Cosnac, *Mémoires*, 1:345.

97. Philippe to Charles II, Saint-Cloud, July 12, 1667, PRO, SP 78/123, fols. 140–41. Some have alleged, or at least implied, that the prince left the army out of boredom and merely used Henriette's miscarriage as an excuse (La Batut, *Cour de Monsieur*, p. 83; Erlanger, *Monsieur*, p. 106). Philippe's letter, however, reported that "for a quarter of an hour" Madame

had been thought dead. Her convalescence was prolonged. She did not again appear in public until August 15, when she went to the monastery of the Ursulines at Saint-Cloud to render thanks for her recovery (*Gazette de France*, August 30, 1667). What would his critics have said if in fact she had died and the prince had not hastened to her side?

98. Louis XIV, *Mémoires*, in *Oeuvres*, ed. P. H. Grimoard and P. A. Grouvelle, 6 vols. (Paris, 1806), 2:324–25, 349; *Gazette de France*, February 4, 1668. Belatedly, Philippe set out to join Louis in Franche-Comté but, learning en route that the campaign was so advanced that it would be over by the time he arrived, he turned back (*Gazette de France*, February 25, 1668).

99. Choisy, *Mémoires*, ed. Montgrédien, pp. 194–95; Cosnac, *Mémoires*, pp. 337–45.

100. Victor Cousin, *Madame de Sablé* (Paris, 1854), p. 152; see also Baillon, *Henriette-Anne*, pp. 261–63.

101. Philippe to Mme de Sablé, from the camp before Lille, August 24 [1667], BN, Fonds Français, 17043, fol. 213.

FIVE   MADAME IS DYING! MADAME IS DEAD!

1. Philippe to Charles II, July 16, 1664, PRO, SP 78/119, fols. 8–8v.

2. Cosnac, *Mémoires*, 1:323–24. This report is suspect because Cosnac, earlier a supporter of the prince, had become his enemy by the time he wrote his memoirs. Equally unreliable is his assertion that Madame was inconsolable over the child's death.

3. Abbé de Montigy, MS de Valentin Conrart, 9:652, Bibliothèque de l'Arsenal (hereafter BA), cited in Baillon, *Henriette-Anne*, p. 83.

4. Cosnac, *Mémoires*, 1:317; Baillon, *Henriette-Anne*, pp. 267–68.

5. Abbé de Montigny, MS de Conrart, 9:1109, BA; Baillon, *Henriette-Anne*, pp. 327–28.

6. Saint-Simon, *Mémoires*, 8:342. See Boislisle's n. 1, ibid., p. 343, for details on the background of the chevalier and his attachment to Monsieur.

7. According to personality theorists, such transvestite behavior might be a form of the "gender discontent" experienced by many bisexuals and homosexuals (West, *Homosexuality Re-examined*, p. 56). It might also be the ultimate and unconscious identification with his mother.

8. Choisy, *Mémoires*, ed. Montgrédien, pp. 325–26.

9. Hartmann, *The King My Brother*, pp. 290–92.

10. Twentieth-century scholarly investigation has strongly reinforced the contemporary impression that the "Treaty of Madame" gained its momentum from Henriette and lost it after her death. See Keith Feiling, "Henrietta Stuart, Duchess of Orléans, and the Origins of the Treaty of Dover," *English Historical Review* 47(1932): 642–45.

11. AMAE, MD, Angleterre, vol. 26. Many have been published in a modernized English by Hartmann, *The King My Brother*. In my citations I have retained the language of the originals.

12. August 9, 1668, Whitehall, als, AMAE, MD, Angleterre, vol. 26, fol. 135.

13. Hartmann, *The King My Brother*, p. 274.

14. Louis XIV to Colbert de Croissy, Saint-Germain, January 29, 1670, AMAE, Correspondance politique (hereafter CP), Angleterre, vol. 99, fol. 37.

15. De Villers-Cottrès (*sic*), February 2, 1670. This letter has been published a number of times. For exact references see Saint-Simon, *Mémoires*, 8:372, n. 1. The version used in the translation above, which appears to be the most correct one (Philippe's writing, never easy to read, was particularly illegible in this letter, probably as a result of his emotional state) is in Jean-François Champollion-Figeac, ed. *Documents historiques inédits tirés des collections manuscrites de la bibliothèque royale*, 4 vols. (Paris, 1841–48), 2:513–15. The translation is my own.

16. According to some (La Fare, *Mémoires*, pp. 178–79; Visconti [San Maiolo], *Mémoires*, pp. 27–28), Louis's anger was caused by the penetration of the secret of the Anglo-French negotiations by the chevalier, who allegedly learned of it from the mistress of Marshal Turenne, one of the few privy to the affair. Others, among them Mademoiselle, held that the chevalier encouraged Philippe to defy the king after he had been refused the governorship of Languedoc (Montpensier, *Mémoires*, 4:137). Another version, which cites a letter allegedly written by Louis to his minister Arnaud de Pomponne (Saint-Germain-en-Laye, February 7, 1670, BA), maintains that Philippe's defiance grew out of the king's refusal to permit him to grant his favorite the income from a rich abbey in his appanage and the king's belief that it was the chevalier who was instigating Monsieur's rebellion (La Batut, *Cour de Monsieur*, pp. 120–21).

17. Montpensier, *Mémoires*, 4:137.

18. Louis himself wrote to Colbert de Croissy to inform him of the return of Monsieur and Madame and to assure him that the two brothers were reconciled (*attendris*), February 26, 1670, AMAE, CP, Angleterre, vol. 99, fol. 79.

19. M. de Lionne to Colbert, February 26, 1670, AMAE, CP, Angleterre, vol. 99, fol. 80.

20. Colbert de Croissy to Louis XIV, no date, but by context between January 30 and February 26, 1670, AMAE, CP, Angleterre, vol. 99, fols. 68–69. Philippe's letter to Charles has not been preserved, but its contents may be inferred from that of Croissy to Louis.

21. Montpensier, *Mémoires*, 4:156.

22. Ibid.

23. The chevalier obtained the information from Mme de Coetquen, mistress of Turenne, who had indiscreetly let her in on the secret. See Visconti [San Maiolo], *Mémoires*, pp. 27–28, and Choisy, *Mémoires*, ed. Montgrédien, pp. 208–9.

24. PRO, SP 78, France, vols. 115–30 (1660–70).

25. June 19, 1665, PRO, SP 78, France, vol. 120, fol. 211.

26. January 16, 1666, PRO, SP 78, France, vol. 122, fols. 11–12.

27. Charles II to Henriette, Hamilton Court, July 13, 1665, AMAE, MD, Angleterre, vol. 26, fols. 99–102.

28. Paris, January 15, 1666, PRO, SP 78, France, cited in Baillon, *Henriette-Anne*, p. 251.

29. Hampton Court, January 27, 1666, PRO, SP 78, France, cited in Baillon, *Henriette-Anne*, pp. 258–59.

30. Details on the negotiation and provisions of the secret Treaty of Dover, sometimes known as the Traité de Madame, of May 22–June 1, 1670, and the Traité Simulé, signed December 21–31, 1670, are in Hartmann, *The King My Brother*, pp. 309–39. See also François Auguste Marie Alexis Mignet, *Négociations relatives à la succession d'Espagne*, 4 vols. (Paris, 1835–42), 3:150–202.

31. Lionne to Colbert de Croissy, St. Germain, March 22, 1670, AMAE, CP, Angleterre, vol. 99, fols. 107–8.

32. Colbert de Croissy to Lionne, London, March 27, 1670; Louis XIV to Colbert de Croissy, March 29, 1670; Colbert de Croissy to Louis XIV, London, April 3, 1670, AMAE, CP, Angleterre, vol. 99, fols. 116–17, 119, 121–22.

33. Choisy, *Mémoires*, ed. Petitot, p. 415.

34. Montpensier, *Mémoires*, 4:177.

35. Ibid.

36. Ibid.

37. Many accounts exist. For the negotiations and accompanying documents see Mignet, *Négociations relatives à la succession d'Espagne*, 3:176–202; see also Paul Pellisson-Fontanier, *Lettres historiques de Pellisson*, 3 vols. (Paris, 1729), 1:43, 48, 53–54; and Hartmann, *The King My Brother*, pp. 312–19. Among the memoirs, see those of Pomponne, Choisy, and Cosnac. The Boislisle edition of the memoirs of Saint-Simon lists an extended bibliography, 8:373, n. 5.

38. The revenue of the "great" noblemen for an entire year in seventeenth-century France is estimated as between 50,000 and 250,000 livres (Pierre Goubert, *The Ancien Régime: French Society, 1600–1750*, trans. Steve Cox [New York, 1973], p. 169).

39. Montpensier, *Mémoires*, 4:184.

40. La Fayette, "Relation de la mort de Madame," in *Henriette d'Angleterre*, p. 81.

41. Ibid.

42. Those present who were part of the French court and who recorded their impressions in memoirs were Mlle de Montpensier and Mme de La Fayette. The English ambassador, Sir Ralph Montagu, visited the princess briefly before her death and recounted the scene in a report to Lord Arlington, secretary of state of Charles II. Although hostile to Philippe, he did not accuse him of poisoning the princess (Paris, June 30, 1670, and July 15, La Fayette, *Henriette d'Angleterre*, appendix, 1:91–92, and 4:97–99).

43. Montpensier, *Mémoires*, 4:192.

44. Montagu reported that he had asked Madame repeatedly if she be-

lieved herself poisoned. Before she could answer her confessor intervened, warning her to accuse no one and to offer her death to God as a sacrifice. The ambassador could elicit nothing from her beyond a shrug of the shoulders (Montagu to Arlington, Paris, July 15, 1670, La Fayette, *Henriette d'Angleterre*, appendix, 4:98. Hartmann, *The King My Brother*, p. 329.

45. La Fayette, "Relation de la mort de Madame," in *Henriette d'Angleterre*, p. 90.

46. *Gazette de France*, July 5, 1670.

47. My translation of this famous eulogy. For the French original see Saint-Simon, *Mémoires*, 8:376, n. 1.

48. Mme de Sévigné to Bussy-Rabutin, Paris, July 6, 1670, *Correspondance*, ed. Roger Duchêne, 3 vols. (Paris, 1972–78), 1:128.

49. Montpensier, *Mémoires*, 4:194.

50. The readiness of the public to believe in death by poisoning was well recognized at the time (Lionne to Colbert de Croissy, Paris, AMAE, CP, Angleterre, vol. 16, quoted in Baillon, *Henriette-Anne*, pp. 429–30).

51. Le Roy Ladurie, "Auprès du roi, la cour," pp. 28–30.

52. Colbert de Croissy to Lionne, July 3, 1670, AMAE, CP, Angleterre, quoted in Baillon, *Henriette-Anne*, p. 432.

53. Montagu to Arlington, Paris, July 15, 1670, "Lettres relatives à la mort de Madame," no. 5, appendix, La Fayette, *Henriette d'Angleterre*, p. 100.

54. *Gazette de France*, July 5, 1670.

55. Montpensier, *Mémoires*, 4:195.

56. Elizabeth Charlotte to Countess Luise, [Paris], July 13, 1716, *Correspondance*, p. 252.

57. Ibid.; Saint-Simon, *Mémoires*, 8:370–78. In the appendix of this volume, pp. 636–66, Boislisle has exhaustively explored the existing evidence and followed the enormous literature surrounding the alleged poisoning.

58. Mme de Sévigné to Mme de Grignan, Paris, February 12, 1672, *Correspondance*, 1:439.

59. Boislisle's "appendix" on the death of Madame, Saint-Simon, *Mémoires*, 8:662–65.

60. Hartmann, *The King My Brother*, p. 333; Jean Fabre, *Sur la vie et principalement sur la mort de Madame* (Paris, 1912); for a more recent account designed for the general reader see Antonia Fraser, *Royal Charles: Charles II and the Restoration* (New York, 1979). An exception is the French academician and specialist of diseases of the blood, Jean Bernard, who has asserted (without the slightest contemporary evidence) that Henriette was a victim of porphyria, a disease that ran in the English royal family and later caused the death of George III. See Jean Bernard, *Le sang et l'histoire* (Paris, 1983), pp. 138–40. A major problem with his diagnosis is that although the princess did indeed experience the severe abdominal pain characteristic of that disease, she evinced none, or very few, of the other symptoms, among which are paralysis and intermittent psychosis amounting to insanity.

61. Bruch, *Eating Disorders*, p. 223.

62. Not long after the birth of the duke of Valois in 1664 Patin had written: "[Henriette] is thin, delicate, and of those that were said by Hippocrates to have a tendency toward consumption. The English are subject to this disease of consumption [tuberculosis]" (Gui Patin to André Falconet, Paris, September 26, 1664, *Lettres*, vol. 3, no. 643, p. 484.

63. Paul E. Garfinkel, *Anorexia Nervosa: A Multidimensional Perspective* (New York, 1982), p. 318; William A. R. Thomson, *Black's Medical Dictionary*, 34th ed. (London, 1984), p. 697.

64. *Gazette de France*, July and August 1670, passim.

65. Montpensier, *Mémoires*, 4:198.

66. Montagu to count of Arlington, Paris, July 6, 1670, La Fayette, *Henriette d'Angleterre*, appendix, 3, pp. 94–97. Montagu is a hostile source of information. Clearly he and Monsieur regarded each other with mutual loathing. Nonetheless, the facts must have been pretty much as he described, as it was through the prince's seizure of Madame's correspondence that Charles's letters remained in French hands and found their way into the archives of the French Foreign Ministry.

67. AMAE, CP, Angleterre, vol. 14, fol. 122; Baillon, *Henriette-Anne*, p. 366.

68. Gay, *Freud for Historians*, p. 110.

SIX LISELOTTE

1. Montpensier, *Mémoires*, 4:194.

2. See Barker, "Philippe d'Orléans, Frère Unique du Roi," pp. 151–52.

3. Montpensier, *Mémoires*, 4:203.

4. Ibid., 4:206–7.

5. Ibid., 4:206. Louis was already thinking of marrying the dauphin to one of the daughters of the elector of Bavaria. Ezéchiel Spanheim's memoirs maintain that the king still bore a grudge against Mademoiselle for her role in the Fronde and for that reason had always opposed her projects of marriage in high places (*Relation de la cour de France en 1690*, p. 72). Because he was writing at a much later date and apparently was not aware of this episode, his opinion is not convincing.

6. The correspondence between Anne of Gonzaga and her brother-in-law the elector concerning the marriage of Elizabeth Charlotte is published in Sophie of Hanover, *Briefwechsel der Herzogin Sophie von Hannover mit ihrem Bruder, dem Kurfürsten Karl Ludwig von der Pfalz, und des Letzteren mit seiner Schwägerin, der Pfalzgräfin Anna*, ed. Eduard Bodeman, Publicationen aus den K. Preussischen Staats Archiven, vol. 26 (Leipzig, 1885), nos. 1–33, pp. 445–76. The letters are in French. Excerpts may be found in Arvède Barine, *Madame: Mère du régent* (Paris, 1923), pp. 62–69.

7. Ludwig Haüsser, *Geschichte der Reinischen Pfalz nach ihren politischen, kirchlichen und litterarischen Verhältnesse*, 2 vols. (Heidelberg, 1845), 2:616.

8. Wolf (*Louis XIV*, p. 313) believes, in my opinion correctly, that Louis had as yet no comprehension of German feudal law and had not yet con-

ceived a design on the Palatine inheritance. Erlanger (*Monsieur*, p. 176) maintains the opposite.

9. Barine, *Madame*, pp. 66–67.

10. When Philippe had proposed the idea of a childless marriage to Mademoiselle, Louis had told his brother that he would do better to hope for children (Montpensier, *Mémoires*, 4:206). The Venetian ambassador at the French court also believed that the need for progeny was the principal reason for the match ("Relation de l'ambassadeur vénitien, 1671," Saint-Simon, *Mémoires*, vol. 8, appendix 25, p. 626.

11. An écu was a gold coin that ranged between three and six times the value of a livre. The dowry greatly exceeded the capacity of the Spanish treasury, and it was never paid.

12. How much Philippe had received of Henriette's dowry by 1671 is not known. However, when his younger daughter Henriette married the duke of Savoy in 1684, 270,000 livres was still outstanding. See the marriage contract of Anne d'Orléans, April 9, 1864, Papiers personnels [of Monsieur], AN 300 AP I 115.

13. Contrat de mariage de S.A.R. Monsieur ... à la princesse Elisabeth Charlotte, palatine du Rhin, November 6, 1671, Papiers personnels [of Monsieur], AN 300 AP I 115. Another copy may be found in AN K 542, no. 9.

14. AN K 542, no. 10.

15. Barine, *Madame*, p. 70. In addition to the jewelry and other precious articles, the elector promised to pay 32,000 German florins, that is, 64,000 livres (AN K 542, no. 14). But judging from subsequent correspondence, this sum was never, or was only partially, paid. See the Electress Sophie of Hanover to Charles Ludwig, Osnabrück, November 23, 1679, *Briefwechsel der Herzogin Sophie*, no. 394, p. 390. Wolf (*Louis XIV*, p. 313) is in error to imply that the princess brought with her a dowry of value.

16. Contrat de mariage, March 31, 1661, Papiers personnels [of Monsieur], AN 300 AP I 115.

17. A chronic complaint. See Elizabeth Charlotte to Countess Luise, Versailles, December 10, 1701, *Correspondance*, 2:58. At other times Elizabeth Charlotte blamed Anne of Gonzaga for the alleged deficiencies of the contract. See same to same, [Paris], February 2, 1717, ibid., p. 291.

18. Barine (*Madame*, p. 70) erred in believing that Monsieur had a vast fortune in 1671. Apparently she misread, or misconstrued, the notes of Boislisle (Saint-Simon, *Mémoires*, 8:357, nos. 1 and 2), cited as her authority.

19. After the death of Monsieur, Liselotte was at least once sufficiently honest to confess her ignorance of things financial. To her half-sister Luise she wrote: "It would be very fortunate if I could understand financial affairs as well as you, but I can understand nothing of such things and at age fifty am much too old to learn" (Versailles, October 12, 1701, *Correspondance*, 1:54).

20. *Gazette de France*, January 1671.

21. Ibid., April 4, 1671.

22. Montpensier, *Mémoires*, 4:315.
23. Ibid., May 16, July 4, and August 1, 1671.
24. Mme de Sévigné to Mme de Grignan, Vitré, August 16, 1671, *Correspondance*, 1:323.
25. *Gazette de France*, November 28, 1671.
26. Visconti [San Maiolo], *Mémoires*, p. 30.
27. Mme de Sévigné to Mme de Grignan, Paris, January 13 [1672], *Correspondance*, 1:415.
28. Montpensier, *Mémoires*, 4:334.
29. Louis had long since abandoned falconry. Instead he hunted stags and other wild game on horseback or shot fowl with guns. See Jacques Levron, *La vie quotidienne à la cour de Versailles aux XVIIe et XVIIIe siècles* (Paris, 1965), pp. 54–55.
30. Barine, *Madame*, pp. 91–92.
31. Häusser, *Geschichte der Reinischen Pfalz*, 2:660.
32. "Inventaire des titres du duc d'Orléans [Monsieur], brevets, dons, régie et des charges d'évaluation," AN 300 AP I 748.
33. "Supplément d'apanage, 24 avril 1672, déclaration du roy" [imprimé], AN 300 AP I 199.
34. Elizabeth Charlotte to Duchess Sophie, Saint-Germain, February 5, 1672, *A Woman's Life in the Court of the Sun King: Letters of Liselotte von der Pfalz, 1652–1722, Elizabeth Charlotte, Duchesse d'Orléans*, trans. and intro. Elborg Forster (Baltimore, 1984), p. 7. (Hereafter cited as *Letters of Liselotte.*)
35. Same to same, Saint-Germain, December 14, 1676, *Letters of Liselotte*, p. 17.
36. Elizabeth Charlotte to Duchess Sophie, February 5, 1672, trans. from Barine, *Madame*, p. 73.
37. Barine, *Madame*, pp. 17–20.
38. Elizabeth Charlotte to Duchess Sophie, Versailles, June 6, 1709, *Aus den Briefen der Herzogin Elisabeth Charlotte von Orleans an die Kurfürstin Sophie von Hannover: Ein Beitrag zur Kulturgeschichte des 17. und 18. Jahrhunderts*, ed. Eduard Bodemann (Hanover, 1891), vol. 1, no. 696, pp. 215–16. At the time of this letter Liselotte was reminiscing over the events of 1679 when both Sophie and Monsieur desired to bring Charlotte to the French court. See also Sophie to Karl Ludwig, Osnabrück, November 23, 1679, *Briefwechsel der Herzogin Sophie*, no. 394, p. 390.
39. Sophie to Karl Ludwig, December 1, 1670, quoted in Barine, *Madame*, p. 37.
40. Sophie to Karl Ludwig, June 6, 1663, quoted in Barine, *Madame*, p. 35.
41. Sophie to Karl Ludwig, Diffhols, September 1673, *Briefwechsel der Herzogin Sophie*, no. 175, p. 167.
42. *Letters of Liselotte*, p. xii.
43. Elizabeth Charlotte to the Raugräfin Luise (half-sister), June 22, 1719, *Briefe der Herzogin Elisabeth Charlotte*, in *Die Litterarischen Vereins in Stuttgard*, ed. W. Menzel and L. Holland, cited by Barine, *Madame*, p. 53.

44. Elizabeth Charlotte to the Raugräfin Luise, [Paris], December 9, 1718, *Correspondance*, 2:38.

45. Elizabeth Charlotte to Duchess Sophie, Fontainebleau, October 10, 1699, *Letters of Liselotte*, p. 117.

46. For Elizabeth Charlotte's views of medical practice and illness see, in addition to her letters passim, Elborg Forster, "From the Patient's Point of View: Illness and Health in the Letters of Liselotte von der Pfalz (1652–1722)," *Bulletin of the History of Medicine* 60(1986): 297–320.

47. Elizabeth Charlotte to Duchess Sophie, Fontainebleau, October 10, 1699, *Letters of Liselotte*, p. 117.

48. A frequently expressed opinion in her late years. For examples see Elizabeth Charlotte to the Raugräfin Luise, March 16, 1699; April 3, 1699; June 12, 1699, and November 19, 1706, *Correspondance*, 1:35–36, 37, 92.

49. Sophie to Karl Ludwig, Osnabrück, December 28, 1673, *Briefwechsel der Herzogin Sophie*, no. 179, p. 170; Elizabeth Charlotte to Mme von Harling [Liselotte's former governess in Hanover], November 23, 1672, *Correspondance*, 1:2.

50. Elizabeth Charlotte to Raugräfin Luise, June 30, 1718, quoted in Barine, *Madame*, p. 154.

51. J. H. Shennan, *Philippe, Duke of Orléans: Regent of France 1715–1723* (London, 1979), p. 12.

52. Elizabeth Charlotte to Sophie, Saint-Germain, December 3, 1672, *Briefe . . . an die Kurfürstin Sophie von Hannover*, vol. 1, no. 2, p. 2.

53. Sophie to Karl Ludwig, Diffhols, September 19, 1673, *Briefwechsel des Herzogin Sophie*, no. 175, p. 167.

54. Same to same, ibid., no. 179, p. 170.

55. Elizabeth Charlotte to Raugräfin Luise, October 18, 1720, *Correspondance*, 2:275–76.

56. Elizabeth Charlotte to Sophie, Fontainebleau, September 29, 1683, *Die Briefe der Liselotte von der Pfalz, Herzogin von Orleans*, ed. C. Künzel (Munich, n.d.), p. 84.

57. Montpensier, *Mémoires*, 4:213.

58. Mme de Sévigné to Mme de Grignan, Paris, February 12, 1672, *Correspondance*, vol. 1, no. 245, p. 439. Mme de Sévigné assured her daughter that she had learned of the conversation from a very sure source and that "nothing is more true."

59. Barine, *Madame*, pp. 144–47.

60. C. Rousset, *Histoire de Louvois*, 4 vols. (Paris, 1862), 2:18–19.

61. Karl Ludwig to Sophie, May 23, 1674, *Briefwechsel der Herzogin Sophie*, no. 198, pp. 187–88.

62. Philippe to Karl Ludwig, Saint-Cloud, July 13, 1674, ibid., no. 198, p. 197, n. 7.

63. Sophie to Karl Ludwig, Osnabrück, August 25, 1674, ibid., no. 213, p. 205.

64. Sophie to Karl Ludwig, Osnabrück, October 21, 1677, ibid., no. 310, p. 306.

65. Forster, "From the Patient's Point of View," p. 307.

66. Elizabeth Charlotte to Frau von Harling, Saint-Cloud, April 20, 1676, *Letters of Liselotte*, p. 13.
67. Elizabeth Charlotte to Frau von Harling, Saint-Cloud, May 30, 1676, ibid., pp. 14–15.
68. Mme de Sévigné to Mme de Grignan, July 8, 1676, *Correspondance*, vol. 2, no. 526, p. 339.
69. Elizabeth Charlotte to Frau von Harling, Saint-Cloud, October 10, 1676, *Briefe der Liselotte von der Pfalz*, p. 38.
70. *Gazette de France*, April 6, 1675.
71. Sophie to Karl Ludwig, Osnabrück, April 10, 1675, *Briefwechsel der Herzogin Sophie*, no. 234, p. 225.
72. Elizabeth Charlotte to Sophie, Paris, May 22, 1675, *Briefe . . . an die Kurfürstin Sophie*, vol. 1, no. 7, p. 6.
73. Philippe to Karl Ludwig, Paris, March 30, 1675, *Briefwechsel der Herzogin Sophie*, p. 226, n. 1. Emphasis mine.

SEVEN   LONG LIVE . . . MONSIEUR

1. For several recent studies of Louis's war and diplomacy see Theodore K. Rabb, *The Struggle for Stability in Early Modern Europe* (New York, 1975); Carl J. Ekberg, *The Failure of Louis XIV's Dutch War* (Chapel Hill, N.C., 1979); Ragnhild Hatton, ed., *Louis XIV and Europe* (Columbus, Ohio, 1976), especially the article by Paul Sonnino, "Louis XIV and the Dutch War," pp. 153–78.
2. Spanheim, *Relation de la cour de France en 1690*, p. 57.
3. Visconti [San Maiolo], *Mémoires*, p. 189.
4. Voltaire (François Marie Arouet), *Siècle de Louis XIV*, 2 vols. (Paris, 1830), 1:432.
5. Plessis-Praslin, *Mémoires*, p. 424.
6. Elizabeth Charlotte to Philippe, duke of Chartres, Paris, March 24, 1691, *Briefe der Herzogin Elisabeth Charlotte*, vol. 1, no. 67, p. 115.
7. Elizabeth Charlotte to Raugräfin Luise, April 22, 1719, *Correspondance*, 2:96.
8. Sigmund Freud, "Group Psychology and the Analysis of the Ego," in *Standard Edition*, 18:122.
9. *Mémoire du roy à Monsieur du 30 mars 1677 au camp devant Cambray*, Archives du Ministère de la Guerre (hereafter AMG), A1/544, fol. 174.
10. *Mémoire du roy à Monsieur du 29 mars 1677 au camp devant Cambray*, AMG, A1/544, fol. 158.
11. Luxembourg to the marquise de Sablé, April 16, 1677, quoted in Pierre de Ségur, *Le maréchal de Luxembourg et le prince d'Orange, 1668–1678* (Paris, n.d.), p. 442.
12. The "Reglement" of Turenne for the campaign of 1672 states the order of command explicitly. Louis XIV, *Oeuvres*, 3:124.
13. The *Gazette de France*, June 13, 1672, contains a long article with

details on the sieges and surrender of the four cities. See also Charles Sevin Quincy, *Histoire militaire du règne de Louis le Grand*, 7 vols. (Paris, 1726), 1:311–26.

14. Pellisson to Mme de Scudéry, at the camp at Rées, June 11, 1672, Paul Pellisson-Fontanier, *Lettres historiques*, 1:119–20.

15. "Mémoire inédit de Louis XIV relatif à la campagne de 1672," Papers of M. de Chamlay in AMG, A1/1112, quoted in Rousset, *Histoire de Louvois*, 1:527.

16. Wolf, *Louis XIV*, p. 222.

17. Quincy, *Histoire militaire*, 1:325–26; the *Gazette de France*, July 14, 1672, ran a fourteen-page account of the siege and surrender of Zutphen.

18. Philippe to Louvois, copy, June 22, 1672, in camp before Zutphen, AMG, A1/284, no. 155. The original is preserved as A1/276, fol. 121.

19. "Articles et conditions qu'il a pleu à Monsieur, . . . lieutenant general et commandant en chef des armées de Sa Majesté aux Bourgomestre et habitans de la ville de Zutphen," AMG, A1/284.

20. Pellisson to Mme de Scudéry, June 26, 1672, Pellisson-Fontanier, *Lettres historiques*, 1:203.

21. The party is described in much detail in the *Gazette de France*, August 17, 1672.

22. Albert Sorel, *L'Europe et la révolution française*, part 1, *Moeurs politiques et les traditions*, 4th ed. (Paris, 1897), pp. 280–83; Ekberg, *Dutch War*, pp. 13–14; Wolf, *Louis XIV*, pp. 222–23.

23. Rousset, *Histoire de Louvois*, 1:453–64.

24. Louis XIV, *Oeuvres*, 3:326–71.

25. *Gazette de France*, June 24, 1673.

26. Louis's own account of the campaign of 1673, Louis XIV, *Oeuvres*, 3:370.

27. *Gazette de France*, June 10 and June 17, 1673.

28. *Gazette de France*, August 5, 1673.

29. *Gazette de France*, June 16, 1674.

30. Rousset, *Histoire de Louvois*, 2:22–24.

31. *Gazette de France*, May–July 1675.

32. Sophie to Karl Ludwig, Brückhausen, May 23, 1674, *Briefwechsel der Herzogin Sophie*, no. 199, p. 188.

33. The only indication I have found to the contrary is a cryptic order of Louis XIV to Colbert of June 15, 1675, that reads: "I am astonished that my brother reacted in the way you said he did in the matter of the gold and silver, as you write me. Watch closely to see if he keeps the promise he made me, and if he breaks it let me know that I may write him about it" (Colbert, *Lettres*, vol. 6, no. 91, p. 328).

34. *Gazette de France*, April 14, 1674.

35. *Gazette de France*, June 16 and June 30, 1674.

36. Wolf, *Louis XIV*, pp. 236–37.

37. List of order of command for the campaign of 1676, Louis XIV, *Oeuvres*, 4:54.

38. Louvois to Le Tellier, *Mémoire* . . . *1676*, AMG, AI/499, fol. 153. The same account may be found almost verbatim in *Gazette de France*, May 21, 1676.

39. "Relation de ce qui s'est passé pendant le siège de Bouchain," Heurtebise, May 13, 1676, Colbert, *Lettres*, 6:461–62, appendix; Guillaume Temple, *Mémoires de ce qui s'est passé dans la chrétienté depuis le commencement de la guerre en 1672, jusqu'à la paix conclue en 1679*, trans. from English, ed. MM. Michaud and Poujoulat, Nouvelles collections des mémoires à l'histoire de France, vol. 8 (Paris, 1839), pp. 116–17.

40. Louis XIV, *Oeuvres*, 4:26. The official account of the event is the *Abrégé historique de la campagne (1676)*, BN, Fonds Français, 7892, fol. 8. Wolf, *Louis XIV*, has a long analysis of the king's actions and probable motives, pp. 249–53.

41. La Fare, *Mémoires*, p. 228; Rousset, *Histoire de Louvois*, 2:220–25.

42. Philippe, duke of Orléans to Mme de Sablé, in camp before Bouchain, May 7, [1676], BN, Français, 17048, fol. 164.

43. "Relation de M. le duc de la Feuillade à M. le maréchal de Villeroy," Pellisson-Fontanier, *Lettres historiques*, 3:72. Feuillade was at Heurtebise with the army and was present at the king's council of war. See also ibid., 3:51, 53, which gives Pellisson's views. He too was on the field that day.

44. "Relation de ce qui s'est passé pendant le siège de Bouchain," Camp de Hurtebize [*sic*], May 13, 1676, AMG, *Ordres du roi pour la marine*, 1676, fol. 126, reproduced in Colbert, *Lettres*, 6:461–62, appendix; *Mercure Galant*, June 1701, fol. 285.

45. *Mémoire du roy à Monsieur du 30 mars 1677 au camp devant Cambray*, AMG, A1/544, fol. 174.

46. Louvois to Chamblay, April 3, 1677, Lille, AMG, A1/545, fol. 21; Louvois to Humières, April 8, 1677, Cambray, AMG, A1/545, fol. 80.

47. Louvois to Humières, April 10, 1677, AMG A1/545, fol. 102.

48. *Mémoire du roy pour Monsieur du 7 avril 1677 au camp devant . . . Cambray*, AMG, A1/545, fol. 71.

49. Philippe to Mme de Sablé, April 3, 1677, reproduced in Edouard de Barthélemy, *Les amis de la marquise de Sablé: Recueil de lettres des principaux habitués de son salon*, (Paris, 1865), p. 260.

50. The number of combatants in belligerent armies is generally very difficult to ascertain with accuracy, the enumeration usually being much influenced by political considerations. We know that on April 3, 1677, Louvois estimated Monsieur's army as having 20,000 infantry and 15,000 cavalry. After that date Monsieur received an additional nine battalions of probably about 1,000 men each. At Cassel, therefore, he must have commanded some 44,000 men (Rousset, *Histoire de Louvois*, 2:195). Rousset believed that the prince of Orange had an army of approximately the same size. Others report him as having had as few as 30,000 to 35,000 men.

51. *Relation de la Bataille de Péene [Cassel]*, by Cardinal d'Estrées, BN, Clairamboult, vol. 582, fol. 385. Estrées was present when Philippe's emissary, the marquis d'Effiat, gave his report of the battle to the king. The official account is the *Abrégé historique de la campagne [1677]*, BN, Français,

vol. 7893, fol. 6. Another eyewitness account, perhaps by the chevalier de Lorraine, is *Détail de ce qui s'est passé à la Bataille de Cassel gagnée par S.A.R. Monsieur contre M. le prince d'Orange, le 11 avril 1677,* AMG, A1/545, fol. 107. See also *Gazette de France,* April 23, 1677.

52. Ségur, *Le maréchal de Luxembourg,* p. 436.

53. *Détail de ce qui s'est passé à la Bataille de Cassel,* AMG, A1/545, fol. 107.

54. Temple, *Mémoires,* p. 124. Temple was the ambassador from England to the United Netherlands and was present at the battle.

55. Luxembourg to Mme de Sablé, April 16, 1677, *Les amis de la marquise de Sablé,* p. 237; also reproduced in Ségur, *Maréchal de Luxembourg,* p. 442.

56. Visconti [San Maiolo], *Mémoires,* pp. 189–90.

57. Sigmund Freud, *Group Psychology and the Analysis of the Ego,* trans. James Strachey (London, 1922), pp. 8–35.

58. Freud, "Why War?" in *Collected Papers,* trans. and ed. James Strachey (New York, 1959), 5:282.

59. *Mercure Galant,* April 1677, fol. 198.

60. Visconti [San Maiolo], *Mémoires,* p. 189.

61. Pellisson to Mme de Scudéry, Cambray, April 12, 1677, Pellisson-Fontanier, *Lettres historiques,* 3:233.

62. Louis XIV to the prince de Condé, Cambray, April 15, 1677, *Oeuvres,* 4:17.

63. Louvois to Humières, Cambray, April 8, 1677, AMG A1/545, fol. 80.

64. Louvois to Humières, March 27, 1677, AMG, A1/531, quoted by Rousset, *Louvois,* 2:293–94. Humières was instructed specifically to combat "the pernicious influence" of the chevalier de Lorraine and the marquis d'Effiat. The letter concluded: "I beg you to burn this letter when you have read it and to tell no one what I have written you in this regard."

65. *Mercure Galant,* June 1701. A eulogy after Philippe's death. Emphasis in original.

66. Louvois to Humières, Cambray, March 31, 1677, AMG A1/544, fol. 172.

67. Ségur, *Luxembourg,* pp. 355–56.

68. Louis XIV, *Oeuvres,* 4:104–5.

69. La Fare, *Mémoires,* p. 229; see also Visconti [San Maiolo], *Mémoires,* p. 189. The Venetian ambassador at the French court was another who believed the king was jealous ("Relation de l'ambassadeur vénitien, 1676 [*sic*; from the context it is clear it was written in 1679]," Saint-Simon, *Mémoires,* vol. 8, appendix 25, pp. 626–27).

70. *Abrégé historique . . . 1677,* BN, Fonds Français, 7893, fol. 6.

71. Louis XIV, *Oeuvres,* 4:145. See also the official account of the campaign of 1678 that attributes its success entirely to Louis and is unusually sycophantic even for an official report. *Abrégé historique de la campagne (1678),* BN, Fonds Français, 7894, fol. 1. Neither account mentions Philippe.

72. *Oraison funèbre, cathédrale de Chartres,* by M. Gontier, *avec permission,* BN, Clairamboult, vol. 1144, fol. 63.

73. Oliver Brachfeld, *Inferiority Feelings in the Individual and the Group* (Westport, Conn., 1977), p. 137. Brachfeld is referring to theories of inferiority developed by Alfred Adler and others.

74. Ernest Lavisse, ed., *Histoire de France illustrée depuis les origines jusqu'à la révolution* (Paris, 1911), vol. 7, part 2, p. 338.

EIGHT   SERVICE TO MAMMON

1. Bernard, *Emerging City*, pp. 99–101.

2. "Brevet du roi en faveur de Guichard, intendant des bâtiments et jardins du duc d'Orléans," August 1674, *Correspondance administrative sous le règne de Louis XIV*, ed. G. B. Depping, 4 vols. (Paris, 1850–55), 4:595–596; Lionel de Laurencie, *Lully: Les maîtres de la musique* (Paris, 1919), pp. 38–48.

3. Espezel, *Palais-Royal*, p. 81; Champier and Sandoz, *Palais-Royal*, 1:176; Erlanger, *Monsieur*, p. 274; AN, Registre du Secrétariat de la Maison du Roi O1 36, passim. It is true that one finds no documentary confirmation of a bargain struck between the king linking the donation of the Palais Royal to the marriage of the future regent. (Nor would one expect to find evidence of this kind.) Nonetheless, given Monsieur's well-established opposition to the match and the equally well-established pattern of using expensive gifts as a means of obtaining the prince's cooperation, the connection seemed obvious to contemporaries. Dangeau, diarist of the court, recorded it dispassionately as a part of the financial arrangements of the marriage that included the handsome dowry to be brought by the bride (Philippe de Dangeau, *Journal publié en entier pour la première fois par MM. Soulié, Dussieux, de Chennevières, Mantz, de Montaiglon avec les additions inédites du duc de Saint-Simon publiées par M. Feuillet de Conches*, 19 vols. (Paris, 1854–60), 4:6–8 (January 9, 1962). See also Saint-Simon, *Mémoires*, vol. 1, no. 5, pp. 74–75. Another part of the bargain was favored treatment of the chevalier de Lorraine (see chap. 9).

4. Royal edict of March 13, 1693, granting the Palais Cardinal (as it was sometimes still known) to Philippe, duke of Orléans, BN, Fonds Français, 15533, fols. 23–24.

5. Champier and Sandoz, *Palais-Royal*, 1:175–88; Espezel, *Palais Royal*, pp. 82–83. Although other writers have held that the king did much of this work at an earlier date, a comparison of the palace in 1679 (see plate 19) with a plan of it in the Cabinet des Estampes, BN, of 1692 indicates that the authors above are correct. Louis visited Monsieur in Paris in April 1701 and viewed the *galerie nouvelle*, which he had not yet seen. He was heard to say he was "very satisfied" with both the architecture and the decoration of the new addition (Dangeau, *Journal*, 8:105). As early as October 1693 Monsieur was inspecting the progress of his new additions (ibid., 4:382). The best recent work on the Palais Royal has been done by Tony Sauvel. See "Palais-Royal," pp. 179–80.

6. *Compte de la trésorerie de Monsieur*, AN R4, 1066, fols. 231–32.

7. Saint-Simon, *Mémoires*, 8:334–39.

8. *Mercure Galant*, July 1689, pp. 178–86.

9. Martin Lister, "A Journey to Paris in the Year 1698," in *A General Collection of the Best and Most Interesting Voyages and Travels in All Parts of the World*, ed. John Pinkerton, 4 vols. (London, 1809), 4:58.

10. Espezel, *Palais-Royal*, pp. 86–88; Frantz Funck-Brentano with Paul d'Estrée, *Figaro et ses devanciers* (Paris, 1909), p. 116. At this time the arrival of French Protestants in Holland gave impetus to a critical Dutch press that circulated in Paris. See Louis Trenard, "La presse française des origines à 1788," in *Histoire générale de la presse française*, ed. Claude Bellanger et al. (Paris, 1969), 1:143–46.

11. The *Journal* of Dangeau, which describes the comings and goings of the king, Monsieur, the grand dauphin, and so on, in much detail shows, for example, that in the years 1697 and 1698 Monsieur spent most of the fall and winter in the Palais Royal, although he made frequent visits to the king at Versailles. He was invariably in Paris over the Christmas season. In spring and summer he was usually at Saint-Cloud except for excursions with the court to Compiègne (vol. 6, passim). The grand dauphin often visited him in the Palais Royal. A typical visit (Dangeau, *Journal*, 5:151–52) would begin with gambling followed by the opera, after which gambling was resumed until supper. The evening ended with a masked ball that lasted until the small hours of the morning.

12. From 1671 to 1693 Louis attended only twenty ceremonies in Paris and did not return again until 1701, after which he came to Paris only four more times in his reign. He became increasingly hostile to the city and tried to keep the members of his court out of it. Ranum, *Paris in the Age of Absolutism*, pp. 289–90.

13. Saint-Simon, *Mémoires*, 11:94–96, text and n. 6; Dangeau, *Journal*, 1:238. See also "Maison de Monsieur, 1698," *Estat de la France*, 2:65–114; and AN 300 AP I 130, containing a chronological list of Monsieur's chief officers of his household.

14. "Etat des biens de la succession du Régent," AN 300 AP I 761. A valuable volume providing a wealth of statistics and historical information on the real property of the house of Orléans.

15. AN O1 3870—Saint-Cloud.

16. Historians of architecture have disagreed on when and by whom the château was constructed and designed. Documentation is almost non-existent (the series O1 3870 on Saint-Cloud in AN contains very little for the period of Monsieur). The surviving engravings (many in the BN, Cabinet des Estampes) often do not settle the questions conclusively, since even if dated they carry no proof whether the buildings portrayed were in fact already in existence or were instead designs for future construction. Emile Magne (*Le château de Saint-Cloud, d'après des documents inédits* [Paris, 1932], pp. 117–25) and others place the building of the great château in the latter half of the 1670s but maintain that the Gondi Maison was not part of it and was subsequently razed. In Magne's opinion Hardouin-Mansart was the principal architect, while Le Pautre worked only on the

upper waterfall. Louis Hautecoeur (*Histoire de l'architecture classique en France*, 2:155–62), on the other hand, asserts that Monsieur built the central corps and both wings, one of which subsumed the Gondi Maison, in the 1660s before Henriette died and that Le Pautre, not Hardouin-Mansart and others, was the principal architect.

Magne and Hautecoeur seem to have both been partially right and partially wrong. A comparison of two paintings of Saint-Cloud in the Museum of Versailles, one by Van der Meulen in approximately 1671 (MV 6265) and the other by Allegrain in approximately 1677 (MV 743), prove that the great transformation of the château and building of the central corps and north wing took place in the latter half of the 1670s, contrary to the assertions of Hautecoeur. On the other hand, these paintings also establish that the Gondi Maison was incorporated within the south wing and did not stand apart to be later razed, as Magne maintained. As for the timing, the publication in 1681 of two descriptions of the château specifically authorized by Monsieur (Laurent, abbé de Morellet, *Explication historique de ce qu'il y a de plus remarquable dans la maison royale de Versailles et en celle de Monsieur à Saint-Cloud* [Paris, 1681], and Morellet, *Saint-Clou* [*sic*] *et les devises du salon, à Son Altesse Royale, Monsieur, fils de France, frère unique de Sa Majesté* [Paris, 1681]) provide independent evidence of its construction in the late 1670s. Many details of the decor evoked the prince's great victory at Cassel in 1677. Other reasons, not the least of which were financial, made it unlikely that Monsieur could have undertaken so ambitious a project in the 1660s. During the years 1665–67 the prince was acquiring property to expand the garden and park at Villers-Cotterêts (AN 300 AP I 164, Villers-Cotterêts). It is also difficult to believe that Louis would have permitted his brother to build on so grand a scale before he himself had begun major work at Versailles.

The best recent work on Saint-Cloud has been done by Daniel Meyer, conservateur au château de Versailles et des Trianons. See his "Le domaine national de Saint-Cloud," *Revue des Monuments Historiques de la France*, no. 3 (1975): 40–57; and *Le domaine national de Saint-Cloud* (Paris, n.d.). Meyer has been able to establish not only the approximate dates of the major construction but also the principal architects: Le Pautre, Thomas Gobert, and Hardouin-Mansart. Independent evidence of Le Pautre's involvement is his title *controlleur général des bâtiments* of Monsieur, which he held in the 1670s ("Estat général de la maison de monsieur," *Etat de la France*, 1:409–56).

17. *Mercure Galant*, January–March 1677, pp. 136–37.

18. Magne, *Saint-Cloud*, p. 135.

19. The waterfalls are described in detail in a booklet authorized by Monsieur and written by Harcouet de Longeville, *Description des grandes cascades de la maison royale de Saint Cloud: Dédiée à Son Altesse Royale Monseigneur duc d'Orléans* (Paris, 1706). A foreword explains that the author was ordered to undertake the description in July 1698.

20. Although the inventory gives the subject and dimensions of each

canvas, it does not provide the name of the painters. "Inventaire après décès de Monsieur," AN 300 AP I 746.

21. Lister, "Journey," p. 63.

22. Herzogin Sophie von Hannover, *Memoiren der Herzogin Sophie nachmals Kurfürstin von Hannover*, ed. Adolf Köcher, Publicationen aus den K. Preussischen Staatsarchiven (Leipzig, 1879), 4:116.

23. Ibid., p. 123.

24. Ibid., p. 127. The following November Liselotte conveyed to Sophie a similar gift from the king and noted, with an irreverent aside, that Monsieur regretted that he was unable to show her himself precisely how they were to be worn but would have a paper pattern sent (Elizabeth Charlotte to Duchess Sophie, Saint-Germain, November 1679, *Letters of Liselotte*, p. 27.

25. *Inventaire après décès de Monsieur*, June 17, 1701, AN 300 AP I 746. For a published summary of the jewel collection see Champier and Sandoz, *Palais-Royal*, pp. 191–92.

26. Saint-Simon, *Mémoires*, 8:335–36.

27. Lister, "Journey," pp. 62–63.

28. Sophie, *Memoiren*, 4:125.

29. Ibid, p. 126.

30. Morellet, *Explication historique*, p. 150.

31. Longeville, *Description des grandes cascades*.

32. Dangeau, *Journal*, 7:112–13.

33. *Mercure Galant*, July 1699, pp. 243–44.

34. *Mercure Galant*, March 1702, pp. 201–6. For detail see AN KK, 388. The auction brought in only 500,801 livres.

35. Champier and Sandoz, *Palais-Royal*, 1:339–59. In 1788, several years before the sale, the paintings in the possession of Philippe Egalité, most of which were in the Palais Royal, numbered 481 and were appraised at 2,201,600 livres: Italian school, 1,431,698 livres; Dutch school, 450,432 livres; and French school, 319,470 livres ("Etat général des tableaux appartenants à S.A.S. Mgr. le duc d'Orléans, dressé au mois de mars 1788, AN "Succession du duc d'Orléans," AN 300 AP I 28. A note appended to the register noted that a total of fifty-eight paintings listed in a register of 1726 were unaccounted for.

36. Robert Mandrou, *La France au XVIIe et au XVIIIe siècles* (Paris, 1970), pp. 128–29; Goubert, *Louis XIV et vingt millions de Français* p. 66. An analysis of the wealth of the princes of Condé on the eve of the eighteenth century by Daniel Roche demonstrates clearly how dependent the family was on the generosity of the Crown ("Aperçus sur la fortune et les revenus des princes de Condé à l'aube du 18e siècle," *Revue d'Histoire Moderne et Contemporaine* 14 July–September 1967]: 217–43). See also Barker, "Philippe d'Orléans," pp. 147–51.

37. "Inventaire des titres du duc d'Orléans [Monsieur], brevets, dons, régie et des charges d'évaluation," AN 300 AP I 749. The dowries from his two wives are omitted from this enumeration of income, since they

yielded little cash income. Of the 840,000 livres the king of England promised with the hand of Henriette, 270,000 livres was still unpaid in 1684, fourteen years after her death when Anne d'Orléans, her younger daughter by Monsieur, married the duke of Savoy. At the most, Philippe could not have received more than 25,000 livres annually from the dowry. See the "Contrat de mariage 31 mars 1661 [of Monsieur]," AN 300 AP I 115; and "contrat de mariage 9 avril 1684," of Anne d'Orléans, ibid. Of the paltry sum promised by the elector of the Palatinate, little or nothing was paid (see chap. 6).

38. *Apanage, mars 1661, edit du roy*, in *Apanage de la maison d'Orléans* (Paris, 1762), pp. 3–11, AN 300 AP I 199.

39. *Supplément* [*sic*] *d'apanage 24 avril 1672, déclaration du roy*, ibid., pp. 11–15.

40. Labatut, *Ducs et pairs de France au XVIIe siècle*, p. 285. In 1710 the duc de Berry also was in possession of an appanage with a revenue of 200,000 livres (ibid.).

41. According to Pierre Goubert, the annual revenue of "the great" ranged between 50,000 and 250,000 livres in the seventeenth century and twice that amount in the eighteenth century (*Ancien Régime*, p. 169).

42. See chap. 4, n. 5.

43. The succession was not formally granted to Monsieur and to his male and female descendants until Louis XIV issued letters patent of March 1695 ("Etat des biens de la succession du régent," AN 300 AP I 761). A copy of her testament appeared in the *Mercure Galant*, April 1693, pp. 152–60. See also "Succession Montpensier," "Papiers de Mlle de Montpensier," AN 300 AP I 93; and "Principauté de Dombes," AN 300 AP I 438.

44. Saint-Simon, *Mémoires*, 1:123. *Mercure Galant*, March and April 1693.

45. Mademoiselle told her own story at length. *Mémoires*, vol. 4 (the years 1680–82): 400–464.

46. "Etat des biens de la succession du régent," AN 300 AP I 761.

47. Spanheim, *Relation de la cour de France*, p. 75; Saint-Simon, *Mémoires*, 1:124, editorial note.

48. "Inventaire après décès de Monsieur," AN 300 AP I 746.

49. "Estat géneral de la maison de Monsieur, duc d'Orléans," *Estat de la France*, 1:409–56 (1672); 1:498–564 (1682); 2:65–132 (1698).

50. For a discussion of "enthusiasm" in the seventeenth century, see the review article by Michael Heyd, "The Reaction to Enthusiasm in the Seventeenth Century: Toward an Integrative Approach," *Journal of Modern History* 53(June 1981): 258–80.

51. This review of Monsieur's charities is drawn from the following sources: "Papiers personnels, fondation de l'hôpital de Triel," May 22, 1693, AN 300 AP I 115; "Contrat de constitution de . . . rente," May 29, 1696, ibid., "Contrat, hôpital de Triel," February 15, 1707, ibid.; "Etat des Biens . . . succession du Régent," AN 300 AP I 761; and "Inventaire des titres du duc d'Orléans (Monsieur)," AN 300 AP I 748.

52. "Testament de feu SAS Monsieur duc d'Orléans," June 14, 1701, AN 300 AP I 115; "Inventaire après décès de Monsieur," AN 300 AP I 746.

53. Dangeau, *Journal*, 4:259–60.

54. Patrice Berger, "Rural Charity in Late Seventeenth-Century France: The Pontchartrain Case," *French Historical Studies*, 10(Spring 1978): 399, 403.

55. J. Grancolas, *Oraison funèbre de très haut, très puissant, et très-excellent prince Philippe, fils de France, frère unique du roy* (Paris, 1701), pp. 31–32, 35. François de Clermont-Tonnere, *Oraison funèbre de très-haut et très puissant* [*etc.*] . . . *prononcée dans l'église de l'abbaye de S. Denis le 23 juillet* (Paris 1701), p. 20.

56. See, for example, December 11, 1662, March 23, 1672, December 22, 1672, September 1, 1677, October 20, 1677, "Inventaire des minutes de conseil," AN 300 AP I 814.

57. Magne, *Saint-Cloud*, pp. 171–72.

58. Vatout, *Souvenirs historiques des résidences royales*, p. 99.

59. "Maison de Monsieur," *Estat de la France*, for the year 1682, 1:498–545; for the year 1698, 2:65–114. During Monsieur's lifetime the chancellors and superintendents of finance of the house of Orléans were as follows: Guillaume de Bautru de Serrant, to 1671; Duhousset, 1671–85; Joachim Seiglière de Boifranc and Seiglière fils, 1685–88; Louis de Béchameil, 1688; Gaston-Jean-Baptiste Terrat, 1688–1719 (AN 300 AP I 130).

60. Goubert, *Louis XIV et vingt millions de Français*, pp. 139–41.

61. Jean-Claude Waquet, *Les grands maîtres des eaux et forêts de France de 1689 à la révolution suivi d'un dictionnaire des grands maîtres* (Geneva, 1978), pp. 1–2.

62. "Le 'Mémoire' sur l'apanage," AN D X2, fols. 13–19. This memoir was prepared by the Comité des Domaines for the National Assembly either in 1790 or 1791 when, the princely appanages having all been abolished, the question of indemnification was being studied. For forest conditions see principally Michel Devèze, *Histoire des forêts: Que sais-je?* (Paris, 1965), pp. 50–52; J. B. Plinquet, *Traité sur les réformations et les aménagemens des forêts avec une application à celles d'Orléans et de Montargis* (Orléans, 1789), pp. 23–24, 35–36; Paul Domet, *Histoire de la forêt d'Orléans* (Orléans, 1892), pp. 291–92.

63. In addition to "Le 'Mémoire' sur l'apanage," AN D X2, see the "Inventaire des minutes de conseil" of Monsieur for the years 1662–76, AN 300 AP I 814, passim.

64. Alexandre Michaux, *Essai historique sur la forêt de Retz* (Soissons, 1876), pp. 30–47; Louis Le Pelletier, "Étude sur la forêt de Villers-Cotterêts," *Bulletin de la Société Archéologique, Historique et Scientifique de Soissons*, 3d ser., 11 (1901–02): 1–202; Domet, *Histoire de la forêt d'Orléans*, passim.

65. Domet, *Histoire de la forêt d'Orléans*, p. 291.

66. Two excellent authorities are Michel Devèze, *La grande réformation des forêts sous Colbert (1661–1683)* (Nancy, 1962); and John Croumbie

Brown, *French Forest Ordinance of 1669, with Historical Sketch of Previous Treatment of Forests in France* (London, 1883).

67. Waquet, *Grands maîtres des eaux et forêts*, pp. 2, 8.

68. "'Mémoire' sur l'apanage," AN D X2.

69. "Papiers de Louis-Philippe, duc d'Orléans," AN 300 AP I 48, "Etat des biens possédés en 1757 avec mention de l'origine et dates des acquisitions"; and ibid., "Biens de la maison d'Orléans"; "Etat des Biens de la maison d'Orléans, 1748," AN 300 AP I 826, fol. 57; see also "'Mémoire' sur l'apanage," AN D X2.

70. All the documents in the previous note yield information on La Ferté-Milon.

71. The best published authority on the construction of the Orléans Canal is Hubert Pinsseau, *Histoire de la construction, de l'administration et de l'exploitation du Canal d'Orléans de 1676 à 1954: Un aspect du développement économique de la France* (Paris, 1963). A series of articles in the *Journal du Loiret*, October 23, 1913, no. 244; October 26, 1913, no. 247; October 27–28, no. 248; and November 5, 1913, no. 254 gives useful detail from the departmental archives. See also E. J. M. Vignon, *Etudes historiques sur l'administration des voies publiques en France au XVIIe et XVIIIe siècles*, 3 vols. (Paris, 1862), 1:45, 65–66, 112–25, 302. For documents in the archives of the house of Orléans see "Inventaire des minutes du conseil" of Monsieur, AN 300 AP I 814, April 24 or 25, 1676, March 8, 15, and 22, 1697; "Etat des biens... succession du régent," AN 300 AP I 761; and "Canal d'Orléans, emprunt," May 15, 1699, AN 300 AP I 115.

72. Edict of September 1687, Archives du Loiret C 272, cited by Pinsseau, *Canal d'Orléans*, pp. 46–47.

73. "Edit du roy donné à Saint-Germain en Laye au mois de mars 1679," AN H 3148 (imprimé).

74. André Jubert de Bouville to President Harlay, August 2, 1694, AN G7 419, quoted in Charles de Beaucorps, *L'administration des intendants d'Orléans de 1686 à 1713: Jean de Creil, André Jubert de Bouville, Yves de La Bourdonnaye* (reprinting of the Orléans edition of 1911 in Geneva, 1978), p. 216. See also Georges Lefebvre, *Etudes orléanaises*, 2 vols. (Paris, 1961–63), 1:83.

75. "Etats des biens... succession du régent," "Rivière d'Ourque [*sic*]," AN 300 AP I 761. See also Le Pelletier, "Etude sur la forêt de Villers-Cotterêts," pp. 1–202.

76. For the acquisitions above see respectively fols. 65, 30, 58, and 65 of the "Etat des biens de la maison d'Orléans, 1748," AN 300 AP I 826.

77. "Notes et observations sur la formation des officiers de la chancellerie et du conseil de l'apanage," February 14, 1825, by order of Louis Philippe, AN 300 AP 130.

78. René-Louis Voyer, marquis d'Argenson, *Mémoires et journal inédit*, 5 vols. (Paris, 1857–58), 1:248.

79. For examples of Liselotte's complaints see Elizabeth Charlotte to Sophie, Versailles, June 28, 1693, and March 7, 1696, *Briefe der Liselotte von der Pfalz*, pp. 153, and 166–70; same to same, Versailles, June 12, June 30,

July 7, and July 21, *Letters of Liselotte*, pp. 131–32, 133–34, 134, 135, and 135–36.

80. Liselotte did in fact understand that her marriage contract, about which she frequently complained, was at the root of her financial problems. That knowledge did not prevent her from accusing Monsieur of improvidence. See Elizabeth Charlotte to Sophie, Versailles, July 7, 1701, *Letters of Liselotte*, p. 134.

81. "Etat des biens de la maison d'Orléans, 1748," AN 300 AP I 826, fol. 36.

82. Magne, *Château de Saint-Cloud*, p. 192.

83. "Canal d'Orléans: Emprunt de 400,000 livres," May 15, 1699, AN 300 AP I 115. The revenues from the canal provided the collateral for the loan.

84. Visconti [San Maiolo], *Mémoires*, p. 158.

85. Monsieur's love of money was also a trait recognized by his contemporaries. A pen portrait of him written shortly after his death reads in part: "Always avid for money and almost always embroiled in monetary affairs, [he was] inordinately fond of himself" ("Portraits divers de Monsieur, appendix 25, Saint-Simon, *Mémoires*, 8:629).

86. Louis XIV had four main councils: the Council of State (the most important, which treated of high policy); the Privy Council; the Council of Dispatches; and the Council of Finances. For descriptions of the responsibilities and meetings of the Council of Dispatches see Spanheim, *Relation de la cour*, p. 236, and Saint-Simon, *Mémoires*, 5:443, 446, 468–69, Boislisle's appendixes.

87. Dangeau, *Journal*, 4:381–82; Saint-Simon, *Mémoires*, 2:80.

NINE   THE END OF THE TETHER

1. Elizabeth Charlotte to Luise, [Paris], November 18, 1718, *Correspondance*, 2:25.

2. Elizabeth Charlotte to the Raugräfin Luise [Paris], June 11, 1717, ibid., 2:300.

3. Elizabeth Charlotte to Sophie, Versailles, July 21, 1682, *Briefe der Liselotte von der Pfalz*, p. 72. In the letter cited previously, written in 1717, Liselotte had implied that the termination of marital relations had begun sometime after the birth of her third child in 1676. The letter above, somewhat more precise, implies that husband and wife continued sleeping together until 1677 or 1678. For a published English translation of the letter see *Letters of Liselotte*, p. 35.

4. Elizabeth Charlotte to Sophie, November 24, 1682, Barine, *Madame*, pp. 210–11.

5. Elizabeth Charlotte to Sophie, Paris, November 14, 1678, *Letters of Liselotte*, p. 25; *Briefe... an die Kurfürstin Sophie*, vol. 1, no. 23, pp. 25–26.

6. Mme de Sévigné to Mme de Grignan, Rochers, September 18 [1680], *Correspondance*, vol. 3, no. 808, p. 16.

7. Elizabeth Charlotte to Sophie, Saint-Cloud, September 24, 1680, *Letters of Liselotte*, pp. 27–28.

8. Same to same, Saint-Germain, December 11, 1680, ibid., pp. 29–30.

9. Elizabeth Charlotte to Sophie, April 3, 1710, Barine, *Madame*, p. 194.

10. Sophie to Karl Ludwig, Palais Royal, September 13, 1679, *Briefwechsel der Herzogin Sophie*, no. 376, p. 376.

11. Sophie to Karl Ludwig, Osnabrück, November 23, 1679, ibid., no. 394, p. 390; Barine, *Madame*, pp. 174–77.

12. Elizabeth Charlotte to Sophie, Saint-Germain, November 1, 1679, *Letters of Liselotte*, p. 27.

13. Elizabeth Charlotte to Sophie, Saint-Germain, December 15, 1679, *Briefe der Liselotte*, pp. 56–57; see also Barine, *Madame*, pp. 185–88.

14. Elizabeth Charlotte to Sophie, Saint-Cloud, August 1, 1683, *Letters of Liselotte*, p. 41.

15. For a discussion of the marriage and its scholarly documentation see Wolf, *Louis XIV*, pp. 329–33.

16. Such complaints are sprinkled throughout her correspondence. See, for example, Elizabeth Charlotte to Sophie, Saint-Cloud, August 2, 1688, *Briefe . . . an die Kurfürstin Sophie*, vol. 1, no. 81, pp. 97–98.

17. Elizabeth Charlotte to Sophie, Saint-Cloud, May 18, 1686, *Briefe . . . an die Kurfürstin Sophie*, vol. 1, no. 56, p. 68.

18. Mme de Sévigné to Mme de Grignan, Rochers, July 7 [1680], *Correspondance*, vol. 2, no. 782, pp. 1001–2. Mme de Maintenon thought so too, as is evidenced from a malicious comment in one of her letters to a good friend, Mme de Brinon, December 25, 1686; Mme de Maintenon, *Correspondance générale*, ed. Théophile Lavallée, 5 vols. (Paris, 1865), vol. 3, no. 84, p. 55.

19. A voluminous letter from Elizabeth Charlotte to Sophie tells the entire story—at least so far as Liselotte saw it (Saint-Cloud, September 19, 1682, *Briefe . . . an die Kurfürstin Sophie*, vol. 1, no. 41, pp. 45–54). A shorter letter from same to same of September 12, 1682, reproduced in English translation in *Letters of Liselotte*, pp. 36–37, alludes to the same incident.

20. Sophie to Raugraf Karl-Lutz, November 7, 1682, *Briefe der Kurfürstin Sophie von Hannover an die Raugräfin*, quoted in Barine, *Madame*, p. 209.

21. These themes are developed and repeated continually in the letters of Elizabeth Charlotte to Sophie in the 1680s and 1690s. A convenient English translation of a typical letter that hits upon most of the complaints in the paragraph above is in *Letters of Liselotte*, pp. 90–92.

22. Elizabeth Charlotte to Raugräfin Luise, Saint-Cloud, May 15, 1697, *Letters of Liselotte*, p. 101.

23. Elizabeth Charlotte to Mme de Harling, April 15, 1696, Barine, *Madame*, p. 282.

24. A pen portrait of Philippe written at the beginning of the War of the Spanish Succession states: "[Monsieur] does not appear to approve of the policy of persecution of religious dissenters, of which he never speaks" (Arthur-Michel de Boislisle, ed., *Portraits et caractères, 1703* [Paris, 1897], p.

24). Boislisle believes that the author of the portrait was a Protestant refugee in England.

25. Obeying the king, Philippe corresponded with his son-in-law, attempting to win him to the French side. Occasionally Victor Amadeus wrote to Monsieur imploring him to intercede on his behalf with Louis. An example of such a letter is that of June 24, 1690, BN, Morel de Thoisy, vol. 63, fol. 212. Such intervention was invariably useless. See Dangeau, *Journal*, 3:120–21.

26. Elizabeth Charlotte to Sophie, November 10, 1688, *Briefe... an die Kurfürstin Sophie*, vol. 1, no. 84, p. 102.

27. On occasion the duke of Savoy attempted to use Monsieur as an intermediary in his negotiations with Louis, but to no avail. See Victor Amadeus to Philippe, copy, June 24, 1690, BN, Morel de Thoisy, vol. 63, fol. 212; and Dangeau, *Journal*, 3:120–21.

28. Erlanger, *Monsieur*, p. 253.

29. Saint-Simon, *Mémoires*, 8:348–49, 340.

30. For accounts of the marriage see *Mercure Galant*, September 1679, pp. 259–337; October 1679, pp. 289–392; and *Gazette de France*, September 12 and 13, 1679. The formal account of the ceremonies by the Spanish ambassador, marquis de los Balbaces, is in AMAE, MD, nouvelle acquisition (without call number). See also AMAE, MD Espagne, vol. 73, "Relation des ceremonies observées au mariage du roy d'Espagne, 1679," fol. 48.

31. Sophie, *Memoiren*, p. 120.

32. Mme de Sévigné to Mme de Grignan, Paris, September 27 [1679], *Correspondance*, vol. 2, no. 693, p. 688.

33. Ibid.

34. *Gazette de France*, September 12, 1679; *Mercure Galant*, September 1679, September 1679, fol. 338, and October 1679, pp. 289–302; marquis de los Balbaces, AMAE, MD, France, nouvelle acquisition (no call number). Balbaces was the Spanish ambassador at the French court.

35. *Mercure Galant*, July 1679, p. 235.

36. Prince of Harcourt to Pomponne, copy, AMAE, MD, Espagne, vol. 73, fol. 103. Harcourt was a passenger in the coach with Marie Louise and Monsieur.

37. Sophie, *Memoiren*, p. 120.

38. Ibid.

39. See for example Dangeau, *Journal*, 1:207. Marie Louise wrote to Monsieur that she believed her life was in danger.

40. After receiving a letter from his daughter, Monsieur told the French court that she had received the *clave de tres dobles* to all the apartments of the palace, the highest mark of esteem that a king of Spain could award his queen. Dangeau, *Journal*, 1:256.

41. Rebenac to Louis XIV, February 12, 1689, AMAE, MD, Espagne, vol. 73, fols. 256–57; Dangeau, *Journal*, 2:334–35; Mme de Sévigné to Mme de Grignan, February 21, [1689], *Correspondance*, vol. 3, no. 1073, p. 509, ed. note, p. 1400.

42. Elizabeth Charlotte to Raugräfin Amalie Elizabeth, Fontainebleau, November 4, 1701, *Letters of Liselotte*, p. 138.

43. Wolf, *Louis XIV*, pp. 422–423.

44. For the *contrat de mariage*, October 15, 1696, see AN K 543 (Papiers des princes).

45. Appendix 13, "Négociations avec la Savoie," Saint-Simon, *Mémoires*, 3:419–49 Wolf, *Louis XIV*, pp. 480–81.

46. Louis-François de Bouschet, marquis de Sourches, *Mémoires du marquis de Sourches sur le règne de Louis XIV*, ed. Gabriel Jules Cosnac and Edoudrel Pontal (Paris, 1885), 5:212.

47. Elizabeth Charlotte to Sophie, Paris, November 8, 1696, *Letters of Liselotte*, p. 95.

48. Saint-Simon, *Mémoires*, 8:368–69.

49. Ibid., 1:60.

50. Marie Anne de Bourbon, styled Mlle de Blois, married Louis Armand de Bourbon, prince of Conti, on January 16, 1680. She was widowed in 1685. Louise Françoise de Bourbon, styled Mlle de Nantes, married Louis III, duke of Bourbon-Condé, son of the Grand Condé, on July 24, 1685.

51. Elizabeth Charlotte to Luise, [Paris], May 17, 1720, *Correspondance*, 2:239.

52. Dangeau, *Journal*, 2:442, August 5, 1689; Elizabeth Charlotte to Sophie, Versailles, August 26, 1689, *Briefe... an die Kurfürstin Sophie*, vol. 1, no. 92, pp. 111–14.

53. Saint-Simon, *Mémoires*, 8:267; Liselotte complained frequently about Monsieur's indulgence of his son and his alleged desire to put him in bad company. Elizabeth Charlotte to Sophie, Versailles, March 7, 1696, *Letters of Liselotte*, p. 90.

54. *Contrat de mariage*, February 17, 1692, AN K 543 (Papiers des princes).

55. Elizabeth Charlotte to Sophie, Versailles, January 10, 1692, *Briefe... an die Kurfürstin Sophie*, vol. 1, no. 125, p. 143; English translation in *Letters of Liselotte*, p. 74. The marriage was the talk of the court for weeks. See Caylus, *Souvenirs*, p. 509; Dangeau, *Journal*, 4:6–8; Saint-Simon, *Mémoires*, 1:60–61, 74–75.

56. Marthe-Marguérite de Villette de Murçay, marquise de Caylus, *Souvenirs*, ed. A. Petitot and L. J. N. Monmerqué, Collection des mémoires relatifs à l'histoire de France, vol. 66 (Paris, 1928), p. 470.

57. Mme de Maintenon wrote piously to a friend that although she knew the marriage of Chartres was not to Madame's liking she hoped that the lady would nonetheless accept with good grace what she could not prevent (Mme de Maintenon to duchess of Ventadour, February 1692, Maintenon, *Correspondance générale*, vol. 3, no. 273, p. 324).

58. *Mercure Galant*, February 1692, pp. 303–35.

59. Ibid., March 1692, pp. 7–20.

60. Elizabeth Charlotte to Sophie, Saint-Cloud, August 7, 1692, *Letters of Liselotte*, p. 78.

61. Saint-Simon, *Mémoires*, 2:181–82.

62. In a ceremony at the château of Amboise (Indre-et-Loire) on September 27, 1987, the count of Paris, then seventy-nine years of age, designated his grandson, Prince Jean, as his heir to the crown and conferred on him the title of duke of Vendôme. Prince Henri, father of Jean and oldest son of the count of Paris, was excluded from the succession as a consequence of his divorce from his wife, mother of Jean, and of his remarriage in 1984, in a civil ceremony and without the consent of his father.

63. Elizabeth Charlotte to Sophie, Fontainebleau, September 29, 1683, *Letters of Liselotte*, p. 42.

64. Dangeau, *Journal*, 6:419. For the contrat de mariage, October 12, 1699, see AN K 543 (Papiers des princes).

65. Saint-Simon, *Mémoires*, 6:5.

66. Elizabeth Charlotte to Sophie, November 16, 1698, *Letters of Liselotte*, p. 110. A year later Elizabeth Charlotte reported: "My daughter is very happy with her duke; he anticipates her every wish and they love each other with all their hearts" (Elizabeth Charlotte to Raugräfin Luise, Fontainebleau, October 11, 1699, ibid., p. 117).

67. Elizabeth Charlotte to Sophie, Paris, December 27, 1691, *Briefe der Herzogin Elisabeth Charlotte*, vol. 1, no. 70, pp. 119–20.

68. Isherwood, *Music in the Service of the King*, p. 254.

69. Dangeau, *Journal*, 5:151–52.

70. Peter Loewenberg, *Decoding the Past: The Psychohistorical Approach* (New York, 1983), p. 108.

71. Saint-Simon, *Mémoires*, 12:284.

72. Ibid., 8:333.

73. Monsieur's tour of duty is reported intermittently in the *Journal* of Dangeau in the spring and summer of 1693, vol. 4, pp. 267–337. See also *Gazette de France*, May 30 to August 1, 1693.

74. La Fare, *Mémoires*, p. 276.

75. Elizabeth Charlotte to Sophie, Versailles, June 28, 1693, *Briefe der Liselotte von der Pfalz*, p. 153.

76. Mme de Sévigné to Mme de Grignan, [Paris], April 21, [1694], *Correspondance*, vol. 3, no. 1300, p. 1039. The lady in question was very likely the marquise de Châteaufremont, wife of the president *à mortier* of the Parlement of Brittany. In the spring of 1694 she turned up at the Palais Royal and was the object of much gossip.

77. Dangeau, *Journal*, 6:86–87; 7:124, 133.

78. Ibid., 7:412–13.

79. Shennan, *Philippe, Duke of Orléans*, p. 18; A. Baudrillart, *Philippe V et la cour d'Espagne*, 5 vols. (Paris, 1890–1910), 2:21.

80. Dangeau, *Journal*, 4:318–19.

81. Elizabeth Charlotte to Raugräfin Luise, [Paris], February 15, 1716, *Correspondance*, 1:216.

82. Liselotte did not inform her relatives of Monsieur's gift until many years later. Elizabeth Charlotte to Luise, [Paris], June 11, 1717, *Correspondance*, 1:300.

83. Elizabeth Charlotte to Sophie, Port Royal, July 26, 1699, *Letters of Liselotte*, p. 114.

84. Elizabeth Charlotte to Sophie, Marly, May 6, 1700, *Letters of Liselotte*, p. 121.

85. Elizabeth Charlotte to Sophie, Versailles, January 1, 1693, *Letters of Liselotte*, p. 80.

86. Elizabeth Charlotte to Sophie, Saint-Cloud, August 7, 1692, *Letters of Liselotte*, p. 77.

87. Elizabeth Charlotte to Chartres, Marly, June 18, 1696; same to Abbé Dubois, Saint-Cloud, June 21, 1696; same to same, Port-Royal, August 10, 1696, *Briefe der Herzogin Elisabeth Charlotte*, 1:157–58, no. 105; ibid., 1:158–59, no. 106; and ibid., 1:162–63, no. 110. Details on Chartres's misdeeds with bibliographical references are supplied by Boislisle in Saint-Simon, *Mémoires*, 8:314–15, n. 6.

88. Elizabeth Charlotte to Sophie, Marly, May 6, 1700, *Letters of Liselotte*, p. 121.

89. Saint-Simon, *Mémoires*, 8:313.

90. According to Saint-Simon, who wrote from hearsay in the court, often based on information received from Chartres, Monsieur obeyed his confessor out of fear of the devil. Ibid.

91. Testament of Monsieur, April 11, 1699, Papiers personnels [of Monsieur], AN 300 AP I 115.

92. Saint-Simon, *Mémoires*, 2:254–59.

93. Ibid., 8:267–68.

94. Dangeau, *Journal*, 8:122–23.

95. The report of the chevalier de Lorraine. *Mercure Galant*, June 1701, fol. 285.

96. Once again the reporter of the scene is Saint-Simon. He could have learned of the conversation not only from Philippe II, who supped with his father a few hours after it took place, but from the many within the palace who overheard it. Neither Dangeau, ever the courtier, nor Liselotte, confined at Saint-Cloud with fever, mentions a quarrel between the brothers, but both confirmed Philippe's presence at Marly for dinner with the king. The former, confirming Saint-Simon, noted that Monsieur's choleric appearance caused those present to urge him to be bled (*Journal*, 8:119). The latter, who saw Philippe after his return from Marly, found him "hale and hearty" but in a state of excitement and exhilaration (Elizabeth Charlotte to Sophie, Versailles, June 12, 1701, *Letters of Liselotte*, p. 131).

97. Elizabeth Charlotte to Sophie, Versailles, June 12, 1701, *Letters of Liselotte*, p. 131.

98. Elizabeth Charlotte to Sophie, Saint-Cloud, June 9, 1701, *Letters of Liselotte*, p. 130.

99. For details on the funeral services see, among other places, *Mercure Galant*, June 1701, fol. 316–72, and July 1701, fol. 295–333.

100. *Mercure Galant*, July 1701, fol. 65. *Pour Monsieur, duc d'Orléans. Cassel le vit briller dans un fameux combat, La gloire l'élevait, et la parque l'abbat.*

EPILOGUE: A PRINCE FOR POSTERITY

1. Saint-Simon, *Mémoires*, 8:330.
2. Ibid., 8:327–28.
3. Elizabeth Charlotte to Luise, [Paris], March 11, 1719, *Correspondance*, 2:79.
4. Elizabeth Charlotte to Countess Luise, July 15, 1718, *Correspondance*, 1:428.
5. Saint-Simon, *Mémoires*, 8:325.
6. The view of Saint-Simon and therefore probably also of Chartres, with whom he was closely associated. For the death of Monsieur the memoirist is therefore a privileged source of information on the emotions of the family. Saint-Simon, *Mémoires*, 8:359–60.
7. Ibid., p. 356.
8. Ibid., pp. 356–60; Dangeau, *Journal*, 8:127–30, contains much of the same detail.
9. Elizabeth Charlotte to Countess Luise, August 11, 1701, *Correspondance*, 1:53.
10. Dangeau, *Journal*, 8:128.
11. Erlanger, *Monsieur*, p. 309.
12. Boislisle, *Portraits et caractères*, p. 24.
13. Voltaire, *Siècle de Louis XIV*, 1:432.
14. Wolf, *Louis XIV*, p. 606.
15. Jean Meyer, *Le régent* (Paris, 1985), p. 15.
16. Apostolidès, *Le roi-machine*, p. 42.
17. Grancolas, *Oraison funèbre*, p. 10; see also Clermont-Tonnere, *Oraison funèbre*, pp. 7–8; *Abrégé de la vie et des actions héroiques de très haut et très-puissant prince Philippe de France frère unique du roy, duc d'Orléans* (Paris, 1701), p. 2. The *Abrégé* was the official eulogy of the prince.
18. Hyslop, *Apanage de Philippe-Egalité duc d'Orléans*, p. 77. The appanage alone yielded an annual income of 4,368,000 livres in 1790 (AN R4 268 [Apanages]).
19. For a recent scholarly review of Philippe Egalité's political activities see George Armstrong Kelly, "The Machine of the Duc d'Orléans and the New Politics," *Journal of Modern History* 51(December 1979): 667–84.
20. In 1824 the former appanage was yielding an annual income of 2,288,000 francs (AN R4 268 [Apanages]).
21. Guillaume de Bertier de Sauvigny, *The Bourbon Restoration*, trans. Lynn M. Case (Philadelphia, 1966), p. 373.

Bibliography

MANUSCRIPT SOURCES

Archives du Ministère des Affaires Etrangères [Paris]
  Correspondance politique: Angleterre, 1669–70, vols. 94–99.
  Mémoires et documents: correspondance Mazarin, vols. 269, 272, 274, 275, 277, 279, 280, 281, 283, 284, 290, 291, 292, 896, 2193; Angleterre, lettres autographes de Charles II à Henriette d'Angleterre; Espagne, vol. 73, mariage de Marie Louise d'Orléans avec Charles II, 1665–89; nouvelle acquisition (without volume number), journal du marquis de los Balbaces.
Archives du Ministère de la Guerre [Paris]
  Series A/1, vols. 276, 284, 489, 499, 531, 536, 537, 544, 545, 2538.
Archives Nationales [Paris]
  Fonds de Dreux, Archives de la maison de France (branche d'Orléans) 300 AP I, nos. 1–2634. (Family papers of the house of Orléans deposited by the count of Paris in the Archives Nationales. A published inventory, prepared by Suzanne d'Huart, appeared in 1976, after which date the papers became available to scholars who were authorized by the count.)
  Series K 542, K 543 (papiers des princes); O1 36 (Maison du roi); O 1, 3870 (Saint-Cloud); R 4, 268 (Apanages); 292 (Palais-Royal et dépendances); 645 (Réformation des eaux et forêts); 1066 (Compte de la trésorerie de Monsieur): *D X2 ("Mémoire" sur l'apanage)*.
Bibliothèque Nationale [Paris]
  Salle des manuscrits: Fonds Français; Baluze; Clairamboult; Mélanges Colbert; Morel de Thoisy; Nouvelles acquisitions françaises.

Public Record Office [London]
State Papers 78. France, 1577–1780, vols. 115–30, 307, 308.

PRINTED PRIMARY SOURCES

Abrégé de la vie et des actions héroiques de très haut et très-puissant prince Philippe de France frère unique du roy, duc d'Orléans. Paris, 1701. (An official eulogy.)

Argenson, René-Louis Voyer, marquis d'. *Mémoires et journal inédit*. 5 vols. Paris, 1857–58.

Brice, Germain. *Description nouvelle de la ville de Paris*. 4 vols. Paris, 1752.

Brienne, Louis-Henri de Loménie de. *Mémoires inédits*. 2 vols. Paris, 1828.

Caylus, Marthe-Marguérite de Villette de Murçay, marquise de. *Souvenirs*. Ed. A. Petitot and L. J. N. Monmerqué. Collection des mémoires relatifs à l'histoire de France, vol. 66. Paris, 1828.

Champollion-Figeac, Jean-François, ed. *Documents historiques inédits tirés des collections manuscrites de la bibliothèque royale*. 4 vols. Paris, 1841–48.

Chéruel, Pierre Adolphe. "Les carnets de Mazarin pendant la Fronde, septembre-octobre 1648." *Revue Historique* 4 (1877): 103–16.

Choisy, abbé de. *Mémoires pour servir à l'histoire de Louis XIV*. Ed. A. Petitot and L. J. N. Monmerqué. Collection des mémoires relatifs à l'histoire de France, vol. 63. Paris, 1828.

———. *Mémoires de l'abbé de Choisy habillé en femme*. Ed. Georges Mongrédien. Paris, 1966.

Clermont-Tonnerre, François de. *Oraison funèbre de très-haut et très puissant prince monseigneur Philippe fils de France frère unique du Roy, duc d'Orléans prononcée dans l'église de l'abbaye de S. Denis le 23 juillet*. Paris, 1701.

Colbert, Jean Baptiste. *Lettres, instructions et mémoires de Colbert*. Ed. Pierre Clément. 7 vols. Paris, 1861.

Cordey, Jean. "L'inventaire après décès d'Anne d'Autriche et le mobilier du Louvre." *Bulletin de la Société de l'Histoire de l'Art Français*, 1930, pp. 209–75.

Cosnac, Daniel de. *Mémoires publiés pour la Société de l'Histoire de France par le Comte Jules de Cosnac*. 2 vols. Paris, 1852.

Dangeau, Philippe de Courcillon, marquis de. *Journal publié en entier pour la première fois par MM. Soulié, Dussieux, de Chennevières, Mantz, de Montaiglon avec les additions inédites du duc de Saint-Simon publiées par M. Feuillet de Conches*. 19 vols. Paris, 1854–60.

Depping, G. B., ed. *Correspondance administrative sous le règne de Louis XIV*. 4 vols. Paris, 1850–55.

Dubois de Lestourmière, Marie. *Mémoire fidèle des choses qui se sont passées à la mort de Louis XIII*. Ed MM. Michaud and Poujoulat. Nouvelle collection des mémoires pour servir à l'histoire de France, vol. 11. Paris, 1838.

L'éstat de la France . . . dédié au roy. 2 vols. Paris, 1662–1701.

Furetière, Antoine. *Dictionnaire universel*. La Haye, 1701 and 1727.

La Gazette de France. 1638–1701.

Grancolas, J. *Oraison funèbre de très haut, très puissant et très-excellent prince Philippe, fils de France, frère unique du roy.* Paris, 1701.

Guiffrey, M. Jules. *Comptes des bâtiments du roi sous le règne de Louis XIV.* 5 vols. Paris, 1881–91.

[Hanover] Sophie, Herzogin von Hannover. *Briefwechsel der Herzogin Sophie von Hannover mit ihrem Bruder, dem Kurfürsten Karl Ludwig von der Pfalz, und des Letzteren mit seiner Schwägerin, der Pfalzgräfin Anna.* Ed. Eduard Bodemann. Publicationen aus den K. Preussischen Staatsarchiven, vol. 26. Leipzig, 1885.

———. *Memoiren der Herzogin Sophie nachmals Kurfürstin von Hannover.* Ed. Adolf Köcher. Vol 4. *Publicationen aus den K. Preussischen Staatsarchiven.* Leipzig, 1879.

Heroard, Jean. *Journal sur l'enfance et la jeunesse de Louis XIII (1601–1628).* 2 vols. Paris, 1868.

La Fare, Charles-Auguste, marquis de. *Mémoires et réflexions sur les principaux événements du règne de Louis XIV, et sur le caractère de ceux qui y ont eu la principale part.* Ed. A. Petitot et L. J. N. de Monmerqué. Collection des mémoires relatifs à l'histoire de France, vol. 65. Paris, 1828.

La Fayette, Marie-Madeleine, Mme de. *Histoire de Madame Henriette d'Angleterre suivie de mémoires de la cour de France pour les années 1688 et 1689.* Ed. Gilbert Sigaux. Paris, 1965.

La Porte, Pierre de. *Mémoires.* Ed. A. Petitot et L. J. N. de Monmerqué. Collection des mémoires relatifs à l'histoire de France, vol. 59. Paris, 1827.

Lister, Martin. "A Journey to Paris in the Year 1698." In *A General Collection of the Best and Most Interesting Travels in All Parts of the World,* ed. John Pinkerton. 4 vols. London, 1809.

Locatelli, Sébastien. *Voyage de France: Moeurs et coutumes françaises (1664–1665).* Trans. and ed. Adolphe Vautier. Paris, 1905.

Longeville, Harcouet de, avocat au Parlement. *Description des grandes cascades de la maison royale de Saint Cloud: Dédiée à Son Altesse Royale Monseigneur duc d'Orléans.* Paris, 1706.

Louis XIV. *Mémoires pour les années 1661 et 1666 suivis des réflexions sur le métier de roi; des instructions au duc d'Anjou, et d'un projet de harangue.* Ed. Jean Longnon. Paris, 1923.

———. *Oeuvres.* Ed. P. H. Grimoard and P. A. Grouvelle. 6 vols. Paris, 1806.

Maintenon, Mme de. *Correspondance générale.* Ed. Théophile Lavallée. 5 vols. Paris, 1865.

Mazarin, Jules, cardinal. *Lettres du cardinal Mazarin pendant son ministère.* Ed. M. A. Chéruel. 9 vols. Paris, 1872–1906.

———. *Lettres du cardinal Mazarin où l'on voit le secret de la négotiation de la paix des Pirenées; et la relation des conferences qu'il a eues pour ce sujet avec dom Louis de Haro, ministre d'Espagne. Avec d'autres lettres très-curieuses écrites au roi et la reine par le même cardinal, pendant son voyage.* Amsterdam, 1692.

Mercure François (before 1672). *Mercure Galant* (1672–74).

Molière, Jean-Baptiste Poquelin. *Oeuvres complètes*. Ed. Louis Moland. 2d ed. 12 vols. Paris, 1880–85.

Montpensier, Anne Marie Louise d'Orléans, duchesse de [Mademoiselle, or la Grande Mademoiselle]. *Mémoires*. Ed. A. Petitot et L. J. N. de Monmerqué. Collection des mémoires relatifs à l'histoire de France, vols. 39–43. Paris, 1826.

Morellet, Laurent, abbé de. *Explication historique de ce qu'il y a de plus remarquable dans la maison royale de Versailles et en celle de Monsieur à Saint-Cloud*. Paris, 1681.

————. *Saint-Clou* [*sic*] *et les devises du salon, à Son Altesse Royale, Monsieur, fils de France, frère unique de Sa Majesté*. Paris, 1681.

Motteville, Françoise Bertaut de. *Mémoires*. Ed. C. B. Petitot. Collection des mémoires relatifs à l'histoire de France, vols. 36–39. Paris, 1824.

La Muse Historique.

[Orléans] Elizabeth Charlotte, duchesse d'. *Aus den Briefen der Herzogin Elisabeth Charlotte von Orleans an die Kurfürstin Sophie von Hannover: Ein Beitrag zur Kulturgeschichte des 17. und 18. Jahrhunderts*. Ed. Eduard Bodemann. Hanover, 1891.

————. *Briefe der Herzogin Elisabeth Charlotte von Orleans*. Ed. Hans F. Helmolt. 2 vols. Leipzig, 1908.

————. *Die Briefe der Liselotte von der Pfalz, Herzogin von Orleans*. Ed. C. Künzel. Munich, n.d.

————. *Correspondance complète de Madame duchesse d'Orléans née Princesse Palatine, mère du régent*. Trans. and ed. M. G. Brunet. 2 vols. Paris, n.d. (The title is misleading. No complete edition of Liselotte's letters has ever been published).

————. *A Woman's Life in the Court of the Sun King: Letters of Liselotte von der Pfalz, 1652–1722, Élisabeth Charlotte, Duchesse d'Orléans*. Trans. and intro. Elborg Forster. Baltimore, 1984.

Patin, Gui. *Lettres de Gui Patin à Charles Spon, médecin à Lyon*. Ed. J. B. Baillière. 3 vols. Paris, 1846.

Pellisson-Fontanier, Paul. *Lettres historiques de Pellisson*. 3 vols. Paris, 1729.

Piganiol de la Force, Jean-Aymar. *Description historique de la ville de Paris et ses environs*. 10 vols. Paris, 1742.

Plessis-Praslin, César de Choiseul, comte du. *Mémoires des divers emplois et des principales actions du maréchal du Plessis*. Ed. A. Petitot et L. J. N. de Monmerqué. Collection des mémoires relatifs à l'histoire de France. vol. 57. Paris, 1827.

Racine, Jean. *Oeuvres complètes*. 5 vols. Paris, 1922.

Révérend, Père. *Les dits notables de Monsieur Philippe de France, duc d'Anjou, frère unique du roy*. Paris, 1655.

Le sacre et couronnement de Louis XIV, roy de France et de navarre dans l'eglise de Reims, le septième juin 1654. Reims, 1652. (One of the many printed accounts of the coronation preserved in the BN.)

Saint-Simon, Louis de Rouvroy, duc de. *Mémoires*. Ed. A. de Boislisle. 41 vols. Paris, 1879–1928.

San Maiolo, Giovanni Battista Primi Visconti Fassola di Rossa. *Mémoires sur la cour de Louis XIV.* Trans. from Italian and ed. Jean Lemoine. Paris, 1908.

Sévigné, Marie de Rabutin-Chantal, marquise de. *Correspondance.* Ed. Roger Duchêne. 3 vols. Paris, 1972–78.

Sourches, Louis-François de Bouschet, marquis de. *Mémoires secrets et inédits de la cour de France sur la fin du règne de Louis XIV.* Ed. Adhelm Bernier. 2 vols. Paris, 1836.

Spanheim, Ezéchiel. *Relation de la cour de France en 1690.* Ed. Charles Schefer. Paris, 1882.

Temple, Guillaume, chevalier de. *Mémoires de ce qui s'est passé dans la chrétienté depuis le commencement de la guerre en 1672, jusqu'à la paix conclue en 1679.* Trans. from English. Ed. MM. Michaud and Poujoulat. Nouvelles collections des memoires a l'histoire de France, vol. 8., Paris, 1839.

Turenne, Henri de la Tour, maréchal de. *Mémoires.* Ed. Paul Maréchal. 2 vols. Paris, 1909–14.

Visconti. *See* San Maiolo, Giovanni Battista Primi Visconti Fassola di Rossa.

Voltaire (François-Marie Arouet). *Siècle de Louis XIV.* 2 vols. Paris, 1830.

SECONDARY SOURCES

Adler, Alfred. *The Practice and Theory of Individual Psychology.* Trans. P. Radin. London, 1955.

Apostolidès, Jean-Marie. *Le roi-machine: Spectacle et politique au temps de Louis XIV.* Paris, 1981.

Ariès, Philippe. *Centuries of Childhood: A Social History of Family Life.* Trans. Robert Baldick. New York, 1965.

Baillon, comte de. *Henriette-Anne d'Angleterre, duchesse d'Orléans: Sa vie et sa correspondance avec son frère Charles II.* Paris, 1886.

Barine, Arvède. *Madame: Mère du régent.* Paris, 1923.

Barker, Nancy N. "Philippe d'Orléans, Frère Unique du Roi: Founder of the Family Fortune." *French Historical Studies* 13, no. 2 (1983): 145–71.

Barrault, Jean-Louis, Georges Montgrédien, et al. *Molière.* Paris, 1976.

Barthélemy, Edouard de, ed. *Les amis de la marquise de Sablé: Recueil de lettres des principaux habitués de son salon.* Paris, 1865.

Baudrillart, A. *Philippe V et la cour d'Espagne.* 5 vols. Paris, 1890–1910.

Beaucorps, Charles de. *L'administration des intendants d'Orléans de 1686 à 1713: Jean de Creil, André Jubert de Bouville, Yves de La Bourdonnaye.* Geneva, 1978. (Reprint of 1911 Orléans edition.)

Bell, Alan P., Martin S. Weinberg, and Sue Kiefer Hammersmith. *Sexual Preference: Its Development in Men and Women.* Bloomington, Ind., 1981.

Berger, Patrice. "Rural Charity in Late Seventeenth-Century France: The Pontchartrain Case." *French Historical Studies* 10(Spring 1978): 393–415.

Bernard, Jean. *Le sang et l'histoire.* Paris, 1983.

Bernard, Leon. *The Emerging City: Paris in the Age of Louis XIV.* Durham, N.C., 1970.

Bertier de Sauvigny, Guillaume de. *The Bourbon Restoration.* Trans. Lynn M. Case. Philadelphia, 1966.

Bieber, Irving, et al. *Homosexuality: A Psychoanalytic Study.* New York, 1962.

Bluche, François. *Louis XIV.* Paris, 1986.

———. *La vie quotidienne au temps de Louis XIV.* Paris, 1984.

Boislisle, Arthur-Michel de. *Les conseils du roi sous Louis XIV.* Paris, 1884. (Geneva reprint, 1977.)

———, ed. *Portraits et caractères, 1703.* Paris, 1897.

Bowles, Emily. *Madame de Maintenon.* London, 1888.

Brachfeld, Oliver. *Inferiority Feelings in the Individual and the Group.* Westport, Conn., 1977.

Brim, O. G., Jr., and J. Kagan, eds. *Constancy and Change in Human Development.* Cambridge, Mass., 1980.

Broglie, Gabriel de. *L'Orléanism: La ressource libérale de la France.* Paris, 1981.

Brown, John Croumbie. *French Forest Ordinance of 1669, with Historical Sketch of Previous Treatment of Forests in France.* London, 1883.

Bruch, Hilde. *Eating Disorders: Obesity, Anorexia Nervosa, and the Person Within.* New York, 1973.

Brunswick, Ruth Mack. "The Preoedipal Phase of the Libido Development." *Psychoanalytic Quarterly* 9(1940): 293–319.

Bullough, Vern L. *Homosexuality: A History.* New York, 1979.

Carré, Henri. *L'enfance et la première jeunesse de Louis XIV, 1638–1661.* Paris, 1944.

Champier, Victor, and G. Roger Sandoz. *Le Palais-Royal d'après des documents inédits (1629–1900).* 2 vols. Paris, 1900. Vol. 1: *Du cardinal de Richelieu à la révolution.*

Chérot, P. Henri. *La première jeunesse de Louis XIV (1649–1653) d'après la correspondance inédite du P. Charles Paulin, son premier confesseur.* Lille, 1892.

Cousin, Victor. *Madame de Hautefort.* 2d ed. Paris, 1868.

———. *Madame de Sablé.* Paris, 1854.

Crozet, René. *Histoire de l'Orléanais.* Paris, 1936.

Derblay, Claude. *Henriette d'Angleterre et sa légende.* Paris, 1950.

Dethan, Georges. *Gaston d'Orléans: Conspirateur et prince charmant.* Paris, 1959.

———. *Mazarin: Un homme de paix à l'âge baroque, 1602–1661.* Paris, 1981.

———. *Mazarin et ses amis: Etude sur la jeunesse du cardinal d'après ses papiers conservés aux archives du Quai d'Orsay suivie d'un choix de lettres inédites.* Paris, 1968.

Deutsch, Helene. *The Psychology of Women: A Psychoanalytic Interpretation.* New York, 1944.

Devèze, Michel. "Les forêts françaises à la veille de la révolution de 1789." *Revue d'Histoire Moderne et Contemporaine.* 13(October–December, 1966): 241–72.

———. *La grande réformation des forêts sous Colbert (1661–1683).* Nancy, 1962.

————. *Histoire des forêts: Que sais-je?* Paris, 1965.

Dézallier d'Argenville, Antoine Nicolas. *Vies des fameux architectes depuis la renaissance des arts avec la description de leurs ouvrages.* Paris, 1787. (Geneva reprint, 1972).

Dinfreville, Jacques. *Louis XIV: Les saisons d'un grand règne.* Paris, 1977.

Domet, Paul. *Histoire de la forêt d'Orléans.* Orléans, 1892.

Druon, H. *Histoire de l'éducation des princes dans la maison des Bourbons de France.* 2 vols. Paris, 1897.

Dulong, Claude. *Anne d'Autriche: Mère de Louis XIV.* Paris, 1980.

Dupezard, E. *Le Palais-Royal de Paris.* Paris, 1911.

Dupin, André M. J. J. *Des apanages en général et en particulier de l'apanage d'Orléans.* Paris, 1827.

Durand, G. "What Is Absolutism?" In *Louis XIV and Absolutism,* ed. Ragnhild Hatton. London, 1976.

Dutens, Louis. *Histoire de la navigation intérieure de la France.* 2 vols. Paris, 1829.

Ekberg, Carl J. *The Failure of Louis XIV's Dutch War.* Chapel Hill, N.C., 1979.

Engel, Claire Eliane. *Le régent.* Paris, 1969.

Erikson, Erik H. *Childhood and Society.* 2d ed. New York, 1950.

Erlanger, Philippe. *Monsieur: Frère de Louis XIV.* Paris, 1953.

————. *Le régent.* Paris, 1938.

Espezel, Pierre d'. *Le Palais-Royal.* Paris, 1936.

Fabre, Jean. *Sur la vie et principalement sur la mort de Madame.* Paris, 1912.

Feiling, Keith. "Henrietta Stuart, Duchess of Orléans, and the Origins of the Treaty of Dover." *English Historical Review* 47(1932): 642–45.

Forster, Elborg. "From the Patient's Point of View: Illness and Health in the Letters of Liselotte von der Pfalz (1652–1722)." *Bulletin of the History of Medecine* 60(1986): 297–320.

Fox, Vivian C. "Is Adolescence a Phenomenon of Modern Times?" *Journal of Psychohistory* 5, no. 2 (1977): 271–90.

Fraser, Antonia. *Royal Charles: Charles II and the Restoration.* New York, 1979.

Freud, Sigmund. "Dostoevsky and Parricide." In *Collected Papers,* ed. James Strachey, 5:222–42. New York, 1959.

————. *Group Psychology and the Analysis of the Ego.* Trans. and ed. James Strachey. London, 1922.

————. *The Standard Edition of the Complete Psychological Works of Sigmund Freud.* Trans. and ed. James Strachey et al. 24 vols. London, 1953–75.

————. *Three Contributions to the Theory of Sex.* Trans. A. A. Brill. New York, 1920.

————. "Why War?" In *Collected Papers,* Trans. and ed. James Strachey, 5:273–87. New York, 1959.

Fruhauf, Christian. *Forêt et société de la forêt paysanne à la forêt capitaliste en pays de Sault sous l'ancien régime (vers 1670–1791).* Paris, 1980.

Funck-Brentano, Frantz. *La cour du roi soleil.* Paris, 1937.

Funck-Brentano, Frantz, with Paul d'Estrée. *Figaro et ses devanciers*. Paris, 1909.

Garfinkel, Paul E. *Anorexia Nervosa: A Multidimensional Perspective*. New York, 1982.

Gay, Peter. *Freud for Historians*. New York, 1985.

Gélis, Jacques, Mireille Laget, and Marie-France Morel. *Entrer dans la vie: Naissances et enfances dans la France traditionnelle*. Paris, 1978.

Godard, Charles. *Les pouvoirs des intendants sous Louis XIV particulièrement dans les pays d'élections de 1661 à 1715*. Paris, 1901.

Goodich, Michael. *The Unmentionable Vice: Homosexuality in the Later Medieval Period*. Santa Barbara, Calif., 1979.

Goubert, Pierre. *The Ancien Régime: French Society, 1600–1750*. Trans. Steve Cox. New York, 1973.

———. *Louis XIV et vingt millions de Français*. Paris, 1966.

Green, Richard, M. D. *Sexual Identity Conflict in Children and Adults*. New York, 1974.

Hamscher, Albert. "Ouvrages sur la Fronde parus en anglais depuis 1970." *XVIIe Siècle* 36(1984): 380–83.

Harding, Robert R. *Anatomy of a Power Elite: The Provincial Governors of Early Modern France*. New Haven, 1978.

Hartmann, Cyril Hughes. *The King My Brother*. London, 1954.

Hatton, Ragnhild, ed. *Louis XIV and Absolutism*. London and Basinstoke, 1976.

———. *Louis XIV and Europe*. Columbus, Ohio, 1976.

Häusser, Ludwig. *Geschichte der Reinischen Pfalz nach ihren politischen, kirchlichen, und litterarischen Verhältnesse*. 2 vols. Heidelberg, 1845.

Hautecoeur, Louis. *Histoire de l'architecture classique en France*. 7 vols. Paris, 1943–55.

Henry, Louis, and Mlle Claude Lévy. "Ducs et pairs sous l'ancien régime: Caractéristiques démographiques d'une caste." *Population: Revue Trimestrielle de l'Institut National d'Etudes Démographiques* 15(October–December 1960): 807–30.

Heyd, Michael. "The Reaction to Enthusiasm in the Seventeenth Century: Toward an Integrative Approach." *Journal of Modern History* 53(June 1981): 258–80.

Hunt, David. *Parents and Children in History: The Psychology of Family Life in Early Modern France*. New York, 1970.

Hyslop, Beatrice F. *L'apanage de Philippe-Egalité duc d'Orléans*. Paris, 1965.

Isherwood, Robert M. *Music in the Service of the King: France in the Seventeenth Century*. Ithaca, 1973.

Jackson, Richard A. *Vive le Roi: A History of the French Coronations from Charles V to Charles X*. Chapel Hill, N.C., 1984.

Jager-Schmidt, J. "La Sologne forestière." *Revue des Eaux et Forêts* 61(January 1923): 54–63.

Jouhaud, Christian. *Mazarinades: La Fronde des mots*. Paris, 1985.

Journal du Loiret.

Kantorowicz, Ernst. *The King's Two Bodies*. Princeton, 1957.

Kelly, George Armstrong. "The Machine of the Duc D'Orléans and the New Politics." *Journal of Modern History* 51(December 1979): 667–84.

Kettering, Sharon. "Patronage and Politics during the Fronde." *French Historical Review* 14, no. 3 (1986): 409–41.

Kleinman, Ruth. *Anne of Austria: Queen of France*. Columbus, Ohio, 1985.

Kohut, Heinz. *The Search for the Self: Selected Writings of Heinz Kohut, 1950–1978*. Ed. Paul H. Ornstein. 2 vols. New York, 1978.

Kohut, Thomas A. "Psychohistory as History." *American Historical Review* 91, no 2 (1986): 336–54.

Kossman, E. H. *La Fronde*. Leiden, 1954.

La Batut, Guy de. *La cour de Monsieur, frère de Louis XIV*. Paris, 1927.

Labatut, Jean-Pierre. *Les ducs et pairs de France au XVIIe siècle: Etude sociale*. Paris, 1972.

Lafenestre, Georges. *Les grands écrivains français: Molière*. Paris, 1909.

Lampl de Groot, Jeanne. "The Pre-oedipal Phase in the Development of the Male Child." *Psychoanalytic Study of the Child* 2(1947): 75–83.

Laurencie, Lionel de. *Lully: Les maîtres de la musique*. Paris, 1919.

Lavisse, Ernest, A. de Saint-Léger, A. Rébelliau, and P. Sagnac. *Louis XIV—la fin du règne (1685–1715)*. Vol. 8 of *Histoire de France illustrée depuis les origines jusqu'à la révolution*. Ed. Ernest Lavisse. Paris, 1911.

Lefebvre, Georges. *Etudes orléanaises*. 2 vols. Paris, 1961–63.

Leloup, Gaston. "La maîtrise de la forêt de Montargis en 1670." *Bulletin de la Société d'Emulation de l'Arrondissement de Montargis* 44(December 1978): 31–39.

Le Pelletier, le baron Louis. "Etude sur la forêt de Villers-Cotterêts." *Bulletin de la Société Archéologique, Historique et Scientifique de Soissons*, 3d ser., 11(1901–2): 1–202.

Le Roy Ladurie, Emmanuel. "Auprès du roi, la cour." *Annales: Economies, Sociétés, Civilisations* 38(January 1983): 21–41.

Levron, Jacques. *La vie quotidienne à la cour de Versailles aux XVIIe et XVIIIe siècles*. Paris, 1965.

Lizerand, Georges. *Le régime rural de l'ancienne France*. Paris, 1942.

Loewenberg, Peter. *Decoding the Past: The Psychohistorical Approach*. New York, 1983.

Lottin, D., Père. *Recherches historiques de la ville d'Orléans, depuis Aurélien, l'an 274, jusqu'en 1789 dédiées à ses concitoyens*. 3 vols. Orléans, 1837–38.

Maffert, A. *Les apanages en France du XVIe au XIXe siècle*. Paris, 1900.

Magne, Emile. *Le château de Saint-Cloud, d'après des documents inédits*. Paris, 1932.

Mandrou, Robert. *La France au XVIIe et au XVIIIe siècles*. Paris, 1970.

———. *Louis XIV en son temps, 1661–1715*. Paris, 1973.

Marvick, Elizabeth Wirth. *The Young Richelieu: A Psychoanalytic Approach to Leadership*. Chicago, 1980.

Melchior-Bonnet, Bernardine. *La Grande Mademoiselle: Héroïne et amoureuse*. Paris, 1985.

Meyer, Daniel. *Le domaine national de Saint-Cloud*. Paris, n.d.

———. "Le domaine national de Saint-Cloud." In *Revue des Monuments Historiques de la France*, no. 3 (1975): 40–57.

Meyer, Jean. *Le régent*. Paris, 1985.

Michaux, Alexandre. *Essai historique sur la forêt de Retz*. Soissons, 1876.

Mignet, François Auguste Marie Alexis. *Négociations relatives à la succession d'Espagne*. 4 vols. Paris, 1835–42.

Picard, Raymond. *La carrière de Jean Racine: Bibliothèque des idées*. 4th ed. Paris, 1956.

Pinsseau, Hubert. *Histoire de la construction, de l'administration et de l'exploitation du Canal d'Orléans de 1676 à 1954: Un aspect du développement économique de la France*. Paris, 1963.

———. *Le canal Henri IV ou canal de Briare, 1604–1943*. Orléans, 1944.

Plinquet, J. B. *Traité sur les réformations et les aménagemens des forêts avec une application à celles d'Orléans et de Montargis*. Orléans, 1789.

Pouradier, Gabriel. "Le canal d'Orléans." *Journal du Loiret*, 23, 26, 28 October, 5 November 1913.

Quincy, Charles Sevin, marquis de. *Histoire militaire du règne de Louis le Grand*. 7 vols. Paris, 1726.

Rabb, Theodore K. *The Struggle for Stability in Early Modern Europe*. New York, 1975.

Ranum, Orest. *Paris in the Age of Absolutism*. Bloomington, Ind. 1968.

Richet, Denis. *La France moderne: L'esprit des institutions*. Paris, 1973.

Robins, Beatrice. "Molière's Attitude toward Court and Courtier as Revealed in His Comedies." M.A. thesis, University of Texas, 1940.

Roche, Daniel. "Aperçus sur la fortune et les revenus des princes de Condé à l'aube du 18e siècle." *Revue d'Histoire Moderne et Contemporaine* 14(July–September 1967): 217–43.

Rousset, C. *Histoire de Louvois*. 4 vols. Paris, 1862.

Runyan, William McKinley. *Life Histories and Psychobiography: Explorations in Theory and Method*. New York, 1982.

Rutter, M. *Maternal Deprivation Reassessed*. 2d ed. New York, 1981.

Sainte-Beuve, C. A. *Causeries de lundi*. 2 vols. London, n.d.

Sauvel, Tony. "Le Palais-Royal de la mort de Richelieu à l'incendie en 1763." *Bulletin Monumental* 120(1962): 173–90.

Schalk, Ellery. "Clientage, Elites and Absolutism in Seventeenth-Century France." *French Historical Studies* 14, no. 3 (1986): 442–46.

———. *From Valor to Pedigree: Ideas of Nobility in France in the Sixteenth and Seventeenth Centuries*. Princeton, 1986.

Ségur, Pierre de. *Le maréchal de Luxembourg et le prince d'Orange, 1668–1678*. Paris, n.d.

Shennan, J. H. *Philippe, Duke of Orléans: Regent of France 1715–1723*. London, 1979.

Sorel, Albert. *L'Europe et la révolution française*. Part 1. *Moeurs politiques et les traditions*. 4th ed. Paris, 1897.

Stoller, Robert J., M.D. *Sex and Gender*. 2 vols. New York, 1968–74.

Taillandier, Mme Saint-René. *La jeunesse du grand roi Louis XIV et Anne d'Autriche.* Paris, 1945.

Thompson, Norman L., et al. "Parent-Child Relationships and Sexual Identity in Male and Female Homosexuals and Heterosexuals." *Journal of Consulting and Clinical Psychology* 41, no. 1 (1973): 120–27.

Thomson, William A. R. *Black's Medical Dictionary.* 34th ed. London, 1984.

Trenard, Louis. "La presse française des origines à 1788." In *Histoire générale de la presse française,* ed. Claude Bellanger et al., 1:27–402. Paris, 1969.

Vatout, Jean, dit Julien. *Souvenirs historiques des résidences royales: Le Palais-Royal.* Paris, 1838.

Vignon, E. J. M. *Etudes historiques sur l'administration des voies publiques en France au XVIIe et XVIIIe siècles.* 3 vols. Paris, 1862.

Wachtel, P. "Psychodynamics, Behavior Therapy, and the Implacable Experimenter: An Inquiry into the Consistency of Personality." *Journal of Abnormal Psychology* 82(1973): 323–34.

Waquet, Jean-Claude. *Les grands maîtres des eaux et forêts de France de 1689 à la révolution suivi d'un dictionnaire des grands maîtres.* Geneva, 1978.

West, D. J. *Homosexuality Re-examined.* Minneapolis, 1977.

Wolf, John B. *Louis XIV.* New York, 1968.

———. "The Reign of Louis XIV." *Journal of Modern History* 36, no. 2 (1964): 128–44.

Index